Mastering PHP 7

Design, configure, build, and test professional web
applications in PHP 7

Branko Ajzele

BIRMINGHAM - MUMBAI

Mastering PHP 7

First published: June 2017

Production reference: 1220617

Published by Packt Publishing Ltd.
Livery Place
35 Livery Street
Birmingham
B3 2PB, UK.

ISBN 978-1-78588-281-4

www.packtpub.com

Credits

Author

Branko Ajzele

Reviewers

Martin Beaudry

Andrew Caya

Alexandru-Emil Lupu

Mario Magdic

Commissioning Editor

Kunal Parikh

Acquisition Editor

Chaitanya Nair

Content Development Editor

Siddhi Chavan

Technical Editor

Dhiraj Chandanshive

Copy Editor

Safis Editing

Project Coordinator

Vaidehi Sawant

Proofreader

Safis Editing

Indexer

Pratik Shirodkar

Production Coordinator

Nilesh Mohite

About the Author

Branko Ajzele is an internationally respected and highly accomplished software developer, book author, solution specialist, consultant, and team leader.

Strong technical knowledge coupled with the ability to communicate those technicalities frequently and clearly with strong direction has enabled him to architect, develop, and launch numerous successful businesses. He often feels comfortable proposing alternatives to demands that he feels can be improved, even when it means pulling a late shift to meet deadlines.

He holds several respected IT certifications, such as Zend Certified PHP Engineer, Magento Certified Developer, Magento Certified Developer Plus, Magento Certified Solution Specialist, and a few more.

Branko was crowned E-commerce Developer of the Year by Digital Entrepreneur Awards in October 2014 for his excellent knowledge and expertise in e-commerce development. His work is second to none, and he is truly dedicated to helping fellow developers around the world.

He currently works as a full-time contractor for Lab Lateral Ltd, an award-winning team of innovative thinkers, artists, and developers specializing in customer-centric websites, digital consultancy, and marketing. Here, he holds the role of a lead developer and the head of Lab's Croatia office.

The book, *Instant E-Commerce with Magento: Build a Shop,* by Packt was his first Magento-related book oriented toward Magento newcomers, after which he decided to write his second book, *Getting Started with Magento Extension Development*. The third book, *Magento 2 Developers Guide*, was released days after the official Magento 2 release. His fourth book, *Modular Programming with PHP 7*, describes modular design techniques to help developers build readable, manageable, reusable, and more efficient code, and doing so on a mini web shop application written in the Symfony framework.

About the Reviewers

Martin Beaudry started his programming career 7 years ago by creating a software in C after going through the K&R book. He then switched to PHP to work as a web developer, becoming a Zend Certified PHP Engineer and Zend Certified Architect along the way. Before learning computer languages, he worked with human ones as a professional translator and editor.

Martin works in his own start-up and is one of Linux for PHP's contributors.

> *I want to thank my friend, Andrew Caya, for teaching me everything I needed to know to review this book.*

Andrew Caya discovered his passion for computers at the age of 11 and started programming in GW-BASIC and QBASIC in the early 90s. He earned a master's degree in Information Science and master's short program in public administration. After doing some software development in C, C++, and Perl, and some Linux system administration, he became a PHP developer more than 7 years ago. He is also a Zend Certified PHP Engineer and a Zend Certified Architect.

He is the creator of Linux for PHP, a lightweight, Docker-based, custom Linux project that allows PHP developers to easily compile and use recent versions of PHP in a variety of ways. He is also the lead developer of a popular Joomla! extension and has the great pleasure of contributing code to many open source projects.

He is currently a professional contract programmer in Montreal, Canada, a technical reviewer for Packt, and a loving husband and father.

Alexandru-Emil Lupu has about 10 years experience in the Web Development area. During this time, he got a lot of skills from the implementation of e-commerce platforms and presentation sites' code writing to online games. He is one of the developers who are constantly learning new programming languages, and he has no problem in understanding Ruby, PHP, Python, JavaScript, and Java code.

Alexandru is very passionate about programming and computer science. When he was young, he did not own a computer or an Internet connection (hard to believe, but true). He would go to an Internet cafe in order to read about his programming problems and would then struggle to implement them at home. He fondly remembers those days and hopes he's the same guy from 10 years ago with much more experience. For him, *passion* is the word that describes the challenge he faced while learning. He says it was not easy to be a youngster and one who was willing to learn new stuff. Coming home at 2-3 A.M., determined to install Linux just to learn about it, was not as easy as it sounds. He had a Pentium I at 133 MHz in the Pentium IV in the 1800 MHz era!

He is constantly learning and likes to stay close to well-trained and passionate people who better motivate him every day. This is the reason he joined the eJobs team to face a challenge. He likes teams who work intelligently and are energetic.

Alexandru is a Certified Scrum Master and is passionate about Agile Development. His experience also includes 3 years as a Ruby on Rails developer and CTO at 2Performant Network (2Parale), 4 years at eRepublik.com, an online game, during which he was responsible for a long list of tasks, including feature development, performance optimization, and he was also the tech lead for an internal project. He has learned the hard way the necessary skills to fulfill his day-to-day tasks at 2Performant.com and gained all the experience he needed to face new kind of challenges at eJobs.ro.

In his little free time, he also develops small personal projects. If he still has spare time, he reads some technical or project management books or articles. When he is relaxing, he watches thriller movies and also likes playing shooter or strategy games.

He doesn't talk too much, but he is willing to teach programming to others. If you meet him over a coffee, prepare yourself to be entertained--he likes to tell a lot of contextual jokes.

You can interact with him at `http://github.com/alecslupu`.

Mario Magdic is a full-stack software developer originally from Croatia and currently residing in Dublin, Ireland, where he moved 2 years ago to work for a FinTech company. He was first introduced to the wonderful world of software development in a high school programming class and decided to make it his career.

During his career, he has had an opportunity to work with various technologies and programming languages and is always happy to improve and learn new things.

www.PacktPub.com

For support files and downloads related to your book, please visit www.PacktPub.com.

Did you know that Packt offers eBook versions of every book published, with PDF and ePub files available? You can upgrade to the eBook version at www.PacktPub.com and as a print book customer, you are entitled to a discount on the eBook copy. Get in touch with us at service@packtpub.com for more details.

At www.PacktPub.com, you can also read a collection of free technical articles, sign up for a range of free newsletters and receive exclusive discounts and offers on Packt books and eBooks.

https://www.packtpub.com/mapt

Get the most in-demand software skills with Mapt. Mapt gives you full access to all Packt books and video courses, as well as industry-leading tools to help you plan your personal development and advance your career.

Why subscribe?

- Fully searchable across every book published by Packt
- Copy and paste, print, and bookmark content
- On demand and accessible via a web browser

Customer Feedback

Thanks for purchasing this Packt book. At Packt, quality is at the heart of our editorial process. To help us improve, please leave us an honest review on this book's Amazon page at `https://www.amazon.com/dp/1785882813`.

If you'd like to join our team of regular reviewers, you can e-mail us at `customerreviews@packtpub.com`. We award our regular reviewers with free eBooks and videos in exchange for their valuable feedback. Help us be relentless in improving our products!

I hereby dedicate this book to my loving late grandma, Katarina, whose help throughout my school days will always be remembered and appreciated.

Table of Contents

Preface

The PHP language has been around for quite some time now. What started out as a humble set of scripts, soon turned into a powerful scripting language. The rise of various frameworks and platforms paved the way into the hearts of many developers. Over time, PHP coding standards sprung out, along with numerous testing solutions. These gave it the solid enterprise foothold it has today.

The latest PHP 7.1 release brings forth enormous amount of improvements, both from the language syntax and overall performance perspective. There has never been a better time to dig into a PHP than now.

Throughout this book, we will be covering a wide range of topics. These might seem seemingly random at first, but they reflect a minimum skill level PHP developers are required to possess nowadays.

What this book covers

Chapter 1, *The All New PHP*, talks about the latest changes introduced to the PHP 7.1 language, most of which directly improve the quality and elegancy of written code.

Chapter 2, *Embracing Standards*, introduces you to important standards in the PHP ecosystem. Presented standards affect the quality and elegancy of code, pushing ypu closer to truly mastering PHP.

Chapter 3, *Error Handling and Logging*, stresses on the importance of robust error handling and effective logging. You will learn how to handle errors and log truly important bits of information--two disciplines that often lack proper attention in everyday PHP coding.

Chapter 4, *Magic Behind Magic Methods*, discusses the magic functions available in PHP classes, and their beauty and importance. You will learn every PHP magic method, and its meaning and use through practical examples.

Chapter 5, *The Realm of CLI*, explores command-line PHP, and its tools and processes. You will learn how to use Symfony's Console component, work with input/output streams, and handle processes.

Chapter 6, *Prominent OOP Features*, looks at a subset of features that turn PHP into a powerful OOP language. You will learn important concepts behind PHP OOP features, part of which may escape everyday code base as they find more use as building blocks of various frameworks.

Chapter 7, *Optimizing for High Performance*, talks about the importance of performance optimization, providing hands-on solutions along the way. You will learn about details of the PHP performance optimization, where small configuration changes can affect the overall application performance.

Chapter 8, *Going Serverless*, outlines using PHP and its use in serverless infrastructure. You will gain an insight into the emerging serverless architecture, along with utilizing it via two of the dominant PaaS (platform as a service) solutions in the market.

Chapter 9, *Reactive Programming*, covers the emerging reactive programming paradigm that found its way into the PHP ecosystem. You will learn the basic principles of reactive programming using the synchronous coding techniques to write asynchronous code via icicle, one of the most dominant libraries in the ecosystem now.

Chapter 10, *Common Design Patterns*, focuses on the subset of design patterns, and the most common ones used in PHP programming. You will learn the practical implementation of several important design patterns, which, in turn, will result in more elegant, readable, manageable, and testable code.

Chapter 11, *Building Services*, takes you through REST, SOAP, and RPC style services, alongside with the microservice architecture. You will learn how to create a SOAP and REST web server, alongside their respective client counterparts.

Chapter 12, *Working with Databases*, explains the several types of database PHP programmers need to interact with, such as transactional SQL, NoSQL, key-value, and search databases. You will learn how to query the MySQL, Mongo, and Redis databases.

Chapter 13, *Resolving Dependencies*, explores the dependency issue and the means to resolve it. You will learn how to solve the dependency issue using the dependency injection and dependency container techniques.

Chapter 14, *Working with Packages*, covers the ecosystem around PHP packages, and their creation and distribution. You will learn how to find and use third-party packages to enrich applications, along with a quick glimpse of possibly creating and distributing its own packages.

Chapter 15, *Testing the Important Bits*, dives into several types of testing, emphasizing where one might be more important than the other. You will learn several most common types of testing done for PHP web applications.

Chapter 16, *Debugging, Tracing, and Profiling*, teaches you the most common tools for debugging, tracing, and profiling PHP applications. You will learn how to utilize several various tools to achieve effective debugging, tracing, and profiling of your application.

Chapter 17, *Hosting, Provisioning, and Deployment*, discusses making an informed decision for hosting the application, along with provisioning, deployment, and continuous integration processes in place. You will learn about the difference between hosting solutions and the automated process of getting the code from local to production machines.

What you need for this book

Throughout this book, there are a number of simple and self-contained code and configuration examples. To successfully run these, we can easily make use of the Ubuntu powered desktop (https://www.ubuntu.com/desktop) and server (https://www.ubuntu.com/server) machines. Those of you using Windows or OSX machines can easily install Ubuntu within a VirtualBox. Installation instructions for VirtualBox can be found on the official VirtualBox page (https://www.virtualbox.org/).

Who this book is for

Target readers are assumed to be intermediate-level PHP developers. This book will embark you on a journey to become a master in PHP. Solid knowledge of PHP is implied across areas such as basic syntax, types, variables, constants, expressions, operators, control structures, and functions.

Conventions

In this book, you will find a number of text styles that distinguish between different kinds of information. Here are some examples of these styles and an explanation of their meaning.

Code words in text, database table names, folder names, filenames, file extensions, pathnames, dummy URLs, user input, and Twitter handles are shown as follows: "Objects might utilize the PHP `Serializable` interface, `__sleep()` or `__wakeup()` magic methods."

A block of code is set as follows:

```
interface RequestInterface extends MessageInterface
{
  public function getRequestTarget();
  public function withRequestTarget($requestTarget);
}
```

Any command-line input or output is written as follows:

```
php index.php
serverless invoke local --function hello
```

New terms and **important words** are shown in bold. Words that you see on the screen, for example, in menus or dialog boxes, appear in the text like this: "We start by clicking the **New Project** button under the **Iron.io** dashboard."

Warnings or important notes appear in a box like this.

Tips and tricks appear like this.

Reader feedback

Feedback from our readers is always welcome. Let us know what you think about this book-what you liked or disliked. Reader feedback is important for us as it helps us develop titles that you will really get the most out of.

To send us general feedback, simply e-mail feedback@packtpub.com, and mention the book's title in the subject of your message.

If there is a topic that you have expertise in and you are interested in either writing or contributing to a book, see our author guide at www.packtpub.com/authors.

Customer support

Now that you are the proud owner of a Packt book, we have a number of things to help you to get the most from your purchase.

Downloading the example code

You can download the example code files for this book from your account at http://www.packtpub.com. If you purchased this book elsewhere, you can visit http://www.packtpub.com/support and register to have the files e-mailed directly to you.

You can download the code files by following these steps:

1. Log in or register to our website using your e-mail address and password.
2. Hover the mouse pointer on the **SUPPORT** tab at the top.
3. Click on **Code Downloads & Errata**.
4. Enter the name of the book in the **Search** box.
5. Select the book for which you're looking to download the code files.
6. Choose from the drop-down menu where you purchased this book from.
7. Click on **Code Download**.

Once the file is downloaded, please make sure that you unzip or extract the folder using the latest version of:

- WinRAR / 7-Zip for Windows
- Zipeg / iZip / UnRarX for Mac
- 7-Zip / PeaZip for Linux

The code bundle for the book is also hosted on GitHub at https://github.com/PacktPublishing/Mastering-PHP-7. We also have other code bundles from our rich catalog of books and videos available at https://github.com/PacktPublishing/. Check them out!

Errata

Although we have taken every care to ensure the accuracy of our content, mistakes do happen. If you find a mistake in one of our books-maybe a mistake in the text or the code-we would be grateful if you could report this to us. By doing so, you can save other readers from frustration and help us improve subsequent versions of this book. If you find any errata, please report them by visiting `http://www.packtpub.com/submit-errata`, selecting your book, clicking on the **Errata Submission Form** link, and entering the details of your errata. Once your errata are verified, your submission will be accepted and the errata will be uploaded to our website or added to any list of existing errata under the Errata section of that title.

To view the previously submitted errata, go to `https://www.packtpub.com/books/content/support` and enter the name of the book in the search field. The required information will appear under the **Errata** section.

Piracy

Piracy of copyrighted material on the Internet is an ongoing problem across all media. At Packt, we take the protection of our copyright and licenses very seriously. If you come across any illegal copies of our works in any form on the Internet, please provide us with the location address or website name immediately so that we can pursue a remedy.

Please contact us at `copyright@packtpub.com` with a link to the suspected pirated material.

We appreciate your help in protecting our authors and our ability to bring you valuable content.

Questions

If you have a problem with any aspect of this book, you can contact us at `questions@packtpub.com`, and we will do our best to address the problem.

1
The All New PHP

Programming languages nowadays are a dime a dozen. New languages spring into existence every so often. Choosing the right one for the job is so much more than just a checklist of its features. Some of them target specific problem domains, others try to position themselves for more general use. This goes to say that software development is a dynamic ecosystem where languages need to constantly adapt to ever-changing industry in order to stay relevant to its consumers. These changes are particularly challenging for already established languages such as PHP, where backward compatibility is an important consideration.

Originally created by Rasmus Lerdorf around 1995, PHP started its life as nothing more than a few **Common Gateway Interface** (**CGI**) programs in C. At that time, it was a simple scripting solution that empowered developers to build dynamic HTML pages with ease. Without the need to compile, developers could easily throw in a few lines of code into a file and see the results in the browser. This gave a rise to its early popularity. Two decades later, PHP matured into a rich general-purpose scripting language suited to web development. Throughout all these years, PHP managed to yield an impressive set of features with each new release whilst maintaining a trustworthy level of backward compatibility. Nowadays, large number of its core extensions ultimately simplify working with files, sessions, cookies, databases, web services, cryptography, and many other features common to web development. Its outstanding support for the **object-oriented programming** (**OOP**) paradigm made it truly competitive with other leading industry languages.

The decade-old ruling of PHP 5 has been overthrown by the release of PHP 7 in December 2015. It brought forth the all new execution engine, **Zend** Engine 3.0, which significantly improved performance and reduced memory consumption. This simple software update now allowed us to serve more concurrent users without adding any physical hardware to the mix. Acceptance among developers has been almost instant, all the more so because backward incompatibility was minimal, making migration as painless as possible.

In this chapter, we will take a detailed look into some of the new features introduced in PHP 7 and 7.1 releases:

- Scalar type hints
- Return type hints
- Anonymous classes
- Generator delegation
- Generator return expressions
- The null coalesce operator
- The spaceship operator
- Constant arrays
- Uniform variable syntax
- Throwables
- Group use declarations
- Class constant visibility modifiers
- Catching multiple exceptions types
- Iterable pseudo-type
- Nullable types
- Void return types

It is features like these that are bound to make a mark on the next generation of PHP frameworks and libraries, as well as how we write our own code.

Scalar type hints

By classification, PHP is a dynamically typed and weakly typed language. These are two different concepts that often get mixed together. Dynamically typed languages do not require the explicit declaration of a variable before it is used. Weakly typed languages are those in which the variable is not of any specific data type, that is, its type can change through different value-type reassignments.

Let's take a look at the following example:

```
// dynamic typed (no specific type defined, directly assigning value)
$name = "Branko"; // string
$salary = 4200.00; // float
$age = 33; // int

// weak typed (variable value reassigned into different type)
$salary = 4200.00; // float
$salary = $salary + "USD"; // float
$salary = $salary . "USD"; // string
```

In the preceding code, we see three different variables being used, none of which are predefined with a certain type. We just have values declared into them. PHP then determines the type on the go. Even when the variable type is determined, it can still be changed by simply assigning another type of value to it. These are two very powerful concepts, which, when used wisely, can save us lines and lines of code.

However, these powerful features often indirectly encourage bad design. This is particularly noticeable when writing functions, either by forcing function designers into multiple data type checks, or forcing them into multiple function return types.

Let's take a look at the following example:

```
function addTab($tab) {
   if (is_array($tab)) {

   } elseif (is_object($tab)) {

   } elseif (is_string($tab)) {

   } else {

   }
}
```

Given the type uncertainty of the input argument, the addTab function was forced to branch its logic. Similarly, the same function might decide to return different types of data, depending on the logic branch. Designs like these are usually a result of functions that simply try to do too much. The real problem is not even in the function, it is on the consumer side of things. If it happens that the developer using a function is not aware enough of the passing parameter type, unexpected results might occur.

To help us write more correct and self-documenting programs, PHP introduced **type hinting**.

PHP has supported function parameter type hinting from version 5.0, but only for objects, and from version 5.1 for arrays as well. With PHP 7, scalar types can be type-hinted as well, making it one of the more exciting features of the release. The following are the scalar type hints that are supported by PHP:

- `int`
- `float`
- `string`
- `bool`

We can now write functions in either of the following ways:

- It can be `function register($email, $age, $notify) { /* ... */}`
- It can be `function register($email, int $age, $notify) { /* ... */}`
- It can be `function register(string $email, int $age, bool $notify) { /* ... */}`

However, simply hinting scalar types is not enough as type declarations are not enforced by default. PHP will simply attempt to convert to the specified type without complaint. By adding the `declare(strict_types=1);` directive as the first statement in a PHP file, we can enforce the strict type checking behavior. It is worth noting that this directive only affects the specific file it is used in, and does not affect other included files. The **file-level** directive was used to preserve the backward compatibility with numerous extensions and built-in PHP functions.

Let's take a look at the following example:

```
declare(strict_types=1);

function register(string $email, int $age, bool $notify) {
 // body
}

register('user@mail.com', '33', true);
```

With strict types directive turned on, trying to pass an improper data type to a hinted scalar parameter would result in a \TypeError exception, as per the following output:

```
Fatal error: Uncaught TypeError: Argument 2 passed to register() must be of
the type integer, string given, called in /test.php on line 11 and defined
in /test.php:5 Stack trace: #0 /test.php(11): register('user@mail.co...',
'33', true) #1 {main} thrown in /test.php on line 5.
```

Scalar type hints are a powerful new addition to the PHP language. They empower developers with an extra layer of protection during runtime, without really sacrificing the weak type system in general.

Return type hints

Type hinting features are not limited to function parameters only; as of PHP 7, they expand to function return values as well. The same rules that apply to function parameters hinting, apply to function return type hinting. To specify a function return type, we simply follow the parameter list with a colon and the return type, as shown in the following example:

```
function register(string $user, int $age) : bool {
  // logic ...
  return true;
}
```

Developers can still write functions with multiple conditioned return statements; its just that in this case, each of these return statements, when reached, will have to match the hinted return type, otherwise \TypeError will be thrown.

The function return type hints play nicely with super types. Let's take a look at the following example:

```
class A {}
class B extends A {}
class C extends B {}

function getInstance(string $type) : A {
    if ($type == 'A') {
        return new A();
        } elseif ($type == 'B') {
            return new B();
        } else {
            return new C();
        }
    }
```

```
getInstance('A'); #object(A)#1 (0) { }
getInstance('B'); #object(B)#1 (0) { }
getInstance('XYZ'); #object(C)#1 (0) { }
```

We see that the function executes nicely for all three types. Given that B extends A directly, and C extends B, the function accepts them as the return value.

Given the dynamic nature of PHP, function return types might seem like a step in the wrong direction at first, more so because a lot of PHP code out there already uses the PHPDoc @return annotation, which plays nicely with modern IDE tools, such as PhpStorm. However, the @return annotation is merely informative, it does not enforce an actual return type during runtime, and it really makes sense only with a powerful IDE. Using the function return type hints ensures that our functions return what we intended them to return. They do not stand in the way of PHP's dynamic nature; they merely enrich it from a function consumer point of use.

Anonymous classes

Instantiating objects from classes is a pretty straightforward action. We use the new keyword, followed by a class name and possible constructor parameters. The class name part implies the existence of a previously defined class. Though rare, there are cases where classes are only used during execution. These rare cases make it verbose to force a class definition separately when we know that the class is only being used once. To address this verbosity challenge, PHP introduced a new functionality called **anonymous classes**. While the concept of anonymous classes has been around for quite some time in other languages, PHP only got to it in the PHP 7 release.

The syntax of anonymous classes is pretty straightforward, which is as follows:

```
$obj = new class() {};
$obj2 = new class($a, $b) {
    private $a;
    private $b;
    public function __construct($a, $b) {
        $this->a = $a;
        $this->b = $b;
    }
};
```

We use the `new` keyword , followed by the `class` keyword, followed by optional constructor parameters, and finally the body of the class packed in curly braces. Both objects are instantiated as a `class@anonymous` type. The functionality of objects instantiated through anonymous classes is no different from those instantiated via named classes.

Compared to named classes, anonymous classes are pretty much equal, in that, they can pass contractor parameters, extend other classes, implement interfaces, and use traits. However, anonymous classes cannot be serialized. Trying to serialize an instance of an anonymous class, as shown in the following code snippet, throws a fatal `Serialization of class@anonymous is not allowed...` error.

There are few other caveats to keep in mind when using anonymous classes. Nesting an anonymous class within another class hides the private and protected methods or properties of that outer class. To circumvent the limitation, we can pass the outer class' private and protected properties into an anonymous class constructor, as follows:

```php
interface Salary {
    public function pay();
}

trait Util {
    public function format(float $number) {
        return number_format($number, 2);
    }
}

class User {
    private $IBAN;
    protected $salary;
    public function __construct($IBAN, $salary) {
        $this->IBAN = $IBAN;
        $this->salary = $salary;
    }

    function salary() {
      return new class($this->IBAN, $this->salary) implements Salary {
        use Util;
        private $_IBAN;
        protected $_salary;

        public function __construct($IBAN, $salary) {
            $this->_IBAN = $IBAN;
            $this->_salary = $salary;
        }
```

```
        public function pay() {
            echo $this->_IBAN . ' ' . $this->format($this->_salary);
        }
    };
  }
}
$user = new User('GB29NWBK60161331926819', 4500.00);
$user->salary()->pay();
```

In this strip down User class example, we have a salary method that returns an anonymous class. To showcase the more robust use of anonymous classes, we make it implement the Salary interface and use the Util trait. The Salary interface forces the anonymous class to implement the pay method. Our implementation of pay method requires IBAN and salary member values from the outer class. Since an anonymous class does not allow access to private and protected members of the outer class, we pass those through anonymous class constructors. While the overall example certainly does not reflect notions of a good class design, it does showcase how to bypass the member visibility limitation.

There is also an option for an anonymous class to fetch the private and protected members of the outer class by extending the outer class itself. However, this requires the anonymous class constructor to properly instantiate the outer class; otherwise, we might end up with a warning, such as a missing argument, for User::__construct().

Even though they are namelessly defined, anonymous classes still get an internal name. Using the core PHP get_class method on an instance of an anonymous class, gets us that name, as shown in the following examples:

```
class User {}
class Salary {}

function gen() {
  return new class() {};
}

$obj = new class() {};
$obj2 = new class() {};
$obj3 = new class() extends User {};
$obj4 = new class() extends Salary {};
$obj5 = gen();
$obj6 = gen();

echo get_class($obj); // class@anonymous/var/www/index.php0x27fe03a
echo get_class($obj2); // class@anonymous/var/www/index.php0x27fe052
echo get_class($obj3); // class@anonymous/var/www/index.php0x27fe077
echo get_class($obj4); // class@anonymous/var/www/index.php0x27fe09e
```

```php
echo get_class($obj5); // class@anonymous/var/www/index.php0x27fe04f
echo get_class($obj6); // class@anonymous/var/www/index.php0x27fe04f

for ($i=0; $i<=5; $i++) {
  echo get_class(new class() {}); // 5 x
    class@anonymous/var/www/index.php0x27fe2d3
}
```

Observing these outputs, we see that the anonymous classes created in the same position (function or a loop) will yield the same internal name. Those with the same name return `true` for the equal (==) operator and `false` for the identity operator (===), an important consideration in order to avoid potential bugs.

Support for an anonymous classes opens a door to some interesting use cases, such as mocking tests and doing the inline class overrides, both of which, when used wisely, can improve code quality and readability.

Generator delegation

Iterating through a list of items is among the most common things in any programming language. PHP makes it easy to iterate over a diverse collection of data using the `foreach` construct. Many languages differentiate various data types of collection data, such as dictionary, list, set, tuple, and alike. PHP, however, does not dwell that much on data structures and simply uses the `array()` or `[]` constructs most of the time for its collections. This, in turn, can have a negative impact on creating large arrays in memory, which could cause exceeding memory limits or even increased processing times.

 Aside from the primitive *array* type, PHP also provides the `ArrayObject` and `ArrayIterator` classes. These turn arrays into a first class citizens in an OOP application.

Generators allow us to write code that uses `foreach` to iterate over a set of data without needing to build an array. They are like a function that yields as many values as needed, instead of returning just one, which gives them an iterator-like behavior. While generators have been around from PHP 5.5, they lacked more advanced functionality. **Generator delegation** is one of the improvements made available with the release of PHP 7.

Let's take a look at the following example:

```php
function even() {
    for ($i = 1; $i <= 10; $i++) {
      if ($i % 2 == 0) {
         yield $i;
      }
    }
}

function odd() {
    for ($i = 1; $i <= 10; $i++) {
        if ($i % 2 != 0) {
            yield $i;
        }
      }
}

function mix() {
    yield -1;
    yield from odd();
    yield 17;
    yield from even();
    yield 33;
}

// 2 4 6 8 1 0
foreach (even() as $even) {
   echo $even;
}

// 1 3 5 7 9
foreach (odd() as $odd) {
   echo $odd;
}

// -1 1 3 5 7 9 17 2 4 6 8 10 33
foreach (mix() as $mix) {
   echo $mix;
}
```

Here, we define three generator functions: even, odd, and mix. The mix function demonstrates the concept of generator delegation via the use of yield from <expr>. Whereas, <expr> is any expression that evaluates to a traversable object or array. We can see that the result of looping through the mix function echoes all of the yielded values from both itself as well as the even and odd functions.

The generator delegation syntax allows the factoring of yield statements into smaller conceptual units, giving generators the similar organizational functionality as methods give to classes. Used carefully, this can improve our code quality and readability.

Generator return expressions

Though PHP 5.5 enriched the language by introducing generator functions functionality, it lacked the return expressions alongside their yielded values. This inability of generator functions to specify return values limited their usefulness with coroutines. The PHP 7 version addressed this limitation by adding support for the return expressions. Generators are basically interruptible functions, where the yield statement flags the interruption point. Let's take a look at the following simple generator, written in the form of a self-invoking anonymous function:

```php
$letters = (function () {
  yield 'A';
  yield 'B';
  return 'C';
})();

// Outputs: A B
foreach ($letters as $letter) {
  echo $letter;
}

// Outputs: C
echo $letters->getReturn();
```

Though the $letters variable is defined as a self-invoking anonymous function, the yield statements are preventing immediate function execution, turning the function into the generator. Generator itself stands still until we try to iterate over it. Once the iteration kicks in, generator yields value A followed by value B, but not C. What this means is that when used in the foreach construct, the iteration will only encompass yielded values, not the returned ones. Once the iteration is done, we are free to call the getReturn() method to retrieve the actual return value. Calling the getReturn() method prior to iterating over generator results cannot get the return value of a generator that hasn't returned an exception.

The great thing about the generators is that they are not a one-way street; they are not limited to only yielding values, they can accept them as well. By being the instances of a \Generator class, they operate with several useful methods, two of which are getReturn and send. The send method enables us to send values back to the generator, which turns the one-way communication from the generator to the caller into a two-way channel between the two, effectively, turning generators into coroutines. The addition of the getReturn method empowered generators with the return statements, giving more flexibility with coroutines.

The null coalesce operator

Working with variables in PHP is quite easy. Variable declaration and initialization is done via a single expression. For example, the expression $user['name'] = 'John'; will automatically declare variable $user of type array and initialize that array with a single key name of value John.

Day-to-day development often includes checking for the existence of a variable value for various branching decisions, such as if ($user['name'] =='John') { ... } else { ... }. As we write our code ourselves, we tend to make sure that our code does not use non-declared variables and non-initialized array keys. There are cases, however, where variables come from outside, so we are not really in a position to guarantee their existence at runtime. Calling for $user['name'] when $user is not set, or is set but with keys other than name, will result in notice undefined index--name. Like any unexpected state in code, notices are bad, more so because they do not actually break your code, they allow it to execute further. When a notice occurs, unless we have the display_errors configuration set to true, and error reporting configured to show E_ALL, we would not even see the notice in the browser.

This is bad, as we might depend on the existence of variables and their values that are not there. This dependency might not even be handled in our code, and we would not even notice it because the code will continue to execute unless a specific variable check is put in place.

The PHP language has a certain number of predefined variables called **superglobals**, which we can use from any function, class, or file, regardless of the scope. The most used ones are probably $_POST and $_GET superglobals, which are used to fetch the data submitted via forms or URL parameters. Since we cannot guarantee the existence of $_GET['name'] in such cases, we need to check for it. Usually, this is done using the isset and empty functions in PHP, as shown in the following code block:

```
// #1
if (isset($_GET['name']) && !empty($_GET['name']))
    {
        $name = $_GET['name'];
    }
else {
        $name = 'N/A';
    }

// #2
if (!empty($_GET['name']))
    {
        $name = $_GET['name'];
    }
else {
        $name = 'N/A';
    }

// #3

$name = ((isset($_GET['name']) && !empty($_GET['name']))) ? $_GET['name'] :
'N/A';

// #4
$name = (!empty($_GET['name'])) ? $_GET['name'] : 'N/A';
```

The first example is the most robust one, as it uses both, the isset and empty functions. These functions are not the same, so it's important to understand what each of them does. The good thing about an empty function is that it will not trigger a notice if we try to pass it a variable that might not be set, such as $_GET['name']; it will simply return true or false. This makes the empty function a nice helper for most cases. However, even the fourth example, written via the use of the ternary operator, is somewhat robust.

PHP 7 introduced a new type of operator called the **null coalesce** (??) operator. It empowers us with the ability of writing shorter expressions. The following example demonstrates the elegance of its use:

```
$name = $_GET['name'] ?? 'N/A';
```

It returns the result of its first operand if it exists and is not null, or else its second operand. In other words, reading it from left to right, the first existing value, which is not null, is the value that will be returned.

The spaceship operator

Comparing two values is a frequent operation in any programming language. We use various language operators to express the type of comparison we wish to execute between two variables. In PHP, these operators include equal ($a == $b), identical ($a === $b), not equal ($a != $b or $a <> $b), not identical ($a !== $b), less than ($a < $b), greater than ($a > $b), less than or equal to ($a <= $b), and greater than or equal to ($a >= $b) comparisons.

All of these comparison operators result in Boolean true or false. Sometimes, however, there are cases where a three-way comparison is needed, in which case, the result of the comparison is more than just a Boolean true or false. While we can achieve a three-way comparison using various operators through various expressions, the solution is all but elegant.

With the release of PHP 7, a new spaceship <=> operator has been introduced, with a syntax as follows:

```
(expr) <=> (expr)
```

The spaceship <=> operator offers combined comparison. After comparison, it follows these conditions:

- It returns 0 if both operands are equal
- It returns 1 if the left operand is greater
- It returns -1 if the right operand is greater

Comparison rules used to yield the preceding results are the same as those used by existing comparison operators: <, <=, ==, >=, and >.

The usefulness of the new operator is especially apparent with ordering functions. Without it, the ordering functions were quite robust, as per the following example:

```
$users = ['branko', 'ivana', 'luka', 'ivano'];

usort($users, function ($a, $b) {
  return ($a < $b) ? -1 : (($a > $b) ? 1 : 0);
});
```

We can shorten the preceding example by applying the new operator to it, as follows:

```
$users = ['branko', 'ivana', 'luka', 'ivano'];

usort($users, function ($a, $b) {
  return $a <=> $b;
});
```

Applying the spaceship <=> operator, where applicable, gives the expressions simplicity and elegance.

Constant arrays

There are two types of constants in PHP, the **constants** and the **class constants**. The constants can be defined pretty much anywhere using the define construct, while the class constants are defined within the individual class or interface using the const keyword.

While we cannot say that one type of constant is more important than the other, PHP 5.6 made the difference between the two by allowing class constants with the array data type. Aside from that difference, both types of constants supported scalar values (integer, float, string, Boolean, or null).

The PHP 7 release addressed this inequality by adding the array data type to constants as well, making the following into valid expressions:

```
// The class constant - using 'const' keyword
class Rift {
  const APP = [
    'name' => 'Rift',
    'edition' => 'Community',
    'version' => '2.1.2',
    'licence' => 'OSL'
  ];
}

// The class constant - using 'const' keyword
```

```
interface IRift {
  const APP = [
    'name' => 'Rift',
    'edition' => 'Community',
    'version' => '2.1.2',
    'licence' => 'OSL'
  ];
}

// The constant - using 'define' construct
define('APP', [
  'name' => 'Rift',
  'edition' => 'Community',
  'version' => '2.1.2',
  'licence' => 'OSL'
]);

echo Rift::APP['version'];
echo IRift::APP['version'];
echo APP['version'];
```

Though having constants with the array data type might not be an exciting type of feature, it adds a certain flavor to the overall constant use.

Uniform variable syntax

The new variable syntax is probably one of the most impacting features of the PHP 7 release. It brings greater order into variable dereferencing. The impacting part, however, not only affects changes for better as it also introduces certain **backwards compatibility (BC)** breaks. Among the main reasons for these changes were inconsistencies with *variable variable* syntax.

Observing the $foo['bar']->baz expression, first a variable named $foo is fetched, then the bar offset is taken from the result, and, finally, the baz property is accessed. This is how normally variable accesses is interpreted, from left to right. However, the *variable variable* syntax goes against this principle. Observing the $$foo['baz'] variable, $foo is fetched first, then its baz offset, and finally looking for the variable with the name of the result is done.

The newly introduced uniform variable syntax addresses these inconsistencies as per the following example:

```
/*** expression syntax ***/
$$foo['bar']['baz']
```

```
// PHP 5.x meaning
${$foo['bar']['baz']}

// PHP 7.x meaning
($$foo)['bar']['baz']

/*** expression syntax ***/
$foo->$bar['baz']

// PHP 5.x meaning
$foo->{$bar['baz']}

// PHP 7.x meaning
($foo->$bar)['baz']

/*** expression syntax ***/
$foo->$bar['baz']()

// PHP 5.x meaning
$foo->{$bar['baz']}()

// PHP 7.x meaning
($foo->$bar)['baz']()

/*** expression syntax ***/
Foo::$bar['baz']()

// PHP 5.x meaning
Foo::{$bar['baz']}()

// PHP 7.x meaning
(Foo::$bar)['baz']()
```

Other than addressing the preceding inconsistencies, several new syntax combinations have been added that make the following expressions now valid:

```
$foo()['bar']();
[$obj1, $obj2][0]->prop;
getStr(){0}
$foo['bar']::$baz;
$foo::$bar::$baz;
$foo->bar()::baz()
// Assuming extension that implements actual toLower behavior
"PHP"->toLower();
[$obj, 'method']();
'Foo'::$bar;
```

There are quite a few different syntaxes here. While some of this might seem overwhelming and hard to find use for, it opens a door for new ways of thinking and code use.

Throwables

The exceptions in PHP are not a new concept. They have been around ever since PHP 5 was released. However, they did not encompass all of PHP's error handling because errors were not considered to be exceptions. PHP, at the time, had two-error handling systems. This made it tricky to deal with, as traditional errors were not catchable via the try...catch blocks exceptions. Certain tricks were possible, where one could have used the set_error_handler() function in order to set a user-defined error handler function, basically listening for errors and turning them into exceptions.

Let's look at the following example:

```php
<?php

class Mailer
{
    private $transport;

    public function __construct(Transport $transport)
    {
        $this->transport = $transport;
    }
}

$transport = new stdClass();

try {
    $mailer = new Mailer($transport);
} catch (\Exception $e) {
    echo 'Caught!';
} finally {
    echo 'Cleanup!';
}
```

PHP 5 would not be able to catch this, and instead throws Catchable fatal error, as shown here:

```
Catchable fatal error: Argument 1 passed to Mailer::__construct() must be
an instance of Transport, instance of stdClass given, called in /index.php
on line 18 and defined in /index.php on line 6.
```

By adding the implementation of `set_error_handler()` before this code, as follows, we could turn that fatal error into an exception:

```
set_error_handler(function ($errno, $errstr) {
  throw new \Exception($errstr, $errno);
});
```

With the preceding code in place, the `try...catch...finally` blocks would now kick in as intended. However, there were error types that could not be caught with `set_error_handler`, such as `E_ERROR`, `E_PARSE`, `E_CORE_ERROR`, `E_CORE_WARNING`, `E_COMPILE_ERROR`, `E_COMPILE_WARNING`, and most of `E_STRICT` raised in the file where `set_error_handler` is called.

The PHP 7 release improved the overall error handling system by introducing the `Throwable` interface, and moving the errors and exceptions under its umbrella. It is now the base interface for any object that can be thrown via a `throw` statement. While we cannot extend it directly, we can extend the `\Exception` and `\Error` classes. While `\Exception` is the base class for all PHP and user exceptions, `\Error` is the base class for all internal PHP errors.

We could now easily rewrite our preceding `try...catch...finally` block into one of the following:

```php
<?php

// Case 1
try {
    $mailer = new Mailer($transport);
} catch (\Throwable $e) {
    echo 'Caught!';
} finally {
    echo 'Cleanup!';
}

// Case 2
try {
    $mailer = new Mailer($transport);
} catch (\Error $e) {
    echo 'Caught!';
} finally {
    echo 'Cleanup!';
}
```

Notice the use of `\Throwable` in the first example `catch` block. Even though we cannot extend it, we can use it as a shorthand for catching both `\Error` and `\Exception` in a single `catch` statement.

Implementation of `\Throwable` brings a much needed alignment between errors and exceptions, making them easier to reason with.

Group use declarations

PHP introduced namespaces as part of the 5.3 release. It provided a way to group related classes, interfaces, functions, and constants, thus making our code base more organized and readable. However, dealing with modern libraries usually involves a lot of verbosity in terms of numerous `use` statements used to import classes from various namespaces, as shown in the following example:

```
use Magento\Backend\Block\Widget\Grid;
use Magento\Backend\Block\Widget\Grid\Column;
use Magento\Backend\Block\Widget\Grid\Extended;
```

To address this verbosity, the PHP 7 release introduced the group use declarations, allowing the following syntax:

```
use Magento\Backend\Block\Widget\Grid;
use Magento\Backend\Block\Widget\Grid\{
  Column,
  Extended
};
```

Here, we condensed `Column` and `Extend` under a single declaration. We can further condense this using the following compound namespaces:

```
use Magento\Backend\Block\Widget\{
  Grid
  Grid\Column,
  Grid\Extended
};
```

The group use declarations act as a shorthand to condense `use` declarations, making it slightly easier to import classes, constants, and functions in a concise way. While their benefits seem somewhat marginal, their use is completely optional.

Catching multiple exceptions types

With the introduction of throwables, PHP pretty much aligned its efforts around error detection, reporting, and handling. Developers are able to use the try...catch...finally blocks to handle the exceptions as they see fit. The possibility to use multiple catch blocks can give finer control over the response to certain types of exceptions. Sometimes, however, there are groups of exceptions we would like to respond equally. In PHP 7.1, exception handling was further refined to accommodate this challenge.

Let's take a look at the following PHP 5.x example:

```
try {
    // ...
    }
catch (\InvalidArgumentException $e)
    {
        // ...
    }
catch (\LengthException $e)
    {
        // ...
    }
catch (Exception $e)
    {
        // ...
    }
finally
    {
        // ...
    }
```

Here, we are handling three exceptions, two of which are quite specific, and a third one that catches in if the previous two are not matched. The finally block is merely a cleanup, if it happens that one is needed. Imagine now that the same response is needed for both the \InvalidArgumentException and \LengthException blocks. The solution would be to either copy an entire chunk of code from one exception block into another, or, at best, write a function that wraps the response code and then calls that function within each exception block.

The newly added exception handling syntax is enabled to catch multiple exception types. By using a single vertical bar (|), we can define multiple exception types for the catch parameter, as per the following PHP 7.x example:

```
try {
    // ...
```

```
    }
catch (\InvalidArgumentException | \LengthException $e)
    {
      // ...
    }
catch (\Exception $e)
    {
      // ...
    }
  finally
    {
      // ...
    }
```

Aside from a touch of elegance, the new syntax directly affects code reuse for the better.

Class constant visibility modifiers

There are five types of access modifier in PHP: public, private, protected, abstract, and final. Often called **visibility modifiers**, not all of them are equally applicable. Their use is spread across classes, functions, and variables, as follows:

- **Functions**: public, private, protected, abstract, and final
- **Classes**: abstract and final
- **Variables**: public, private, and protected

Class constants, however, are not on the list. The older versions of PHP did not allow a visibility modifier on the class constant. By default, class constants were merely assigned public visibility.

The PHP 7.1 release addresses this limitation by introducing the public, private, and protected class constant visibility modifiers, as per the following example:

```
class Visibility
  {
    // Constants without defined visibility
    const THE_DEFAULT_PUBLIC_CONST = 'PHP';

    // Constants with defined visibility
    private const THE_PRIVATE_CONST = 'PHP';
    protected const THE_PROTECTED_CONST = 'PHP';
    public const THE_PUBLIC_CONST = 'PHP';
  }
```

Similar to the old behavior, class constants declared without any explicit visibility default to `public`.

Iterable pseudo-type

Quite often, functions in PHP either accept or return an array or object implementing the `\Traversable` interface. Though both types can be used in the `foreach` constructs, fundamentally, an array is a primitive type; objects are not. This made it difficult for functions to reason about these types of iterative parameters and return values.

PHP 7.1 addresses this need by introducing the iterable pseudo-type to the mix. The idea is to use it as a type declaration on a parameter or return type to indicate that the value is `iterable`. The `iterable` type accepts any array, any object implementing Traversable, and generators.

The following example demonstrates the use of `iterable` as a function parameter:

```
function import(iterable $users)
  {
    // ...
  }

function import(iterable $users = null)
  {
    // ...
  }

function import(iterable $users = [])
  {
    // ...
  }
```

Trying to pass the value to the preceding `import` function other than an array instance of Traversable or generator will throw `\TypeError`. If, however, the default value is assigned, be it null or an empty array, the function will work.

The following examples demonstrates the use of `iterable` as a function return value:

```
function export(): iterable {
  return [
    'Johny',
    'Tom',
    'Matt'
  ];
```

```
    }

    function mix(): iterable {
      return [
        'Welcome',
         33,
         4200.00
      ];
    }

    function numbers(): iterable {
       for ($i = 0; $i <= 5; $i++) {
          yield $i;
       }
    }
```

One thing to be careful about is that `iterable` is implemented as a reserved class name in PHP. What this means is that any user class, interface, or trait named `iterable` will throw an error.

Nullable types

Many programming languages allow some sort of optional or nullable types, depending on terminology. The PHP dynamic type already supports this notion via the built-in null type. A variable is considered to be of the null type if it has been assigned a constant value null, it has not been assigned any value, or it has been unset using the `unset()` construct. Aside from variables, the null type can also be used against the function parameters, by assigning them a default value of null.

However, this imposed a certain limitation, as we could not declare a parameter that might be null without flagging it as optional at the same time.

PHP 7.1 addressed this limitation by adding a leading question mark symbol (?) to indicate that a type can be null, unless specifically assigned to some other value. This also means that type could be null and mandatory at the same type. These nullable types are now permitted pretty much anywhere where type declarations are permitted.

The following is an example of the nullable type with a mandatory parameter value:

```
function welcome(?string $name) {
    echo $name;
}

welcome(); // invalid
welcome(null); // valid
```

The first call to the `welcome` function throws an `\Error`, because its declaration is making the parameter mandatory. Goes to say that the nullable type should not be mistaken with `null` being passed as a value.

The following is an example of a nullable type with an optional parameter value, optional in the sense that it has been assigned a default value of `null` already:

```
function goodbye(?string $name = null)
{
    if (is_null($name))
    {
        echo 'Goodbye!';
    }
    else
    {
        echo "Goodbye $name!";
    }
}

goodbye(); // valid
goodbye(null); // valid
goodbye('John'); // valid
```

The following is an example of function declaration using the nullable return type:

```
function welcome($name): ?string
{
    return null; // valid
}

function welcome($name): ?string
{
    return 'Welcome ' . $name; // valid
}

function welcome($name): ?string
{
    return 33; // invalid
}
```

The nullable types work both with scalar types (Boolean, Integer, Float, String) and compound types (Array, Object, Callable).

Void return types

With all the power of function parameter types and function return types introduced in PHP 7, there was one thing missing from the mix function. While function return types allowed specifying a desired return type, they did not allow specifying the lack of return value. To address this inconsistency, the PHP 7.1 release introduced a void return type feature.

Why is this important, we might ask ourselves? As with previously mentioned function return types, this feature can be extremely useful for documentation and error-checking purposes. By its nature, PHP does not require a return statement in its function definitions, making it unclear at first look if the function simply executes certain actions or returns a value. Using the void return type makes it clearer that a function's purpose is to perform an action, rather than producing a result.

Let's take a look at the following example:

```
function A(): void {
    // valid
}

function B(): void {
    return; // valid
}

function C(): void {
    return null; // invalid
}

function D(): void {
    return 1; // invalid
}
```

The `function A` and `function B` methods showcase a valid use of the `void` type parameter. The `function A` method has no explicitly set return value, but that's OK, as PHP implicitly always returns `null`. The `function B` method simply uses the `return` statement without any following type, which also makes it valid. The `function C` method is a bit strange, as it looks like it might be valid at first, but it's not. How is it that `function C` is invalid while the `function A` method is, even though they do the same thing? Even though `return` and `return null` are technically equivalent in PHP, they are not really the same. The existence of a return type, or its lack, denotes a function intent. Specifying return values, even if its `null`, suggests the value is significant. With a void return type, the return value is insignificant. The use of the `void` return type, therefore, signifies an unimportant return value, the one that won't be used anywhere after the function is called.

The differentiation between explicit void and implicit null return might come as somewhat foggy. The takeaway here is that using void return types conveys that the function is not supposed to return any kind of value. While they do not make any major impact on the code itself, and their use is fully optional, they do bring a certain richness to the language.

Summary

The PHP 7 and 7.1 releases have introduced quite a few changes. Some of these changes transform the language beyond what PHP once was. While still pertaining the dynamic typing system, function parameters and return types can now be strictly defined. This changes the way we look and work with functions. Among function-related changes, there are several others targeting improvements over a decade old PHP 5. The ecosystem, as a whole, will take some time to catch up. For developers with experience in PHP 5, these changes are not merely technical in nature; they require change of mindset in order to successfully apply what is now possible.

Moving forward, we will look into the current state of PHP standards, who defines them, what they describe, and how can we benefit from embracing them.

2
Embracing Standards

Every profession and industry has its own set of standards. Whether formal or informal, they govern the way of doing things. The software industry tends to formalize standards into documents that establish various specifications and procedures designed to ensure the quality and reliability of products and services. They further incite the compatibility and interoperability processes, which otherwise might not be possible.

Putting the code into the context of products, various coding standards have emerged over the years. Their use yields greater code quality and reduced cognitive friction over our codebase. With code quality being one of the pillars of sustainable software development, it's no surprise standards are of impeccable importance to any professional developer.

When it comes to PHP, there are several layers of standards we need to take into consideration. There are coding standards specific to the language itself, and those specific to the individual library, framework, or platform. While some of these standards follow each other, others tend to clash sometimes. Usually, this clash is about little things, such as putting the opening function bracket in a new line or leaving it on the same line. That being the case, specific library, framework, and platform standards should take precedence over the pure language standards.

Back in 2009, at the **php[tek]** conference in Chicago, a number of developers joined forces and founded the *PHP Standards Group*. Organized around the mailing list at standards@lists.php.net, the initial goal was to establish the proper autoloading standard. Autoloading was a serious challenge for framework and platform developers. Different developers were using different conventions when naming their class files. This had a serious impact on interoperability. The **PHP Standards Recommendations**, codenamed **PSR-0**, set out to solve this issue by outlining practices and constraints that must be followed for autoloader interoperability. At its early stages, group acceptance into the PHP community was quite reserved. They had yet to earn the right to call themselves that in the eyes of the community. Two years later, the group renamed itself into **Framework Interoperability Group**, abbreviated to **PHP-FIG**. To this date, PHP-FIG has produced several PSRs, reaffirming its position among developers with each of them.

The PHP-FIG and its PSRs were predated by the PEAR Coding Standard, which is still quite dominant today. It focuses mostly on the elements of the PHP language itself. These elements address the way we write functions, variables, classes, and so on. The PSRs on the other hand mostly focus on the interoperability side of things. The PHP-FIG and PEAR intersect within the bounds of PSR-1 and PSR-2; this makes developers free to follow a single set of standards now, the ones provided by the PHP-FIG group.

In this chapter, we will take a detailed look at currently published and accepted PSR standards:

- PSR-1 - basic coding standard
- PSR-2 - coding style guide
- PSR-3 - logger interface
- PSR-4 - autoloading standard
- PSR-6 - caching interface
- PSR-7 - HTTP message interface
- PSR-13 - hypermedia links

Throughout the PSRs, there is an extensive use of the **MUST, MUST NOT, REQUIRED, SHALL, SHALL NOT, SHOULD, SHOULD NOT, RECOMMENDED, MAY**, and **OPTIONAL** keywords. The meaning of these keywords is described in more detail under RFC 2119 (http://www.ietf.org/rfc/rfc2119.txt).

PSR-1 - basic coding standard

PSR-1 is the basic coding standard. It outlines the rules our code should follow, as seen by the members of PHP-FIG. The standard itself is quite short.

Files MUST use only <?php and <?= tags. At one time, PHP supported several different tags (`<?php ?>`, `<? ?>`, `<?= ?>`, `<% %>`, `<%= %>`, `<script language="php"></script>`). The use of some depend on the configuration directives `short_open_tag` (`<? ?>`) and `asp_tags` (`<% %>`, `<%= %>`). The PHP 7 release removed ASP tags (`<%`, `<%=`), and the script tag (`<script language="php">`) altogether. The use of only `<?php ?>` and `<?= ?>` tags is now recommended in order to maximize compatibility.

Files MUST use only UTF-8 without BOM for PHP code. The **byte order mark** (**BOM**) is a Unicode character, **U+FEFF BYTE ORDER MARK** (BOM), appearing at the beginning of a document. When used correctly, BOM is invisible. The HTML5 browsers are required to recognize the UTF-8 BOM and use it to detect the encoding of the page. PHP, on the other hand, can experience issues with BOM. Positioned at the start of the file, BOM clashes with PHP headers by causing the page to begin output before the header command is interpreted.

Files SHOULD either declare symbols (classes, functions, constants, and so on) or cause side-effects (for example, generate output, change .ini settings, and so on) but SHOULD NOT do both. Quite often, the simplicity of PHP becomes its downside. The language is quite loose when it comes to its use. We can easily start from a blank file and code an entire application in it. This implies having dozens of different classes, functions, constants, variables, includes, requires, and other directives, all stacked one next to another. While this might come in handy for a quick prototyping, it is, by no means, an approach to be taken when building our applications.

The following lines of code demonstrate an example to avoid:

```php
<?php

// side effect: change ini settings
ini_set('error_reporting', E_ALL);

// side effect: loads a file
include 'authenticate.php';

// side effect: generates output
echo "<h1>Hello</h1>";

// declaration
function log($msg)
```

```
{
  // body
}
```

The following lines of code demonstrate an example to follow:

```php
<?php

// declaration
function log()
{
  // body
}

// conditional declaration is *not* a side effect
if (!function_exists('hello')) {
 function hello($msg)
 {
   // body
 }
}
```

Namespaces and classes MUST follow an autoloading PSR: [PSR-0, PSR-4]. Autoloading plays a big role in PHP. The concept cuts down the use of require constructs by pulling in our classes and functions automatically from various files. By default, the language itself provides the __autoload() and spl_autoload_register() functions to assist with that. The PHP-FIG group produced two autoloading standards. The PSR-0 standard was the first PSR to come out, and it soon became widely adopted across many PHP frameworks. As of October 2014, PSR-0 has been marked as deprecated, leaving PSR-4 as an alternative. We will touch upon PSR-4 in more detail later on. For the moment, it's suffice to say that the code written for PHP 5.3 and after must use formal namespaces.

The following lines of code demonstrate an example to avoid:

```php
<?php

class Foggyline_User_Model
{
  // body
}
```

The following lines of code demonstrate an example to follow:

```php
<?php

namespace Foggyline\Model;
```

```
class User
{
  // body
}
```

Class names MUST be declared in **StudlyCaps**. The class names, among other things, sometimes comprise of multiple words. Imagine, for example, the class in charge of XML parsing. Reasonably enough, we might call it `Xml_Parser`, `XmlParser`, `XML_Parser`, `XMLParser`, or some similar combination. There are many different rules used to squeeze together multiple words that contribute to better readability of the code, such as camel case, kebab case, snake case, and so on. This standard proposes the use of StudlyCaps, where capitalization of letters varies arbitrarily. They resemble the , but might be carried out in a more random fashion.

The following lines of code demonstrate an example to avoid:

```
<?php

class xmlParser
{
  // body
}

class XML_Parser
{
  // body
}
```

The following lines of code demonstrate an example to follow:

```
<?php

class XmlParser
{
  // body
}

class XMLParser
{
  // body
}
```

Class constants MUST be declared in all upper case with underscore separators. The PHP system has two types of constants, the ones that live outside the class and are defined using the define construct, and the other ones that live inside the class. Given that constants represent immutable variables, their name is supposed to stand out. This standard clearly states that any class constant name should be fully capitalized. It, however, avoids any recommendation regarding the property names. We are free to use any of the following combinations ($StudlyCaps, $camelCase, or $under_score) as long as we are being consistent.

The following lines of code demonstrate an example to avoid:

```php
<?php

class XmlParser
{
  public const APPVERSION = 1.2;
  private const app_package = 'net.foggyline.xml.parser';
  protected const appLicence = 'OSL';
}
```

The following lines of code demonstrate an example to follow:

```php
<?php

class XmlParser
{
  public const APP_VERSION = 1.2;
  private const APP_PACKAGE = 'net.foggyline.xml.parser';
  protected const APP_LICENCE = 'OSL';
}
```

Method names MUST be declared in camelCase. Functions enclosed within a class are called **methods**. The naming pattern here differs from previously mentioned StudlyCaps, as it uses camelCase, which is less arbitrary. More specifically, lowercase camelCase is used, which implies method names starting with lowercase letters.

The following lines of code demonstrate an example to avoid:

```php
<?php

class User
{
  function say_hello($name) { /* … */ }
  function Pay($salary) { /* … */ }
  function RegisterBankAccount($account) { /* … */ }
}
```

The following lines of code demonstrate an example to follow:

```php
<?php

class User
{
    function sayHello($name) { /* … */ }
    function pay($salary) { /* … */ }
    function registerBankAccount($account) { /* … */ }
}
```

 The official, full-length *PSR-1 Basic Coding Standard* guide is available at `ht` `tp://www.php-fig.org/psr/psr-1/`.

PSR-2 - coding style guide

PSR-2 is an extension of PSR-1. This means that when talking about PSR-2, the PSR-1 standard is sort of implicitly understood. The difference is that PSR-2 expands beyond basic class and function formatting by enumerating a set of rules on how to format PHP code. The outlined style rules are derived shared similarities across the various PFP-FIG member projects.

Code MUST follow a coding style guide PSR (PSR-1). Goes to say that every PSR-2 code is implicitly PSR-1 compliant.

Code MUST use 4 spaces for indenting, not tabs. The spaces versus tabs dilemma is quite an old one in the programming world. There are those who the PHP-FIG group voted for the use of spaces, whereas 4 spaces represent what is usually a single tab indent. The benefit of a space over a tab is consistency. Whereas, a tab could show up as a different number of columns depending on the environment, a single space is always one column. While this might not be the most convincing argument of all, the standards goes on to say that 4 spaces constitute for a single indent. Think of it as 4 spaces for what was once a single indent. Most modern IDE editors nowadays, such as PhpStorm, handle this automatically for us.

There MUST NOT be a hard limit on line length; the soft limit MUST be 120 characters; lines SHOULD be 80 characters or less. The 80 characters line length argument is as old as programming itself. The IBM punch card, designed in 1928, had the 80 columns with 12 punch locations each, one character to each column. This 80 characters per row design choice was later passed on to character-based terminals. Although the display device advancements are far beyond these limitations, even today, some command prompts remain set at 80 columns. This standard basically says that while we might use any length we want, it is highly preferable to keep it below 80 characters.

There MUST be one blank line after the namespace declaration, and there MUST be one blank line after the block of use declarations. Although this is not a technical requirement imposed by the language itself, the standard mandates it. The requirement itself is more of a cosmetic nature. The resulting use impacts code readability for the better.

The following lines of code demonstrate an example to avoid:

```php
<?php
namespace Foggyline\User\Model;
use Foggyline\User\Model\Director;

class Employee
{
}
```

The following lines of code demonstrate an example to follow:

```php
<?php
namespace Foggyline\User\Model;
use Foggyline\User\Model\Director;

class Employee
{
}
```

Opening braces for classes MUST go on the next line, and closing braces MUST go on the next line after the body. Similarly, this is not a technical requirement of the language, rather a cosmetic one.

The following lines of code demonstrate an example to avoid:

```php
<?php

class Employee {
  // body
}
```

The following lines of code demonstrate an example to follow:

```php
<?php

class Employee
{
  // body
}
```

Opening braces for methods MUST go on the next line, and closing braces MUST go on the next line after the body. Again, this is a cosmetic type of requirement, it is not really imposed by the language itself.

The following lines of code demonstrate an example to avoid:

```php
<?php

class Employee {
  public function pay() {
    // body
  }
}
```

The following lines of code demonstrate an example to follow:

```php
<?php

class Employee
{
  public function pay()
  {
    // body
  }
}
```

Visibility MUST be declared on all properties and methods; abstract and final MUST be declared before the visibility; static MUST be declared after the visibility. Visibility is merely a shorthand for what is officially called **access modifiers**. The class methods in PHP can use more than one access modifier. The order of access modifiers in such cases is not relevant; we can easily say `abstract public function` and `public abstract function` or `final public function` and `public final function`. The same goes when we add the `static` access modifier to the mix, where we effectively might have three different access modifiers on a single method. This standard clearly specifies that the `abstract` and `final` modifiers, if used, need to be set first, while the `static` modifiers, if used, need to follow `public` and `private` modifiers.

The following block of code demonstrates an example to avoid:

```php
<?php

abstract class User
{
  public function func1()
  {
    // body
  }

  private function func2()
  {
    // body
  }

  protected function func3()
  {
    // body
  }

  public static abstract function func4();

  static public final function func5()
  {
    // body
  }
}

class Employee extends User
{
  public function func4()
  {
    // body
  }
}
```

The following block of code demonstrates an example to follow:

```php
<?php

abstract class User
{
  public function func1()
  {
    // body
  }
```

```php
  private function func2()
  {
    // body
  }

  protected function func3()
  {
    // body
  }

  abstract public static function func4();

  final public static function func5()
  {
    // body
  }
}

class Employee extends User
{
  public static function func4()
  {
    // body
  }
}
```

Control structure keywords MUST have one space after them; method and function calls MUST NOT. This is a rather cosmetic requirement, which merely affects code readability.

The following lines of code demonstrate an example to avoid:

```php
<?php

class Logger
{
  public function log($msg, $code)
  {
    if($code >= 500) {
      // logic
    }
  }
}
```

The following lines of code demonstrate an example to follow:

```php
<?php

class Logger
```

```
  {
    public function log($msg, $code)
    {
      if ($code >= 500)
      {

      }
    }
  }
```

Opening braces for control structures MUST go on the same line, and closing braces MUST go on the next line after the body.

The following block of code demonstrates an example to avoid:

```php
<?php

class Logger
{
  public function log($msg, $code)
  {
    if ($code === 500)
    {
      // logic
    }
    elseif ($code === 600)
    {
      // logic
    }
    elseif ($code === 700)
    {
      // logic
    }
    else
    {
      // logic
    }
  }
}
```

The following block of code demonstrates an example to follow:

```php
<?php

class Logger
{
  public function log($msg, $code)
  {
```

```
    if ($code === 500) {
        // logic
    } elseif ($code === 600) {
        // logic
    } elseif ($code === 700) {
        // logic
    } else {
        // logic
    }
  }
}
```

Opening parenthesis for control structures MUST NOT have a space after them, and closing parenthesis for control structures MUST NOT have a space before them. The closing parenthesis space might be a bit confusing here to grasp, because, earlier, we saw the standard enforcing spaces for indention instead of tabs. This means that we will have spaces preceding closing brackets. However, there should only be enough space to represent the actual indention at the point of the closing bracket, nothing more.

The demonstrates an example to avoid (notice the space on line 7, after the opening curly brace):

```
1   <?php
2
3   class Logger
4   {
5       public function log($msg, $code)
6       {
7           if ($code === 500) {
8               // logic
9           } elseif ($code === 600) {
10              // logic
11          } elseif ($code === 700) {
12              // logic
13          } else {
14              // logic
15          }
16      }
17  }
```

The demonstrates an example to follow:

```php
1  <?php
2
3  class Logger
4  {
5      public function log($msg, $code)
6      {
7          if ($code === 500) {
8              // logic
9          } elseif ($code === 600) {
10             // logic
11         } elseif ($code === 700) {
12             // logic
13         } else {
14             // logic
15         }
16     }
17 }
```

The official, full-length *PSR-2 Coding Style* guide is available at http://www.php-fig.org/psr/psr-2/.

PSR-3 - logger interface

Logging different type of events is a common practice for applications. While one application might categorize these types of events into errors, informational events, and warnings, others might throw in more elaborate levels of severity logging. The same goes for the actual format of the log message itself. Goes to say that every application might easily have its own flavor of logging mechanism. This stands in a way of interoperability.

The PSR-3 standard sets out to fix this by defining a standard for the actual logger interface. Such a standardized interface then enables us to write PHP application logs in a simple and universal way.

The *syslog protocol* (RFC 5424), defined by **Internet Engineering Task Force (IETF)**, differentiates the following eight severity levels:

- emergency: This states the system is unusable
- alert: This states action must be taken immediately
- critical: This states critical conditions
- error: This states error conditions
- warning: This states warning conditions
- notice: This states normal but significant condition
- info: This states informational messages
- debug: This states debug-level messages

The PSR-3 standard builds upon the RFC 5424 by specifying LoggerInterface, which exposes a special method for each of the eight severity levels, shown as follows:

```php
<?php

interface LoggerInterface
{
  public function emergency($message, array $context = array());
  public function alert($message, array $context = array());
  public function critical($message, array $context = array());
  public function error($message, array $context = array());
  public function warning($message, array $context = array());
  public function notice($message, array $context = array());
  public function info($message, array $context = array());
  public function debug($message, array $context = array());
  public function log($level, $message, array $context = array());
}
```

We can also notice the ninth log() method, whose signature differs than the first eight. The log() method is more of a convenience method, whose level parameter needs to indicate one of the eight severity levels. Calling this method must have the same result as calling the level-specific methods. Every method accepts a string as $message, or an object with a __toString() method. Trying to call these methods with an unknown severity level must throw Psr\Log\InvalidArgumentException.

The `$message` string may contain one or more placeholders, which the interface implementors might interpolate with key-value parameters passed into the `$context` string, as shown in the following abstract example:

```php
<?php

//...
$message = "User {email} created, with role {role}.";
//...
$context = array('email' => 'john@mail.com', 'role' => 'CUSTOMER');
//...
```

Without going into the implementation details, it's suffice to say that PSR-3 is a simple standard set to sort an important role of a logger mechanism. Using the logger interface, we are freed from having to rely on a specific logger implementation. We can type-hint our application code against `LoggerInterface` to acquire a PSR-3 compliant logger.

If we were using **Composer** with our project, we could easily include the `psr/log` package into it. This would enable us to integrate a PSR compliant logger with our project in one of the following ways:

- Implementing the `LoggerInterface` interface and defining all of its methods
- Inheriting the `AbstractLogger` class and defining the `log` method
- Using `LoggerTrait` and defining the `log` method

However, it is much easier to use an existing Composer package, such as `monolog/monolog` or `katzgrau/klogger`, and avoid writing our own logger implementation altogether.

The *Monolog* project is a nice example of a popular and robust PHP library that implements the PSR-3 logger interface. It can be used to send our logs to files, sockets, inboxes, databases, and various web services.

The official, full-length *PSR-3: Logger Interface* guide is available at http://www.php-fig.org/psr/psr-3/.

PSR-4 - autoloading standard

To this date, the PHP-FIG group has released two autoloading standards. Predating PSR-4 was PSR-0. It was the first standard released by the PHP-FIG group. Its class naming had certain backward compatibility features aligned with an even older PEAR standard. Whereas, each level of the hierarchy was separated with a single underscore, indicating pseudo-namespaces and directory structure. The PHP 5.3 release then brought official namespace support to the language. PSR-0 allowed both the old PEAR underscore mode and the use of the new namespace notation. Allowing the underscores for some time to follow eased the transition to namespaces and encouraged wider adoption. Pretty soon, Composer came on the scene.

> Composer is a popular dependency manager for PHP that deals with packages and libraries by installing them in a `vendor/` directory of our project.

With Composer's `vendor/` directory philosophy, there was no single main directory for PHP sources as with PEAR. PSR-0 became a bottleneck and was marked as deprecated as of October 2014.

PSR-4 is the recommended autoloading standard nowadays.

According to PSR-4, a fully qualified class name now has the form as per the following example:

```
\<NamespaceName>(\<SubNamespaceNames>)*\<ClassName>
```

The term *class* here does not just refer to classes. It also refers to *interfaces*, *traits*, and other similar structures.

To put this into context, let's take a look at the partial class code taken from the *Magento 2* commerce platform, which is shown as follows:

```php
<?php

namespace Magento\Newsletter\Model;

use Magento\Customer\Api\AccountManagementInterface;
use Magento\Customer\Api\CustomerRepositoryInterface;

class Subscriber extends \Magento\Framework\Model\AbstractModel
{
    // ...
```

```
    public function __construct(
      \Magento\Framework\Model\Context $context,
      \Magento\Framework\Registry $registry,
      \Magento\Newsletter\Helper\Data $newsletterData,
      \Magento\Framework\App\Config\ScopeConfigInterface $scopeConfig,
      \Magento\Framework\Mail\Template\TransportBuilder
        $transportBuilder,
      \Magento\Store\Model\StoreManagerInterface $storeManager,
      \Magento\Customer\Model\Session $customerSession,
      CustomerRepositoryInterface $customerRepository,
        AccountManagementInterface $customerAccountManagement,
      \Magento\Framework\Translate\Inline\StateInterface
        $inlineTranslation,
      \Magento\Framework\Model\ResourceModel\AbstractResource
        $resource = null,
      \Magento\Framework\Data\Collection\AbstractDb
        $resourceCollection = null,
      array $data = []
    ) {
      // ...
    }

    // ...
  }
```

The preceding `Subscriber` class is defined within the `Subscriber.php` file present at `vendor\Magento\module-newsletter\Model\`, relative to the root of the *Magento* project. We can see `__construct` using all sorts of fully classified class names. The Magento platform has these types of robust constructors all over its codebase because of the way it handles dependency injection. We can imagine the amount of additional code needed to individually `require` all of these classes manually if it weren't for the unified autoloading standard.

The PSR-4 standard also states that the autoloader implementation must not throw an exception or raise an error of any level. This is to ensure that possible multiple autoloaders do not break one another.

The official, full-length *PSR-4: Autoloader Standard* guide is available at `http://www.php-fig.org/psr/psr-4/`.

PSR-6 - caching interface

Performance issues are the ever-hot topic of application development. The effects of poorly performing applications can sometimes have serious financial impact. Back in 2007, Amazon reported a 100 ms increase in `https://www.amazon.com/` load time and their sales decreased by 1%. Several studies have also shown that nearly half of the users are likely to abandon the website if the page load time is over 3 seconds. To address the performance issues, we look into caching solutions.

Both browsers and servers allow caching of various resources, such as images, web pages, CSS/JS files. Sometimes, however, this is not enough as we need to be able to control the caching of various other bits on the application level, such as objects themselves. Over time, various libraries rolled out their own caching solutions. This made it tough for developers, as they needed to implement specific caching solutions in their code. This made it impossible to easily change caching implementation later on.

To solve these problems, the PHP-FIG group brought forth the PSR-6 standard.

This standard defines two main interfaces, `CacheItemPoolInterface` and `CacheItemInterface`, for working with **Pool** and **Items**. The pool represents a collection of items in the caching system. Whereas, item represents a single **key**/value pair stored within the pool. The key part acts as a unique identifier, so it must be immutable.

The following code snippet reflects the PSR-6 `CacheItemInterface` definition:

```php
<?php

namespace Psr\Cache;

interface CacheItemInterface
{
  public function getKey();
  public function get();
  public function isHit();
  public function set($value);
  public function expiresAt($expiration);
  public function expiresAfter($time);
}
```

The following code snippet reflects the PSR-6 `CacheItemPoolInterface` definition:

```php
<?php

namespace Psr\Cache;
```

```
interface CacheItemPoolInterface
{
  public function getItem($key);
  public function getItems(array $keys = array());
  public function hasItem($key);
  public function clear();
  public function deleteItem($key);
  public function deleteItems(array $keys);
  public function save(CacheItemInterface $item);
  public function saveDeferred(CacheItemInterface $item);
  public function commit();
}
```

Libraries that implement the PSR-6 standard must support the following serializable PHP data types:

- Strings
- Integers
- Floats
- Boolean
- Null
- Arrays
- Object

The compound structures such as arrays and objects are always tricky ones. The standard says that the indexed, associative, and multidimensional arrays of arbitrary depth must be supported. Since arrays in PHP are not necessarily of a single data type, this is the one to be careful about. Objects might utilize the PHP Serializable interface, __sleep() or __wakeup() magic methods, or similar language functionality. The important bit is that any data passed to libraries that implement PSR-6 is expected to come back exactly as passed.

There are several PSR-6 cache implementations available via Composer, all of which support tags. The following is a partial list of the most popular ones:

- cache/filesystem-adapter: Using filesystem
- cache/array-adapter: Using a PHP array
- cache/memcached-adapter: Using Memcached
- cache/redis-adapter: Using Redis
- cache/predis-adapter: Using Redis (Predis)

- `cache/void-adapter`: Using Void
- `cache/apcu-adapter`: Using APCu
- `cache/chain-adapter`: Using chain
- `cache/doctrine-adapter`: Using Doctrine

We can easily add any one of these caching libraries to our project just by using `Composer require new/package`. The PSR-6 compliance makes it possible for us to easily swap these libraries in our project without changing any of its code.

The *Redis* is an open source in-memory data structure store used as a database, cache, and message broker. It is quite popular with PHP developers as a caching solution. The official *Redis* page is available at `https://redis.io/`.

The official, full-length *PSR-6: Caching Interface* guide is available at `http://www.php-fig.org/psr/psr-6/`.

PSR-7 - HTTP message interface

The HTTP protocol has been around for quite some time now. Its development was initiated by Tim Berners-Lee at CERN way back in 1989. Throughout the years, **Internet Engineering Task Force (IETF)** and the **World Wide Web Consortium (W3C)** defined series of standards for it, known as **Requests for Comments (RFCs)**. The first definition of HTTP/1.1 occurred in RFC 2068 in 1997, and was later deprecated by RFC 2616 in 1999. Over a decade later, HTTP/2 was standardized in 2015. Although HTTP/2 is now supported by major web servers, HTTP/1.1 is still widely used.

The underlying HTTP communication comes down to requests and responses, commonly referred to as **HTTP messages**. Abstracted away from average consumers, these messages form the foundation of web development, and are therefore of interest to every web application developer. While RFC 7230, RFC 7231, and RFC 3986 spec out the details of HTTP itself, PSR-7 describes common interfaces for representing the HTTP messages in accordance with these RFCs.

PSR-7 defines a total of the following seven interfaces:

- `Psr\Http\Message\MessageInterface`
- `Psr\Http\Message\RequestInterface`
- `Psr\Http\Message\ServerRequestInterface`
- `Psr\Http\Message\ResponseInterface`
- `Psr\Http\Message\StreamInterface`
- `Psr\Http\Message\UriInterface`
- `Psr\Http\Message\UploadedFileInterface`

They can be fetched via Composer as a part of the `psr/http-message` package.

The following block of code reflects the PSR-7 `Psr\Http\Message\MessageInterface` definition:

```php
<?php

namespace Psr\Http\Message;

interface MessageInterface
{
    public function getProtocolVersion();
    public function withProtocolVersion($version);
    public function getHeaders();
    public function hasHeader($name);
    public function getHeader($name);
    public function getHeaderLine($name);
    public function withHeader($name, $value);
    public function withAddedHeader($name, $value);
    public function withoutHeader($name);
    public function getBody();
    public function withBody(StreamInterface $body);
}
```

The preceding `MessageInterface` methods common to both the request and response type of message. Messages are considered immutable. A class that implements the `MessageInterface` interface needs to assure this immutability by returning a new message instance for every method call that changes the message state.

The following block of code reflects the
PSR-7 `Psr\Http\Message\RequestInterface` definition:

```php
<?php

namespace Psr\Http\Message;

interface RequestInterface extends MessageInterface
{
    public function getRequestTarget();
    public function withRequestTarget($requestTarget);
    public function getMethod();
    public function withMethod($method);
    public function getUri();
    public function withUri(UriInterface $uri, $preserveHost = false);
}
```

The `RequestInterface` interface extends `MessageInterface` serving as a representation of an outgoing, client-side request. Like previously mentioned messages, requests are also considered immutable. This means that the same class behavior applies. If the class method is to change the request state, the new instance of request needs to be returned for every such method call.

The following `Psr\Http\Message\ServerRequestInterface` definition reflects the PSR-7 standard:

```php
<?php

namespace Psr\Http\Message;

interface ServerRequestInterface extends RequestInterface
{
    public function getServerParams();
    public function getCookieParams();
    public function withCookieParams(array $cookies);
    public function getQueryParams();
    public function withQueryParams(array $query);
    public function getUploadedFiles();
    public function withUploadedFiles(array $uploadedFiles);
    public function getParsedBody();
    public function withParsedBody($data);
    public function getAttributes();
    public function getAttribute($name, $default = null);
    public function withAttribute($name, $value);
    public function withoutAttribute($name);
}
```

The implementations of `ServerRequestInterface` serve as a representation of an incoming server-side HTTP request. They too are considered immutable; this means that the same rules of state changing methods apply as previously mentioned.

The following code snippet reflects the PSR-7 `Psr\Http\Message\ResponseInterface` definition:

```php
<?php

namespace Psr\Http\Message;

interface ResponseInterface extends MessageInterface
{
  public function getStatusCode();
  public function withStatus($code, $reasonPhrase = '');
  public function getReasonPhrase();
}
```

With only three methods defined, the implementations of `ResponseInterface` serve as a representation of an outgoing server-side response. These types of messages are considered immutable as well.

The following piece of code reflects the PSR-7 `Psr\Http\Message\StreamInterface` definition:

```php
<?php

namespace Psr\Http\Message;

interface StreamInterface
{
  public function __toString();
  public function close();
  public function detach();
  public function getSize();
  public function tell();
  public function eof();
  public function isSeekable();
  public function seek($offset, $whence = SEEK_SET);
  public function rewind();
  public function isWritable();
  public function write($string);
  public function isReadable();
  public function read($length);
  public function getContents();
  public function getMetadata($key = null);
}
```

`StreamInterface` provides a wrapper around the common PHP stream operations, including serialization of the entire stream to a string.

The following piece of code reflects the PSR-7 `Psr\Http\Message\UriInterface` definition:

```php
<?php

namespace Psr\Http\Message;

interface UriInterface
{
  public function getScheme();
  public function getAuthority();
  public function getUserInfo();
  public function getHost();
  public function getPort();
  public function getPath();
  public function getQuery();
  public function getFragment();
  public function withScheme($scheme);
  public function withUserInfo($user, $password = null);
  public function withHost($host);
  public function withPort($port);
  public function withPath($path);
  public function withQuery($query);
  public function withFragment($fragment);
  public function __toString();
}
```

The `UriInterface` interface here represents the URIs according to RFC 3986. The interface methods force the implementor to provide methods for most common operations around the URI object. The instances of URI objects are also considered immutable.

The following code snippet reflects the PSR-7 `Psr\Http\Message\UploadedFileInterface` definition:

```php
<?php

namespace Psr\Http\Message;

interface UploadedFileInterface
{
  public function getStream();
  public function moveTo($targetPath);
  public function getSize();
  public function getError();
```

```
    public function getClientFilename();
    public function getClientMediaType();
}
```

The `UploadedFileInterface` interface represents a file uploaded through an HTTP request, which is a frequent role of web applications. The handful of methods force the class implementation to cover the most common actions performed on files. Like with all of the previous interfaces, class implementation needs to ensure object immutability.

Guzzle is a popular PSR-7 compliant HTTP client library that makes it easy to work with requests, responses, and streams. It is available at `https://github.com/guzzle/guzzle`, or as a Composer `guzzlehttp/guzzle` package.

The official, full-length *PSR-7: HTTP Message Interface* guide is available at `http://www.php-fig.org/psr/psr-7/`.

PSR-13 - hypermedia links

The hypermedia links form an essential part of any web application, whether we are speaking about HTML or API formats. At the very minimum, each hypermedia link consists of a URI representing the target resource and a relationship defining how the target resource relates to the source. The target link must be an absolute URI or a relative URI, as defined by RFC 5988, or possibly a URI template as defined by RFC 6570.

The PSR-13 standard defines a series of interfaces that outline a common hypermedia format and a way to represent links between these formats:

- `Psr\Link\LinkInterface`
- `Psr\Link\EvolvableLinkInterface`
- `Psr\Link\LinkProviderInterface`
- `Psr\Link\EvolvableLinkProviderInterface`

These interfaces can be fetched via Composer as a part of the `psr/link` package.

The following code snippet reflects the PSR-13 `Psr\Link\LinkInterface` definition, which represents a single readable link object:

```php
<?php

namespace Psr\Link;

interface LinkInterface
{
  public function getHref();
  public function isTemplated();
  public function getRels();
  public function getAttributes();
}
```

The following code snippet reflects the
PSR-13 `Psr\Link\LinkProviderInterface` definition, which represents a single link
provider object:

```php
<?php

namespace Psr\Link;

interface LinkProviderInterface
{
  public function getLinks();
  public function getLinksByRel($rel);
}
```

The following code snippet reflects the PSR-13
`Psr\Link\EvolvableLinkInterface` definition, which represents a single evolvable link
value object:

```php
<?php

namespace Psr\Link;

interface EvolvableLinkInterface extends LinkInterface
{
  public function withHref($href);
  public function withRel($rel);
  public function withoutRel($rel);
  public function withAttribute($attribute, $value);
  public function withoutAttribute($attribute);
}
```

The following code snippet reflects the PSR-13 `Psr\Link\EvolvableLinkProviderInterface` definition, which represents a single evolvable link provider value object:

```php
<?php

namespace Psr\Link;

interface EvolvableLinkProviderInterface extends LinkProviderInterface
{
  public function withLink(LinkInterface $link);
  public function withoutLink(LinkInterface $link);
}
```

here means that object instances of these interfaces exhibit the same behavior as those in PSR-7. By default, objects need to be immutable. The moment an object state needs to change, that change should be reflected into a new object instance. Thanks to PHP's copy-on-write behavior, this is easy for the class to implement.

The copy-on-write behavior is a built-in mechanism of PHP code, whereas PHP takes care of avoiding unnecessary variable duplicates. Until one or more bytes of variable are changed, the variable is not being copied.

The official, full-length *PSR-13: Hypermedia Links* guide is available at `http://www.php-fig.org/psr/psr-13/`.

Summary

The PHP-FIG group addresses a wide range of things through its PSRs. Some of them focus on the structure and readability of the code, others strive for increased interoperability by defining numerous interfaces. These PSRs, directly or indirectly, contribute to improved quality of our project and the third-party libraries we might use. The RFC 2119 standard was a common base for each of the PSR. It removes any ambiguity around may, must, should, and similar words that describe the standard. This ensures that the documentation gets read just as PHP-FIG intended it. While we might not be in touch with each of the standards on a day-to-day basis, it is worth paying attention to them when choosing the libraries for our project. Standard compliant libraries, such as Monolog, usually mean more flexibility, as we can easily switch between different libraries in later stages of the project.

Moving forward, we will look into configuration options, mechanisms, and libraries behind error handling and logging.

3
Error Handling and Logging

Effective error handling and logging are essential parts of an application. Early versions of PHP lacked the support for exceptions and only used errors to flag faulty application states. The PHP 5 version brought forth the OOP features to the language and, with it, the exception model. This empowered PHP with the `try...catch` blocks like other programming languages. Later, the PHP 5.5 version brought support for the `finally` block, which always executed after the `try...catch` blocks, regardless of whether an exception was thrown or not.

Nowadays, the PHP language differentiates errors and exceptions as faulty states of an application. Both are raised as unexpected to our application logic. There are numerous types of errors, such as `E_ERROR`, `E_WARNING`, `E_NOTICE`, and others. When speaking of errors, we default to the `E_ERROR` type that tends to signal the end of our application, an unexpected state that an application should not try to catch and continue executing. This might be due to a lack of memory, IO errors, TCP/IP errors, null reference errors and many others. Exceptions, on the other hand, indicate an unexpected state that an application might want to catch and still carry on executing. This might be due to the inability to save an entry in a database at a given time, an unexpected e-mail sending failure, and many others. This helps to think of an exception as an OO concept of an error.

PHP has its own mechanisms that allow interaction with some of the error types and exceptions. Using `set_error_handler`, we can define the custom error handler to possibly log or display an appropriate message to the user. Using the `try...catch...finally` blocks, we can safely catch possible exceptions and continue executing the application. The exceptions we don't catch automatically turn into a standard error and break our application execution.

Handling errors would not really be complete without proper logging mechanism. While PHP itself provides an interesting and useful `error_log()` function, there are far more robust logging solutions available in the form of free community libraries, such as Mongo.

Moving forward, we will take a detailed look into the following areas of error handling and logging:

- Error handling
    - Error
        - ArithmeticError
        - DivisionByZeroError
        - AssertionError
        - ParseError
        - TypeError
    - Exception
- Logging
    - Native logging
    - Logging with Monolog

 NASA lost a $125 million Mars orbiter on September 1999 because engineers failed to convert units from English to metric. While the system had nothing to do with PHP or the fatal runtime errors as such, it goes to say how great the impact a faulty software might have in real life.

Error handling

Having errors and exceptions as two different error handling system introduces a certain level of confusion among developers. The older versions of PHP made it difficult to reason with E_ERROR as they could not be caught with custom error handlers. The PHP 7 version tried to address this confusion by introducing the Throwable interface, which is summarized as follows:

```
Throwable {
  abstract public string getMessage (void)
  abstract public int getCode (void)
  abstract public string getFile (void)
  abstract public int getLine (void)
  abstract public array getTrace (void)
  abstract public string getTraceAsString (void)
  abstract public Throwable getPrevious (void)
  abstract public string __toString (void)
}
```

The `Throwable` interface is now the base interface for `Error`, `Exception`, and any other object that can be thrown via a `throw` statement. The methods defined in this interface are nearly identical to those of `Exception`. The PHP classes themselves cannot implement the `Throwable` interface directly or extend from `Error`; they can only extend `Exception`, as shown in the following example:

```php
<?php

class Glitch extends \Error
{
}

try {
    throw new Glitch('Glitch!');
}
catch (\Exception $e) {
    echo 'Caught ' . $e->getMessage();
}
```

The preceding code will result in the following output:

```
PHP Fatal error: Uncaught Glitch: Glitch! in index.php:7
Stack trace:
#0 {main}
thrown in /root/app/index.php on line 7
```

What's happening here is that the `Glitch` class is trying to extend the `Error` class, which is not allowed and results in a `Fatal error` that does not get caught by our `try...catch` block here:

```php
<?php

class Flaw extends \Exception
{
}

try {
    throw new Flaw('Flaw!');
}
catch (\Exception $e) {
    echo 'Caught ' . $e->getMessage();
}
```

The preceding example is a valid use of PHP `Throwable`, whereas, our custom `Flaw` class extends the `Exception` class. The `catch` block is triggered, resulting in the following output message:

```
Caught Flaw!
```

The new exception hierarchy in PHP 7 is as follows:

```
interface Throwable
 | Error implements Throwable
   | TypeError extends Error
   | ParseError extends Error
   | ArithmeticError extends Error
     | DivisionByZeroError extends ArithmeticError
   | AssertionError extends Error
 | Exception implements Throwable
   | ...
```

The obvious benefit of the new `Throwable` interface is that we can now easily catch both `Exception` and `Error` objects in a single `try...catch` block, as per the following example:

```php
<?php

try {
  throw new ArithmeticError('Missing numbers!');
}
catch (Throwable $t) {
  echo $t->getMessage();
}
```

`AssertionError` extends `Error`, which in turn implements the `Throwable` interface. The signature of the preceding `catch` block targets the `Throwable` interface, so the thrown `ArithmeticError` would be caught and the output of `Missing numbers!` shown.

Though our classes cannot implement the `Throwable` interface, we can define the interface that extends it. Such an interface can then only be implemented by a class extending either `Exception` or `Error`, as per the following example:

```php
<?php

interface MyThrowable extends Throwable
{
  //...
}

class MyException extends Exception implements MyThrowable
```

```
    {
      //...
    }

    throw new MyException();
```

While it might not be a common practice, such an approach might be useful with package-specific interfaces.

Error

The `Error` class is the base class for internal PHP errors in PHP 7. Nearly all fatal and recoverable fatal errors in PHP 5.x now throw instances of the `Error` object, making themselves catchable via the `try...catch` blocks.

The `Error` class implements the `Throwable` interface, as per the following class synopsis:

```
Error implements Throwable {
    /* Properties */
    protected string $message ;
    protected int $code ;
    protected string $file ;
    protected int $line ;

    /* Methods */
    public __construct (
      [ string $message = ""
      [, int $code = 0
      [, Throwable $previous = NULL ]]]
    )

    final public string getMessage (void)
    final public Throwable getPrevious (void)
    final public mixed getCode (void)
    final public string getFile (void)
    final public int getLine (void)
    final public array getTrace (void)
    final public string getTraceAsString (void)
    public string __toString (void)
    final private void __clone (void)
}
```

The following example demonstrates the use of the `Error` instance in the `catch` block:

```php
<?php

class User
{
  function hello($name)
  {
    return 'Hello ' . $name;
  }
}

// Case 1 - working
try {
  $user = new User();
  $user->greeting('John');
}
catch (Error $e) {
  echo 'Caught: ' . $e->getMessage();
}

// Case 2 - working
try {
  $user = new User();
  $user->greeting('John');
}
catch (Throwable $t) {
  echo 'Caught: ' . $t->getMessage();
}
```

However, there are still cases where some errors are not catchable:

```php
<?php

ini_set('memory_limit', '1M');

try {
  $content = '';
  while (true) {
    $content .= 'content';
  }
}
catch (\Error $e) {
  echo 'Caught ' . $e->getMessage();
}
```

The preceding example triggers the `PHP Fatal error: Allowed memory size of 2097152 bytes exhausted...` error.

Furthermore, even warnings get passed by, as shown in the following example:

```php
<?php

error_reporting(E_ALL);
ini_set('display_errors', 1);
ini_set('memory_limit', '1M');

try {
    str_pad('', PHP_INT_MAX);
}
catch (Throwable $t) {
    echo 'Caught ' . $t->getMessage();
}
```

The preceding example triggers the `PHP Warning:  str_pad(): Padding length is too long...` error.

It goes to say that we should be careful with our expectations towards catching core language errors, as some might slip through. Those that get caught are usually of the base `Error` class. However, some errors will throw a more specific subclass of `Error`: `ArithmeticError`, `DivisionByZeroError`, `AssertionError`, `ParseError`, and `TypeError`.

ArithmeticError

The `ArithmeticError` class addresses the possibly faulty outcomes of performing mathematical operations. PHP uses it for two situations--bit shifting by a negative number or calling `intdiv()` with a dividend of `PHP_INT_MIN` and a divisor of -1.

The `ArithmeticError` class has no methods of its own; they are all inherited from the parent `Error` class, as per the following class synopsis:

```
ArithmeticError extends Error {
    final public string Error::getMessage (void)
    final public Throwable Error::getPrevious (void)
    final public mixed Error::getCode (void)
    final public string Error::getFile (void)
    final public int Error::getLine (void)
    final public array Error::getTrace (void)
    final public string Error::getTraceAsString (void)
    public string Error::__toString (void)
    final private void Error::__clone (void)
}
```

The following example demonstrates the `try...catch` block with `ArithmeticError` being thrown for bit shifting by a negative number:

```php
<?php

try {
  $value = 5 << -1;
}
catch (ArithmeticError $e) {
  echo 'Caught: ' . $e->getMessage();
}
```

The resulting output is as follows :

```
Caught: Bit shift by negative number
```

The following example demonstrates the `try...catch` block with `ArithmeticError` being thrown for calling `intdiv()` with a dividend of `PHP_INT_MIN` and divisor of `-1`:

```php
<?php

try {
  intdiv(PHP_INT_MIN, -1);
}
catch (ArithmeticError $e) {
  echo 'Caught: ' . $e->getMessage();
}
```

The resulting output is as follows:

```
Caught: Division of PHP_INT_MIN by -1 is not an integer
```

DivisionByZeroError

Division by zero is an undefined mathematical expression, at least in elementary arithmetic; hence, PHP needed a way to respond to such cases. `DivisionByZeroError` is thrown when we try to divide a number by zero.

The `DivisionByZeroError` class has no methods of its own, they are all inherited from the parent `ArithmeticError` class, as per the following class synopsis:

```
DivisionByZeroError extends ArithmeticError {
    final public string Error::getMessage (void)
    final public Throwable Error::getPrevious (void)
    final public mixed Error::getCode (void)
    final public string Error::getFile (void)
```

```
    final public int Error::getLine (void)
    final public array Error::getTrace (void)
    final public string Error::getTraceAsString (void)
    public string Error::__toString (void)
    final private void Error::__clone (void)
}
```

We need to be careful what expression we are using for division. Simply dividing dividend number with 0 divisor number using the / operator will not yield the same result as using the intdiv() function. Consider the following code snippet:

```php
<?php

try {
  $x = 5 / 0;
}
catch (DivisionByZeroError $e) {
  echo 'Caught: ' . $e->getMessage();
}
```

The preceding example will not trigger the DivisionByZeroError catch block. Instead, the following warning is raised.

```
PHP Warning: Division by zero
```

Using the intdiv() function instead of the / operator will trigger the catch block as shown in the following code snippet:

```php
<?php

try {
  $x = intdiv(5, 0);
}
catch (DivisionByZeroError $e) {
  echo 'Caught: ' . $e->getMessage();
}
```

The intdiv() function throws the DivisionByZeroError exception if the divisor is 0. If the dividend is PHP_INT_MIN and the divisor is -1, then an ArithmeticError exception is thrown, as shown in the preceding section.

AssertionError

Assertions are runtime checks used as a debugging feature. Using the PHP 7 assert() language construct, we can confirm whether certain PHP expressions are true or false. Whenever the assertion fails, AssertionError is thrown.

The AssertionError class has no methods of its own, they are all inherited from the parent Error class, as per the following class synopsis:

```
AssertionError extends Error {
    final public string Error::getMessage (void)
    final public Throwable Error::getPrevious (void)
    final public mixed Error::getCode (void)
    final public string Error::getFile (void)
    final public int Error::getLine (void)
    final public array Error::getTrace (void)
    final public string Error::getTraceAsString (void)
    public string Error::__toString (void)
    final private void Error::__clone (void)
}
```

PHP 7 provides two configuration directives to control the behavior of assert()--zend.assertions and assert.exception. The assert() function will only get executed and possibly throw AssertionError if zend.assertions = 1 and assert.exception = 1, as per the following example:

```
<?php

try {
    assert('developer' === 'programmer');
}
catch (AssertionError $e) {
    echo 'Caught: ' . $e->getMessage();
}
```

Assuming the configuration directives are all set, the preceding code will output the Caught: assert('developer' === 'programmer') message. If only zend.assertions = 1 but assert.exception = 0, then the catch block will have no effect and the following warning is raised: Warning: assert(): assert('developer' === 'programmer') failed.

The zend.assertions derivative may be completely enabled or disabled only in the php.ini file.

ParseError

The `eval()` language construct enables us to execute any arbitrary PHP code. The only requirement is that the code must not be wrapped in opening and closing PHP tags. Apart from that, the passed code itself must be a valid PHP code. If it happens that the passed code is invalid, then `ParseError` is thrown.

The `ParseError` class has no methods of its own, they are all inherited from the parent `Error` class, as per the following class synopsis:

```
ParseError extends Error {
    final public string Error::getMessage (void)
    final public Throwable Error::getPrevious (void)
    final public mixed Error::getCode (void)
    final public string Error::getFile (void)
    final public int Error::getLine (void)
    final public array Error::getTrace (void)
    final public string Error::getTraceAsString (void)
    public string Error::__toString (void)
    final private void Error::__clone (void)
}
```

The following code snippet demonstrates the valid `eval()` expression:

```
<?php

try {
    $now = eval("return date('D, d M Y H:i:s');");
    echo $now;
}
catch (ParseError $e) {
    echo 'Caught: ' . $e->getMessage();
}
```

The following code block demonstrates a parse error in the evaluated code:

```
<?php

try {
    $now = eval("return date(D, d M Y H:i:s);");
    echo $now;
}
catch (ParseError $e) {
    echo 'Caught: ' . $e->getMessage();
}
```

Seeming nearly identical as a working example, you can notice the lack of the opening and closing (') character around the date function parameter. This breaks the eval function, triggering the `ParseError` catch block with the following output:

```
Caught: syntax error, unexpected 'M' (T_STRING), expecting ',' or ')'
```

Now, let's take a look at the following code snippet:

```php
<?php

try {
    $now = date(D, d M Y H:i:s);
    echo $now;
}
catch (ParseError $e) {
    echo 'Caught: ' . $e->getMessage();
}
```

Here, we are not using the `eval()` expression, but have intentionally broken the code. The resulting output triggers the parse error, but this time not through reacting to the `catch` block, which is sort of expected. It is highly unlikely that this specific case would even happen in the modern IDE environments, such as PhpStorm, Netbeans, and alike, as they automatically alert us on broken syntax.

TypeError

PHP 7 brought forth the *function type parameters* and *function return types*. This, in turn, implied the need to properly handle errors around their misuse. `TypeError` was introduced to target these errors.

The `TypeError` class has no methods of its own, they are all inherited from the parent `Error` class, as per the following class synopsis:

```
ParseError extends Error {
    final public string Error::getMessage (void)
    final public Throwable Error::getPrevious (void)
    final public mixed Error::getCode (void)
    final public string Error::getFile (void)
    final public int Error::getLine (void)
    final public array Error::getTrace (void)
    final public string Error::getTraceAsString (void)
    public string Error::__toString (void)
    final private void Error::__clone (void)
}
```

There are at least three possible error scenarios that throw `TypeError`, which are as follows:

- The type of argument passed to a function does not match the declared type
- The function return value does not match the declared function return type
- An invalid number of arguments is being passed to a built-in PHP function

The following code demonstrates the wrong function argument type:

```php
<?php

declare(strict_types = 1);

function hello(string $name) {
    return "Hello $name!";
}
try {
    echo hello(34);
}
catch (TypeError $e) {
    echo 'Caught: ' . $e->getMessage();
}
```

Here, we defined the `hello()` function that expects to receive a single string argument. However, the function is passed to the integer value. The `declare(strict_types = 1);` expression is required if we want the `catch` block to actually catch `TypeError`. The preceding example results in the following output:

```
Caught: Argument 1 passed to hello() must be of the type string, integer
given, called in...
```

The following code demonstrates the wrong function return type:

```php
<?php

declare(strict_types = 1);

function hello($name): string {
    return strlen($name);
}

try {
    echo hello('branko');
}
catch (TypeError $e) {
    echo 'Caught: ' . $e->getMessage();
}
```

Here, the defined `hello()` function has no specific argument types defined, but it does have a function return type defined. To simulate the faulty scenario, we changed the body of the function to return the integer value rather than the string. Same as with the previous example, the `strict_types = 1` declaration was needed to trigger `TypeError`, resulting in the following output:

```
Caught: Return value of hello() must be of the type string, integer
returned
```

The following code demonstrates the invalid number of arguments that are passed to a built-in PHP function:

```php
<?php

declare(strict_types = 1);

try {
   echo strlen('test', 'extra');
}
catch (TypeError $e) {
   echo 'Caught: ' . $e->getMessage();
}
```

Here, we are calling the `strlen()` function with two parameters. Though this core PHP function itself is defined such that it accepts only one parameter, the `strict_types = 1` declaration turns the standard warning into `TypeError`, thus triggering the `catch` block.

Uncaught error handler

While a great deal of `Error` can now be caught via `try...catch`, there is also an extra mechanism to handle errors. PHP provides a mechanism in the form of a `set_error_handler()` function that allows us to define a custom handler function for all uncaught errors. The `set_error_handler()` function accepts two parameters, as per the following description:

```
mixed set_error_handler (
   callable $error_handler
   [, int $error_types = E_ALL | E_STRICT ]
)
```

The `$error_handler` function is either a handler function name passed as string, or entire anonymous handler function, whereas `$error_types` is one or more (separated by |) masks specifying the type of error. The handler function itself also accepts several parameters, as per the following description:

```
bool handler (
   int $errno ,
   string $errstr
   [, string $errfile
     [, int $errline
       [, array $errcontext ]]]
)
```

Let's take a look at the following two examples:

```php
<?php

function handler($errno, $errstr, $errfile, $errline, $errcontext)

{
  echo 'Handler: ' . $errstr;
}

set_error_handler('handler', E_USER_ERROR | E_USER_WARNING);

echo 'start';
  trigger_error('Ups!', E_USER_ERROR);
echo 'end';

<?php

set_error_handler(function ($errno, $errstr, $errfile, $errline,
  $errcontext) {
  echo 'Handler: ' . $errstr;
}, E_USER_ERROR | E_USER_WARNING);

echo 'start';
  trigger_error('Ups!', E_USER_WARNING);
echo 'end';
```

These examples are nearly identical. The first one is using a separately defined handler function, which is then passed as a string argument to `set_error_handler()`. The second example uses the anonymous function with the same definition. Both examples use the `trigger_error()` function, one triggering `E_USER_ERROR` and the other `E_USER_WARNING`. When executed, both outputs will contain the `end` string.

While the custom handler function enables us to handle all sorts of runtime errors, there are some errors we cannot handle. The following error types cannot be handled with a user-defined function: E_ERROR, E_PARSE, E_CORE_ERROR, E_CORE_WARNING, E_COMPILE_ERROR, E_COMPILE_WARNING, and most of E_STRICT raised in the file where set_error_handler() is called.

Triggering errors

The PHP trigger_error() function provides a way to trigger a user-level error/warning/notice message. It can be used in conjunction with the built-in error handler, or with a user-defined error handler, as we saw in the previous section.

The trigger_error() function accepts two parameters, as per the following description:

```
bool trigger_error (
  string $error_msg
  [, int $error_type = E_USER_NOTICE ]
)
```

The $error_msg parameter has a limitation of 1024 bytes, whereas $error_type is limited to the E_USER_ERROR, E_USER_WARNING, E_USER_NOTICE, and E_USER_DEPRECATED constants.

Let's take a look at the following example:

```php
<?php

set_error_handler(function ($errno, $errstr) {
  echo 'Handler: ' . $errstr;
});

echo 'start';
trigger_error('E_USER_ERROR!', E_USER_ERROR);
trigger_error('E_USER_ERROR!', E_USER_WARNING);
trigger_error('E_USER_ERROR!', E_USER_NOTICE);
trigger_error('E_USER_ERROR!', E_USER_DEPRECATED);
echo 'end';
```

Here, we have four different trigger_error() function calls, each accepting different error types. The custom error handler kicks in for all four errors, and our code continues executing all the way to show end as the output.

There are certain conceptual similarities between **error model** (set_error_handler and trigger_error) on one side and **throwable model** (try...catch and throw new ...) on the other. Seemingly, both can catch and trigger errors. The main difference is that the throwable model is a more modern, object-oriented way. That being said, we should limit our use of trigger_error() to when it's absolutely needed for some contextual reasons.

Exception

Exceptions were originally introduced in PHP 5, which brought forth the OOP model as well. They remain pretty much unchanged throughout the time. Among significant changes was the one added by PHP 5.5, which added the finally block, and PHP 7, which added the possibility to use the | operator in order to catch multiple exception types via a single catch block.

Exception is the base class for all user exceptions in PHP 7. Same as Error, Exception implements the Throwable interface, as per the following class synopsis:

```
Exception implements Throwable {
    /* Properties */
    protected string $message ;
    protected int $code ;
    protected string $file ;
    protected int $line ;

    /* Methods */
    public __construct (
      [ string $message = ""
        [, int $code = 0
          [, Throwable $previous = NULL ]]]
    )

    final public string getMessage (void)
    final public Throwable getPrevious (void)
    final public mixed getCode (void)
    final public string getFile (void)
    final public int getLine (void)
    final public array getTrace (void)
    final public string getTraceAsString (void)
    public string __toString (void)
    final private void __clone (void)
}
```

Exceptions remain the backbone of OO error handling. The simplicity of extending, throwing, and catching exceptions makes them easy to work with.

Creating a custom exception handler

By extending the built-in `Exception` class, PHP lets us throw any object as if it were an exception. Let's take a look at the following example:

```php
<?php

class UsernameException extends Exception {}

class PasswordException extends Exception {}

$username = 'john';
$password = '';

try {
  if (empty($username)) {
    throw new UsernameException();
  }
  if (empty($password)) {
    throw new PasswordException();
  }
  throw new Exception();
}
catch (UsernameException $e) {
  echo 'Caught UsernameException.';
}
catch (PasswordException $e) {
  echo 'Caught PasswordException.';
}
catch (Exception $e) {
  echo 'Caught Exception.';
}
finally {
  echo 'Finally.';
}
```

Here, we defined two custom exceptions, `UsernameException` and `PasswordException`. They merely extended the built-in `Exception`, not really introducing any new methods or functionality. We then defined two variables, `$username` and `$password`. The `$password` variable was set to be an empty string. Finally, we set the `try...catch...finally` blocks, with three different `catch` blocks. The first two `catch` blocks are targeted to our custom exceptions, and the third targets the built-in `Exception`. Due to an empty password, the preceding example would throw `new PasswordException`, and, therefore, output the `Caught PasswordException. Finally.` string.

Rethrowing exceptions

Rethrowing exceptions is a relatively common practice in development. Sometimes, we wish to catch an exception, look into it, do a bit of an extra logic, and then rethrow the exception back so that the parent catch block might handle it further.

Let's take a look at the following example:

```php
<?php

class FileNotExistException extends Exception {}

class FileReadException extends Exception {}

class FileEmptyException extends Exception {}

$file = 'story.txt';

try {
  try {
    $content = file_get_contents($file);
    if (!$content) {
      throw new Exception();
    }
  }
  catch (Exception $e) {
    if (!file_exists($file)) {
      throw new FileNotExistException();
    }
    elseif (!is_readable($file)) {
      throw new FileReadException();
    }
    elseif (empty($content)) {
      throw new FileEmptyException();
    }
    else {
      throw new Exception();
    }
  }
}

catch (FileNotExistException $e) {
  echo 'Caught FileNotExistException.';
}
catch (FileReadException $e) {
  echo 'Caught FileReadException.';
}
catch (FileEmptyException $e) {
```

```
      echo 'Caught FileEmptyException.';
  }
  catch (Exception $e) {
    echo 'Caught Exception.';
  }
  finally {
    echo 'Finally.';
  }
```

Here, we defined three simple exceptions--`FileNotExistException`, `FileReadException`, and `FileEmptyException`. These correspond to three different faulty outcomes we might expect when dealing with our file. We then added some logic around the `file_get_contents` function call, trying to wrap it in the `try...catch` blocks. The `file_get_contents` function results in Boolean `false` if the file cannot be read. Knowing that, and knowing that `empty` function call results in `false` if the file is found empty, we can easily check if the file is alright or not in a single `if (!$content)` statement. There are several possible scenarios once the general `Exception` is thrown. The first and the most obvious one is the missing file. Surprisingly, even with the `try...catch` blocks in place, if the file is missing, PHP would output the following:

```
Warning: file_get_contents(story.txt): failed to open stream: No such file
or directory in /index.php on line 13
Caught FileNotExistException.Finally.
```

We can clearly see that the core PHP language `Warning` has been raised, along with triggering the proper `catch` and `finally` block. Ideally, we would like to get away with the warning output. One possible way is to use the error control operator--the at sign (@). It suppresses both errors and warnings. This is quite dangerous and should be used with the utmost care. Generally speaking, errors and warnings are triggered to be handled, not to be suppressed. However, in this case, we might just call it justified, as we are wrapping everything in `try...catch` blocks. The last general `catch` block is merely there to catch an unexpected faulty state that is not covered by our three custom exceptions.

Uncaught Exception handler

PHP provides a mechanism in the form of a `set_exception_handler` function that allows us to define a custom handler function for all uncaught throwables, including exceptions. The `set_exception_handler` function accepts a single callable parameter--either a *function name passed as string*, or an entire *anonymous function*.

Let's take a look at the following *function name passed as string* example:

```php
<?php

function throwableHandler(Throwable $t)
{
    echo 'Throwable Handler: ' . $t->getMessage();
}

set_exception_handler('throwableHandler');

echo 'start';
    throw new Exception('Ups!');
echo 'end';
```

Let's take a look at the following *anonymous function* example:

```php
<?php

set_exception_handler(function (Throwable $t) {
    echo 'Throwable Handler: ' . $t->getMessage();
});

echo 'start';
  throw new Exception('Ups!');
echo 'end';
```

Both of these code examples do the same thing, there is no difference to them. Other than the second example being more ascetically pleasing, as there is no need to define a separate function like `throwableHandler()` that will only get used in one place. The important thing to note here is that unlike the `try...catch` blocks, the call to the handler function is the last thing that our application executes, which, in this case, means that we will never see the `end` string on screen.

Logging

Logging is an important aspect of every application. Knowing how to catch errors does not necessarily mean we are handling the faulty situation as best as we should. If we are not logging the right details, and passing them on to the right consumer, then we are not really handling the situation right.

Let's consider the following catch and generate user message example:

```php
try {
    //...
```

```
    }
    catch (\Exception $e) {
       $messages[] = __('We can't add this item to your shopping cart right
now.');
    }
```

Let's consider the following example:

```php
<?php

try {
    //...
} catch (\Exception $e) {
    $this->logger->critical($e);
    $messages[] = __("We can't add this item to your shopping cart right
now . ");
}
```

Both examples react to the exception by storing the message into a $messages variable, which is later shown on screen to the current user. This is great as the application does not crash, the user is shown what happened, and the application is allowed to execute. However, is it great? The examples are nearly identical, aside from one minor detail. The first example merely responds to the error and reacts to it in the moment. The second example uses the $this->logger->critical($e); expression to log the error, presumably, but necessarily, to a file. By logging the error, we make it possible for the consumer to review it later. The consumer is most likely a developer who might take a look into log files every now and then. Notice how the $messages array is not passed directly to the $e variable, rather, a custom message that fits the user situation. This is because the user should never be shown the level of detail we might pass onto our logs. The more details we pass to our log, the easier it gets to troubleshoot our application. By logging an entire exception instance object, in this case, we pretty much provide all the details the developer needs to know to try and prevent an error in the future.

Thoughtfully used, logging can provide quality analytics insight upon which we might periodically reiterate over our codebase and prevent issues that might not be visible during initial development. Aside from logging errors, we could easily log other analytical, or otherwise important bits.

The open source Elastic stack, available at https://www.elastic.co, enables us to reliably and securely take data from any source, in any format, and search, analyse, and visualize it in real time. The Kibana product, available at https://www.elastic.co/products/kibana, gives shape to our data through its interactive visualizations.

Native logging

PHP has a built-in `error_log()` function that sends an error message to the defined error handling routines; thus, providing an out-of-the-box solution for simple logging.

The following code snippet describes the `error_log()` function definition:

```
bool error_log (
    string $message
  [, int $message_type = 0
    [, string $destination
      [, string $extra_headers ] ]]
)
```

The parameters are defined as follows:

- `$message`: This is a string type value, and a message we want to log
- `$message_type`: This is an integer type value; it has one of four possible values, which are as follows:
  - `0`: This is an operating system logging mechanism
  - `1`: This is sent by e-mail to the address in the destination parameter
  - `2`: This is no longer an option
  - `3`: This message is appended to the file destination
  - `4`: This is sent directly to the SAPI logging handler
- `$destination`: This string type value kicks in only for `$message_type = 1` and denotes an e-mail address
- `$extra_headers`: This string type value kicks in only for `$message_type = 1` and denotes e-mail headers

The `error_log()` function works closely with the `log_errors` and `error_log` configuration options defined in `php.ini`:

- `log_errors`: This is a boolean type configuration option. It tells if error messages should be logged to the server error log or `error_log`. To log to a file specified with the `error_log` configuration option, set this to 1.
- `error_log`: This is a string type configuration option. It specifies the name of the file where errors should be logged. If `syslog` is used, errors are logged to the system logger. If no value is set, errors are sent to the SAPI error logger, which is most likely an error log in Apache or stderr in CLI.

The following example demonstrates logging to a file:

```php
<?php

ini_set('log_errors', 1);
ini_set('error_log', dirname(__FILE__) . '/app-error.log');

error_log('Test!');
```

The `log_errors` and `error_log` options might be defined in the `.php` file itself; however, it is recommended to do so in `php.ini`, otherwise, logging won't log any errors if the script has parse errors or cannot be run at all. The resulting output of the preceding example would be an `app-error.log` file, located in the same directory as the executing script itself with the following content:

```
[26-Dec-2016 08:11:32 UTC] Test!
[26-Dec-2016 08:11:39 UTC] Test!
[26-Dec-2016 08:11:42 UTC] Test!
```

The following example demonstrates logging to an e-mail:

```php
<?php

ini_set('log_errors', 1);
ini_set('error_log', dirname(__FILE__) . '/app-error.log');

$headers = "From: john@server.loc\r\n";
$headers .= "Subject: My PHP email logger\r\n";
$headers .= "MIME-Version: 1.0\r\n";
$headers .= "Content-Type: text/html; charset=ISO-8859-1\r\n";

error_log('<html><h2>Test!</h2></html>', 1, 'john@mail.com', $headers);
```

Here, we are first building the raw `$headers` string, which we then pass to the `error_log()` function, along with the destination e-mail address. This is an obvious downside of the `error_log()` function, as we are required to be familiar with e-mail message headers standards.

The `error_log()` function is not binary-safe, which means the `$message` argument should not contain a null character, otherwise, it will be truncated. To bypass this limitation, we can use one of the conversion/escape functions, such as `base64_encode()`, `rawurlencode()`, or `addslashes()` before calling `error_log()`. The following RFCs might be useful for dealing with e-mail message headers: RFC 1896, RFC 2045, RFC 2046, RFC 2047, RFC 2048, RFC 2049, and RFC 2822.

Understanding the `error_log()` function, we can easily wrap it into a custom function of ours, let's say `app_error_log()`, thus abstracting the entire e-mails' boilerplate, such as the address and headers. We can also make our `app_error_log()` function log into file and e-mail at once, thus making for a simple, one-line logging expression such as the following, possibly across our application:

```
try {
  //...
}
catch (\Exception $e) {
  app_error_log($e);
}
```

Writing simple loggers such as these is quite easy. However, simplicity in development usually comes with the cost of reduced modularity. Luckily, there are third-party libraries out there that are quite robust when it comes to logging features. Best of all, they comply to a certain logging standard, as we will see in the next section.

Logging with Monolog

The PHP community provides several logging libraries for us to choose, such as Monolog, Analog, KLogger, Log4PHP, and others. Choosing the right library can be a daunting task. More so because we might decide to change the logging mechanism later on, which might leave us with a substantial amount of code to change. This is where the PSR-3 logging standard helps. Choosing a library that is standards-compliant makes it easier to reason with.

Monolog is one of the most popular PHP logging libraries. It is a free, MIT-licensed library that implements the PSR-3 logging standard. It allows us to easily sends our logs to files, sockets, inboxes, databases, and various web services.

We can easily install the Monolog library as a `composer` package by running the following console command within our projects folder:

```
composer require monolog/monolog
```

If `composer` is not an option, we can download Monolog from the GitHub at `https://github.com/Seldaek/monolog`. Those using leading PHP frameworks, such as Symfony or Laravel, get the Monolog out-of-the-box.

The compliance to the PSR-3 logging standard also means that Monolog supports the logging levels described by RFC 5424, as follows:

- `DEBUG (100)`: Debug-level messages
- `INFO (200)`: Informational messages
- `NOTICE (250)`: Normal but significant condition
- `WARNING (300)`: Warning conditions
- `ERROR (400)`: Error conditions
- `CRITICAL (500)`: Critical conditions
- `ALERT (550)`: Action must be taken immediately
- `EMERGENCY (600)`: System is unusable

These constants are defined as part of the `vendor/monolog/monolog/src/Monolog/Logger.php` file, alongside a practical use case example for most of them.

The core concept behind every Monolog logger instance is that the instance itself has a channel (name) and a stack of handlers. We can instantiate multiple loggers, each defining a certain channel (db, request, router, and alike). Each channel can combine various handlers. The handlers themselves can be shared across channels. The channel is reflected in the logs and allows us to easily see or filter records. Finally, each handler also has a formatter. The formatter normalizes and formats incoming records so that they can be used by the handlers to output useful information.

The following diagram visualizes this logger-channel-formatter structure:

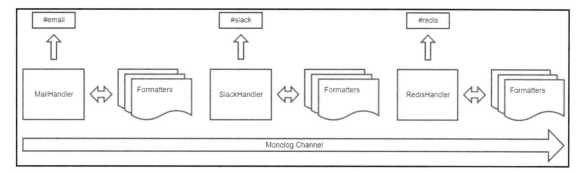

Monolog provides quite an extensive list of loggers and formatters.

- Loggers:
    - Log to files and syslog (StreamHandler, RotatingFileHandler, SyslogHandler, ...)
    - Send alerts and e-mails (SwiftMailerHandler, SlackbotHandler, SendGridHandler, ...)
    - Log-specific servers and networked logging (SocketHandler, CubeHandler, NewRelicHandler, ...)
    - Logging in development (FirePHPHandler, ChromePHPHandler, BrowserConsoleHandler, ...)
    - Log to databases (RedisHandler, MongoDBHandler, ElasticSearchHandler, ...)
- Formatters:
    - LineFormatter
    - HtmlFormatter
    - JsonFormatter
    - ...

A full list of Monolog loggers and formatters can be obtained through the official Monolog project page at https://github.com/Seldaek/monolog.

Let's take a look at the following simple example:

```php
<?php

require 'vendor/autoload.php';

use Monolog\Logger;
use Monolog\Handler\RotatingFileHandler;
use Monolog\Handler\BrowserConsoleHandler;

$logger = new Logger('foggyline');

$logger->pushHandler(new RotatingFileHandler(__DIR__ .
  '/foggyline.log'), 7);
$logger->pushHandler(new BrowserConsoleHandler());

$context = [
  'user' => 'john',
  'salary' => 4500.00
];

$logger->addDebug('Logging debug', $context);
$logger->addInfo('Logging info', $context);
$logger->addNotice('Logging notice', $context);
$logger->addWarning('Logging warning', $context);
$logger->addError('Logging error', $context);
$logger->addCritical('Logging critical', $context);
$logger->addAlert('Logging alert', $context);
$logger->addEmergency('Logging emergency', $context);
```

Here, we are creating an instance of `Logger` and naming it `foggyline`. We then use the `pushHandler` method to push inline instantiated instances of two different handlers.

The `RotatingFileHandler` logs records to a file and creates one log file per day. It also deletes files older than the `$maxFiles` argument, which, in our example, is set to 7. Regardless of the log file name being set to `foggyline.log`, the actual log file created by `RotatingFileHandler` contains the timestamp in it, resulting in a name such as `foggyline-2016-12-26.log`. When we think about it, the role of this handler is remarkable. Aside from just creating new log entries, it also takes care of deleting old logs.

The following is an output of our `foggyline-2016-12-26.log` file:

```
    [2016-12-26 12:36:46] foggyline.DEBUG: Logging debug
{"user":"john","salary":4500} []
    [2016-12-26 12:36:46] foggyline.INFO: Logging info
{"user":"john","salary":4500} []
    [2016-12-26 12:36:46] foggyline.NOTICE: Logging notice
```

```
{"user":"john","salary":4500} []
    [2016-12-26 12:36:46] foggyline.WARNING: Logging warning
{"user":"john","salary":4500} []
    [2016-12-26 12:36:46] foggyline.ERROR: Logging error
{"user":"john","salary":4500} []
    [2016-12-26 12:36:46] foggyline.CRITICAL: Logging critical
{"user":"john","salary":4500} []
    [2016-12-26 12:36:46] foggyline.ALERT: Logging alert
{"user":"john","salary":4500} []
    [2016-12-26 12:36:46] foggyline.EMERGENCY: Logging emergency
{"user":"john","salary":4500} []
```

The second handler we pushed to stack, `BrowserConsoleHandler`, sends logs to the browser's JavaScript console with no browser extension required. This works on most modern browsers that support the console API. The resulting output of this handler is shown in the following screenshot:

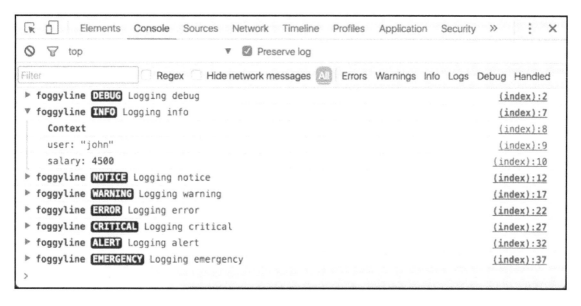

With these few simple lines of code, we have added quite an impressive set of logging capabilities to our application. `RotatingFileHandler` seems perfect for a later state analysis of a production running application, while `BrowserConsoleHandler` might serve as a convenient way to speed up ongoing development. Goes to say that logs serve a wider purpose of just logging for errors. Logging various pieces of information at various log levels, we can easily use the Monolog library as sort of an analytics bridge. All it takes is to push proper handlers to the stack, which in turn push logs to various destinations, such as Elasticsearch and alike.

Summary

Throughout this chapter, we took a detailed look through the PHP error handling mechanism. PHP 7 made quite a cleanup of its error handling model by wrapping most of it under the `Throwable` interface. This makes it possible to catch core errors via `try...catch` blocks that were, prior to PHP 7, reserved for `Exception` only. This leaves a bit of a terminology fuzz to digest now, as we come across `Throwable`, `Error`, `Exception`, system-errors, user-errors, notices, warnings and alike. Speaking high level, we might say that any faulty state is error. More specifically, we now have throwables on one side and errors on the other. Throwables encompass thrown and catchable instances of `Error` and `Exception`, whereas, errors encompass basically anything not catchable as `Throwable`.

Handling faulty states would not really be complete without proper logging. While the built-in `error_log()` function provides enough to get us started, more robust solutions are available in the form of various third-party libraries. The Monolog library is among the most popular ones and is used across dozens of community projects.

Moving forward, we will look into the magic methods and the enormous power they bring to the PHP language.

4
Magic Behind Magic Methods

The PHP language allows for both, a procedural and an **object-oriented** (**OO**) way of writing code. Whereas the procedural way is more of a remnant of initial versions of PHP, nothing really stops us from writing fully procedural applications even today. While both approaches have their advantages and disadvantages, the OO way is by far the most dominant one nowadays, the advantages of which are more evident in robust and modular applications, which are nearly impossible to work on with the procedural style.

Knowing the individual features of the PHP OO model is vital to understand, write, and debug modern applications. The **magic methods** are one of the more interesting and often mystic features of the PHP language. They are the predefined class methods that the PHP compiler executes under some event, such as object initialized, object destroyed, object converted to string, object method accessed, object property accessed, object serialized, object deserialized, and more.

In this chapter, we will cover the use of each of the magic methods available in PHP, as per the following list of sections:

- Using __construct()
- Using __destruct()
- Using __call()
- Using __callStatic()
- Using __set()
- Using __get()
- Using __isset()
- Using __unset()
- Using __sleep()
- Using __wakeup()
- Using __toString()

- Using __invoke()
- Using __set_state()
- Using __clone()
- Using __debugInfo()
- Usage statistic across popular platforms

 The PHP language reserves all function names starting with __ as magical.

Using __construct()

The __construct() magic method represents a PHP constructor concept similar to that of other OO languages. It allows developers to tap into the object creation process. Classes that have the __construct() method declared, call it on each newly-created object. This allows us to deal with any initialization that the object may need before it is used.

The following code snippet shows the simplest possible use of the __construct() method:

```php
<?php

class User
{
  public function __construct()
  {
    var_dump('__construct');
  }
}

new User;
new User();
```

Both User instances will yield the same string(11) "__construct" output to the screen. The more complex example might include constructor parameters. Consider the following code snippet:

```php
<?php

class User
{
  protected $name;
  protected $age;
```

```
public function __construct($name, $age)
{
    $this->name = $name;
    $this->age = $age;
    var_dump($this->name);
    var_dump($this->age);
}
}

new User; #1
new User('John'); #2
new User('John', 34); #3
new User('John', 34, 4200.00); #4
```

Here, we see a __construct() method that accepts the two parameters--$name and $age.
Right after the User class definition, we have four different object initialization attempts.
Attempt #3 is the only valid initialization attempt. Attempts #1 and #2 trigger the
following error:

```
Warning: Missing argument 1 for User::__construct() // #1
Warning: Missing argument 2 for User::__construct() // #1 & #2
```

Attempt #4, even though invalid, does not trigger the error. PHP does not generate an error
message, unlike with other methods, when __construct() is overridden with
extra parameters.

Another interesting case for the __construct() method is with the parent classes. Let's
consider the following example:

```
<?php

class User
{
    protected $name;
    protected $age;

    public function __construct($name, $age)
    {
        $this->name = $name;
        $this->age = $age;
    }
}

class Employee extends User
{
    public function __construct($employeeName, $employeeAge)
    {
```

```
      var_dump($this->name);
      var_dump($this->age);
    }
}

new Employee('John', 34);
```

The output of the preceding code is as follows:

```
NULL NULL
```

The reason for this is that parent constructors are not called implicitly if the child class defines a constructor. To trigger the parent constructor, we need to run `parent::__construct()` within the child constructor. Let's amend our `Employee` class to do just that:

```
class Employee extends User
{
 public function __construct($employeeName, $employeeAge)
 {
   parent::__construct($employeeName, $employeeAge);
   var_dump($this->name);
   var_dump($this->age);
 }
}
```

This will be the output now:

```
string(4) "John" int(34)
```

Let's take a look at the following example:

```
<?php

class User
{
  public function __construct()
  {
    var_dump('__construct');
  }

  public static function hello($name)
  {
    return 'Hello ' . $name;
  }
}

echo User::hello('John');
```

Here, we have a simple `User` class with a magic `__construct()` and a static `hello()` method. Right after the class definition, we have a call towards the static `hello()` method. This does not trigger the `__construct()` method.

The only output from the preceding example is as follows:

```
Hello John
```

The `__construct()` method only triggers when an object is being initiated via the `new` keyword.

We would want to keep our `__construct()` method, as well as other magic methods, under `public` access modifier only. However, if the situation demands it, we are free to throw in the `finally` access modifier in the mix as well.

Consider the following example:

```php
<?php

class User
{
 public final function __construct($name)
 {
 var_dump($name);
 }
}

class Director extends User
{

}

class Employee extends User
{
 public function __construct($name)
 {
 var_dump($name);
 }
}

new User('John'); #1
new Director('John'); #2
new Employee('John'); #3
```

Unusual as it is, the initialization attempts #1 and #2 would operate even with the `final` access modifier. This is because #1 instantiates the original `User` class that defines the final `__construct()` method, and #2 instantiates the empty `Director` class that does not try to implement its own `__construct()` method. The initialization attempt #3 would fail, resulting in the following error:

```
Fatal error: Cannot override final method User::__construct()
```

This is really the basis of access modifiers and overrides, not specific to the `__construct()` magic method itself. However, it is worth knowing that it is possible to use the `final` modifier with the constructor, as it might come in handy.

Aside from instantiating simple objects, the practical use of the `__construct()` method in OOP comes in the form of **dependency injection**. Nowadays, it is generally accepted that injecting dependencies is a best-practice for dealing with dependencies. While dependencies can be injected into an object through various setter methods, the use of the `__construct()` method prevails as a dominant approach with some of the leading PHP platforms, such as Magento.

The following code block demonstrates the `__construct()` method of Magento's `vendor/magento/module-gift-message/Model/Save.php` file:

```php
public function __construct(
    \Magento\Catalog\Api\ProductRepositoryInterface $productRepository,
    \Magento\GiftMessage\Model\MessageFactory $messageFactory,
    \Magento\Backend\Model\Session\Quote $session,
    \Magento\GiftMessage\Helper\Message $giftMessageMessage
) {
    $this->productRepository = $productRepository;
    $this->_messageFactory = $messageFactory;
    $this->_session = $session;
    $this->_giftMessageMessage = $giftMessageMessage;
}
```

There are several dependencies being passed here via the `__construct()` method, which seems quite a step up from previous examples. Even so, the majority of Magento's `__construct()` methods are much more robust than this, passing on tens of parameters to the object.

We could easily summarize the role of the `__construct()` method as sort of a class signature that represents how a consumer should fully instantiate a particular object.

Using __destruct()

Alongside the constructor, the destructor is a common feature of the OO language. The __destruct() magic method represents this concept. The method gets triggered as soon as there are no other references to a particular object. This can happen either when PHP decides to explicitly free the object, or when we force it using the unset() language construct.

As with constructors, parent destructors don't get called implicitly by PHP. In order to run a parent destructor, we need to explicitly call parent::__destruct(). Furthermore, the child class inherits the parent's destructor if it does not implement one for itself.

Let's say we have a following simple User class:

```php
<?php

class User
{
    public function __destruct()
    {
        echo '__destruct';
    }
}
```

With the User class in place, let's go ahead and look through instance creation examples:

```
echo 'A';
new User();
echo 'B';

// outputs "A__destructB"
```

The new User(); expression here instantiates an instance of the User class into *thin air* as it does not assign the newly instantiated object into the variable. This is a trigger for PHP to explicitly call the __destruct() method right there on the same line, resulting in the A__destructB string output:

```
echo 'A';
$user = new User();
echo 'B';

// outputs "AB__destruct"
```

The `new User();` expression here instantiates an instance of `User` class into the `$user` variable. This prevents PHP from triggering instantly, as the script might use the `$user` variable further down the path. Still, PHP explicitly calls the `__destruct()` method when it concludes that the `$user` variable is not being referenced, resulting in the `AB__destruct` string output:

```
echo 'A';
$user = new User();
echo 'B';
unset($user);
echo 'C';

// outputs "AB__destructC"
```

Here, we are extending the previous example a little bit. We are using the `unset()` language construct to force the destruction of the `$user` variable in between expressions. The call to `unset()` is basically an implicit trigger for PHP to execute the object's `__destruct()` method, resulting in the `AB__destructC` string output:

```
echo 'A';
$user = new User();
echo 'B';
exit;
echo 'C';

// outputs "AB__destruct"
```

Here, we are calling the `exit()` language construct right before the `C` string output. This serves as an implicit trigger for PHP that there are no more references towards the `$user` variable, and, therefore, the object's `__destruct()` method can be executed. The resulting output is the `AB__destruct` string.

Certain situations might tempt us to call the `exit()` constructor from within the `__destruct()` method itself. We should never do this, because calling `exit()` within `__destruct()` prevents the remaining shutdown routines from executing. Likewise, throwing an exception from the `__destruct()` method will trigger a fatal error, but only if thrown at the time of script termination. This is, by no means, a way to handle our application states.

Most of the time, destructors are not something we will want or need to implement on our own. Chances are that a great majority of our classes won't have a need for it, as PHP itself does a pretty good job of cleaning up. There are, however, cases where we might want to instantly release the resource consumed by the object after the object is not being referenced anymore. The __destruct() method allows certain follow-up actions during the object's termination.

Using __call()

Overloading is a familiar term in OOP. However, not all programming languages interpret it in the same way. The PHP notion of overloading is quite different than that of other OO languages. Where traditionally overloading provides the ability to have multiple methods with the same name but different arguments, in PHP overloading means to dynamically create methods and properties.

 The unfortunate misuse of the term overloading adds a layer of confusion for some developers, as the more proper term for this type of functionality might have been *interpreter hooks*.

There are two magic methods in PHP supporting method overloading: __call() and __callStatic(). Throughout this section, we will take a closer look at the __call() method.

The __call() magic method is triggered when invoking inaccessible methods in an *object context*. This method accepts two parameters, as per the following synopsis:

```
public mixed __call(string $name, array $arguments)
```

However the __call() method parameters have the following meaning:

- $name: This is the name of the method being called
- $arguments: This is an enumerated array containing the parameters passed to the $name method

The following example demonstrates the use of the __call() method in the object context:

```php
<?php

class User
{
 public function __call($name, $arguments)
 {
 echo $name . ': ' . implode(', ', $arguments) . PHP_EOL;
 }

 public function bonus($amount)
 {
 echo 'bonus: ' . $amount . PHP_EOL;
 }
}

$user = new User();
$user->hello('John', 34);
$user->bonus(560.00);
$user->salary(4200.00);
```

The User class itself declared only the __call() and bonus() methods. The $user object tries to call the hello(), bonus(), and salary() methods. This effectively means the object is trying to call two missing methods: hello() and salary(). The __call() method kicks in for the missing two methods, thus yielding the following output:

```
__call => hello: John, 34
bonus: 560
__call => salary: 4200
```

We can find a nice use case example of the __call() method in the Magento platform, as per the following entry taken from the vendor/magento/framework/DataObject.php class file:

```php
public function __call($method, $args)
{
    switch (substr($method, 0, 3)) {
      case 'get':
        $key = $this->_underscore(substr($method, 3));
        $index = isset($args[0]) ? $args[0] : null;
      return $this->getData($key, $index);
      case 'set':
        $key = $this->_underscore(substr($method, 3));
        $value = isset($args[0]) ? $args[0] : null;
      return $this->setData($key, $value);
      case 'uns':
```

```
      $key = $this->_underscore(substr($method, 3));
    return $this->unsetData($key);
    case 'has':
      $key = $this->_underscore(substr($method, 3));
    return isset($this->_data[$key]);
  }
  // ...
}
```

Without getting into the details of Magneto itself, it's suffice to say that
their DataObject class serves as a root data object throughout the entire framework. The
code within the __call() method enables it to magically *get, set, unset,* and *check* for the
existence of the property on the object instance. This is used later in expressions, such as the
following entry taken from the vendor/magento/module-
checkout/Controller/Cart/Configure.php file:

```
$params = new \Magento\Framework\DataObject();
$params->setCategoryId(false);
$params->setConfigureMode(true);
$params->setBuyRequest($quoteItem->getBuyRequest());
```

The benefit is that we have easily empowered instances of DataObject here with magical
methods that might and might not exist. For example, setCategoryId() is a method that
does not exist on the DataObject class. Since it does not exist, calling it triggers the
__call() method. This might not be that obvious at first, so let's consider
another imaginary example where our custom class extends from DataObject:

```
<?php

class User extends \Magento\Framework\DataObject
{

}

$user = new User();

$user->setName('John');
$user->setAge(34);
$user->setSalary(4200.00);

echo $user->getName();
echo $user->getAge();
echo $user->getSalary();
```

Notice the *beauty and simplicity* of *setters* and *getters* we have achieved here with the help of the __call() magic method. Even though our User class is basically empty, we have inherited the magic behind the parent's __call() implementation.

The __call() method empowers us with some truly interesting possibilities, most of which will fit right in as a part of frameworks or libraries.

Using __callStatic()

The __callStatic() magic is nearly identical to the __call() method. Where the __call() method is bound to the *object context*, the __callStatic() method is bound to the *static context*, which means this method is triggered when invoking inaccessible methods via the scope resolution operator (::).

The method accepts two parameters as per the following synopsis:

```
public static mixed __callStatic (string $name, array $arguments)
```

Notice the use of the static access modifier in the method declaration that is required by the static context upon which this method operates. The following example demonstrates the use of the __callStatic() method in the static context:

```php
<?php

class User
{
  public static function __callStatic($name, $arguments)
  {
    echo '__callStatic => ' . $name . ': ' . implode(', ', $arguments)
      . PHP_EOL;
  }

  public static function bonus($amount)
  {
  echo 'bonus: ' . $amount . PHP_EOL;
  }
}
```

The preceding code will yield the following output:

```
User::hello('John', 34);
User::bonus(560.00);
User::salary(4200.00);
```

The User class itself declared only the __callStatic() and bonus() methods. The User class tries to call static hello(), bonus(), and salary() methods. This effectively means that the class is trying to call two missing methods: hello() and salary(). The __callStatic() method kicks in for the missing two methods, thus yielding the following output:

```
__callStatic => hello: John, 34
bonus: 560
__callStatic => salary: 4200
```

In OO programming, the static context is less frequent than the object context, which makes the __callStatic() method less frequently used than the __call() method.

Using __set()

Aside from *method overloading*, *property overloading* is another aspect of the PHP overloading capabilities. There are four magic methods in PHP that support the property overloading: __set(), __get(), __isset(), and __unset(). Throughout this section, we will take a closer look at the __set() method.

The __set() magic method is triggered when trying to write data to inaccessible properties.

The method accepts two parameters, as per the following synopsis:

```
public void __set(string $name, mixed $value)
```

Whereas, the __set() method parameters have the following meaning:

- $name: This is the name of the property being interacted with
- $value: This is the value that the $name property should be set to

Let's take a look at the following object context example:

```php
<?php

class User
{
    private $data = array();

    private $name;
    protected $age;
    public $salary;
```

```
    public function __set($name, $value)
    {
        $this->data[$name] = $value;
    }
}

$user = new User();
$user->name = 'John';
$user->age = 34;
$user->salary = 4200.00;
$user->message = 'hello';

var_dump($user);
```

The User class declares four properties with various access modifiers. It further declares the __set() method that intercepts all the property write attempts on the object context. Attempting to set a non-existing ($message) or inaccessible ($name, $age) property triggers the __set() method. The inner workings of the __set() method push the inaccessible data into the $data property array, which is visible in the following output:

```
object(User)#1 (4) {
  ["data":"User":private]=> array(3) {
    ["name"]=> string(4) "John"
    ["age"]=> int(34)
    ["message"]=> string(5) "hello"
  }
  ["name":"User":private]=> NULL
  ["age":protected]=> NULL
  ["salary"]=> float(4200)
}
```

One practical use of the __set() method might be allowing the setting of a property if some allow modifications parameter was set to true during object construction; otherwise, throw an exception.

Trying to use any of the four property overloading methods (__set(), __get(), __isset(), and __unset()) in a static context would result in the following error:

```
PHP Warning: The magic method __set() must have public visibility and
cannot be static...
```

Using __get()

The __get() magic method is triggered when trying to read the data from an inaccessible property. The method accepts a single parameter, as per the following synopsis:

```
public mixed __get(string $name)
```

The $name argument is the name of the property being interacted with.

Let's take a look at the following object context example:

```php
<?php

class User
{
  private $data = [
    'name' => 'Marry',
    'age' => 32,
    'salary' => 5300.00,
  ];

  private $name = 'John';
  protected $age = 34;
  public $salary = 4200.00;

  public function __get($name)
  {
    if (array_key_exists($name, $this->data)) {
      echo '__get => ' . $name . ': ' . $this->data[$name] . PHP_EOL;
    } else {
      trigger_error('Undefined property: ' . $name, E_USER_NOTICE);
    }
  }
}

$user = new User();

echo $user->name . PHP_EOL;
echo $user->age . PHP_EOL;
echo $user->salary . PHP_EOL;
echo $user->message . PHP_EOL;
```

The `User` class defines four different properties, across three different visibility access modifiers. Since we don't have getter methods to access all of the individual properties, the only directly accessible property is `public $salary`. This is where the `__get()` method comes in handy, as it kicks in as soon as we try to access a nonexistent or otherwise inaccessible property. The resulting output of the preceding code comes down to the following four lines:

```
__get => name: Marry

__get => age: 32

4200

PHP Notice: Undefined property: message in...
```

The `age` and the `name` values are fetched from within the `$data` property as a result of the `__get()` method's inner workings.

Using __isset()

The `__isset()` magic method is triggered by calling the `isset()` or `empty()` language constructs on inaccessible properties. The method accepts a single parameter, as per the following synopsis:

```
public bool __isset(string $name)
```

The `$name` argument is the name of the property being interacted with.

Let's take a look at the following object context example:

```php
<?php

class User
{
  private $data = [
    'name' => 'John',
    'age' => 34,
  ];

  public function __isset($name)
  {
    if (array_key_exists($name, $this->data)) {
      return true;
    }
```

```
        return false;
    }
}

$user = new User();

var_dump(isset($user->name));
```

The User class defines a single protected array property called $data, and a magic __isset() method. The current method's inner workings simply do a name lookup against the $data array key names and return true if the key is found in the array, otherwise, false. The resulting output of the example is bool(true).

The Magento platform provides an interesting and practical use case for the __isset() method as part of its vendor/magento/framework/HTTP/PhpEnvironment/Request.php class file:

```
public function __isset($key)
{
  switch (true) {
    case isset($this->params[$key]):
    return true;

    case isset($this->queryParams[$key]):
    return true;

    case isset($this->postParams[$key]):
    return true;

    case isset($_COOKIE[$key]):
    return true;

    case isset($this->serverParams[$key]):
    return true;

    case isset($this->envParams[$key]):
    return true;

    default:
    return false;
  }
}
```

The `Magento\Framework\HTTP\PhpEnvironment\Request` class here represents the PHP environment and all of its possible request data. The request data can come from many sources: a query string, `$_GET`, `$_POST`, and others. The `switch` case traverses through several of these source data variables (`$params`, `$queryParams`, `$postParams`, `$serverParams`, `$envParams`, `$_COOKIE`) in order to find and confirm the existence of the request parameter.

Using __unset()

The `__unset()` magic method is triggered by calling the `unset()` language constructs on inaccessible properties. The method accepts a single parameter, as per the following synopsis:

```
public bool __unset(string $name)
```

The `$name` argument is the name of the property being interacted with.

Let's take a look at the following object context example:

```php
<?php

class User
{
  private $data = [
    'name' => 'John',
    'age' => 34,
  ];

  public function __unset($name)
  {
    unset($this->data[$name]);
  }
}

$user = new User();

var_dump($user);
unset($user->age);
unset($user->salary);
var_dump($user);
```

The `User` class declares a single private `$data` array property, alongside the `__unset()` magic method. The method itself is quite simple; it merely calls for the `unset()` constructor, passing it the value at a given array key. We are trying to unset to the `$age` and `$salary` properties here. The `$salary` property does not really exist, neither as a class property nor as a `data` array key. Luckily, `unset()` won't throw an `Undefined index` notice type of error, so we do not need additional `array_key_exists()` checks. The following resulting output shows the `$age` property being removed from the object instance:

```
object(User)#1 (1) {
  ["data":"User":private]=> array(2) {
    ["name"]=> string(4) "John"
    ["age"]=> int(34)
  }
}

object(User)#1 (1) {
  ["data":"User":private]=> array(1) {
    ["name"]=> string(4) "John"
  }
}
```

We should not confuse the use of the `unset()` construct with the `(unset)` casting. These two are different operations, and as such the `(unset)` casting will not trigger the `__unset()` magic method:

```
unset($user->age); // will trigger __unset()
((unset) $user->age); // won't trigger __unset()
```

Using __sleep()

Object serialization is another important aspect of OOP. PHP provides a `serialize()` function that allows us to serialize a value passed to it. The result is a string containing a byte-stream representation of any value that can be stored in PHP. Serializing the scalar data types and simple objects is pretty straightforward, as per the following example:

```php
<?php

$age = 34;
$name = 'John';

$obj = new stdClass();
$obj->age = 34;
$obj->name = 'John';
```

```
var_dump(serialize($age));
var_dump(serialize($name));
var_dump(serialize($obj));
```

The resulting output is shown as follows:

```
string(5) "i:34;"
string(11) "s:4:"John";"
string(56) "O:8:"stdClass":2:{s:3:"age";i:34;s:4:"name";s:4:"John";}"
```

Even a simple custom class can be easily serialized:

```php
<?php

class User
{
  public $name = 'John';
  private $age = 34;
  protected $salary = 4200.00;
}

$user = new User();

var_dump(serialize($user));
```

The preceding code results in the following output:

```
string(81)
"O:4:"User":3:{s:4:"name";s:4:"John";s:9:"Userage";i:34;s:9:"*salary";d:420
0;}"
```

The issue occurs when our classes are either significant in size, or contain resource-type references. The __sleep() magic method addresses these challenges in a way. Its intended use is to commit pending data or perform related cleanup tasks. The function is useful when we have large objects that do not need to be serialized completely.

The serialize() function triggers the object's __sleep() method if it exists. The actual triggering is done before the serialization process starts. This empowers the object to specifically list the fields it wants to allow for serialization. The return value of the __sleep() method must be an array with the names of all the object properties that we want to serialize. If the method doesn't return a serializable property name array, then NULL is serialized and E_NOTICE is issued.

The following example demonstrates a simple `User` class with a simple `__sleep()` method implementation:

```php
<?php

class User
{
    public $name = 'John';
    private $age = 34;
    protected $salary = 4200.00;

    public function __sleep()
    {
        // Cleanup & other operations???
        return ['name', 'salary'];
    }
}

$user = new User();

var_dump(serialize($user));
```

The implementation of the `__sleep()` method clearly states that the only two serializable properties of a `User` class are `name` and `salary`. Notice how the actual names are provided as a string, without a `$` sign, which results in an output as follows:

```
string(60) "O:4:"User":2:{s:4:"name";s:4:"John";s:9:"*salary";d:4200;}"
```

Serializing objects in order to store them in a database is a dangerous practice, and should be avoided by any means possible. Rare are the cases that require complex object serialization. Even those are likely a mark of improper application design.

Using __wakeup()

The topic of serializable objects would not be complete without the `serialize()` method counterpart--the `unserialize()` method. If the `serialize()` method call triggers the object's `__sleep()` magic method, it is logical to expect there is a similar behavior for deserialization. Rightfully so, calling the `unserialize()` method upon a given object triggers its `__wakeup()` magic method.

The intended use of `__wakeup()` is to reestablish any resources that might have been lost during serialization and perform other reinitialization tasks.

Let's take a look at the following example:

```php
<?php

class Backup
{
  protected $ftpClient;
  protected $ftpHost;
  protected $ftpUser;
  protected $ftpPass;

  public function __construct($host, $username, $password)
  {
    $this->ftpHost = $host;
    $this->ftpUser = $username;
    $this->ftpPass = $password;

    echo 'TEST!!!' . PHP_EOL;

    $this->connect();
  }

  public function connect()
  {
    $this->ftpClient = ftp_connect($this->ftpHost, 21, 5);
    ftp_login($this->ftpClient, $this->ftpUser, $this->ftpPass);
  }

  public function __sleep()
  {
    return ['ftpHost', 'ftpUser', 'ftpPass'];
  }

  public function __wakeup()
  {
    $this->connect();
  }
}

$backup = new Backup('test.rebex.net', 'demo', 'password');
$serialized = serialize($backup);
$unserialized = unserialize($serialized);

var_dump($backup);
var_dump($serialized);
var_dump($unserialized);
```

The `Backup` class accepts host, username, and password information through its constructor. Internally, it sets the core PHP `ftp_connect()` function to establish a connection towards the FTP server. A successfully established connection returns a resource we store into a protected `$ftpClient` property of a class. Since resources are not serializable, we made sure to exclude it from the __sleep() method return array. This ensures that our serialized string does not contain the `$ftpHost` property. We have further set a `$this->connect();` call within the __wakeup() method to reinitialize the `$ftpHost` resource. The overall example results in the following output:

```
object(Backup)#1 (4) {
  ["ftpClient":protected]=> resource(4) of type (FTP Buffer)
  ["ftpHost":protected]=> string(14) "test.rebex.net"
  ["ftpUser":protected]=> string(4) "demo"
  ["ftpPass":protected]=> string(8) "password"
}

string(119)
"O:6:"Backup":3:{s:10:"*ftpHost";s:14:"test.rebex.net";s:10:"*ftpUser";s:4:
"demo";s:10:"*ftpPass";s:8:"password";}"

object(Backup)#2 (4) {
  ["ftpClient":protected]=> resource(5) of type (FTP Buffer)
  ["ftpHost":protected]=> string(14) "test.rebex.net"
  ["ftpUser":protected]=> string(4) "demo"
  ["ftpPass":protected]=> string(8) "password"
}
```

The __wakeup() method sort of takes on the role of constructor during the unserialize() function call. Because the object's __construct() method is not called during deserialization, we need to be careful to implement the necessary __wakeup() method logic so that the object can reconstruct any resources it might need.

Using __toString()

The __toString() magic method triggers when we use an object in a string context. It allows us to decide how the object will react when it is treated like a string.

Let's take a look at the following example:

```php
<?php

class User
{
  protected $name;
```

```
    protected $age;

    public function __construct($name, $age)
    {
      $this->name = $name;
      $this->age = $age;
    }
}

$user = new User('John', 34);
echo $user;
```

Here, we have a simple User class that accepts the $name and $age parameters through its constructor method. Other than that, there is nothing else to indicate how the class should respond to the attempt of using it in the string context, which is exactly what we are doing right after the class declaration, as we are trying to echo the object instance itself.

In its current form, the resulting output would be as follows:

```
Catchable fatal error: Object of class User could not be converted to
string in...
```

The __toString() magic method allows us to circumvent this error in a simple and elegant way:

```
<?php

class User
{
  protected $name;
  protected $age;

  public function __construct($name, $age)
  {
    $this->name = $name;
    $this->age = $age;
  }

  public function __toString()
  {
    return $this->name . ', age ' . $this->age;
  }
}

$user = new User('John', 34);
echo $user;
```

By adding the __toString() magic method, we were able to tailor the resulting string representation of our object into the following code line:

```
John, age 34
```

The Guzzle HTTP client provides a practical use case example of the __toString() method through its PSR7 HTTP messaging interface implementations; whereas, some of the implementations make use of the __toString() method. The following code snippet is a partial extract of Guzzle's vendor/guzzlehttp/psr7/src/Stream.php class file that implements the Psr\Http\Message\StreamInterface interface:

```php
public function __toString()
{
  try {
    $this->seek(0);
    return (string) stream_get_contents($this->stream);
  } catch (\Exception $e) {
    return '';
  }
}
```

The try...catch block is pretty much a norm in the case of any logic-rich __toString() implementations. This is because we cannot throw an exception from within a __toString() method. Therefore, we need to make sure no error escapes.

Using __invoke()

The __invoke() magic method gets triggered when the object is being called as a function. The method accepts an optional number of parameters and is is able to return various types of data, or no data at all, as per the following synopsis:

```
mixed __invoke([ $... ])
```

If an object class implements the __invoke() method, we can call the method by specifying parentheses () right after the object's name. This type of object is known as a functor or function object.

 The Wikipedia page (https://en.wikipedia.org/wiki/Functor) provides more information on the functor.

The following block of code illustrates the simple __invoke() implementation:

```php
<?php

class User
{
  public function __invoke($name, $age)
  {
    echo $name . ', ' . $age;
  }
}
```

The __invoke() method can be triggered either by using the object instance as a function or by calling call_user_func(), as shown in the following code snippet:

```php
$user = new User();

$user('John', 34); // outputs: John, 34

call_user_func($user, 'John', 34); // outputs: John, 34
```

Using the __invoke() method, we *masquerade* our classes as callable.

```php
var_dump(is_callable($user)); // true
```

One of the benefits of using __invoke() is that it makes it possible to create a standard callback type across the language. This is much more convenient than using combinations of strings, objects, and arrays when referencing a function, object instance method, or class static method via the call_user_func() function.

The __invoke() method makes for powerful language additions as we perceive opportunities for new development patterns; although, its misuse can lead towards an unclear and messy code.

Using __set_state()

The __set_state() magic method is triggered (not really) for classes exported by the var_export() function. The method accepts a single array type parameter and returns an object, as per the following synopsis:

```php
static object __set_state(array $properties)
```

The `var_export()` function outputs or returns a parsable string representation of a given variable. It is somewhat similar to the `var_dump()` function, except that the returned representation is a valid PHP code:

```php
<?php

class User
{
   public $name = 'John';
   public $age = 34;
   private $salary = 4200.00;
   protected $identifier = 'ABC';
}

$user = new User();
var_export($user); // outputs string "User::__set_state..."
var_export($user, true); // returns string "User::__set_state..."
```

This results in the following output:

```
User::__set_state(array(
  'name' => 'John',
  'age' => 34,
  'salary' => 4200.0,
  'identifier' => 'ABC',
))

string(113) "User::__set_state(array(
  'name' => 'John',
  'age' => 34,
  'salary' => 4200.0,
  'identifier' => 'ABC',
))"
```

Using the `var_export()` function does not actually trigger the `__set_state()` method of our `User` class. It merely yields a string representation of the `User::__set_state(array(...))` expression that we can either log, output, or pass through the `eval()` language construct for execution.

The following piece of code is a more robust example demonstrating the use of `eval()`:

```php
<?php

class User
{
   public $name = 'John';
   public $age = 34;
```

```
    private $salary = 4200.00;
    protected $identifier = 'ABC';

    public static function __set_state($properties)
    {
      $user = new User();

      $user->name = $properties['name'];
      $user->age = $properties['age'];
      $user->salary = $properties['salary'];
      $user->identifier = $properties['identifier'];

      return $user;
    }
}

$user = new User();
$user->name = 'Mariya';
$user->age = 32;

eval('$obj = ' . var_export($user, true) . ';');

var_dump($obj);
```

This results in the following output:

```
object(User)#2 (4) {
  ["name"]=> string(6) "Mariya"
  ["age"]=> int(32)
  ["salary":"User":private]=> float(4200)
  ["identifier":protected]=> string(3) "ABC"
}
```

Knowing how the eval() language construct is very dangerous as it allows execution of arbitrary PHP code, its use is discouraged. Therefore, the use of __set_state() itself becomes questionable for anything other than debugging purposes.

Using __clone()

The __clone() magic method is triggered on newly cloned objects, where cloning is done using the clone keyword. The method does not accept any parameters nor does it return any values, as per the following synopsis:

```
void __clone(void)
```

When it comes to object cloning, we tend to differentiate deep copy and shallow copy. Deep copy copies everything--all of the objects an object might point to. Shallow copy copies as little as possible, leaving the object references as references where possible. While shallow copy might come in handy as a protection against circular references, replicating all properties whether they are references or values is not always the desired behavior.

The following example demonstrates the implementation of the __clone() method and the use of the clone keyword:

```php
<?php

class User
{
  public $identifier;

  public function __clone()
  {
    $this->identifier = null;
  }
}

$user = new User();
$user->identifier = 'john';

$user2 = clone $user;

var_dump($user);
var_dump($user2);
```

This results in the following output:

```
object(User)#1 (1) {
  ["identifier"]=> string(4) "john"
}

object(User)#2 (1) {
  ["identifier"]=> NULL
}
```

The important takeaway when it comes to the __clone() method is that it is not an override of the cloning process. The normal cloning process always occurs. The __clone() method merely takes on the responsibility of amending the wrong doing, where we might not normally be satisfied with the outcome.

Using __debugInfo()

The __debugInfo() magic method gets triggered when the var_dump() function is called. By default, the var_dump() function shows all public, protected, and private properties of an object. However, if an object class implements the __debugInfo() magic method, we get to control the output of the var_dump() function. The method does not accept any parameters, and returns an array of key-values to be shown, as per the following synopsis:

```
array __debugInfo(void)
```

The following example demonstrates the __debugInfo() method implementation:

```php
<?php

class User
{
    public $name = 'John';
    public $age = 34;
    private $salary = 4200.00;
    private $bonus = 680.00;
    protected $identifier = 'ABC';
    protected $logins = 67;

    public function __debugInfo()
    {
        return [
            'name' => $this->name,
            'income' => $this->salary + $this->bonus
        ];
    }
}

$user = new User();

var_dump($user);
```

This results in the following output:

```
object(User)#1 (2) {
    ["name"]=> string(4) "John"
    ["income"]=> float(4880)
}
```

While the __debugInfo() method is useful for tailoring our own var_dump() output, this might not be something we will necessarily be doing in day-to-day development.

Usage statistics across popular platforms

The PHP ecosystem is massive to say the least. There are dozens of free and open source CMS, CRM, shopping cart, blog, and other platforms and libraries out there. WordPress, Drupal, and Magento are probably among the most popular ones when it comes to blogs, content management, and shopping cart solutions. They are all available for download from their respective websites:

- WordPress: `https://wordpress.org`
- Drupal: `https://www.drupal.org`
- Magento: `https://magento.com/`

Considering these popular platforms, the following table puts some perspective around the magic method use:

Magic method	WordPress 4.7 (702 .php files)	Drupal 8.2.4 (8199 .php files)	Magento CE 2.1.3 (29649 .php files)
`__construct()`	343	2547	12218
`__destruct()`	19	19	77
`__call()`	10	35	152
`__callStatic()`	1	2	4
`__get()`	23	31	125
`__set()`	15	24	86
`__isset()`	21	15	57
`__unset()`	11	13	34
`__sleep()`	0	46	103
`__wakeup()`	0	10	94
`__toString()`	15	181	460
`__invoke()`	0	27	112
`__set_state()`	0	3	5
`__clone()`	0	32	68
`__debugInfo()`	0	0	2

The table is a result of a crude `function __[magic-method-name]` search across an entire codebase of individual platforms. It's hard to draw any conclusions on top of it, as platforms differ significantly in number of `.php` files. One thing we can say for sure--not all magic methods are equally popular. WordPress, for example, does not even seem to use the `__sleep()`, `__wakeup()`, and `__invoke()` methods, which are of importance in OOP. This might be because WordPress does not handle as many OO components as Magento, for example, which is much more of an OOP platform in architectural sense. Drupal sort of sits in the middle here, in terms of total `.php` file numbers and the magic methods it uses. Inconclusive or not, the preceding table outlines the active use of pretty much every magic method PHP has to offer.

Summary

Throughout this chapter, we took a detailed look into each and every magic method PHP has to offer. The ease of their use is equally impressive as the power they bring to the language. Simply naming our class methods appropriately, we were able to tap into pretty much every aspect of an object state and behavior. While most of these magic methods are not something we will be using on a day-to-day basis, their existence empowers us with some nifty architectural styles and solutions that are not that easily possible with other languages.

Moving forward, we will step into the realm of CLI and the more elusive use of PHP.

5
The Realm of CLI

A great deal of modern application development evolves around visible bits and pieces. Whether we are talking about the server infrastructure, development tools, or the resulting application itself, graphical interfaces dominate our experience nowadays. While the diversity and overall list of available GUI tools seems endless, the console still remains an important part of development that any self-respectful developer should be familiar with.

There are countless reasons why the console is simply the right tool for the job. Take large database backups, for example. Trying to backup gigabytes of MySQL data via the GUI tool is likely to result in a complete failure or a corrupt backup file, whereas the console-based `mysqldump` tool is impervious to the size of the backup or the time it takes for it to execute. Things such as large and time-consuming data imports, data exports, data synchronizations, and so on are common operations of many PHP applications. These are just some of the operations we would want to move away from the browser and into the console.

In this chapter, we will take a look at the following sections:

- Understanding PHP CLI
- The Console component
- Input/output streams
- Process control:
  - Ticks
  - Signals
  - Alarms
  - Multiprocessing

Understanding PHP CLI

Working with the console in PHP is quite easy via the help of PHP CLI SAPI, or just PHP CLI for short. PHP CLI was first introduced in PHP 4.2.0 as an experimental feature, and, soon after, it became fully supported and enabled by default in the later versions of PHP. The great thing about it is that it is available on all popular operating systems (Linux, Windows, OSX, Solaris). This makes it easy to write console applications that execute pretty much on any platform.

 Check out `https://en.wikipedia.org/wiki/Command-line_interface` and `https://en.wikipedia.org/wiki/Server_Application_Programmi ng_Interface`for more elaborate descriptions of general CLI and SAPI abbreviations.

PHP CLI is not the only SAPI interface supported by PHP. Using the `php_sapi_name()` function, we can get a name of the current interface that PHP is using. Other possible interfaces include aolserver, apache, apache2handler, cgi, cgi-fcgi, cli, cli-server, continuity, embed, fpm-fcgi, and others.

Running a simple `php -v` command within our operating system console should give us an output similar to the following:

```
PHP 7.1.0-3+deb.sury.org~yakkety+1 (cli) ( NTS )
Copyright (c) 1997-2016 The PHP Group
Zend Engine v3.1.0-dev, Copyright (c) 1998-2016 Zend Technologies
 with Zend OPcache v7.1.0-3+deb.sury.org~yakkety+1, Copyright (c)
1999-2016, by Zend Technologies
```

This should serve as confirmation that PHP CLI SAPI is up and running. The CLI version of PHP has its own `php.ini` configuration, separate from other SAPI interfaces. Running the `php --ini` command on console will expose the following details about the currently used `php.ini` file:

```
Configuration File (php.ini) Path: /etc/php/7.1/cli
Loaded Configuration File: /etc/php/7.1/cli/php.ini
Scan for additional .ini files in: /etc/php/7.1/cli/conf.d
Additional .ini files parsed: /etc/php/7.1/cli/conf.d/10-opcache.ini,
/etc/php/7.1/cli/conf.d/10-pdo.ini,
/etc/php/7.1/cli/conf.d/20-calendar.ini,
/etc/php/7.1/cli/conf.d/20-ctype.ini,
...
```

Here, we can see the location of the main configuration file (`php.ini`) and extension-specific configuration files. Chaining the configuration of these configuration files takes immediate effect, as they are loaded each time we invoke PHP.

The Console component

A number of popular PHP frameworks and platforms utilize some sort of console application in order to assist with development, deployment, and maintenance of our projects. The Symfony framework, for example, comes with its own console application empowered with dozens of nifty commands. These can be accessed by executing the `php bin/console` command within the root directory of a Symfony project:

```
$ php bin/console
Symfony 3.2.1 (kernel: app, env: dev, debug: true)

Usage:
  command [options] [arguments]

Options:
  -h, --help            Display this help message
  -q, --quiet           Do not output any message
  -V, --version         Display this application version
      --ansi            Force ANSI output
      --no-ansi         Disable ANSI output
  -n, --no-interaction  Do not ask any interactive question
  -e, --env=ENV         The environment name [default: "dev"]
      --no-debug        Switches off debug mode
  -v|vv|vvv, --verbose  Increase the verbosity of messages: 1 for normal output, 2 for more verbose output and 3 for debug

Available commands:
  help                                Displays help for a command
  list                                Lists commands
assets
  assets:install                      Installs bundles web assets under a public web directory
cache
  cache:clear                         Clears the cache
  cache:pool:clear                    Clears cache pools
  cache:warmup                        Warms up an empty cache
config
  config:dump-reference               Dumps the default configuration for an extension
debug
  debug:config                        Dumps the current configuration for an extension
  debug:container                     Displays current services for an application
  debug:event-dispatcher              Displays configured listeners for an application
  debug:router                        Displays current routes for an application
  debug:swiftmailer                   [swiftmailer:debug] Displays current mailers for an application
  debug:translation                   Displays translation messages information
  debug:twig                          Shows a list of twig functions, filters, globals and tests
doctrine
  doctrine:cache:clear-collection-region   Clear a second-level cache collection region.
  doctrine:cache:clear-entity-region       Clear a second-level cache entity region.
  doctrine:cache:clear-metadata            Clears all metadata cache for an entity manager
  doctrine:cache:clear-query               Clears all query cache for an entity manager
  doctrine:cache:clear-query-region        Clear a second-level cache query region.
  doctrine:cache:clear-result              Clears result cache for an entity manager
  doctrine:database:create                 Creates the configured database
  doctrine:database:drop                   Drops the configured database
  doctrine:database:import                 Import SQL file(s) directly to Database.
  doctrine:ensure-production-settings      Verify that Doctrine is properly configured for a production environment.
  doctrine:generate:crud                   [generate:doctrine:crud] Generates a CRUD based on a Doctrine entity
  doctrine:generate:entities               [generate:doctrine:entities] Generates entity classes and method stubs from your mapping information
  doctrine:generate:entity                 [generate:doctrine:entity] Generates a new Doctrine entity inside a bundle
  doctrine:generate:form                   [generate:doctrine:form] Generates a form type class based on a Doctrine entity
  doctrine:mapping:convert                 [orm:convert:mapping] Convert mapping information between supported formats.
  doctrine:mapping:import                  Imports mapping information from an existing database
  doctrine:mapping:info
  doctrine:query:dql                       Executes arbitrary DQL directly from the command line.
  doctrine:query:sql                       Executes arbitrary SQL directly from the command line.
  doctrine:schema:create                   Executes (or dumps) the SQL needed to generate the database schema
  doctrine:schema:drop                     Executes (or dumps) the SQL needed to drop the current database schema
  doctrine:schema:update                   Executes (or dumps) the SQL needed to update the database schema to match the current mapping metadata.
  doctrine:schema:validate                 Validate the mapping files.
generate
  generate:bundle                     Generates a bundle
  generate:command                    Generates a console command
  generate:controller                 Generates a controller
lint
  lint:twig                           Lints a template and outputs encountered errors
  lint:yaml                           Lints a file and outputs encountered errors
orm
router
  router:match                        Helps debug routes by simulating a path info match
security
  security:check                      Checks security issues in your project dependencies
  security:encode-password            Encodes a password.
server
  server:run                          Runs PHP built-in web server
  server:start                        Starts PHP built-in web server in the background
  server:status                       Outputs the status of the built-in web server for the given address
  server:stop                         Stops PHP's built-in web server that was started with the server:start command
swiftmailer
  swiftmailer:email:send              Send simple email message
  swiftmailer:spool:send              Sends emails from the spool
translation
  translation:update                  Updates the translation file
```

Each of the listed commands executes a very specific purpose; therefore, assisting our project in various ways. While the Symfony framework installation and overall details are out of the scope of this book, there is a component within it that we are interested in. The Console component, while part of the Symfony framework, can also be used as a standalone component to build these types of console applications.

Setting up the Console component

The Console component is available in two flavors:

- Composer package (`symfony/console` on Packagist)
- Git repository (`https://github.com/symfony/console`)

Given that Composer is a de facto standard when it comes to dealing with PHP components, we will use the `composer require` command to quickly kick off our first console application, as follows:

```
mkdir foggyline
cd foggyline
composer require symfony/console
```

Running this command triggers the following output:

```
$ mkdir foggyline
$ cd foggyline/
$ composer require symfony/console
Using version ^3.2 for symfony/console
./composer.json has been created
Loading composer repositories with package information
Updating dependencies (including require-dev)
Package operations: 4 installs, 0 updates, 0 removals
  - Installing psr/log (1.0.2) Downloading: 100%
  - Installing symfony/debug (v3.2.2) Downloading: 100%
  - Installing symfony/polyfill-mbstring (v1.3.0) Downloading: 100%
  - Installing symfony/console (v3.2.2) Loading from cache
symfony/console suggests installing symfony/event-dispatcher ()
symfony/console suggests installing symfony/filesystem ()
symfony/console suggests installing symfony/process ()
Writing lock file
Generating autoload files
```

Upon completion, Composer generates the following structure within our `foggyline` directory:

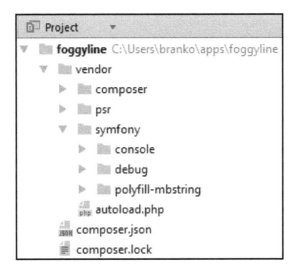

All it takes for us now is to create an application entry file, let's say, `app.php`, and include the `vendor/autoload.php` file generated by Composer, as follows:

The very first line of our file, known as *shebang*, contains the instructions required for autodetection of the type of script. While the line itself is not really necessary, it makes a difference between normally running php app.php or just ./app.php in order to execute our application script. Following the *shebang* line is the PHP code that deals with the inclusion of autoload.php and instantiation of the Console\Application class. The Console\Application class accepts two parameters: the name of the application and the version we wish to assign to it. In between instantiating and running the app, we have a few commented-out lines that merely demonstrate where we would normally register our individual application commands.

> To learn more about the *shebang* character sequence, check out the Wikipedia article at https://en.wikipedia.org/wiki/Shebang_(Unix).

To put the *shebang* line into effect, the app.php file needs to be flagged as executable:

```
$ chmod +x app.php
$ ./app.php
```

With these four lines of PHP code in place, we already have enough to execute our application:

```
$ ./app.php
Foggyline App 1.0.0

Usage:
  command [options] [arguments]

Options:
  -h, --help            Display this help message
  -q, --quiet           Do not output any message
  -V, --version         Display this application version
      --ansi            Force ANSI output
      --no-ansi         Disable ANSI output
  -n, --no-interaction  Do not ask any interactive question
  -v|vv|vvv, --verbose  Increase the verbosity of messages: 1 for normal output, 2 for more verbose output and 3 for debug

Available commands:
  help  Displays help for a command
  list  Lists commands
```

The output comes out colored and nicely formatted, just as we would expect from modern console applications. This is merely but a fraction of things that the Console component takes care for us. With this, we conclude our Console component setup. We can now go ahead and start registering our application commands using the add() method of an $app instance.

Creating a console command

Now that we have our *barebone* console application set up, let's create three commands to handle the following imaginary actions:

- Customer register
- Customer status set
- Customer export

The word imaginary simply flags that we will not actually concern ourselves with the inner details of the executed commands, as our focus is understanding how to reuse the Console component.

We start by creating `CustomerRegisterCommand.php`, `CustomerStatusSetCommand.php`, and `CustomerExportCommand.php` within our project's `src/Foggyline/Console/Command/` directory.

The `CustomerRegisterCommand.php` file has the following content:

```php
<?php

namespace Foggyline\Console\Command;

use Symfony\Component\Console\{
  Command\Command,
  Input\InputInterface,
  Output\OutputInterface
};

class CustomerRegisterCommand extends Command
{
  protected function configure()
  {
    $this->setName('customer:register')
    ->setDescription('Registers new customer.');
  }

  protected function execute(InputInterface $input, OutputInterface
    $output)
  {
    // Some imaginary logic here...
    $output->writeln('Customer registered.');
  }
}
```

The `CustomerStatusSetCommand.php` file has the following content:

```php
<?php

namespace Foggyline\Console\Command;

use Symfony\Component\Console\{
  Command\Command,
  Input\InputInterface,
  Output\OutputInterface
};

class CustomerStatusSetCommand extends Command
{
  protected function configure()
  {
    $this->setName('customer:status:set')
    ->setDescription('Enables of disables existing customer.');
  }

  protected function execute(InputInterface $input, OutputInterface
    $output)
  {
    // Some imaginary logic here...
    $output->writeln('Customer disabled.');
  }
}
```

The `CustomerExportCommand.php` file has the following content:

```php
<?php

namespace Foggyline\Console\Command;

use Symfony\Component\Console\{
  Command\Command,
  Input\InputInterface,
  Output\OutputInterface
};

class CustomerExportCommand extends Command
{
  protected function configure()
  {
    $this->setName('customer:export')
    ->setDescription('Exports one or more customers.');
  }
```

```
   protected function execute(InputInterface $input, OutputInterface
$output)
   {
      // Some imaginary logic here...
      $output->writeln('Customers exported.');
   }
}
```

We can see that all three commands extend
`Symfony\Component\Console\Command\Command` and provide their own
implementation of the `configure()` and `execute()` methods. The `configure()` method
is sort of like the constructor, where we would place our initial configuration, such as name
of the command, its description, options, arguments, and so on. The `execute()` method is
where our actual command logic needs to be implemented, or called if implemented
elsewhere. With these three commands in place, we need to go back to the `app.php` file and
modify its content as follows:

```
#!/usr/bin/env php
<?php

$loader = require __DIR__ . '/vendor/autoload.php';
$loader->add('Foggyline', __DIR__ . '/src/');

use Symfony\Component\Console\Application;
use Foggyline\Console\Command\{
   CustomerExportCommand,
   CustomerRegisterCommand,
   CustomerStatusSetCommand
};

$app = new Application('Foggyline App', '1.0.0');

$app->add(new CustomerRegisterCommand());
$app->add(new CustomerStatusSetCommand());
$app->add(new CustomerExportCommand());

$app->run();
```

Compared to our initial `app.php` file, there are a few changes here. Notice the line where
we require the `autoload.php` file. If we actually took a look at that file, we would see it
returns an instance of the `Composer\Autoload\ClassLoader` class. This is the
Composer's PSR-0, PSR-4, and classmap class loader that we can use to our advantage to
load our commands. This is exactly what the `$loader->add('Foggyline'`... line is
doing. Finally, we register our newly created commands using the application's `add()`
method.

With these changes in place, executing our application yields the following output:

```
$ ./app.php
Foggyline App 1.0.0

Usage:
  command [options] [arguments]

Options:
  -h, --help            Display this help message
  -q, --quiet           Do not output any message
  -V, --version         Display this application version
      --ansi            Force ANSI output
      --no-ansi         Disable ANSI output
  -n, --no-interaction  Do not ask any interactive question
  -v|vv|vvv, --verbose  Increase the verbosity of messages: 1 for normal output, 2 for more verbose output and 3 for debug

Available commands:
  help                  Displays help for a command
  list                  Lists commands
 customer
  customer:export       Exports one or more customers.
  customer:register     Registers new customer.
  customer:status:set   Enables of disables existing customer.
```

Our three commands are now appearing on the list of available commands. The `name` and `description` values we set within the command class `configure()` method are being shown for each command. We can now easily execute one these commands:

```
$ ./app.php customer:status:set
Customer disabled.
```

The `Customer disabled.` label confirms the execution of our `CustomerStatusSetCommand execute()` method. While the overall concept of our console application and its commands was fairly easy to grasp so far, our commands are hardly useful at the moment, as we are not passing any inputs to them.

Dealing with inputs

Making practical and useful commands usually requires the ability to pass on the dynamic information from the operating system console to our application command. The Console component differentiates two types of inputs--`arguments` and `options`:

- Arguments are ordered, space-separated (`John Doe`), optional or required, string types of information. Assignment of arguments comes after the command name itself. We use the `addArgument()` method of the `Symfony\Component\Console\Command\Command` instance to assign arguments to our custom command.

- Options are unordered, two-dashes-separated (`--name=John --surname=Doe`), always optional, assigned type of information. The assignment of options comes after the command name itself. We use the `addOption()` method of the `Symfony\Component\Console\Command\Command` instance to assign options to our custom command.

The `addArgument()` method accepts four parameters, as per the following synopsis:

```
public function addArgument(
    $name,
    $mode = null,
    $description = '',
    $default = null
)
```

Whereas, the `addArgument()` method parameters have the following meanings:

- `$name`: This is the argument name
- `$mode`: This is the argument mode, which can be `InputArgument::REQUIRED` or `InputArgument::OPTIONAL`
- `$description`: This is the description text
- `$default`: This is the default value (for the `InputArgument::OPTIONAL` mode only)

The `addOption()` method accepts five parameters, as per the following synopsis:

```
public function addOption(
    $name,
    $shortcut = null,
    $mode = null,
    $description = '',
    $default = null
)
```

Whereas, the `addOption()` method parameters have the following meanings:

- `$name`: This is the option name
- `$shortcut`: This is the shortcut (it can be `null`)
- `$mode`: This is the option mode, which is one of the `InputOption::VALUE_*` constants
- `$description`: This is the description text
- `$default`: This is the default value (must be `null` for `InputOption::VALUE_NONE`)

We could easily build our commands such that they use the two input types together, as they do not exclude each other.

Let's go ahead and modify our src\Foggyline\Console\Command\CustomerRegisterCommand.php file with the following changes:

```php
<?php

namespace Foggyline\Console\Command;

use Symfony\Component\Console\{
  Command\Command,
  Input\InputInterface,
  Input\InputArgument,
  Input\InputOption,
  Output\OutputInterface
};

class CustomerRegisterCommand extends Command
{
  protected function configure()
  {
    $this->setName('customer:register')
    ->addArgument(
      'name', InputArgument::REQUIRED, 'Customer full name.'
    )
    ->addArgument(
      'email', InputArgument::REQUIRED, 'Customer email address.'
    )
    ->addArgument(
      'dob', InputArgument::OPTIONAL, 'Customer date of birth.'
    )
    ->addOption(
      'email', null, InputOption::VALUE_REQUIRED, 'Send email to
      customer?'
    )
    ->addOption(
      'log', null, InputOption::VALUE_OPTIONAL, 'Log to event system?'
    )
    ->setDescription('Enables or disables existing customer.');
  }

  protected function execute(InputInterface $input, OutputInterface
$output)
  {
    var_dump($input->getArgument('name'));
```

```
        var_dump($input->getArgument('email'));
        var_dump($input->getArgument('dob'));
        var_dump($input->getOption('email'));
        var_dump($input->getOption('log'));
    }
}
```

Our modifications mainly extend the *group use* declaration and the `configure()` method. Within the `configure()` method, we are utilizing the `addArgument()` and `addOption()` instance methods to add the number of inputs to our command.

Trying to execute our console command now, with no arguments, would trigger `RuntimaException`, as shown in the following screenshot:

```
$ ./app.php customer:register

[Symfony\Component\Console\Exception\RuntimeException]
Not enough arguments (missing: "name, email").

customer:register [--email [EMAIL]] [--log [LOG]] [--] <name> <email> [<dob>]
```

The error is descriptive enough to provide a list of missing arguments. However, it does not trigger our own argument and option descriptions. To get those to show up, we could easily run a `./app.php customer:register --help` command. This tells the Console component to show the command details we specified:

```
$ ./app.php customer:register --help
Usage:
  customer:register [options] [--] <name> <email> [<dob>]

Arguments:
  name                      Your full name.
  email                     Your email address.
  dob                       Your date of birth, optionally.

Options:
      --email=EMAIL         Send email to customer?
      --log[=LOG]           Log customer to logging system?
  -h, --help                Display this help message
  -q, --quiet               Do not output any message
  -V, --version             Display this application version
      --ansi                Force ANSI output
      --no-ansi             Disable ANSI output
  -n, --no-interaction      Do not ask any interactive question
  -v|vv|vvv, --verbose      Increase the verbosity of messages: 1 for normal output, 2 for more verbose output and 3 for debug

Help:
  Enables of disables existing customer.
```

Now that we see the exact descriptions behind our arguments and options, we can issue a more valid command that would not trigger an error, such as `./app.php customer:register John Doe --log=true`. Passing all required arguments progresses us to the `execute()` method, which has been modified to do a raw dump of the passed on values for our inspection, as shown in the following screenshot:

```
$ ./app.php customer:register John Doe --log=true
string(4) "John"
string(3) "Doe"
NULL
NULL
string(4) "true"
```

We now have a simple, but working version of a command that is able to accept inputs. The `addArgument()` and `addOption()` methods made it really easy to define and describe these inputs via a single expression. The Console component has proven itself to be a really handy addition to our console application.

Using Console component helpers

Understanding arguments and options is a first step towards utilizing the Console component. Once we understand how to deal with inputs, we turn our attention to other, more advanced features. The helpers feature helps us ease the common tasks, such as format outputs, show running processes, show updatable progress information, provide interactive QA process, display tabular data, and so on.

The following are several Console component helpers available for us to use:

- Formatter Helper
- Process Helper
- Progress Bar
- Question Helper
- Table
- Debug Formatter Helper

 You can see the full helper implementations within our project's `vendor\symfony\console\Helper` directory.

To showcase the ease of use of these helpers, let's go ahead and implement the simple *progress bar* and *table* helper within our *customer export* command.

We do so by modifying the `execute()` method of the `src\Foggyline\Console\Command\CustomerExportCommand.php` class file:

```php
protected function execute(InputInterface $input, OutputInterface $output)
{
    // Fake data source
    $customers = [
        ['John Doe', 'john.doe@mail.loc', '1983-01-16'],
        ['Samantha Smith', 'samantha.smith@mail.loc', '1986-10-23'],
        ['Robert Black', 'robert.black@mail.loc', '1978-11-18'],
    ];

    // Progress Bar Helper
    $progress = new
        \Symfony\Component\Console\Helper\ProgressBar($output,
        count($customers));

    $progress->start();

    for ($i = 1; $i <= count($customers); $i++) {
        sleep(5);
        $progress->advance();
    }

    $progress->finish();

    // Table Helper
    $table = new \Symfony\Component\Console\Helper\Table($output);
    $table->setHeaders(['Name', 'Email', 'DON'])
    ->setRows($customers)
    ->render();
}
```

We start our code by adding a fake customer data. We then instantiate `ProgressBar`, passing it the count of entries in our fake customer data array. The progress bar instance requires explicit `start()`, `advance()`, and `finish()` method calls to actually advance the progress bar. Once the progress bar is done, we instantiate `Table`, passing it proper headers and the row data from our customer data array.

The console component helpers provide great deal of configuration options. To find out more, check out `http://symfony.com/doc/current/components/console/helpers/index.html`.

With the preceding changes in place, triggering the `./app.php customer:export` command on console should now give the following output whilst the command is executing:

```
$ ./app.php customer:export
 2/3 [===================>---------]  66%
```

We will first see the progress par kicking in, showing the exact progress. Once the progress bar is done, the table helper kicks in, making for the final output, as shown in the following screenshot:

```
$ ./app.php customer:export
 3/3 [============================] 100%+----------------+--------------------------+------------+
| Name           | Email                    | DON        |
+----------------+--------------------------+------------+
| John Doe       | john.doe@mail.loc        | 1983-01-16 |
| Samantha Smith | samantha.smith@mail.loc  | 1986-10-23 |
| Robert Black   | robert.black@mail.loc    | 1978-11-18 |
+----------------+--------------------------+------------+
```

Using helpers impacts our console application user experience for better. We are now able to write applications that provide informative and structured feeedback for user.

Input/output streams

Quite early in development, every programmer stumbles upon the **streams** term. This seemingly frightening term represents a form of data. Unlike the typical finite type of data, streams represent a potentially unlimited *sequence* of data. In PHP terms, a stream is a resource object exhibiting streamable behavior. Using various wrappers, the PHP language supports a wide range of streams. The `stream_get_wrappers()` function can retrieve a list of all the registered stream wrappers available on the currently running system, such as the following:

- `php`
- `file`
- `glob`
- `data`
- `http`
- `ftp`
- `zip`
- `compress.zlib`

- `compress.bzip2`
- `https`
- `ftps`
- `phar`

The list of wrappers is quite extensive, but not finite. We can also register our own wrappers using the `stream_wrapper_register()` function. Each wrapper tells the stream how to handle specific protocols and encodings. Each stream is therefore accessed through the `scheme://target` syntax, such as the following:

- `php://stdin`
- `file:///path/to/file.ext`
- `glob://var/www/html/*.php`
- `data://text/plain;base64,Zm9nZ3lsaW51`
- `http://foggyline.net/`

The `scheme` part of the syntax indicates the name of the wrapper to be used, while the `target` part depends on the wrapper used. As a part of this section, we are interested in the `php` wrapper and its target values because they deal with the standard streams.

The standard streams are the following three I/O connections made available to all programs:

- standard input (`stdin`) - file descriptor `0`
- standard output (`stdout`) - file descriptor `1`
- standard error (`stderr`) - file descriptor `2`

The file descriptor is an integer representing a handle used to access an I/O resource. As a part of the POSIX application programming interface, Unix processes are expected to have these three file descriptors. Knowing the file descriptor value, we could use `php://fd` to gain direct access to the given file descriptor, such as `php://fd/1`. However, there is a more elegant way of doing it.

To learn more about POSIX, check out `https://en.wikipedia.org/wiki/POSIX`.

Out of the box, the PHP CLI SAPI provides three constants for these three standard streams:

- `define('STDIN', fopen('php://stdin', 'r'));`: This represents an already opened stream to `stdin`
- `define('STDOUT', fopen('php://stdout', 'w'));`: This represents an already opened stream to `stdout`
- `define('STDERR', fopen('php://stderr', 'w'));`: This represents an already opened stream to `stderr`

The following simple code snippet demonstrates the use of these standard streams:

```php
<?php

fwrite(STDOUT, "Type something: ");
$line = fgets(STDIN);
fwrite(STDOUT, 'You typed: ' . $line);
fwrite(STDERR, 'Triggered STDERR!' . PHP_EOL);
```

Executing it, we would first see **Type something:** on screen, after which, we would need to provide a string and hit *Enter*, which finally gives the following an output:

```
$ ./app.php
Type something: I love PHP
You typed: I love PHP
Triggered STDERR!
```

While the example itself is ultimately simplified, it does showcase the ease of obtaining the stream handles. What we do with those streams, further depends on the functions that utilize the streams (`fopen()`, `fputs()`, and so on) and the actual stream functions.

 PHP provides over forty stream functions, as well as the `streamWrapper` class prototype. These provide us with a means of creating and manipulating streams in pretty much any way imaginable. Check out `http://php.net/manual/en/book.stream.php` for more details.

Process control

Building CLI applications quite often implies working with the system processes. PHP provides a **powerful process control extension** called **PCNTL**. The extension allows us to handle process creation, program execution, signal handling, and process termination. It only works on Unix-like machines, where PHP is compiled with the `--enable-pcntl` configuration option.

To confirm that PCNTL is available on our system, we can execute the following console command:

```
php -m | grep pcntl
```

Given the power it bares, the use of the PCNTL extension is discouraged in production web environments. Writing PHP daemons scripts for command-line applications is what we want to use it for.

To start putting things into perspective, let's go ahead and see how we would use the PCNTL features to handle process signals.

Ticks

PCNTL relies on ticks for its signal handling callback mechanism. The official definition (`http://php.net/manual/en/control-structures.declare.php`) of a tick says:

> *A tick is an event that occurs for every N low-level tickable statements executed by the parser within the declare block. The value for N is specified using ticks=N within the declare block's directive section.*

To elaborate on that, a tick is an event. Using the `declare()` language construct, we control how many statements it takes to set off a tick. We then use `register_ tick_ function()` to execute our function upon each *fired tick*. Ticks are basically a side-effect of a number of evaluated expressions; the side effect we can react to with our custom functions. While most of the statements are tickable, certain condition expressions and argument expressions are not.

 A *statement* is executed, while an *expression* is evaluated.

Alongside the `declare()` language construct, PHP provides the following two functions to work with ticks:

- `register_ tick_ function()`: This registers a function to be executed on each tick
- `unregister_ tick_ function()`: This deregisters a previously registered function

Let's take a look at the following example, where the `declare()` construct uses the `{ }` blocks to wrap the expressions:

```php
<?php

echo 'started' . PHP_EOL;

function tickLogger()
{
   echo 'Tick logged!' . PHP_EOL;
}

register_tick_function('tickLogger');

declare (ticks = 2) {
   for ($i = 1; $i <= 10; $i++) {
     echo '$i => ' . $i . PHP_EOL;
   }
}

echo 'finished' . PHP_EOL;
```

This results in the following output:

```
started
$i => 1
$i => 2
Tick logged!
$i => 3
$i => 4
Tick logged!
$i => 5
$i => 6
Tick logged!
$i => 7
$i => 8
Tick logged!
$i => 9
$i => 10
Tick logged!
finished
```

This is pretty much what we would expect, based on the carefully wrapped expressions within the { } blocks of the declare() construct. A tick is being nicely fired every second iteration of the loop.

Let's take a look at the following example, where the declare() construct is added as the first line of the PHP script without any { } blocks to wrap the expressions:

```php
<?php

declare (ticks = 2);

echo 'started' . PHP_EOL;

function tickLogger()
{
   echo 'Tick logged!' . PHP_EOL;
}

register_tick_function('tickLogger');

for ($i = 1; $i <= 10; $i++) {
   echo '$i => ' . $i . PHP_EOL;
}

echo 'finished' . PHP_EOL;
```

This results in the following output:

```
started
Tick logged!
$i => 1
Tick logged!
$i => 2
Tick logged!
$i => 3
Tick logged!
$i => 4
Tick logged!
$i => 5
Tick logged!
$i => 6
Tick logged!
$i => 7
Tick logged!
$i => 8
Tick logged!
$i => 9
Tick logged!
```

```
$i => 10
Tick logged!
Tick logged!
finished
Tick logged!
```

The output here is not what we might expect at first. The *N* value, `ticks = 2`, does not seem to be respected as the tick seems to be fired after each and every statement. Even the last finished output is followed by one more tick.

Ticks provide the type of feature that may be useful to run monitoring, cleanup, notification, debugging, or other similar tasks. They should be used with utmost care, or else we might get some unexpected results, as we saw in the preceding example.

Signals

Signals are asynchronous messages sent to a running process within the POSIX-compliant operating systems. They can be sent both by users of programs. The following is a list of Linux-supported standard signals:

- `SIGHUP`: Hangup (POSIX)
- `SIGINT`: Terminal interrupt (ANSI)
- `SIGQUIT`: Terminal quit (POSIX)
- `SIGILL`: Illegal instruction (ANSI)
- `SIGTRAP`: Trace trap (POSIX)
- `SIGIOT`: IOT Trap (4.2 BSD)
- `SIGBUS`: BUS error (4.2 BSD)
- `SIGFPE`: Floating point exception (ANSI)
- `SIGKILL`: Kill (can't be caught or ignored) (POSIX)
- `SIGUSR1`: User-defined signal 1 (POSIX)
- `SIGSEGV`: Invalid memory segment access (ANSI)
- `SIGUSR2`: User-defined signal 2 (POSIX)
- `SIGPIPE`: Write on a pipe with no reader, Broken pipe (POSIX)
- `SIGALRM`: Alarm clock (POSIX)
- `SIGTERM`: Termination (ANSI)
- `SIGSTKFLT`: Stack fault
- `SIGCHLD`: Child process has stopped or exited, changed (POSIX)
- `SIGCONT`: Continue executing, if stopped (POSIX)

- `SIGSTOP`: Stop executing (can't be caught or ignored) (POSIX)
- `SIGTSTP`: Terminal stop signal (POSIX)
- `SIGTTIN`: Background process trying to read, from TTY (POSIX)
- `SIGTTOU`: Background process trying to write, to TTY (POSIX)
- `SIGURG`: Urgent condition on socket (4.2 BSD)
- `SIGXCPU`: CPU limit exceeded (4.2 BSD)
- `SIGXFSZ`: File size limit exceeded (4.2 BSD)
- `SIGVTALRM`: Virtual alarm clock (4.2 BSD)
- `SIGPROF`: Profiling alarm clock (4.2 BSD)
- `SIGWINCH`: Window size change (4.3 BSD, Sun)
- `SIGIO`: I/O now possible (4.2 BSD)
- `SIGPWR`: Power failure restart (System V)

The user can initiate a signal message from the console manually using the `kill` command, such as `kill -SIGHUP 4321`.

The signals `SIGKILL` and `SIGSTOP` are the ultimate kill switch as they cannot be caught, blocked, or ignored.

PHP provides several functions to work with signals, some of which are as follows:

- `pcntl_ signal()`: This installs a signal handler
- `pcntl_ signal_ dispatch()`: This calls signal handlers for pending signals
- `pcntl_ sigprocmask()`: This sets and retrieves blocked signals
- `pcntl_ sigtimedwait()`: This waits for signals, with a timeout
- `pcntl_ sigwaitinfo()`: This waits for signals

The `pcntl_ signal()` function is the most interesting one.

Let's take a look at an example utilizing the `pcntl_ signal()` function:

```php
#!/usr/bin/env php
<?php

declare(ticks = 1);

echo 'started' . PHP_EOL;
```

```php
function signalHandler($signal)
{
  echo 'Triggered signalHandler: ' . $signal . PHP_EOL;
  // exit;
}

pcntl_signal(SIGINT, 'signalHandler');

$loop = 0;
while (true) {
  echo 'loop ' . (++$loop) . PHP_EOL;
  flush();
  sleep(2);
}

echo 'finished' . PHP_EOL;
```

We start our code with the *declare ticks* definition. Without it, the installation of our custom `signalHandler` function via the `pcntl_signal()` function would have no effect. The `pcntl_signal()` function itself installs the `signalHandler()` function for the SIGINT signal. Running the preceding code will yield the following output:

```
$ ./app.php
started
loop 1
loop 2
loop 3
^CTriggered signalHandler: 2
loop 4
loop 5
^CTriggered signalHandler: 2
loop 6
loop 7
loop 8
^CTriggered signalHandler: 2
loop 9
loop 10
...
```

The ^C string indicates the moment when we hit *Ctrl* + *C* on our keyboard. We can see that it was immediately followed by a `Triggered signalHandler:` *N* output from our custom `signalHandler()` function. While we were successful at catching the SIGINT signal, we did not follow up and actually execute it once we were done with our `signalHandler()` function, which left the signal to be ignored, and allowed our program to continue executing. As it turns out, we just killed the default operating system functionality by allowing the program to keep executing after *Ctrl* + *C* is pressed.

How do signals help us out? First of, a simple `exit;` call within the `signalHandler()` function would sort out the broken functionality in this case. Beyond that, we are left with a powerful mechanism where we get to tap into (almost) any system signal and execute any arbitrary code we choose to.

Alarms

The `pcntl_alarm()` function enriches the PHP signals functionality by providing an alarm clock for delivery of a signal. Simply put, it creates a timer that sends a `SIGALRM` signal to the process after a given number of seconds.

Once the alarm is fired, the signal handler function kicks in. Once the signal handler function code is done executing, we are taken back to the point in code where the application stopped before jumping into a signal handler function.

Let's take a look at the following piece of code:

```php
#!/usr/bin/env php
<?php

declare(ticks = 1);

echo 'started' . PHP_EOL;

function signalHandler($signal)
{
   echo 'Triggered signalHandler: ' . $signal . PHP_EOL;
}

pcntl_signal(SIGALRM, 'signalHandler');
pcntl_alarm(7);

while (true) {
   echo 'loop ' . date('h:i:sa') . PHP_EOL;
   flush();
   sleep(2);
}

echo 'finished' . PHP_EOL;
```

We are using the `pcntl_signal()` function to register `signalHandler` as a signal handler function for the `SIGALRM` signal. We then call the `pcntl_alarm()` function, passing it the integer value of 7 seconds. The while loop is set to merely output something to the console, in order for us to understand the alarm behavior more easily. Once executed, the following output is shown:

```
$ ./app.php
started
loop 02:17:28pm
loop 02:17:30pm
loop 02:17:32pm
loop 02:17:34pm
Triggered signalHandler: 14
loop 02:17:35pm
loop 02:17:37pm
loop 02:17:39pm
loop 02:17:41pm
loop 02:17:43pm
loop 02:17:45pm
loop 02:17:47pm
loop 02:17:49pm
loop 02:17:51pm
```

We can see that the `Triggered signalHandler: 14` string is shown only once. This is because the alarm was triggered only once. The timing shown in the output indicates the exact seven seconds of delay between the first loop iteration and the alarm. We could easily fire another `pcntl_alarm()` function call within the `signalHandler()` function itself:

```php
function signalHandler($signal)
{
    echo 'Triggered signalHandler: ' . $signal . PHP_EOL;
    pcntl_alarm(3);
}
```

This would then transform our output into something like this:

```
$ ./app.php
started
loop 02:20:46pm
loop 02:20:48pm
loop 02:20:50pm
loop 02:20:52pm
Triggered signalHandler: 14
loop 02:20:53pm
loop 02:20:55pm
Triggered signalHandler: 14
loop 02:20:56pm
```

```
loop 02:20:58pm
Triggered signalHandler: 14
loop 02:20:59pm
loop 02:21:01pm
Triggered signalHandler: 14
loop 02:21:02pm
```

Though specifying multiple alarms is possible, doing so before the previous alarm was reached, makes the new alarm replace the old alarm. The usefulness of alarms becomes obvious when performing a non-linear processing inside our application.
The pcntl_alarm() function is non-blocking, making it easy to toss around, without worrying about blocking the program execution.

Multiprocessing

When speaking of **multiprocessing**, we often come across two seemingly colliding terms: **process** and **thread**. Where the process can be thought of as a currently running instance of an application, a thread is a path of execution within a process. A thread can do pretty much anything a process can do. However, given that threads reside within the process, we look at them as a solution for lightweight tasks, or at least tasks lighter than those employed by a process.

The PHP language leaves a lot to be desired in terms of multiprocessing/multithreading. The following two stand out as the most popular solutions:

- pcntl_fork(): This is a function that forks the currently running process
- pthreads: This is an object-orientated API that provides multithreading based on Posix threads

The pcntl_fork() function is a part of the PCNTL extension, whose functions we used in previous sections as well. The function only forks processes and cannot make threads. While pthreads is a more modern and OOP-aligned solution, we will continue our journey throughout this section with the pcntl_fork() function.

When we run the pcntl_fork() function, it creates a child process for us. This child process differs from the parent process only by its PID and PPID:

- PID: This is the Process ID
- PPID: This is the Parent Process ID, the one that launched this PID

While the actual process forking with the `pcntl_fork()` function is quite easy, it leaves several challenges for us to tackle. Challenges such as *communication between processes* and *zombie children processes* make it tedious to deliver stable applications.

Let's take a look at the following use of the `pcntl_fork()` function:

```php
#!/usr/bin/env php
<?php

for ($i = 1; $i <= 5; $i++) {
  $pid = pcntl_fork();

  if (!$pid) {
    echo 'Child ' . $i . PHP_EOL;
    sleep(2);
    exit;
  }
}
```

The preceding code results in the following output:

```
$ time php ./app.php

real 0m0.031s
user 0m0.012s
sys 0m0.016s
$ Child 1
Child 4
Child 2
Child 3
Child 5

$
```

The console returned the control immediately, despite having five children processes running. The control was first returned right before the **Child 1** string was outputted, and then, a few seconds later, all of the Child strings were outputted and the console returned the control once again. The output clearly shows that the children are not necessarily executed in the order they are forked in. The operating system decides on this, not us. We can further tune the behavior using the `pcntl_waitpid()` and `pcntl_wexitstatus()` functions.

The `pcntl_waitpid()` function instructs PHP to wait for a child, whereas the `pcntl_wexitstatus()` function fetches the value returned by a terminated child. The following example demonstrates this:

```php
#!/usr/bin/env php
<?php

function generatePdf($content, $size)
{
  echo 'Started PDF ' . $size . ' - ' . date('h:i:sa') . PHP_EOL;
  sleep(3); /* simulate PDF generating */
  echo 'Finished PDF ' . $size . ' - ' . date('h:i:sa') . PHP_EOL;
}

$sizes = ['A1', 'A2', 'A3'];
$content = 'foggyline';

for ($i = 0; $i < count($sizes); $i++) {
  $pid = pcntl_fork();

  if (!$pid) {
    generatePdf($content, $sizes[$i]);
    exit($i);
  }
}

while (pcntl_waitpid(0, $status) != -1) {
  $status = pcntl_wexitstatus($status);
  echo "Child $status finished! - " . date('h:i:sa') . PHP_EOL;
}
```

While the majority of this example is similar to the previous one, notice the whole `while` loop at the bottom. The `while` loop will loop until the `pcntl_waitpid()` function returns −1 (no children left). Each iteration of the `while` loop checks for the return code of a terminated child, and stores it into the `$status` variable, which is then again evaluated in the `while` loop expression.

Check out `http://php.net/manual/en/ref.pcntl.php` for more details about the `pcntl_fork()`, `pcntl_waitpid()`, and `pcntl_wexitstatus()` function parameters and return values.

The preceding code results in the following output:

```
$ time ./app.php
Started PDF A2 - 04:52:37pm
Started PDF A3 - 04:52:37pm
Started PDF A1 - 04:52:37pm
Finished PDF A2 - 04:52:40pm
Finished PDF A1 - 04:52:40pm
Finished PDF A3 - 04:52:40pm
Child 2 finished! - 04:52:40pm
Child 1 finished! - 04:52:40pm
Child 0 finished! - 04:52:40pm

real 0m3.053s
user 0m0.016s
sys 0m0.028s
$
```

The console did not return the control now until all of the children finished executing, which is probably the preferred solution for most of the tasks we might be doing.

Though process forking opens up several possibilities for us, we need to ask ourselves, Is it really worth the effort? If simply restructuring our application to use more message queues, CRONs, and other simpler technologies can yield a similar performance with the benefit of easier scaling, maintenance, and debugging, then we should probably avoid forking.

Summary

Throughout this chapter, we have familiarized ourselves with some of the interesting features and tooling around PHP CLI. This chapter started with a basic introduction to PHP CLI SAPI, as one of the many SAPI interfaces in PHP. We then took a look into a simple but powerful Console component, learning how easy it is to create our own console applications. The I/O streams section helped us understand the standard streams, and how they are handled by PHP. Finally, we looked into the process control functions offered by the PCNTL extension. Combined together, these functions open up a wide range of possibilities to write our console applications. While the overall console application development might not seem interesting enough in comparison to more browser-facing applications, it certainly has its role in modern development. The CLI environment simply allows much greater control of our application.

Moving forward, we will take a look into one of the most important and interesting OOP features in PHP.

6
Prominent OOP Features

The term **object-oriented** (**OO**) has been around since the 70s, when it was coined by computer scientist, Alan Kay. The term stood for a programming paradigm based on the concept of objects. At that time, Simula was the first language to exhibit OO features, such as objects, classes, inheritance, subtyping, and so on. Standardized as Simula 67 in 1977, it became an inspiration for later languages. One such inspired language is Smalltalk, created as a product of research led by Alan Kay at Xerox. Compared to Simula, Smalltalk greatly improved the overall OO concept. Over time, Smalltalk became one of the most influential OO programming language.

While there is much more to be said about these early days, the takeaway is that OOP was born out of specific need. Where Simula used static objects for modeling real-world entities, Smalltalk used dynamic objects that could be created, changed, or deleted as the foundation for computation.

 The MVC pattern, one of the most common object-oriented software design patterns, was introduced in Smalltalk.

The ease of mapping physical entities into objects described by classes certainly influenced the overall popularity of the OO paradigm among developers. However, objects are not just about mapped out instances of various properties, they are also about messages and responsibilities. While we may embrace OOP based on the first premise, we certainly start to appreciate the latter one, as the key to making big and scalable systems lies in the ease of object communication.

The PHP language embodies several paradigms, most notably: imperative, functional, object oriented, procedural, and reflective. Whereas, the OOP support in PHP hasn't fully kicked off until the PHP 5 release. The latest versions of PHP 7 brought forth some minor yet noteworthy improvements to what is now considered a stable and mature PHP OOP model.

In this chapter, we will explore some prominent features of object-oriented PHP:

- Object inheritance
- Objects and references
- Object iteration
- Object comparison
- Traits
- Reflection

Object inheritance

The OOP paradigm places objects at the heart of application design, where objects can be looked at as units that contain various properties and methods. Interaction between these properties and methods defines the internal state of an object. Every object is built from a blueprint called a class. There is no such thing as an object without the class, at least not in a class-based OOP.

 We differentiate class-based OOP (PHP, Java, C#, ...) and prototype-based OOP (ECMAScript / JavaScript, Lua, ...). In class-based OOP, objects are created from classes; in prototype-based OOP, objects are created from other objects.

The process of building or creating new objects is called **instantiation**. In PHP, like many other languages, we use the `new` keyword to instantiate an object from a given class. Let's take a look at the following example:

```php
<?php

class JsonOutput
{
  protected $content;

  public function setContent($content)
  {
    $this->content = $content;
  }
```

```php
  public function render()
  {
    return json_encode($this->content);
  }
}

class SerializedOutput
{
  protected $content;

  public function setContent($content)
  {
    $this->content = $content;
  }

  public function render()
  {
    return serialize($this->content);
  }
}

$users = [
  ['user' => 'John', 'age' => 34],
  ['user' => 'Alice', 'age' => 33],
];

$json = new JsonOutput();
$json->setContent($users);
echo $json->render();

$ser = new SerializedOutput();
$ser->setContent($users);
echo $ser->render();
```

Here, we are defining two simple classes, JsonOutput and SerializedOutput. We say simple merely because they have a single property and two methods. These two classes are nearly identical--they only differ in a single line of code within the render() method. One class converts the given content into JSON, while the other converts it to a serialized string. Right after our class declarations, we define a dummy $users array that we then feed to the instances of the JsonOutput and SerializedOutput classes, that is, the $json and $ser objects.

While this is far from an ideal class design, it serves as a nice introduction into inheritance.

Inheritance allows classes and, therefore, objects to inherit properties and methods of another class. Terms such as superclass, base class, or parent class are used to flag the class used as a basis for inheritance. Terms such as subclass, derived class, or child class are used to flag the inheriting class.

The PHP `extends` keyword is used to enable inheritance. Inheritance has its limits. We can only extend from a single class at a time as PHP does not support multiple inheritance. However, having a chain of inheritance is perfectly valid:

```
// valid
class A {}
class B extends A {}
class C extends B {}

// invalid
class A {}
class B {}
class C extends A, B {}
```

The `C` class shown in the valid example will end up inheriting all the allowed properties and methods of classes `B` and `A`. When we say allowed, we refer to the property and method visibility, that is, access modifiers:

```php
<?php

error_reporting(E_ALL);

class A
{
    public $x = 10;
    protected $y = 20;
    private $z = 30;

    public function x()
    {
        return $this->x;
    }

    protected function y()
    {
        return $this->y;
    }

    private function z()
    {
        return $this->z;
    }
```

```
}

class B extends A
{

}

$obj = new B();
var_dump($obj->x); // 10
var_dump($obj->y); // Uncaught Error: Cannot access protected property
B::$y
var_dump($obj->z); // Notice: Undefined property: B::$z
var_dump($obj->x()); // 10
var_dump($obj->y()); // Uncaught Error: Call to protected method A::y()
from context
var_dump($obj->z()); // Uncaught Error: Call to private method A::z() from
context
```

In the object context, the access modifiers behave as per the preceding example, which is pretty much as we would expect them to. The object would exhibit the same behavior, whether it was an instance of class A or class B. Let's observe the behavior of access modifiers on the inner workings of the child class:

```
class B extends A
{
  public function test()
  {
    var_dump($this->x); // 10
    var_dump($this->y); // 20
    var_dump($this->z); // Notice: Undefined property: B::$z
    var_dump($this->x()); // 10
    var_dump($this->y()); // 20
    var_dump($this->z()); // Uncaught Error: Call to private method
      A::z() from context 'B'
  }
}

$obj = new B();
$obj->test();
```

We can see that the public and protected members (property or method) can be accessed from child classes, whereas private members cannot--they are only accessible from the class that defines them.

The `extends` keyword is also applicable to interfaces:

```php
<?php

interface User {}
interface Employee extends User {}
```

Being able to inherit the class and interface properties and methods makes for a powerful overall object inheritance mechanism.

Knowing these simple inheritance rules, let's see how we can rewrite our `JsonOutput` and the `SerializedOutput` classes into a more convenient form using inheritance:

```php
<?php

class Output
{
    protected $content;

    public function setContent($content)
    {
        $this->content = $content;
    }

    public function render()
    {
        return $this->content;
    }
}

class JsonOutput extends Output
{
    public function render()
    {
        return json_encode($this->content);
    }
}

class SerializedOutput extends Output
{
    public function render()
    {
        return serialize($this->content);
    }
}
```

We started off by defining an Output class with the content nearly identical to the previous JsonOutput and SerializedOutput classes, merely changing its render() method to simply return content as-is. We then rewrote the JsonOutput and SerializedOutput classes in such a way that they both extend the Output class. In this setup, an Output class becomes a parent class, whereas JsonOutput and SerializedOutput become child classes. The child classes redefine the render() method, thus overriding the parent class implementation. The $this keyword has access to all of the public and protected modifiers, which makes it easy to access the $content property.

While inheritance might be a quick and powerful way to structure our code into convenient chains of parent/child relationships, one should avoid the danger of misusing or overusing it. This can be especially tricky with larger systems where we might end up spending more time tackling a large class hierarchy than actually maintaining the sub-system interfaces. Therefore, we should use it carefully.

Objects and references

There are two ways to pass arguments within the code:

- **By reference**: This is where both the caller and callee use the same variable for argument.
- **By value**: This is where both the caller and callee have their own copy of the variable for argument. If the callee decides to change the value of the passed argument, the caller would not notice it.

Passing arguments by value is the default PHP behavior, as shown in the following example:

```php
<?php

class Util
{
  function hello($msg)
  {
    $msg = "<p>Welcome $msg</p>";
    return $msg;
  }
}

$str = 'John';

$obj = new Util();
```

```
echo $obj->hello($str); // Welcome John

echo $str; // John
```

Looking at the internals of the `hello()` method, we can see it is resetting the `$msg` argument value to another string value wrapped in HTML tags. The default PHP passed by the value behavior prevents this change to propagate outside the scope of a method. Using the `&` operator just before the argument name in the function definition, we can force the passed by reference behavior:

```php
<?php

class Util
{
  function hello(&$msg)
  {
    $msg = "<p>Welcome $msg</p>";
    return $msg;
  }
}

$str = 'John';

$obj = new Util();
echo $obj->hello($str); // Welcome John

echo $str; // Welcome John
```

Being able to do something does not necessarily mean we should. The passing by reference behavior should be used with caution, only if there's a really good reason to do it. The preceding example clearly shows the side-effect of the internal `hello()` method to a simple scalar type value within the outside scope. Object instance methods, or even plain functions, should not have these types of side-effect to the outside scope.

> Several PHP functions, such as `sort()`, use the `&` operator to force the pass by reference behavior on a given array argument.

With all being said, where do objects fit in? Objects in PHP lean towards the passed by reference behavior. When an object is passed as an argument, it is still being passed as a value, but the value being passed is not the object itself, it is the object identifier. Therefore, the act of passing the object as an argument feels more like it is being passed by reference:

```php
<?php

class User
{
    public $salary = 4200;
}

function bonus(User $u)
{
    $u->salary = $u->salary + 500;
}

$user = new User();
echo $user->salary; // 4200
bonus($user);
echo $user->salary; // 4700
```

 Since objects are bigger structures than scalar values, passing by reference greatly minimizes the memory and CPU footprint.

Object iteration

The PHP arrays are the most frequent collection structure used in PHP. We can squeeze pretty much anything into an array, ranging from scalar values to objects. Iterating through elements of such a structure is trivially easy using the `foreach` statement. However, arrays are not the only iterable types, as objects themselves are iterable.

Let's take a look at the following array-based example:

```php
<?php

$user = [
    'name' => 'John',
    'age' => 34,
    'salary' => 4200.00
];

foreach ($user as $k => $v) {
```

```
    echo "key: $k, value: $v" . PHP_EOL;
}
```

Now let's take a look at the following object-based example:

```php
<?php

class User
{
  public $name = 'John';
  public $age = 34;
  public $salary = 4200.00;
}

$user = new User();

foreach ($user as $k => $v) {
  echo "key: $k, value: $v" . PHP_EOL;
}
```

Executed on the console, both of these examples would yield an identical output:

```
key: name, value: John
key: age, value: 34
key: salary, value: 4200
```

By default, iteration works only with public properties, excluding any private or protected properties from the list.

PHP provides an `Iterator` interface, making it possible to specify what values we want to make available for iterating.

```
Iterator extends Traversable {
  abstract public mixed current(void)
  abstract public scalar key(void)
  abstract public void next(void)
  abstract public void rewind(void)
  abstract public boolean valid(void)
}
```

The following example demonstrates a simple `Iterator` interface implementation:

```php
<?php

class User implements \Iterator
{
  public $name = 'John';
  private $age = 34;
```

```php
    protected $salary = 4200.00;

    private $info = [];

    public function __construct()
    {
      $this->info = [
        'name' => $this->name,
        'age' => $this->age,
        'salary' => $this->salary
      ];
    }

    public function current()
    {
      return current($this->info);
    }

    public function next()
    {
      return next($this->info);
    }

    public function key()
    {
      return key($this->info);
    }

    public function valid()
    {
      $key = key($this->info);
      return ($key !== null && $key !== false);
    }

    public function rewind()
    {
      return reset($this->info);
    }
  }
```

With this implementation, we are now seemingly able to iterate over the User class private and protected properties. Although, this is not really the case. What's happening is that, through the constructor, the class is filling the $info parameter with the data of all other properties we wish to iterate. The interface mandated methods then ensure that our class plays nicely with the foreach construct.

Object iteration is a neat, though often overlooked, feature of PHP when it comes to everyday development.

Object comparison

The PHP language provides several comparison operators that allow us to compare two different values, resulting in either `true` or `false`:

- `==`: equal
- `===`: identical
- `!=`: not equal
- `<>`: not equal
- `!==`: not identical
- `<`: less than
- `>`: greater than
- `<=`: less than or equal to
- `>=`: greater than or equal to

While all of these operators are equally important, let's take a closer look at the behavior of the equal (`==`) and identical (`===`) operators in the context of objects.

Let's take a look at the following example:

```php
<?php

class User {
  public $name = 'N/A';
  public $age = 0;
}

$user = new User();
$employee = new User();

var_dump($user == $employee); // true
var_dump($user === $employee); // false
```

Here, we have a simple User class with two properties set to some default values. We then have two different instances of the same class, $user and $employee. Given that both objects have the same properties, with the same values, the equal (==) operator returns true. The identical (===) operator, on the other hand, returns false. Even though objects are of the same class, and have the same properties and values in those properties, an identical operator sees them as different.

Let's take a look at the following example:

```php
<?php

class User {
  public $name = 'N/A';
  public $age = 0;
}

$user = new User();
$employee = $user;

var_dump($user == $employee); // true
var_dump($user === $employee); // true
```

The identical (===) operator considers two objects to be identical only if they refer to the same instance of the same class. The same operator behavior applies to the counterpart operators, that is, the not equal (<> or !=) and not identical (!==) operators.

Aside from objects, the identical operator is applicable to any other type:

```php
<?php

var_dump(2 == 2); // true
var_dump(2 == "2"); // true
var_dump(2 == "2ABC"); // true

var_dump(2 === 2); // true
var_dump(2 === "2"); // false
var_dump(2 === "2ABC"); // false
```

Looking at the preceding example clearly reveals the importance of an identical operator. The 2 == "2ABC" expression evaluating to true is something that boggles the mind. We might even think of it as a bug in the PHP language itself. While relying on PHP automatic type conversion is mostly fine, there are times where unexpected bugs can squeeze in and disrupt our application logic. The use of the identical operator reaffirms the comparison, assuring that we consider not just the value but the type as well.

Traits

We mentioned previously that PHP is a single inheritance language. We cannot use the `extends` keyword to extend multiple classes in PHP. This very feature is actually a rare commodity only a handful of programming languages support, such as C++. For better or worse, multiple inheritance allows some interesting tinkering with our code structures.

The PHP Traits provide a mechanism by which we can achieve these structures, either in the context of code reuse or the grouping of functionality. The `trait` keyword is used to declare a Trait, as follows:

```php
<?php

trait Formatter
{
    // Trait body
}
```

The body of a Trait can be pretty much anything we would put in a class. While they resemble classes, we cannot instantiate a Trait itself. We can only use the Trait from another class. To do so, we employ the `use` keyword within the class body, as shown in the following example:

```php
class Ups
{
    use Formatter;

    // Class body (properties & methods)
}
```

To better understand how Traits can be helpful, let's take a look at the following example:

```php
<?php

trait Formatter
{
    public function formatPrice($price)
    {
        return sprintf('%.2F', $price);
    }
}

class Ups
{
    use Formatter;
```

```
    private $price = 4.4999; // Base shipping price

    public function getShippingPrice($formatted = false)

        {
            // Shipping cost calc... $this->price = XXX

            if ($formatted) {
                return $this->formatPrice($this->price);
            }

                return $this->price;
        }
}

class Dhl
{
    use Formatter;

    private $price = 9.4999; // Base shipping price

    public function getShippingPrice($formatted = false)
    {
        // Shipping cost calc... $this->price = XXX

        if ($formatted) {
                return $this->formatPrice($this->price);
        }

            return $this->price;
    }
}

$ups = new Ups();
echo $ups->getShippingPrice(true); // 4.50

$dhl = new Dhl();
echo $dhl->getShippingPrice(true); // 9.50
```

The preceding example demonstrates the use of trait in a code reuse context, where two different shipping classes, Ups and Dhl, use the same trait. The trait itself wraps a nice little formatPrice() helper method that formats the given price to two decimal fields.

Like classes, traits have access to $this, 1 which means we could easily rewrite the previous formatPrice() method of the Formatter trait as follows:

```php
<?php

trait Formatter
{
  public function formatPrice()
  {
     return sprintf('%.2F', $this->price);
  }
}
```

This, however, severely limits our trait use, as its formatPrice() method now expects a $price member, which some of the classes using the Formatter trait might not have.

Let's take a look at another example where we use traits in a grouping of functionality context:

```php
<?php

trait SalesOrderCustomer
{
  public function getCustomerFirstname()
  { /* body */
  }

  public function getCustomerEmail()
  { /* body */
  }

  public function getCustomerGender()
  { /* body */
  }
}

trait SalesOrderActions
{
  public function cancel()
  { /* body */
  }

  public function complete()
  { /* body */
  }

  public function hold()
```

```
    { /* body */
    }
}

class SalesOrder
{
  use SalesOrderCustomer;
  use SalesOrderActions;

  /* body */
}
```

What we did here was nothing more than cut and paste our class code into two different traits. We grouped all of the methods related to possible order actions into a single `SalesOrderActions` trait, and all methods related to order customer into the `SalesOrderCustomer` trait. This brings us back to the possible-does-not-necessarily-mean-preferable philosophy.

Using multiple traits can sometimes lead to conflicts, where the same method name can be found in more than one trait. We can use the `insteadof` and `as` keywords to mitigate these types of conflicts, as shown in the following example:

```php
<?php

trait CsvHandler
{
    public function import()
    {
        echo 'CsvHandler > import' . PHP_EOL;
    }

public function export()
    {
        echo 'CsvHandler > export' . PHP_EOL;
    }
}

trait XmlHandler
{
    public function import()
    {
        echo 'XmlHandler > import' . PHP_EOL;
    }

    public function export()
    {
        echo 'XmlHandler > export' . PHP_EOL;
```

```
        }
    }

    class SalesOrder
    {
        use CsvHandler, XmlHandler {
            XmlHandler::import insteadof CsvHandler;
            CsvHandler::export insteadof XmlHandler;
            XmlHandler::export as exp;
        }

        public function initImport()
        {
            $this->import();
        }

        public function initExport()
        {
            $this->export();
            $this->exp();
        }
    }

    $order = new SalesOrder();
    $order->initImport();
    $order->initExport();

    //XmlHandler > import
    //CsvHandler > export
    //XmlHandler > export
```

The as keyword can also be used in conjunction with the public, protected, or private keywords in order to change the method visibility:

```
    <?php

    trait Message
    {
      private function hello()
      {
          return 'Hello!';
      }
    }

    class User
    {
      use Message {
        hello as public;
```

```
    }
}

$user = new User();
echo $user->hello(); // Hello!
```

To make things even more interesting, traits can be further composed of other traits, even supporting the abstract and static members, as shown in the following example:

```php
<?php

trait A
{
  public static $counter = 0;

  public function theA()
  {
    return self::$counter;
  }
}

trait B
{
  use A;

  abstract public function theB();
}

class C
{
  use B;

  public function theB()
  {
    return self::$counter;
  }
}

$c = new C();
$c::$counter++;
echo $c->theA(); // 1
$c::$counter++;
$c::$counter++;
echo $c->theB(); // 3
```

Aside from being non-instantiable, traits share many features with classes. While they provide us with the tooling for some interesting code structuring, they also make it easy to violate the single responsibility principle. The overall impression of trait usage is often that of extending regular classes, which makes it hard to find the right use case. We can use them to describe characteristics that are common to many, but not essential. For example, jet engines are not essential on every airplane, but a lot of airplanes have them, whereas others might have propellers.

Reflection

Reflection is a highly important concept every developer should be wary about. It denotes the ability of a program to inspect itself during runtime, thus allowing easy reverse-engineering of classes, interfaces, functions, methods, and extensions.

We can get a quick taste of the PHP reflection capabilities right from the console. The PHP CLI supports several reflection-based commands:

- `--rf <function name>`: This shows information about a function
- `--rc <class name>`: This shows information about a class
- `--re <extension name>`: This shows information about an extension
- `--rz <extension name>`: This shows information about the Zend extension
- `--ri <extension name>`: This shows the configuration for an extension

The following output demonstrates the result of the `php --rf str_replace` command:

```
Function [ <internal:standard> function str_replace ] {
  - Parameters [4] {
    Parameter #0 [ <required> $search ]
    Parameter #1 [ <required> $replace ]
    Parameter #2 [ <required> $subject ]
    Parameter #3 [ <optional> &$replace_count ]
  }
}
```

The output reflects on the `str_replace()` function, which is a standard PHP function. It clearly describes the total number of parameters, along with their name and required or optional assignment.

The real power of reflection, the one developers get to utilize, comes from the reflection API. Let's take a look at the following example:

```php
<?php

class User
{
  public $name = 'John';
  protected $ssn = 'AAA-GG-SSSS';
  private $salary = 4200.00;
}

$user = new User();

echo $user->name = 'Marc'; // Marc

//echo $user->ssn = 'BBB-GG-SSSS';
// Uncaught Error: Cannot access protected property User::$ssn

//echo $user->salary = 5600.00;
// Uncaught Error: Cannot access private property User::$salary

var_dump($user);
//object(User)[1]
// public 'name' => string 'Marc' (length=4)
// protected 'ssn' => string 'AAA-GG-SSSS' (length=11)
// private 'salary' => float 4200
```

We started off by defining a `User` class with three properties, each of a different visibility. We then instantiated an object of the `User` class and tried changing the value of all three properties. Normally, members that are defined as `protected` or `private` cannot be accessed outside of an object. Trying to access them either in read or write mode would throw a **Cannot access...** error. This is what we would consider a normal behavior.

Using the PHP reflection API, we can circumvent this normal behavior, making it possible to access private and protected members. The reflection API itself provides several classes for us to use:

- Reflection
- ReflectionClass
- ReflectionZendExtension
- ReflectionExtension
- ReflectionFunction
- ReflectionFunctionAbstract

- ReflectionMethod
- ReflectionObject
- ReflectionParameter
- ReflectionProperty
- ReflectionType
- ReflectionGenerator
- Reflector (interface)
- ReflectionException (exception)

Each of these classes expose a diverse set of functionality, allowing us to tinker with internals of other classes, interfaces, functions, methods, and extensions. Assuming our goal is to change the values of `protected` and `private` properties from the previous example, we could use `ReflectionClass` and `ReflectionProperty`, as per the following example:

```php
<?php

// ...

$user = new User();

$reflector = new ReflectionClass('User');

foreach ($reflector->getProperties() as $prop) {
  $prop->setAccessible(true);
  if ($prop->getName() == 'name') $prop->setValue($user, 'Alice');
  if ($prop->getName() == 'ssn') $prop->setValue($user, 'CCC-GG-SSSS');
  if ($prop->getName() == 'salary') $prop->setValue($user, 2600.00);
}

var_dump($user);

//object(User)[1]
// public 'name' => string 'Alice' (length=5)
// protected 'ssn' => string 'CCC-GG-SSSS' (length=11)
// private 'salary' => float 2600
```

We started off by instantiating an object of a User class, as we did in the previous example. We then created an instance of ReflectionClass, passing its constructor the name of the User class. The newly created $reflector instance allows us to fetch a list of all User class properties through its getProperties() method. Looping through properties, one by one, we kick off the real magic of reflection API. Each property ($prop) is an instance of the ReflectionProperty class. Two of the ReflectionProperty methods, setAccessible() and setValue(), provide just the right functionality for us to reach our goal. Using these methods, we are able to set the value of otherwise inaccessible object properties.

Another simple, yet interesting reflection example is that of doc comment extraction:

```php
<?php

class Calc
{
    /**
     * @param $x The number x
     * @param $y The number y
     * @return mixed The number z
     */
    public function sum($x, $y)
    {
        return $x + $y;
    }
}

$calc = new Calc();

$reflector = new ReflectionClass('Calc');
$comment = $reflector->getMethod('sum')->getDocComment();

echo $comment;
```

With merely two lines of code, we were able to reflect upon a Calc class and extract the doc comment from its sum() method. While the practical use of the reflection API might not be obvious at first, it is capabilities such as these that empower us with building powerful and dynamic libraries and platforms.

> The phpDocumentor tool uses the PHP reflection features to automatically generate documentation from the source code. The popular Magento v2.x eCommerce platform extensively uses the PHP reflection features to automatically instantiate objects that are type-hinted as __construct() arguments.

Summary

Throughout this chapter, we took a look into some of the most basic, yet lesser known features of PHP OOP that sometimes do not get enough attention in our day-to-day development. Nowadays, most of the mainstream work is focused around working with frameworks and platforms, which tend to abstract some of these concepts from us. Understanding the inner workings of objects is crucial to successfully developing and debugging a larger system. The reflection API provides a great deal of power when it comes to manipulating objects. Combined with the power of magic methods, which we mentioned in Chapter 4, *Magic Behind Magic Methods*, the PHP OOP model seems quite feature-rich.

Moving forward, we will assume that we have a working application in place and focus on optimizing it for high performance.

7
Optimizing for High Performance

Throughout the years, PHP has grown into a remarkable language we use to build our web applications. An impressive number of language features, alongside countless libraries and frameworks, make our job ever so easier. We often write code which encompasses several layers of stack without giving it a second thought. This makes it easy to overlook one of the most important aspects of every application--performance.

While there are several aspects to performance that developers need to pay attention to, the end user is only interested in one - the time it takes for their web page to be loaded. This is really all that it comes down to. Nowadays, users expect their pages to load in less than 2 seconds. Anything more and we face decreased conversion, which often translates into serious financial loss when it comes to big e-commerce retailers:

> *"A 1 second delay in page response can result in a 7% reduction in conversions."*

> *"If an e-commerce site is making $100,000 per day, a 1 second page delay could potentially cost you $2.5 million in lost sales every year."*
>
> *- kissmetrics.com*

In this chapter, we will address some of the areas of PHP that directly or indirectly impact the application performance and behavior:

- Max execution time
- Memory management
- File uploads
- Session handling
- Output buffering

- Disabling debug messages
- Zend OPcache
- Concurrency

Max execution time

The **maximum execution time** is one of the most common errors developers come across. By default, the maximum execution time of the PHP script executing in the browser is 30 seconds, unless we execute the script within the CLI environment, where there is no such limitation.

We could easily test that through a simple example, given through the index.php and script.php files, as follows:

```php
<?php
// index.php
require_once 'script.php';
error_reporting(E_ALL);
ini_set('display_errors', 'On');
sleep(10);
echo 'Test#1';

?php
// script.php
sleep(25);
echo 'Test#2';
```

Executed from within the browser, this will return the following error:

```
Test#2
Fatal error: Maximum execution time of 30 seconds exceeded in
/var/www/html/index.php on line 5
```

Executed from within the CLI environment, this will return the following output:

```
Test#2Test#1
```

Luckily for us, PHP provides two ways to control the timeout value:

- Using the max_execution_time configuration directive (php.ini file, ini_set() function)
- Using the set_time_limit() function

The `set_time_limit()` function use has an interesting implication. Let's take a look at the following example:

```php
<?php
// index.php
error_reporting(E_ALL);
ini_set('display_errors', 'On');
echo 'Test#1';
sleep(5);
set_time_limit(10);
sleep(15);
echo 'Test#2';
```

The preceding example will result in the following error:

```
Test#1
Fatal error: Maximum execution time of 10 seconds exceeded in
/var/www/html/index.php on line 9
```

Interestingly enough, the `set_time_limit()` function restarts the timeout counter from zero at the point where it was called. What this really means is that using the `set_time_limit()` function throughout the code, in a largely complex system, we can significantly extend the overall timeout beyond the initially imagined boundaries. This is quite dangerous, as PHP timeout is not the only timeout in the mix when it comes to delivering the final web page to a user's browser.

Web servers come with various timeout configurations of their own that might interrupt the PHP execution:

- Apache:
    - `TimeOut` directive, defaults to 60 seconds
- Nginx:
    - `client_header_timeout` directive, defaults to 60 seconds
    - `client_body_timeout` directive, defaults to 60 seconds
    - `fastcgi_read_timeout` directive, defaults to 60 seconds

While we can certainly control script timeouts within the browser context, the important question is *why would we want to do so*? Timeouts are usually a result of resource-intense operations, such as various non-optimized loops, data exports, imports, PDF file generations, and so on. The CLI environment, or ideally, dedicated services, should be our go-to when it comes to all resource-intense jobs. Whereas the browser environment's prime focus should be delivering pages to users in the shortest possible amount of time.

Memory management

Quite often, PHP developers need to deal with a large amount of data. While large is a relative term, memory is not. Certain combinations of functions and language constructs, when used irresponsibly, can clog our server memory in a matter of seconds.

Probably the most notorious function is `file_get_contents()`. This easy-to-use function literally grabs the content of an entire file and puts it into memory. To better understand the issue, let's take a look at the following example:

```php
<?php

$content = file_get_contents('users.csv');
$lines = explode("\r\n", $content);

foreach ($lines as $line) {
  $user = str_getcsv($line);
  // Do something with data from $user...
}
```

While this code is perfectly valid and working, it is a potential performance bottleneck. The `$content` variable will pull the content of the entire `users.csv` file into memory. While this could work for a small file size, of let's say a couple of megabytes, the code is not performance optimized. The moment `users.csv` starts to grow, we will begin experiencing memory issues.

What can we do to mitigate the issue? We can rethink our approach to solving a problem. The moment we shift our mind into the *must optimize performance* mode, other solutions become clear. Instead of reading the content of an entire file into the variable, we can parse the file line by :

```php
<?php

if (($users = fopen('users.csv', 'r')) !== false) {
  while (($user = fgetcsv($users)) !== false) {
    // Do something with data from $user...
  }
  fclose($users);
}
```

Instead of using `file_get_contents()` and `str_getcsv()`, we focus onto using another set of functions, `fopen()` and `fgetcsv()`. The end result is absolutely the same, with the added benefit of being fully performance friendly. Using functions with handles, in this specific case, we have effectively assured that memory limitations are not an issue for our script.

The irresponsible use of loops is another common cause of memory :

```php
<?php

$conn = new PDO('mysql:host=localhost;dbname=eelgar_live_magento',
'root', 'mysql');

$stmt = $conn->query('SELECT * FROM customer_entity');
$users = $stmt->fetchAll();

foreach ($users as $user) {
    if (strstr($user['email'], 'test')) {
        // $user['entity_id']
        // $user['email']
        // Do something with data from $user...
    }
}
```

Now, let's go ahead and see a modified, memory-friendly example with the same effect:

```php
<?php

$conn = new PDO('mysql:host=localhost;dbname=eelgar_live_magento',
  'root', 'mysql');

$stmt = $conn->prepare('SELECT entity_id, email FROM customer_entity WHERE
email LIKE :email');
$stmt->bindValue(':email', '%test%');
$stmt->execute();

while ($user = $stmt->fetch(PDO::FETCH_ASSOC)) {
  // $user['entity_id']
  // $user['email']
  // Do something with data from $user...
}
```

The fetchAll() method is slightly faster than fetch(), but it requires more memory.

When PHP hits the memory limit, it stops the script execution and throws the following error:

```
Fatal error: Allowed memory size of 33554432 bytes exhausted (tried to
allocate 2348617 bytes) ...
```

Luckily, the `memory_limit` directive enables us to control the amount of memory available. The default `memory_limit` value is `128M`, which implies 128 megabytes of memory. The directive is `PHP_INI_ALL` changeable, which means that apart from setting it via the `php.ini` file, we can set it at runtime using `ini_set('memory_limit', '512M');`.

Aside from tuning the `memory_limit` directive, PHP provides the following two functions that return memory usage information:

- `memory_get_usage()`: This returns the amount of memory currently allocated by our PHP script
- `memory_get_peak_usage()`: This returns the peak amount of memory allocated by our PHP script

While we might be tempted to increase this value, we should think twice about doing so. The memory limit is per process, not per server. Web servers themselves can spin up several processes. Using large memory limit values can therefore clog our server. Aside from that, any script that might actually consume a large amount of memory is easily a candidate for performance optimization. Applying simple, thought-through techniques to our code can greatly reduce memory use.

When it comes to actual memory management, things are pretty automated here. Unlike C language, where we get to manage memory ourselves, PHP uses garbage collection in combination with a reference counting mechanism. Without going into the ins and outs of the mechanism itself, it is suffice to say that variables are automatically released when they are not being used any more.

 For more details on garbage collection, check out `http://php.net/manual/en/features.gc.php`.

File uploads

Uploading files is a common functionality to many PHP applications. So common that PHP provides a convenient global `$_FILES` variable we can use to access uploaded files, or errors behind the file upload tries.

Let's take a look at the following simple file upload form:

```
<form method="post" enctype="multipart/form-data">
  <input type="file" name="photo" />
  <input type="file" name="article" />
  <input type="submit" name="submit" value="Upload" />
</form>
```

In order for PHP to pick up the files, we need to set the `form method` value to `post`, and `enctype` to `multipart/form-data`. Once submitted, PHP will pick it up and fill in the `$_FILES` variable appropriately:

```
array(2) {
  ["photo"] => array(5) {
    ["name"] => string(9) "photo.jpg"
    ["type"] => string(10) "image/jpeg"
    ["tmp_name"] => string(14) "/tmp/phpGutI91"
    ["error"] => int(0)
    ["size"] => int(42497)
  }
  ["article"] => array(5) {
    ["name"] => string(11) "article.pdf"
    ["type"] => string(15) "application/pdf"
    ["tmp_name"] => string(14) "/tmp/phpxsnx1e"
    ["error"] => int(0)
    ["size"] => int(433176)
  }
}
```

Without going into the details of the actual post-upload file management, it's suffice to say that `$_FILES` contains enough information for us to either pick up and further manage files, or indicate a possible error code during upload. The following eight error codes can be returned:

- UPLOAD_ERR_OK
- UPLOAD_ERR_INI_SIZE
- UPLOAD_ERR_FORM_SIZE
- UPLOAD_ERR_PARTIAL
- UPLOAD_ERR_NO_FILE
- UPLOAD_ERR_NO_TMP_DIR
- UPLOAD_ERR_CANT_WRITE
- UPLOAD_ERR_EXTENSION

While all of the errors should be equally addressed, two of them (UPLOAD_ERR_FORM_SIZE and UPLOAD_ERR_PARTIAL) open up crucial performance questions: *how big a file can we upload* and *are there any timeouts in the process?*

The answer to these two questions can be found in configuration directives, some of which are directly related to file upload, while others are related to more general PHP options:

- session.gc_maxlifetime: This is the number of seconds after which data will be seen as garbage and cleaned up; it defaults to 1,440 seconds
- session.cookie_lifetime: This is the lifetime of the cookie in seconds; by default, the cookie is valid until the browser is closed
- max_input_time: This is the maximum time in seconds a script is allowed to parse input data, such as POST; by default, this is turned off
- max_execution_time: This is the maximum time a script is allowed to run before it is terminated; it defaults to 30 seconds
- upload_max_filesize: This is the maximum size of an uploaded file; it defaults to 2 megabytes (2M)
- max_file_uploads: This is the maximum number of files allowed to be uploaded in a single request
- post_max_size: This is the maximum size of the post data allowed; it defaults to 8 megabytes (8M)

Tweaking these options ensures that we avoid timeouts and planned size limits. To ensure that we can avoid the maximum file size limitation early in the process, MAX_FILE_SIZE can be used as a hidden form field:

```
<form method="post" enctype="multipart/form-data">
  <input type="hidden" name="MAX_FILE_SIZE" value="100"/>
  <input type="file" name="photo"/>
  <input type="file" name="article"/>
  <input type="submit" name="submit" value="Upload"/>
</form>
```

The MAX_FILE_SIZE field must precede any other file field a form might have. Its value stands for the maximum file size accepted by PHP.

Trying to upload a file larger than defined by the MAX_FILE_SIZE hidden field would now result in a $_FILES variable similar to the one shown here:

```
array(2) {
  ["photo"] => array(5) {
    ["name"] => string(9) "photo.jpg"
    ["type"] => string(0) ""
```

```
      ["tmp_name"] => string(0) ""
      ["error"] => int(2)
      ["size"] => int(0)
    }
  ["article"] => array(5) {
      ["name"] => string(11) "article.pdf"
      ["type"] => string(0) ""
      ["tmp_name"] => string(0) ""
      ["error"] => int(2)
      ["size"] => int(0)
    }
  }
```

We can see that the error has now turned to value 2, which equals the
UPLOAD_ERR_FORM_SIZE constant.

While normally we would address the limitations of default configuration through code
optimization, file uploads are specific; in that, we really need to ensure that large file
uploads are possible if needed.

Session handling

Sessions are an interesting mechanism in PHP, allowing us to maintain state in what is
overall a stateless communication. We might visualize them as a *per-user serialized array of
information* saved to a file. We use them to store user-specific information across various
pages. By default, sessions rely on cookies, although, they can be configured to use the SID
parameter in a browser.

The cookie version of the PHP session works roughly as follows:

1. Read the session token from the cookie.
2. Create or open an existing file on disk.
3. Lock the file for writing.
4. Read the content of the file.
5. Put the file data into the global $_SESSION variable.
6. Set caching headers.
7. Return the cookie to the client.
8. On each page request, repeat steps 1-7.

The *SID version* of the PHP session works pretty much the same way, aside from the cookie part. The cookie here is replaced by the SID value we push via the URL.

The session mechanism can be used for various things, some of which include user login mechanisms, storing minor data caches, parts of templates, and so on. Depending on the usage, this might bring up the question of *maximum session size*.

By default, when a script executes, sessions are read from files into the memory. Therefore, the maximum size of a session file cannot exceed the `memory_limit` directive, which defaults to 128 megabytes. We could bypass this *default* session behavior by defining the custom session handlers. The `session_set_save_handler()` function allows us to register a custom session handler, which must comply to the `SessionHandlerInterface` interface. With custom session handlers, we are able to move away from the file mechanism to storing session data in the database. The added benefit of this is greater performance efficiency, as we are now able to create scalable PHP environments behind a load balancer where all application nodes connect to a central session server.

 Redis and **memcached** are two data stores that are quite popular among PHP developers. The **Magento 2** e-commerce platform supports both Redis and memcached for external session storage.

While the session storage plays a key role in terms of performance, there are a few configuration directives worth keeping an eye on:

- `session.gc_probability`: This defaults to 1
- `session.gc_divisor`: This defaults to 100
- `gc_maxlifetime`: This defaults to 1,440 seconds (24 minutes)

The `gc_probability` and `gc_divisor` directives work in conjunction. Their ratio (*gc_probability/gc_divisor => 1/100 => 1%*) defines a probability of the garbage collector running on each `session_start()` call. Once the garbage collector is run, value of the `gc_maxlifetime` directive tells it if something should be seen as garbage and should be potentially cleaned up.

When it comes to high-performance sites, sessions can easily become a bottleneck. Thoughtful tuning and session storage selection can make just the right performance difference.

Output buffering

Output buffering is a PHP mechanism that controls the output of a script. Imagine we write down echo 'test'; within our PHP script and do not see anything on screen. How is that possible? The answer is **output buffering**.

The following piece of code is a simple example of output buffering:

```php
<?php

ob_start();
sleep(2);
echo 'Chunk#1' . PHP_EOL;
sleep(3);
ob_end_flush();

ob_start();
echo 'Chunk#2' . PHP_EOL;
sleep(5);
ob_end_clean();

ob_start();
echo 'Chunk#3' . PHP_EOL;
ob_end_flush();

ob_start();
sleep(5);
echo 'Chunk#4' . PHP_EOL;

//Chunk#1
//Chunk#3
//Chunk#4
```

When executed within the CLI environment, we will first see Chunk#1 come out after a few seconds, then a few seconds after, we will see Chunk#3 come out, and, finally, a few more seconds after, we will see Chunk#4 come out. Chunk#2 would never be output. This is quite a concept, given that we are used to having the echo construct outputting stuff just after it is called.

There are several output buffering related functions, of which the following five are the most interesting ones:

- `ob_start()`: This triggers a new buffer and creates stacked buffers if called after another *non-closed* buffer
- `ob_end_flush()`: This outputs the topmost buffer and turns this output buffer off
- `ob_end_clean()`: This cleans the output buffer and turns off output buffering
- `ob_get_contents()`: This returns the content of the output buffer
- `ob_gzhandler()`: This is the callback function for use with `ob_start()`, to GZIP the output buffer

The following example demonstrates the stacked buffers:

```php
<?php

ob_start(); // BUFFER#1
sleep(2);
echo 'Chunk #1' . PHP_EOL;

 ob_start(); // BUFFER#2
 sleep(2);
 echo 'Chunk #2' . PHP_EOL;
 ob_start(); // BUFFER#3
 sleep(2);
 echo 'Chunk #3' . PHP_EOL;
 ob_end_flush();
 ob_end_flush();

sleep(2);
echo 'Chunk #4' . PHP_EOL;
ob_end_flush();

//Chunk #1
//Chunk #2
//Chunk #3
//Chunk #4
```

The entire output here is being withheld for roughly 8 seconds, after which all four `Chunk#...` strings are being output at once. This is because the `ob_end_flush()` function is the only one that sends the output to the console, whereas the `ob_end_flush()` function merely closes the buffer, passing it to the parent buffer present in the code.

The use of the `ob_get_contents()` function can add further dynamic to output buffering, as shown in the following example:

```php
<?php

$users = ['John', 'Marcy', 'Alice', 'Jack'];

ob_start();
foreach ($users as $user) {
    echo 'User: ' . $user . PHP_EOL;
}
$report = ob_get_contents();
ob_end_clean();

ob_start();
echo 'Listing users:' . PHP_EOL;
ob_end_flush();

echo $report;

echo 'Total of ' . count($users) . ' users listed' . PHP_EOL;

//Listing users:
//User: John
//User: Marcy
//User: Alice
//User: Jack
//Total of 4 users listed
```

The `ob_get_content()` function allows us to grab a string representation of content stored in the buffer. It is up to us to choose if we want to modify that content further, output it, or pass it on to other constructs.

How does all this apply to web pages? After all, we are interested in the performance of our scripts, mostly, in context of web pages. Without output buffering, HTML is sent to the browser in chunks as PHP progresses through our script. With output buffering, HTML is sent to the browser as one string at the end of our script.

Keeping in mind that the `ob_start()` function accepts a callback function, we can use the callback function to further modify the output. This modification can be anything, either form of filtering or even compression.

The following example demonstrates the use of output filtering:

```php
<?php

ob_start('strip_away');
echo '<h1>', 'Bummer', '</h1>';
echo '<p>', 'I felt foolish and angry about it!', '</p>';
ob_end_flush();

function strip_away($buffer)
{
  $keywords = ['bummer', 'foolish', 'angry'];
  foreach ($keywords as $keyword) {
    $buffer = str_ireplace(
      $keyword,
      str_repeat('X', strlen($keyword)),
      $buffer
    );
  }
  return $buffer;
}

// Outputs:
// <h1>XXXXXX</h1><p>I felt XXXXXXX and XXXXX about it!</p>
```

Nowadays, however, we are not likely to write these kinds of structures ourselves, as the framework abstractions masquerade it for us.

Disabling debug messages

The Ubuntu Server is a popular, free, and open source Linux distribution that we can use to quickly set up a **LAMP (Linux, Apache, MySQL, PHP)** stack. The ease of installation and long-term support of Ubuntu Server makes it a popular choice among PHP developers. With a clean server installation, we can get the LAMP stack up and running just by executing the following commands:

```
sudo apt-get update && sudo apt-get upgrade
sudo apt-get install lamp-server^
```

Once these are done, visiting our external server IP address, we should see an Apache page, as shown in the following screenshot:

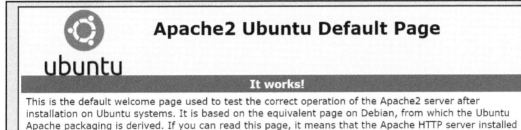

The HTML we are seeing in the browser originates from the `/var/www/html/index.html` file. After replacing `index.html` with `index.php`, we're good to play with the PHP code.

The reason for this Ubuntu Server-like introduction is to emphasize certain server defaults. Out of all configuration directives, we should never blindly accept defaults for *error logging* and *error displaying* directives without truly understanding them. Constant switching between development and production environments makes it way too easy to expose confidential information within the browser or miss logging the right error.

With that in mind, let's assume we have the following broken `index.php` file on our freshly installed Ubuntu Server LAMP stack:

```php
<?php

echo 'Test;
```

On trying to open this in the browser, Apache will send back `HTTP 500 Internal Server Error`, which, depending on the browser, might be visible to the end user, as shown in the following screenshot:

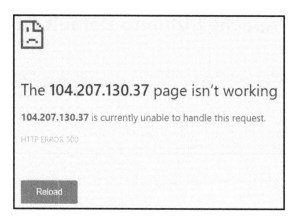

Ideally, we would have our web server configured with a nicely styled generic error page, just to make it more user friendly. While the browser response might satisfy the end user, it certainly does not satisfy the developer in this case. The information returned does not indicate anything about the nature of the error, which makes it difficult to fix it. Luckily, for us, the default LAMP stack configuration in this case includes logging the error to a `/var/log/apache2/error.log` file:

```
[Thu Feb 02 19:23:26.026521 2017] [:error] [pid 5481] [client
93.140.71.25:55229] PHP Parse error: syntax error, unexpected ''Test;'
(T_ENCAPSED_AND_WHITESPACE) in /var/www/html/index.php on line 3
```

While this behavior is perfect for production, it is cumbersome for the development environment. When developing, we would really like our errors to show up in the browser, just to speed things up. PHP allows us to control the error reporting and logging behavior through several configuration directives, the following being the most important:

- `error_reporting`: This is the error level we wish to monitor; we can use the pipe (|) operator to list several error-level constants. Its default value is `E_ALL & ~E_NOTICE & ~E_STRICT & ~E_DEPRECATED`.
- `display_errors`: This specifies if errors should be sent to the browser/CLI or be hidden from the user.
- `error_log`: This is the file where we want to log PHP errors.
- `log_errors`: This tells us if we should log the error to the `error_log` file.

The available error-level constants are defined as follows:

- `E_ERROR (1)`
- `E_WARNING (2)`
- `E_PARSE (4)`
- `E_NOTICE (8)`
- `E_CORE_ERROR (16)`
- `E_CORE_WARNING (32)`
- `E_COMPILE_ERROR (64)`
- `E_COMPILE_WARNING (128)`
- `E_USER_ERROR (256)`
- `E_USER_WARNING (512)`
- `E_USER_NOTICE (1024)`
- `E_STRICT (2048)`
- `E_RECOVERABLE_ERROR (4096)`
- `E_DEPRECATED (8192)`
- `E_USER_DEPRECATED (16384)`
- `E_ALL (32767)`

Using the `error_reporting()` and `ini_set()` functions, we can use some of these directives to configure logging and displaying during runtime:

```php
<?php

error_reporting(E_ALL);
ini_set('display_errors', 'On');
```

careful using `ini_set()` for `display_errors` as it won't have any effect if the script has fatal errors, simply because runtime does not get executed.

Error displaying and error logging are two different mechanisms that work hand in hand with each other. While we are likely to benefit more from error displaying in development environments, error logging is the way to go for production environments.

Zend OPcache

One major downside of PHP is that it loads and parses the PHP script on every request. Written in plain text, the PHP code is first compiled to opcodes, then the opcodes are executed. While this performance impact might not be noticeable with small applications that have one or few scripts in total, it makes a big difference with larger platforms, such as Magento, Drupal, and so on.

Starting from PHP 5.5, there is an out-of-the-box solution to this problem. The Zend OPcache extension addresses the repetitive compilation issue by storing the compiled opcodes in shared memory (RAM). Turning it on or off is simply a matter of changing the configuration directive.

There are quite a few configuration directives, a few of which will get us started:

- `opcache.enable`: This defaults to 1 and is changeable via `PHP_INI_ALL`.
- `opcache.enable_cli`: This defaults to 0 and is changeable via `PHP_INI_SYSTEM`.
- `opcache.memory_consumption`: This defaults to 64 and is changeable via `PHP_INI_SYSTEM`, which defines the size of shared memory used by OPcache.
- `opcache.max_accelerated_files`: This defaults to 2000 and is changeable via `PHP_INI_SYSTEM`, which defines the maximum number of keys/scripts in the OPcache hash table. Its maximum value is 1000000.
- `opcache.max_wasted_percentage`: This defaults to 5 and is changeable via `PHP_INI_SYSTEM`, which defines the maximum percentage of wasted memory allowed before scheduling a restart.

While `opcache.enable` is flagged as `PHP_INI_ALL`, using `ini_set()` to enable it at runtime won't work. Only disabling it with `ini_set()` will work.

Although fully automated, Zend OPcache also provides a few functions for us to use:

- `opcache_compile_file()`: This compiles and caches a script without executing it
- `opcache_get_configuration()`: This fetches the OPcache configuration information
- `opcache_get_status()`: This fetches the OPcache information
- `opcache_invalidate()`: This invalidates OPcache
- `opcache_is_script_cached()`: This tells us if the script is cached via OPcache
- `opcache_reset()`: This resets the OPcache cache

While it is unlikely we will use these methods on our own, they do come in handy for utility tools that deal with OPcache for us.

 The opcache-gui tool shows OPcache statistics, settings, and cached files whilst providing a real-time update. This tool is available for download at `https://github.com/amnuts/opcache-gui`.

One thing to be wary about with OPcache is its potential *cache slam* problem. Using the `memory_consumption`, `max_accelerated_files`, and `max_wasted_percentage` configuration directives, OPcache determines when it is time to flush the cache. When this happens, servers with large amounts of traffic are likely to experience a cache slam problem, with lots of requests simultaneously generating the same cache entries. Therefore, we should try to avoid frequent cache flushing. To do so, we can use the cache monitoring tool and tune the three configuration directives to suit our application size.

Concurrency

While concurrency is a topic applicable to multiple layers of stack, there are a few configuration directives around web servers that every developer should be familiar with. Concurrency refers to handling multiple connections inside a web server. The two most popular web servers for PHP, Apache, and Nginx, both allow some basic configuration for handling multiple connections.

While there are plenty of debates as to which server is faster, Apache with the MPM event module is pretty much on par with the Nginx performance.

The following directives dictate the Apache MPM event concurrency, and are therefore worth keeping an eye on:

- `ThreadsPerChild`: This is the number of threads created by each child process
- `ServerLimit`: This is the limit on the configurable number of processes
- `MaxRequestWorkers`: This is the maximum number of connections to be processed simultaneously
- `AsyncRequestWorkerFactor`: This is the limit on concurrent connections per process

An absolute maximum numbers of possible concurrent connections can be calculated using the following formula:

$$max\_connections = (AsyncRequestWorkerFactor + 1) * MaxRequestWorkers$$

The formula is quite simple; however, changing `AsyncRequestWorkerFactor` is not just a matter of punching in a higher configuration value. We would need to have a solid knowledge about the traffic hitting the web server, which implies extensive testing and data gathering.

The following directives dictate the Nginx concurrency, and are therefore worth keeping an eye on:

- `worker_processes`: This is the number of worker processes; it defaults to 1
- `worker_connections`: This is the maximum number of simultaneous connections that can be opened by a worker process; it defaults to 512

The ideal total number of users Nginx can serve comes down to the following formula:

$$max\_connections = worker\_processes * worker\_connections$$

Though we have barely scratched the surface of web server concurrency and the overall configuration directives for these two web servers, the preceding information should serve us as a starting point. While developers don't usually tune web servers, they should know when to flag misconfiguration that might impact their PHP application performance.

Summary

Throughout this chapter, we have addressed some aspects of the PHP performance optimization. While these merely scratch the surface of the overall performance topic, they outline the most common areas every PHP developer should be deeply familiar with. The broad range of configuration directives allows us to tune application behavior that often works in tandem with the web server itself. The backbone of optimal performance, however, lies in the thoughtful use of resources across the stack, as we got to observe through the simple SQL query example.

Moving forward, we will look into serverless architecture, an emerging abstraction of the standard development environment.

8
Going Serverless

The **serverless** term is probably among the hottest terms in the software industry lately. It may be described as the architecture style that partially or fully abstracts the infrastructure needed to run our software. This abstraction is usually provided by various third-party service providers.

To put it in the context of web application development, let's think about **Single Page Application** (**SPA**). Nowadays, we can easily develop an entire SPA on top of a fully managed infrastructure, such as AWS. Such a SPA may be written in Angular, having client components served from the S3 bucket, managing users through the Amazon Cognito service, whilst using DynamoDB as an application data store. The managed infrastructure abstracts away any hosting or server dealings from us, allowing us to focus our efforts on the application alone. What we end up with is one form of serverless application, depending on how narrow our definition is.

 Like any architectural style, serverless is far from being **<<the solution>>**. While some types of application can benefit from it, others might find it a total mismatch. The long-running applications for example, can easily turn out to be expensive solution for serverless frameworks, rather than running a workload on a dedicated server. The trick is to find the right balance.

A more rigid and narrow definition of serverless is pure code/function hosting, often referred to as **Function as a Service** (**FaaS**). Such infrastructures provide highly concurrent, scalable, yet affordable solutions, given that they are mostly priced by *pay-per-execution* model. AWS Lambda and Iron.io are two platforms that perfectly depict this notion.

In this chapter, we will take a closer look at how we can utilize both the AWS Lambda and the Iron.io platforms to deploy chunks of our code:

- Using the serverless framework
- Using Iron.io IronWorker

Using the serverless framework

The AWS Lambda is a compute service provided by **Amazon Web Services** (**AWS**). What makes it specific is that it lets us run code without provisioning or managing any servers whatsoever. The auto-scaling features enable it to withstand thousands of requests per second. With an added benefit of pay-per-execution pricing, this service caught some traction among developers. Over time, the serverless framework was developed to make the use of the AWS Lambda service easy.

 The serverless framework is available at `https://serverless.com`.

Assuming we have an AWS account created, and a clean installation of the Ubuntu server at hand, let's go ahead and outline the steps needed to set up and utilize the serverless framework.

Before we can deploy applications on the AWS Lambda, we need to make sure we have a user with the right set of permissions. AWS permissions are quite robust, in that we can tune them per resource. The serverless framework uses several other AWS resources aside from AWS Lambda itself, such as S3, API Gateway, and a few others. To make our demonstration simple, we will first create an IAM User with Administrator access:

1. We start by logging into the AWS console at `https://aws.amazon.com/console /`. Once logged in, we need to proceed under the **My Security Credentials** | **Users** screen:

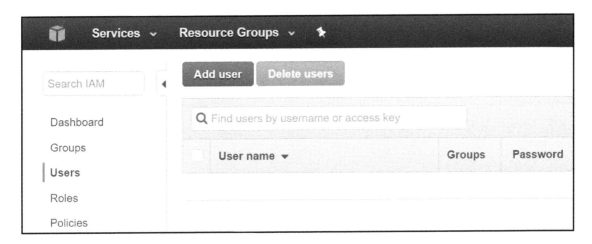

2. To add a new user, we click on the **Add user** button. This triggers a four-step process, as shown in the following screenshot:

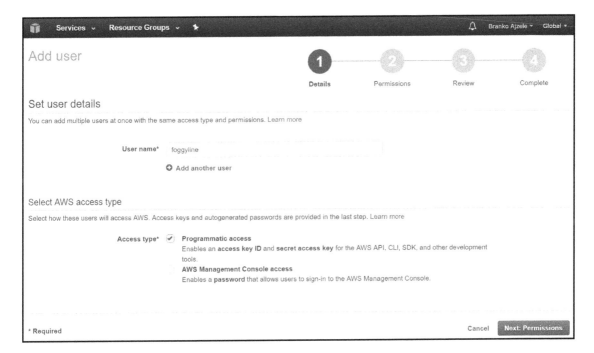

3. We provide two pieces of information here, **User name** and **Access type**. The **Programmatic access** type is what we need for our serverless integration. Clicking on the **Next: Permissions** button gets us to the following screen:

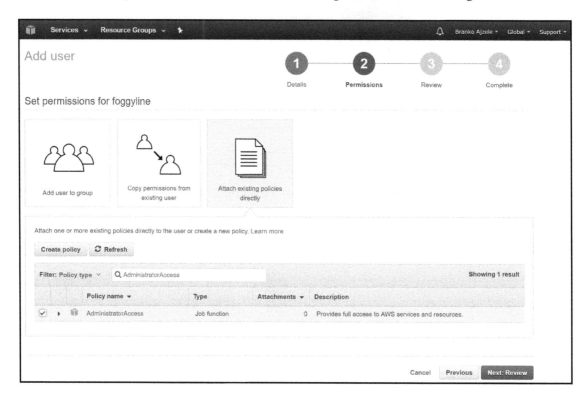

4. There are a few ways we can attach permissions to the user here. To keep things simple, we click on the **Attach existing policies directly** box, and type in **AdministratorAccess** in the **Policy type** field filter. We then simply check the **AdministratorAccess** policy and click on the **Next: Review** button, which gets us to the following screen:

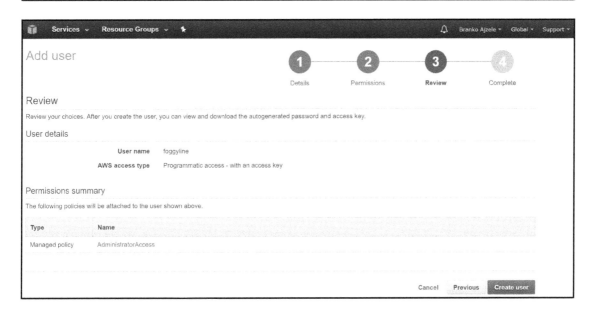

5. Here, we merely review the current progress, and finally click on the **Create user** button, which gets us to the following screen:

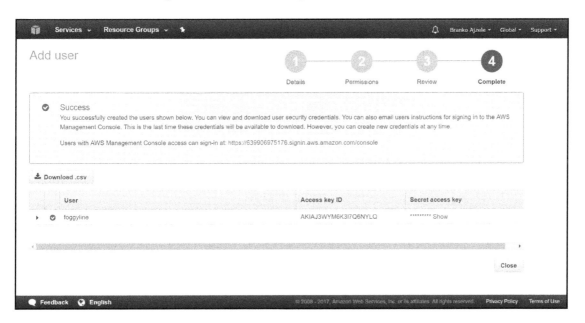

6. We now have **Access key ID** and **Secret access key**, the two pieces of information required by the serverless framework.

 Creating users with full administrative permissions is generally considered a bad security practice. Normally, we would create users with a bare minimum of needed permissions.

With these steps out of the way, we can move forward with setting up the serverless framework itself.

The serverless framework runs on top of Node.js. Assuming we have an instance of a clean Ubuntu server, we can set it up by following these steps:

1. Install Node.js with the following console commands:

   ```
   curl -sL https://deb.nodesource.com/setup_7.x | sudo -E bash -
   sudo apt-get install -y nodejs
   ```

2. Once Node.js is installed, the npm console tool becomes available. The serverless framework itself is available as an npm package at https://www.npmjs.com/package/serverless. Running the following console commands should get it installed on our server:

   ```
   sudo npm install -g serverless
   serverless --version
   ```

   ```
   root@vultr:~# serverless --version
   1.6.1
   root@vultr:~#
   ```

3. With the serverless framework now installed, we need to set the console environment variables: AWS_ACCESS_KEY_ID and AWS_SECRET_ACCESS_KEY. These get used by serverless during deploy:

   ```
   export AWS_ACCESS_KEY_ID=<--AWS_ACCESS_KEY_ID-->
   export AWS_SECRET_ACCESS_KEY=<--AWS_SECRET_ACCESS_KEY-->
   ```

4. We can now address the bits and pieces related to PHP. The official serverless framework example uses an AWS lambda that runs a PHP function, which can be found at `https://github.com/ZeroSharp/serverless-php`. We can install it via the following console command:

```
serverless install --url
https://github.com/ZeroSharp/serverless-php
```

This should give us an output much like the following screenshot:

```
root@vultr:~# serverless install --url https://github.com/ZeroSharp/serverless-php
Serverless: Downloading and installing "serverless-php"...
Serverless: Successfully installed "serverless-php"
root@vultr:~# cd serverless-php
root@vultr:~/serverless-php# ls -al
total 24412
drwxr-xr-x  2 root root      4096 Feb 12 15:50 .
drwx------ 15 root root      4096 Feb 12 15:50 ..
-rw-r--r--  1 root root       644 Feb 12 15:50 buildphp.sh
-rw-r--r--  1 root root      1627 Feb 12 15:50 dockerfile.buildphp
-rw-r--r--  1 root root        63 Feb 12 15:50 event.json
-rw-r--r--  1 root root       148 Feb 12 15:50 .gitignore
-rw-r--r--  1 root root       963 Feb 12 15:50 handler.js
-rw-r--r--  1 root root       140 Feb 12 15:50 index.php
-rw-r--r--  1 root root      1152 Feb 12 15:50 LICENCE.md
-rw-r--r--  1 root root        86 Feb 12 15:50 .npmignore
-rwxr-xr-x  1 root root  24944784 Feb 12 15:50 php
-rw-r--r--  1 root root      1545 Feb 12 15:50 README.md
-rw-r--r--  1 root root      2254 Feb 12 15:50 serverless.yml
root@vultr:~/serverless-php# 
```

The serverless install command merely pulls the content of the Git repository into a local directory. Within the newly created `serverless-php` directory, there is an `index.php` file within which our PHP application code resides. Strangely enough, there are bits and pieces here that, at first, look like they have nothing to do with PHP, such as `handler.js`. A quick look into the `handler.js` reveals something interesting, which is that the AWS Lambda service does not actually run the PHP code directly. The way it works is that `handler.js`, which is a Node.js app, spawns a process with an included `php` binary file. In a nutshell, `index.php` is our application file, the rest is a necessary boilerplate.

As a quick sanity check, let's trigger the following two commands:

```
php index.php
serverless invoke local --function hello
```

These should give us the following output, indicating that serverless is able to see and execute our function:

```
root@vultr:~/serverless-php# php index.php
Go Serverless v1.0! Your PHP function executed successfully!root@vultr:~/serverless-php#
root@vultr:~/serverless-php# serverless invoke local --function hello
{
    "statusCode": 200,
    "body": "{\"message\":\"Go Serverless v1.0! Your PHP function executed successfully!\"}"
}
root@vultr:~/serverless-php#
```

Finally, we are ready to deploy our PHP application to the AWS Lambda service. We do this by executing the following command:

```
serverless deploy
```

```
root@vultr:~/serverless-php# serverless deploy
Serverless: Creating Stack...
Serverless: Checking Stack create progress...
.....
Serverless: Stack create finished...
Serverless: Packaging service...
Serverless: Uploading CloudFormation file to S3...
Serverless: Uploading service .zip file to S3 (8.68 MB)...
Serverless: Updating Stack...
Serverless: Checking Stack update progress...
...............................
Serverless: Stack update finished...
Service Information
service: serverless-php
stage: dev
region: eu-west-1
api keys:
  None
endpoints:
  GET - https://yk1nr9hr4g.execute-api.eu-west-1.amazonaws.com/dev/hello
functions:
  serverless-php-dev-hello
root@vultr:~/serverless-php#
```

This simple command puts in motion a series of events that result in several different AWS services being utilized within the AWS console.

Opening the link listed under **endpoints** shows that our application is publicly available:

```
← → C ⌂   🔒 Secure | https://yk1nr9hr4g.execute-api.eu-west-1.amazonaws.com/dev/hello

{"message":"Go Serverless v1.0! Your PHP function executed successfully!"}
```

This was made possible by the automatically created API entry under the **Amazon API Gateway** service, as shown in the following screenshot:

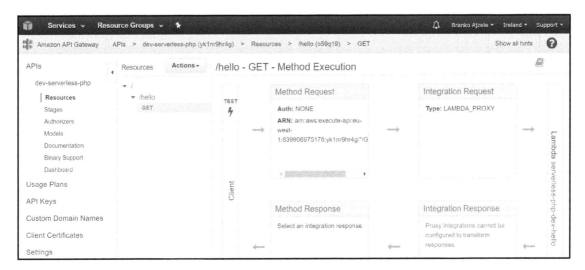

The API Gateway bridges the GET /hello URL action with the AWS Lambda serverless-php-dev-hello application. A look under the **AWS Lambda** screen that reveals this application:

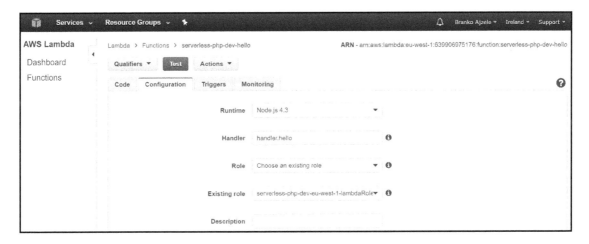

The **CloudFormation** stack has also been created, as shown in the following screenshot:

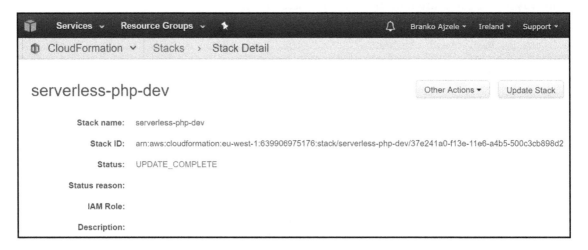

The **S3** bucket has also been created, as shown here:

The **CloudWatch** log group has also been created, as shown in the following screenshot:

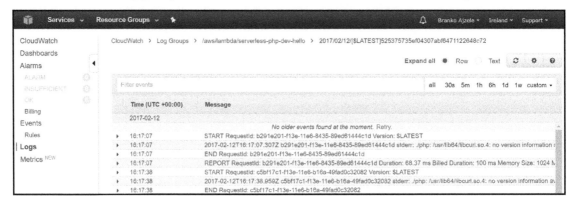

In a nutshell, `serverless deploy` kicked off quite a few services for us, thus giving us time to focus more on actual application development. Although AWS Lambda only charges a fee when a code is run, some of the other services in the mix might be different. This is why it is important to keep an eye on everything that gets automatically triggered for us.

Luckily for us, serverless also provides a cleanup command, which is written as follows:

serverless remove

```
root@vultr:~/serverless-php# serverless remove
Serverless: Getting all objects in S3 bucket...
Serverless: Removing objects in S3 bucket...
Serverless: Removing Stack...
Serverless: Checking Stack removal progress...
.....................
Serverless: Stack removal finished...
root@vultr:~/serverless-php#
```

This command does an overall cleanup by removing all of the services and resources it previously created.

Using Iron.io IronWorker

Iron.io is a serverless job processing platform designed for high performance and concurrency. Built around Docker containers, the platform itself is language-agnostic. We can use it to run pretty much any programming language, including PHP. There are three main features of the Iron.io platform:

- **IronWorker**: This is an elastic task/queue-like worker service that scales out processing
- **IronMQ**: This is a message queueing service designed for distributed systems
- **IronCache**: This is an elastic and durable key/value store

While we cannot run real-time PHP within the Iron.io platform, we could utilize its IronWorker feature for task/queue-like type of applications.

Assuming we have an Iron.io account opened and the Ubuntu server with Docker installed, we'll be able to follow the next steps outlining the IronWorker workflow.

We start by clicking the **New Project** button under the Iron.io dashboard. This opens up a simple screen, where all we need is to punch in the project name:

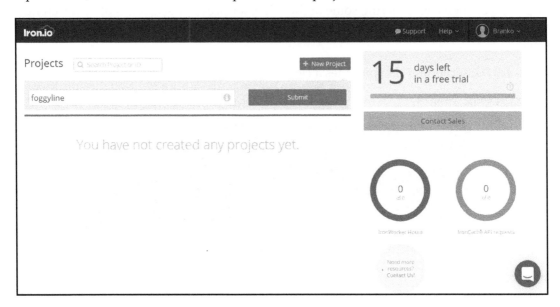

Once the project is created, we can click on the project settings link. This opens up a screen with several pieces of information, including the **Authentication/Configuration** parameters:

We will need these parameters as we will configure the `iron.json` file later on. With these pieces of information at hand, we are ready to proceed with the application bits.

Application-wise, we start of by installing the `iron` console tool:

```
curl -sSL https://cli.iron.io/install | sh
```

Once installed, the `iron` command should be available via the console, as shown in the following screenshot:

```
root@vultr:~/dockerworker/php# iron
usage:  iron [product] [command] [flags] [args]

where [product] is one of:

  mq          Commands to manage messages and queues on IronMQ.
  worker      Commands to queue and view IronWorker tasks.
  docker      Login to Docker Registry.
  register    Register an image or code package with IronWorker.
  lambda      Commands to convert AWS Lambda functions to Docker containers.

run 'iron [product] -help for a list of commands.
run 'iron [product] [command] -help' for [command]'s flags/args.

[flags]:
  -env string
        provide specific dev environment
  -h    show this
  -help
        show this
  -project-id string
        provide project ID
  -token string
        provide OAuth token
  -version
        print the version number
root@vultr:~/dockerworker/php# 
```

We are now ready to kick off our first Iron app.

Assuming we have a clean directory where we want to put our application files, we start by adding `composer.json` with the following content:

```
{
  "require": {
    "iron-io/iron_worker": "2.0.4",
    "iron-io/iron_mq": "2.*",
    "wp-cli/php-cli-tools": "~0.10.3"
  }
}
```

Here, we are just telling Composer what libraries to pull in:

- `iron_worker`: This is the client library for IronWorker (`https://packagist.org/packages/iron-io/iron_worker`)
- `iron_mq`: This is the client binding for IronMQ (`https://packagist.org/packages/iron-io/iron_mq`)
- `php-cli-tools`: These are the console utilities for PHP (`https://packagist.org/packages/wp-cli/php-cli-tools`)

We then create `Dockerfile` with its content as follows:

```
FROM iron/php

WORKDIR /app
ADD . /app

ENTRYPOINT ["php", "greet.php"]
```

These `Dockerfile` instructions help Docker to automatically build the necessary image for us.

We then add the `greet.payload.json` file with its content as follows:

```
{
  "name": "John"
}
```

This is not really a necessary part of the process, but we are using it to simulate the payload our application receives.

We then add the `greet.php` file with its content as follows:

```php
<?php

require 'vendor/autoload.php';

$payload = IronWorker\Runtime::getPayload(true);

echo 'Welcome ', $payload['name'], PHP_EOL;
```

The `greet.php` file is our actual application. The job that gets created on the IronWorker service will be queueing and executing this application. The application itself is simple; it merely grabs the value of a payload variable named `name`, and echoes it out. This should suffice for our IronWorker demonstration purposes.

We then create the `iron.json` file with a similar content, as follows:

```json
{
  "project_id": "589dc552827e8d00072c7e11",
  "token": "Gj5vBCht0BP9MeBUNn5g"
}
```

We ensure that we paste `project_id` and `token` obtained from the **Project settings** screen within the Iron.io dashboard.

With these files in place, we have defined our application, and are now ready to kick off Docker related tasks. The overall idea is that we will first create a local Docker image for testing purposes. Once we are done with the testing, we will push the Docker image to the Docker repository, and then configure the Iron.io platform to use the image from the Docker repository to power its IronWorker job.

We can now install our worker dependencies into Docker, as set by the `composer.json` file. We will do so by running the following command:

```
docker run --rm -v "$PWD":/worker -w /worker iron/php:dev composer install
```

The output should show the Composer installing dependencies, as you can see in the following screenshot:

```
root@vultr:~/dockerworker/php# docker run --rm -v "$PWD":/worker -w /worker iron/php:dev composer install
Unable to find image 'iron/php:dev' locally
dev: Pulling from iron/php

ee54741ab35b: Pull complete
424feef11a88: Pull complete
d0400ab21154: Pull complete
d87fa8ad37ed: Pull complete
b16c22bcf63c: Pull complete
e5cae7ec020a: Pull complete
dcdb50d4acde: Pull complete
Digest: sha256:ca9d80e9c8bdcb70073a085d295741c2516703db2638a75fa1af3faa60aae427
Status: Downloaded newer image for iron/php:dev
Loading composer repositories with package information
Installing dependencies (including require-dev) from lock file
  - Installing iron-io/iron_core (1.0.0)
    Downloading: 100%

  - Installing iron-io/iron_mq (2.0.0)
    Downloading: 100%

  - Installing iron-io/iron_worker (2.0.4)
    Downloading: 100%

  - Installing wp-cli/php-cli-tools (v0.10.5)
    Downloading: 100%

Generating autoload files
root@vultr:~/dockerworker/php#
```

Once Composer is done installing dependencies, we should test to see if our application is executing. We can do this via the following command:

```
docker run --rm -e "PAYLOAD_FILE=greet.payload.json" -v "$PWD":/worker -w
/worker iron/php php greet.php
```

The resulting output of the preceding command should be a **Welcome John** string, as shown in this screenshot:

```
root@vultr:~/dockerworker/php# docker run --rm -e "PAYLOAD_FILE=greet.payload.json" -v "$PWD":/worker -w /worker iron/php php greet.php
Welcome John
root@vultr:~/dockerworker/php#
```

This confirms that our Docker image is working correctly, and we are now ready to build and deploy it to https://hub.docker.com.

 Docker Hub, available at https://hub.docker.com, is a cloud-based service that provides a centralized solution for container image management. While it is a commercial service, there is a free *one-repository* plan available.

Assuming we have opened a Docker Hub account, executing the following command via the console would flag us as logged in:

```
docker login --username=ajzele
```

Where `ajzele` is the username which should be replaced with our own:

```
root@vultr:~# docker login --username=ajzele
Password:
Login Succeeded
root@vultr:~#
```

We can now and package our Docker image by executing the following command:

```
docker build -t ajzele/greet:0.0.1 .
```

This is a standard build command that will create an `ajzele/greet` image, flagged with version `0.0.1`:

```
root@vultr:~/dockerworker/php# docker build -t ajzele/greet:0.0.1 .
Sending build context to Docker daemon 350.2 kB
Step 1 : FROM iron/php
 ---> 9c5f8dee10e0
Step 2 : WORKDIR /app
 ---> Running in 35eb92866504
 ---> 827a2336c6e0
Removing intermediate container 35eb92866504
Step 3 : ADD . /app
 ---> ef7fd786b470
Removing intermediate container 77f150357245
Step 4 : ENTRYPOINT php greet.php
 ---> Running in d41b74b2c0bf
 ---> 078793b597da
Removing intermediate container d41b74b2c0bf
Successfully built 078793b597da
root@vultr:~/dockerworker/php#
```

With the image now created, we should test it first before pushing it to the Docker Hub. Executing the following command confirms that our newly created `ajzele/greet` image is working fine:

```
docker run --rm -it -e "PAYLOAD_FILE=greet.payload.json" ajzele/greet:0.0.1
```

The resulting **Welcome John** output confirms that our image is now ready to be deployed to Docker Hub, which can be done using the following command:

```
docker push ajzele/greet:0.0.1
```

Once the push process is done, we should be able to see our image under the Docker Hub dashboard:

Quite a few steps up until now, but we are nearly there. Now that our application is available as a Docker image within the Docker Hub repository, we can turn our focus back onto the Iron.io platform. The `iron` console tool that we installed early on in the process is able to register the Docker Hub image as a new worker under the Iron.io dashboard:

```
iron register ajzele/greet:0.0.1
```

The following screenshot shows the output of this command:

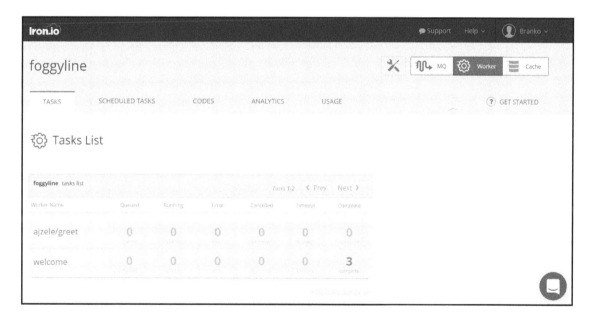

At this point, we should see the `ajzele/greet` worker under the Iron.io dashboard's **TASKS** tab:

Although the worker is registered, it is not executed at this point. The Iron.io platform allows us to execute the worker either as a scheduled or queued task.

The scheduled task, as shown in the following screenshot, allows us to choose the registered Docker image along with the time of execution and a few other options:

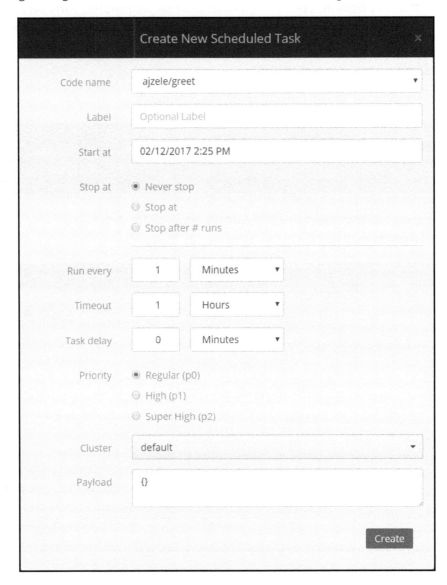

The queued task, as shown in the following screenshot, also allows us to choose the registered Docker image, but this time without any specific timing configuration:

Using the `iron` console tool, we can create both, the schedule and queue tasks based on the `ajzele/greet` worker.

The following command creates a scheduled task based on the `ajzele/greet` worker:

```
iron worker schedule --payload-file greet.payload.json -start-
at="2017-02-12T14:16:28+00:00" ajzele/greet
```

The `start-at` parameter defines a time in the RFC3339 format.

For more information about the RFC3339 format, check out `https://tool`
`s.ietf.org/html/rfc3339`.

The following screenshot shows the output of the preceding command:

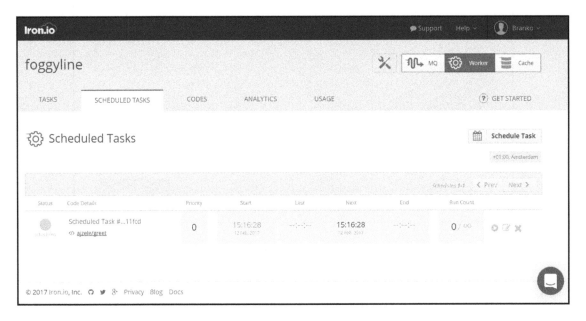

The Iron.io dashboard should now show this as a new entry under the **SCHEDULED
TASKS** section:

When the scheduled time comes, the Iron.io platform will execute this scheduled task.

The following command creates a queued task based on the `ajzele/greet` worker:

```
iron worker queue --payload-file greet.payload.json --wait ajzele/greet
```

The following screenshot shows the output of this command:

```
root@vultr:~/dockerworker/php# iron worker queue --payload-file greet.payload.json --wait ajzele/greet
----->  Configuring client
        Project 'foggyline' with id='589dc552827e8d00072c7e11'
-----> Queueing task 'ajzele/greet'
        Queued task with id='58a06981ed187b000861233e'
        Check https://hud.iron.io/tq/projects/589dc552827e8d00072c7e11/jobs/58a06981ed187b000861233e for more info
----->  Waiting for task to start running
----->  queued: 0:0:1:42
----->  Task running, waiting for completion
----->  running: 0:0:3:99
----->  Done
----->  Printing Log:
Welcome John
root@vultr:~/dockerworker/php# iron worker queue --payload-file greet.payload.json --wait ajzele/greet
----->  Configuring client
        Project 'foggyline' with id='589dc552827e8d00072c7e11'
----->  Queueing task 'ajzele/greet'
        Queued task with id='58a0698a4309aa0007221b70'
        Check https://hud.iron.io/tq/projects/589dc552827e8d00072c7e11/jobs/58a0698a4309aa0007221b70 for more info
----->  Waiting for task to start running
----->  queued: 0:0:1:73
----->  Task running, waiting for completion
----->  running: 0:0:3:11
----->  Done
----->  Printing Log:
Welcome John
root@vultr:~/dockerworker/php#
```

The Iron.io dashboard registers every executed task by increasing the **Complete** counter (currently showing **3** in the following screenshot) under the **TASKS** section:

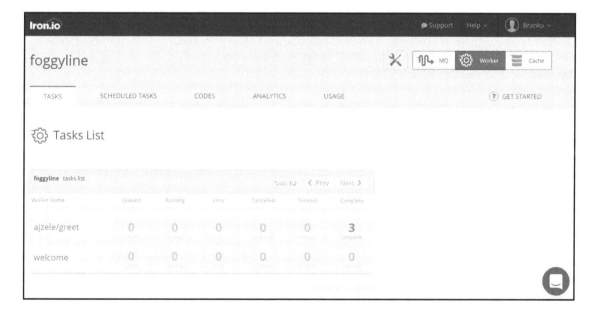

Going into the `ajzele/greet` worker reveals details behind each job, both scheduled and queued:

So far, you have learned how to create a PHP application Docker image, push it to the Docker Hub, register it with the Iron.io platform, and start scheduling and queueing tasks. The part about scheduling and queueing tasks may be a bit tricky as we were doing it from the console and not the PHP code.

Luckily, the `composer.json` file references all of the libraries we need, to be able to schedule and queue tasks from the PHP code. Let's assume, for a moment, that we grabbed the `iron.json` and `composer.json` files and moved onto a completely different server, maybe even our local development machine. All we need to do there is to run `composer install` on the console, and create the `index.php` file with content as follows:

```php
<?php

require './vendor/autoload.php';

$worker = new IronWorker\IronWorker();

$worker->postScheduleAdvanced(
  'ajzele/greet',
  ['name' => 'Mariya'],
  '2017-02-12T14:33:39+00:00'
```

```
);

$worker->postTask(
  'ajzele/greet',
  ['name' => 'Alice']
);
```

Once this code gets executed, it will create one scheduled and one queued task, just as the `iron` console tool does.

While we might not host an entire PHP application with it, the Iron.io platform makes it easy and hassle-free to create and run various isolated jobs, giving developers a worthwhile serverless experience.

Summary

Throughout this chapter, we took a hands-on approach with two popular serverless platforms--AWS and Iron.io. Using the serverless framework, we were able to quickly deploy our code to the AWS Lambda service. The actual deployment involved a few AWS services, exposing our little chunk of code as a REST API endpoint hitting AWS Lambda in the background. With all of the services being managed by AWS, we were left with a true serverless experience. Quite a powerful concept, if we think about it. Aside from AWS, Iron.io is another interesting serverless platform. Unlike real-time code execution on AWS Lamda, the code on Iron.io executes as scheduled/queued tasks (not to say that AWS does not have its own queued solution as well). While AWS Lambda natively supports Node.js, Java, Python, and .NET Core runtimes, Iron.io abstracts the language away by using Docker containers. Still, we were able to run PHP, even on AWS Lambda, by wrapping the PHP binary through Node.js.

The serverless approach certainly has its appeal. While it might not be the complete solution for some of our applications, it can certainly take on the resource-intense bits. The effortless use and pay-per-execution model can be a game changer for some.

Moving forward, we will take a look at what PHP has to offer when it comes to the trending reactive programming paradigm.

9
Reactive Programming

Every so often, there is a shift in the software industry. A shift that enriches the ecosystem with ideas promising easier systems and application development. The driving force behind which is mostly the Internet nowadays, as it is a medium for all connected applications, not just those running in our browser. Majority of mobile users consume a large number of cloud services, without even realizing it. Ensuring consistent user experience in such a connected world is a challenge addressed in multiple ways. One such viewpoint is the reactivity, where programming language itself plays an important role.

Traditionally, PHP follows the synchronous programming model and is not really fit for asynchronous programming. Although the standard library already has everything needed to write asynchronous I/O applications, the reality could not be far from different. Both MySQLi and MySQL (PDO), for example, remain blocking, making asynchronous programming with PHP useless. Luckily, the tides are shifting, and awareness about asynchronous is coming about with PHP.

Reactive programming is an emerging topic of the software industry that builds on top of observables as its primitive. We associate asynchronous behavior with it, as observables provide an ideal way to access asynchronous sequences of multiple items. On a higher level, it's just another programming paradigm, just as procedural, object-oriented, declarative, and functional programming are. While it requires a certain mind shift to adopt observables, operators, observers, and other building blocks, in return, it allows greater expressiveness and unidirectional data flow, leading to cleaner and simpler code.

In this chapter, we will take a closer look at the following sections:

- Similarities with event-driven programming
- Using RxPHP:
    - Installing RxPHP
    - Observable and observer
    - Subject
    - Operator
    - Writing custom operator
- Non-blocking I/O
- Using React:
    - Installing React
    - React event loop
    - Observable and event loop

Similarities with event-driven programming

Wikipedia defines reactive programming as follows:

> *"A programming paradigm oriented around data flows and the propagation of change."*

The very first thought of this may imply some similarities to a well-known event-driven programming. The data flows and the propagation of change sound a bit like something we may implement via the \SplSubject, \SplObjectStorage, and \SplObserver interfaces in PHP, as per the following trivial example. The \SplObjectStorage interface further encapsulates the \Countable, \Iterator, \Traversable, \Serializable, and \ArrayAccess interfaces:

```php
<?php

class UserRegister implements \SplSubject
{
    protected $user;
    protected $observers;

    public function __construct($user)
    {
        $this->user = $user;
        $this->observers = new \SplObjectStorage();
    }
```

```php
    public function attach(\SplObserver $observer)
    {
        $this->observers->attach($observer);
    }

    public function detach(\SplObserver $observer)
    {
        $this->observers->detach($observer);
    }

    public function notify()
    {
        foreach ($this->observers as $observer) {
            $observer->update($this);
        }
    }

    public function getUser()
    {
        return $this->user;
    }
}

class Mailer implements \SplObserver
{
    public function update(\SplSubject $subject)
    {
        if ($subject instanceof UserRegister) {
            echo 'Mailing ', $subject->getUser(), PHP_EOL;
        }
    }
}

class Logger implements \SplObserver
{
    public function update(\SplSubject $subject)
    {
        if ($subject instanceof UserRegister) {
            echo 'Logging ', $subject->getUser(), PHP_EOL;
        }
    }
}

$userRegister = new UserRegister('John');
// some code...
$userRegister->attach(new Mailer());
// some code...
$userRegister->attach(new Logger());
```

```
// some code...
$userRegister->notify();
```

We may say that data flows translate to a sequence of updates coming from the `$userRegister` instance's `notify()` method, the propagation of change translates to triggering the `update()` method of the mailer and logger instances, and the `\SplObjectStorage` method plays an important role This is just a trivial and superficial interpretation of the reactive programming paradigm in the context of the PHP code. Furthermore, there is no asynchronicity here at the moment. The PHP runtime and standard library effectively offer all that is needed to write asynchronous code. Throwing in a *reactivity* in the mix, is merely a matter of choosing the right library.

While the choice of PHP libraries for reactive programming isn't nearly as rich as those of the JavaScript ecosystem, there are a few noteworthy ones, such as **RxPHP** and **React**.

Using RxPHP

Originally developed by Microsoft for the .NET platform, a set of libraries named **ReactiveX** (**reactive extensions**) is available at `http://reactivex.io`. ReactiveX allows us to write asynchronous and event-based programs using observable sequences. They do so by abstracting away low-level concerns such as non-blocking I/O, which we will talk about later. Over time, several programming languages made their own implementations of ReactiveX, following a nearly identical design pattern. The PHP implementation, named RxPHP, can be downloaded from `https://github.com/ReactiveX/RxPHP`:

Installing RxPHP

The RxPHP library is available as a Composer `reactivex/rxphp` package. Assuming we already installed PHP and Composer, we can simply execute the following command in an empty directory:

```
composer require reactivex/rxphp
```

This should give us an output similar to the following one:

```
root@vultr:~/rx# composer require reactivex/rxphp
Do not run Composer as root/super user! See https://getcomposer.org/root for details
Using version ^2.0 for reactivex/rxphp
./composer.json has been created
Loading composer repositories with package information
Updating dependencies (including require-dev)
    Failed to download react/promise from dist: The zip extension and unzip command are both missing, skipping.
The php.ini used by your command-line PHP is: /etc/php/7.0/cli/php.ini
    Now trying to download from source
  - Installing react/promise (v2.5.1)
    Cloning 62785ae604c8d69725d693eb370e1d67e94c4053 from cache

    Failed to download reactivex/rxphp from dist: The zip extension and unzip command are both missing, skipping.
The php.ini used by your command-line PHP is: /etc/php/7.0/cli/php.ini
    Now trying to download from source
  - Installing reactivex/rxphp (2.0.2)
    Cloning 7f5f669850cc035d78f7dafb45fd797fe0ba9e7d from cache

reactivex/rxphp suggests installing react/event-loop (Used for scheduling async operations)
Writing lock file
Generating autoload files
root@vultr:~/rx# 
```

The output suggests installing `react/event-loop`; we need to be sure to follow up on that by executing the following command:

```
composer require react/event-loop
```

This should give us an output much like the following one:

```
root@vultr:~/rx# composer require react/event-loop
Do not run Composer as root/super user! See https://getcomposer.org/root for details
Using version ^0.4.3 for react/event-loop
./composer.json has been updated
Loading composer repositories with package information
Updating dependencies (including require-dev)
    Failed to download react/event-loop from dist: The zip extension and unzip command are both missing, skipping.
The php.ini used by your command-line PHP is: /etc/php/7.0/cli/php.ini
    Now trying to download from source
  - Installing react/event-loop (v0.4.3)
    Cloning 8bde03488ee897dc6bb3d91e4e17c353f9c5252f from cache

react/event-loop suggests installing ext-libevent (>=0.1.0)
react/event-loop suggests installing ext-event (~1.0)
react/event-loop suggests installing ext-libev (*)
Writing lock file
Generating autoload files
```

All that remains now is to create an `index.php` file, which includes `autoload.php` file generated by Composer, and we are ready to start playing with

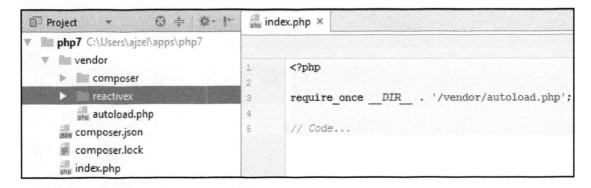

The RxPHP library is comprised of several key components, the most basic ones being the following:

- Observable
- Observer
- Subject
- Operator

Moving forward, let's take a closer look at each of these components.

Observable and observer

In our introduction example, we touched upon the observer pattern using `\SplSubject` and `\SplObserver`. Now, we are introducing an RxPHP observable and observer component. We might say that `\SplSubject` is analogous to `Rx\Observable`, whereas `\SplObserver` is analogous to `Rx\Observer\CallbackObserver`. The whole SPL and Rx, however, are only superficially analogous. `Rx\Observable` is more powerful than `\SplObserver`. We can think of `Rx\Observable` as a lazy source of event, a thing that produces value over time. Observables emit the following three types of events to their observers:

- The current item in the stream
- The error, if one occurred
- The complete state

In a nutshell, it is a reactive data source that knows how to signal internal data changes.

Let's take a look at the following simple example:

```php
<?php

require_once __DIR__ . '/vendor/autoload.php';

use \Rx\Observable;
use \Rx\Observer\CallbackObserver;
use \React\EventLoop\Factory;
use \Rx\Scheduler;

$loop = Factory::create();

Scheduler::setDefaultFactory(function () use ($loop) {
    return new Scheduler\EventLoopScheduler($loop);
});

$users = Observable::fromArray(['John', 'Mariya', 'Marc', 'Lucy']);

$logger = new CallbackObserver(
    function ($user) {
        echo 'Logging: ', $user, PHP_EOL;
    },
    function (\Throwable $t) {
        echo $t->getMessage(), PHP_EOL;
    },
    function () {
        echo 'Stream complete!', PHP_EOL;
    }
);

$users->subscribe($logger);

$loop->run();
```

The output of which is as :

```
Logging: John
Logging: Mariya
Logging: Marc
Logging: Lucy
Stream complete!
```

We see that the subscribe() method of the Observable instance accepts an instance of CallbackObserver. Each of the three parameters of an observer is a callback function. The first callback handles the stream item, the second returns potential error, and the third indicates a completed stream.

RxPHP provides few a type of observables:

- AnonymousObservable
- ArrayObservable
- ConnectableObservable
- EmptyObservable
- ErrorObservable
- ForkJoinObservable
- GroupedObservable
- IntervalObservable
- IteratorObservable
- MulticastObservable
- NeverObservable
- RangeObservable
- RefCountObservable
- ReturnObservable
- TimerObservable

Let's take a look at a more elaborate example of observable and observer:

```php
<?php

require_once __DIR__ . '/vendor/autoload.php';

use \Rx\Observable;
use \Rx\Observer\CallbackObserver;
use \React\EventLoop\Factory;
use \Rx\Scheduler;

$loop = Factory::create();

Scheduler::setDefaultFactory(function () use ($loop) {
    return new Scheduler\EventLoopScheduler($loop);
});

// Generator function, reads CSV file
```

```
function users($file)
{
    $users = fopen($file, 'r');
    while (!feof($users)) {
        yield fgetcsv($users)[0];
    }
    fclose($users);
}

// The RxPHP Observer
$logger = new CallbackObserver(
    function ($user) {
        echo $user, PHP_EOL;
    },
    function (\Throwable $t) {
        echo $t->getMessage(), PHP_EOL;
    },
    function () {
        echo 'stream complete!', PHP_EOL;
    }
);

// Dummy map callback function
$mapper = function ($value) {
    return time() . ' | ' . $value;
};

// Dummy filter callback function
$filter = function ($value) {
    return strstr($value, 'Ma');
};

// Generator function
$users = users(__DIR__ . '/users.csv');

// The RxPHP Observable - from generator
Observable::fromIterator($users)
    ->map($mapper)
    ->filter($filter)
    ->subscribe($logger);

$loop->run();
```

We started off by creating a simple generator function called `users()`. The great thing about generators is that they act as iterator, which makes it easy to create RxPHP observables from them using the `fromIterator()` method. Once we have the observable, we can chain few of its methods, such as `map()` and `filter()`, together. This way, we control the data stream hitting our subscribed observer.

Assume the `users.csv` file with following content:

```
"John"
"Mariya"
"Marc"
"Lucy"
```

The output of the preceding code should be something like this:

```
1487439356 | Mariya
1487439356 | Marc
stream complete!
```

Now, let's assume that we want to attach multiple observers to our `$users` stream:

```
$mailer = new CallbackObserver(
  function ($user) {
    echo 'Mailer: ', $user, PHP_EOL;
  },
  function (\Throwable $t) {
    echo 'Mailer: ', $t->getMessage(), PHP_EOL;
  },
  function () {
    echo 'Mailer stream complete!', PHP_EOL;
  }
);

$logger = new CallbackObserver(
  function ($user) {
    echo 'Logger: ', $user, PHP_EOL;
  },
  function (\Throwable $t) {
    echo 'Logger: ', $t->getMessage(), PHP_EOL;
  },
  function () {
    echo 'Logger stream complete!', PHP_EOL;
  }
);

$users = Observable::fromIterator(users(__DIR__ . '/users.csv'));
```

```
$users->subscribe($mailer);
$users->subscribe($logger);
```

This won't work. The code won't throw any error, but the result might not be what we would expect it to be:

```
Mailer: John
Logger: Mariya
Mailer: Marc
Logger: Lucy
Mailer:
Logger:
Mailer stream complete!
Logger stream complete!
```

We cannot really attach multiple subscribers this way. The first attached observer consumes the stream, which is why the second observer sees it empty. This is where the `Rx\Subject\Subject` component may come in handy.

Subject

`Rx\Subject\Subject` is an interesting component--it's a class that acts both as observable and observer. The benefit of this is seen in the following example:

```php
use \Rx\Subject\Subject;

$mailer = new class() extends Subject
{
    public function onCompleted()
    {
        echo 'mailer.onCompleted', PHP_EOL;
        parent::onCompleted();
    }

    public function onNext($val)
    {
        echo 'mailer.onNext: ', $val, PHP_EOL;
        parent::onNext($val);
    }

    public function onError(\Throwable $error)
    {
        echo 'mailer.onError', $error->getMessage(), PHP_EOL;
        parent::onError($error);
    }
};
```

```php
$logger = new class() extends Subject
{
    public function onCompleted()
    {
        echo 'logger.onCompleted', PHP_EOL;
        parent::onCompleted();
    }

    public function onNext($val)
    {
        echo 'logger.onNext: ', $val, PHP_EOL;
        parent::onNext($val);
    }

    public function onError(\Throwable $error)
    {
        echo 'logger.onError', $error->getMessage(), PHP_EOL;
        parent::onError($error);
    }
};

$users = Observable::fromIterator(users(__DIR__ . '/users.csv'));
$mailer->subscribe($logger);
$users->subscribe($mailer);
```

Using the anonymous classes, we were able to extend the Rx\Subject\Subject class on-the-fly. The underlying onCompleted(), onError(Exception $error), and onNext($value) methods are where we *tap into* our observer-related logic. Once executed, the code results in the following output:

```
mailer.onNext: John
logger.onNext: John
mailer.onNext: Mariya
logger.onNext: Mariya
mailer.onNext: Marc
logger.onNext: Marc
mailer.onNext: Lucy
logger.onNext: Lucy
mailer.onNext:
logger.onNext:
mailer.onCompleted
logger.onCompleted
```

What is happening here is that the mailer first taps into the stream, and then streams back into the logger stream. This is possible because of the dual nature of Rx\Subject\Subject. It is important to note that the logger does not observe the original stream. We can test this easily by adding the filter to $mailer:

```
// ...

$mailer
  ->filter(function ($val) {
    return strstr($val, 'Marc') == false;
  })
  ->subscribe($logger);

$users->subscribe($mailer);
```

The resulting output will now omit the user named on the logger observer:

```
mailer.onNext: John
logger.onNext: John
mailer.onNext: Mariya
logger.onNext: Mariya
mailer.onNext: Marc
mailer.onNext: Lucy
logger.onNext: Lucy
mailer.onNext:
logger.onNext:
mailer.onCompleted
logger.onCompleted
```

Operator

The observable model of RxPHP allows us to treat streams with simple and composable operations. Each of these operations is done by an individual operator. The composition of operators is possible because operators themselves mostly return observable as a result of their operation. A quick peek into the vendor\reactivex\rxphp\lib\Rx\Operator directory reveals 48 different operator implementations, classified in several different categories

- Creating o
- Transforming observables
- Filtering observables
- Combining observables
- Error-handling operators

- Observable utility operators
- Conditional and Boolean operators
- Mathematical and aggregate operators
- Connectable observable operators

The map, filter, and reduce methods are likely the most known and popular operators, so let's start our example with them:

```php
<?php

require_once __DIR__ . '/vendor/autoload.php';

use \Rx\Observable;
use \Rx\Observer\CallbackObserver;
use \React\EventLoop\Factory;
use \Rx\Scheduler;

$loop = Factory::create();

Scheduler::setDefaultFactory(function () use ($loop) {
    return new Scheduler\EventLoopScheduler($loop);
});

// Generator function
function xrange($start, $end, $step = 1)
{
    for ($i = $start; $i <= $end; $i += $step) {
        yield $i;
    }
}

// Observer
$observer = new CallbackObserver(
    function ($item) {
        echo $item, PHP_EOL;
    }
);

echo 'start', PHP_EOL;
// Observable stream, made from iterator/generator
Observable::fromIterator(xrange(1, 10, 1))
    ->map(function ($item) {
        return $item * 2;
    })
    ->filter(function ($item) {
        return $item % 3 == 0;
    })
```

```
    ->reduce(function ($x, $y) {
        return $x + $y;
    })
    ->subscribe($observer);

echo 'end', PHP_EOL;

$loop->run();
```

We started off by writing a simple generator function called `xrange()`. The beauty of the generator here is that the `xrange()` function will always take the same amount of memory, regardless of the range we choose. This gives us a great foundation to play with the ReactiveX operators. We then created a simple `$observer`, utilizing only its `$onNext` callable whilst ignoring the `$onError` and `$onCompleted` callables for the purpose of this section. We then created an observable stream from our `xrange()` function, passing it a range of 1 to 20. Finally, we got to the point where we hooked the `map()`, `filter()`, `reduce()`, and `subscribe()` method calls to our observable instance.

If we were to execute this code now, the resulting output would be number `36`. To understand where this is coming from, let's take a step back and comment out the `filter()` and `reduce()` methods:

```
Observable::fromIterator(xrange(1, 10, 1))
  ->map(function ($item) {
    return $item * 2;
  })
// ->filter(function ($item) {
  // return $item % 3 == 0;
// })
// ->reduce(function ($x, $y) {
  // return $x + $y;
// })
  ->subscribe($observer);
```

The output now is as follows:

```
start
2
4
6
8
10
12
14
16
18
```

```
20
end
```

The `map()` function transforms the emitted items by applying a function to each item. In this case, that function is `$item * 2`. Now, let's go ahead and restore the `filter()` function, but leave the `reduce()` function commented out:

```
Observable::fromIterator(xrange(1, 10, 1))
  ->map(function ($item) {
    return $item * 2;
  })
  ->filter(function ($item) {
    return $item % 3 == 0;
  })
// ->reduce(function ($x, $y) {
  // return $x + $y;
// })
  ->subscribe($observer);
```

Knowing now that the `filter()` function will receive the `map()` function output stream (2, 4, 6, ... 20), we observe the following output:

```
start
6
12
18
end
```

The `filter()` function transforms the emitted items by emitting back only those items that pass a predicate test. In this case, the predicate test is `$item % 3 == 0`, which means, it returns items evenly divisible by 3.

Finally, if we restore the `reduce()` function, the result comes back as `36`. Unlike `map()` and `filter()`, which accept a single emitted item value, the `reduce()` function callback accepts two values.

A quick change to the body of the `reduce()` callback clarifies what's going on:

```
  ->reduce(function ($x, $y) {
    $z = $x + $y;
    echo '$x: ', $x, PHP_EOL;
    echo '$y: ', $y, PHP_EOL;
    echo '$z: ', $z, PHP_EOL, PHP_EOL;
    return $z;
  })
```

This gives output as follows:

```
start
$x: 6
$y: 12
$z: 18

$x: 18
$y: 18
$z: 36

36
end
```

We can see that $x comes in as a value of the first emitted item, whereas $y comes in as a value of the second emitted item. The function then applies sum computation on them, making the return result now a first emitted item in the second iteration, basically, giving (6 + 12) => 18 => (18 + 18) => 36.

Given the sheer number of operators supported by RxPHP, we can imagine the real-life complexities we get to solve in an elegant way by simply composing a number of operators into a chain, as follows:

```
$observable
  ->operator1(function () { /* ...*/ })
  ->operator2(function () { /* ...*/ })
  ->operator3(function () { /* ...*/ })
  // ...
  ->operatorN(function () { /* ...*/ })
  ->subscribe($observer);
```

If existing operators are not enough, we can easily write our own by extending Rx\Operator\OperatorInterface.

Writing custom operators

Though RxPHP provides over 40 operators for us to use, sometimes, there may be a need to use an operator that does not exist. Consider the following case:

```php
<?php

require_once __DIR__ . '/vendor/autoload.php';

use \Rx\Observer\CallbackObserver;
use \React\EventLoop\Factory;
use \Rx\Scheduler;

$loop = Factory::create();

Scheduler::setDefaultFactory(function () use ($loop) {
    return new Scheduler\EventLoopScheduler($loop);
});

// correct
$users = serialize(['John', 'Mariya', 'Marc', 'Lucy']);

// faulty
// $users = str_replace('i:', '', serialize(['John', 'Mariya', 'Marc',
'Lucy']));

$observer = new CallbackObserver(
    function ($value) {
        echo 'Observer.$onNext: ', print_r($value, true), PHP_EOL;
    },
    function (\Throwable $t) {
        echo 'Observer.$onError: ', $t->getMessage(), PHP_EOL;
    },
    function () {
        echo 'Observer.$onCompleted', PHP_EOL;
    }
);

Rx\Observable::just($users)
    ->map(function ($value) {
        return unserialize($value);
    })
    ->subscribe($observer);

$loop->run();
```

Executing this code with the *correct* $users variable gives us the following expected output:

```
$ php index.php
Observer.$onNext: Array
(
    [0] => John
    [1] => Mariya
    [2] => Marc
    [3] => Lucy
)

Observer.$onCompleted
```

However, if we were to remove the comment in front of the *faulty* $user variable, the output comes out slightly unexpected, or at least not how we would like to handle it:

```
$ php index.php
Observer.$onNext:
Observer.$onCompleted
```

What we really want is to shift the unserialize logic into the RxPHP operator, and have it gracefully handle the unsuccessful `unserialize()` attempts. Luckily, writing a custom operator is an easy task. A quick look into the `vendor/reactivex/rxphp/src/Operator/OperatorInterface.php` file reveals the following interface:

```php
<?php

declare(strict_types=1);

namespace Rx\Operator;

use Rx\DisposableInterface;
use Rx\ObservableInterface;
use Rx\ObserverInterface;

interface OperatorInterface
{
    public function __invoke(
        ObservableInterface $observable,
        ObserverInterface $observer
    ): DisposableInterface;
}
```

Easy enough, the interface only requires a single __invoke() method implementation. We wrote about the __invoke() method extensively in Chapter 4, *Magic Behind Magic Methods*. This method gets called when we try to call an object as a function. OperatorInterface, in this case, lists three arguments to the __invoke() method, two of which are mandatory:

- $observable: This will be our input observable to which we subscribe
- $observer: This is where we will emit our output value

With that in mind, the following is an implementation of our custom UnserializeOperator:

```php
<?php

use \Rx\DisposableInterface;
use \Rx\ObservableInterface;
use \Rx\ObserverInterface;
use \Rx\SchedulerInterface;
use \Rx\Observer\CallbackObserver;
use \Rx\Operator\OperatorInterface;

class UnserializeOperator implements OperatorInterface
{
    /**
     * @param \Rx\ObservableInterface $observable
     * @param \Rx\ObserverInterface $observer
     * @param \Rx\SchedulerInterface $scheduler
     * @return \Rx\DisposableInterface
     */
    public function __invoke(
        ObservableInterface $observable,
        ObserverInterface $observer,
        SchedulerInterface $scheduler = null
    ): DisposableInterface
    {
        $callbackObserver = new CallbackObserver(
            function ($value) use ($observer) {
                if ($unsValue = unserialize($value)) {
                    $observer->onNext($unsValue);
                } else {
                    $observer->onError(
                        new InvalidArgumentException('Faulty serialized
string.')
                    );
                }
            },
```

```
        function ($error) use ($observer) {
            $observer->onError($error);
        },
        function () use ($observer) {
            $observer->onCompleted();
        }
    );

    // ->subscribe(...) => DisposableInterface
    return $observable->subscribe($callbackObserver, $scheduler);
    }
}
```

Unfortunately, we cannot chain our operator directly as we chain the RxPHP operators. We need to help ourselves with the `lift()` operator:

```
Rx\Observable::just($users)
  ->lift(function () {
   return new UnserializeOperator();
  })
  ->subscribe($observer);
```

With `UnserializeOperator` in place, the faulty serialized `$users` string now gives the following output:

```
$ php index.php
Observer.$onError: Faulty serialized string.
```

Our operator is now successfully handling errors, in that, it is delegating them onto the observer `onError` callback.

> Making the best out of RxPHP is mostly about knowing the ins and outs of its operators. The `vendor/reactivex/rxphp/demo/` directory provides quite a few operator usage examples. It is worth spending some time going through each.

Non-blocking IO

Using the RxPHP extensions opens up quite a few possibilities. Its observables, operators, and subscribers/observers implementations are certainly powerful. What they don't provide, however, is asynchronicity. This is where the React library comes into play, by providing an event-driven, non-blocking I/O abstraction layer. Before we touch upon React, let's first lay out a trivial example of blocking versus non-blocking I/O in PHP.

We create a small *beacon* script that will merely generate some **standard output (stdout)** over time. Then, we will create a script that reads from the **standard input (stdin)** and see how it behaves when reading is done in the stream blocking and stream non-blocking mode.

We start by creating the `beacon.php` file with the following content:

```php
<?php

$now = time();

while ($now + $argv[1] > time()) {
  echo 'signal ', microtime(), PHP_EOL;
  usleep(200000); // 0.2s
}
```

The use of `$argv[1]` hints that the file is intended to be run from console. Using `$argv[1]`, we provide a number of seconds we wish the script to run. Within the loop, we have a **signal...** output, followed by a short `0.2` seconds of script sleep.

With our beacon script in place, let's go ahead and create `index.php` file with the following content:

```php
<?php

// stream_set_blocking(STDIN, 0);
// stream_set_blocking(STDIN, 1); // default

echo 'start', PHP_EOL;

while (($line = fgets(STDIN)) !== false) {
  echo $line;
}

echo 'end', PHP_EOL;
```

Aside from two obvious start/end outputs, we utilize the `fgets()` function to read from the standard input. `stream_set_blocking()` method is deliberately left commented out for the moment. Notice that the two scripts are completely unrelated to each other. At no point is `index.php` referencing the `beacon.php` file. This is because we will use the console and its pipe (|) to bridge the stdout of the `beacon.php` script to a stdin consumed by the `index.php`:

```
php beacon.php 2 | php index.php
```

The resulting output is shown here:

```
root@vultr:~/php7# php beacon.php 2 | php index.php
start
signal 0.69625400 1487508118
signal 0.89643400 1487508118
signal 0.09701900 1487508119
signal 0.29766900 1487508119
signal 0.49821000 1487508119
signal 0.69866300 1487508119
signal 0.89913000 1487508119
end
root@vultr:~/php7# 
```

There is nothing wrong with this output; this is what we expected. We first see the **start** string showing up, then several occurrences of **signal...**, and finally, the **end** string. However, there lies the catch, all of the **signal...** bits that are pulled by the `fgets()` function from stdout are an example of blocking IO. While we might not perceive it as such in this small example, we could easily imagine a beacon script sending output from a very large file, or a slow database connection. Our `index.php` script would simply hang its execution blocked during that time, or, better to say, it would wait for the `while (($line = fgets(STDIN)`... line to resolve.

How can we resolve the problem? First, we need to understand that this is not really a technical problem as such. There is nothing wrong with waiting to receive data. No matter how much we abstract things, there will always be that someone or something who needs to wait for data somewhere. The trick is positioning the somewhere bit at the right place, so it does not stand in the way of user experience. The JavaScript promises and callbacks are one example of where we may want to place that somewhere. Let's take a look at the simple AJAX call made by the JavaScript jQuery library:

```
console.log('start-time: ' + Date.now());

$.ajax({
  url: 'http://foggyline.net/',
  success: function (result) {
    console.log('result-time: ' + Date.now())
    console.log(result)
  }
});

console.log('end-time: ' + Date.now());
```

The following screenshot shows the resulting output:

```
start-time: 1487510037248
end-time: 1487510037253
result-time: 1487510037771
<!doctype html>
<html>
  <head>
    <meta charset="utf-8">
    <meta http-equiv="X-UA-Compatible" content="chrome=1">
    <title>foggyline by ajzele</title>
```

Notice how `start-time` and `end-time` have been outputted before the `result-time`. The JavaScript did not block the execution at the `$.ajax({...` line, like PHP did on its `while (($line = fgets(STDIN)...` line in the preceding example. This is because JavaScript runtime is fundamentally different than PHP. The asynchronous nature of JavaScript relies on the chunks of code to split off and execute separately, then update what's needed via the callback mechanism, a functionality made possible by JavaScript event loop based concurrency model and message queue mechanism. The callback in this case was the anonymous function assigned to the success property of the `ajax()` method call. Once the AJAX call executed successfully, it called the assigned `success` function, which in turn resulted last on the output as the AJAX call takes time to execute.

Now, let's go back to our little PHP example and modify the `index.php` file by removing the comment we placed in front of the `stream_set_blocking(STDIN, 0);` expression. Running the command again, with the pipe (|) this time, now results in the output much like the following:

```
root@vultr:~/php7# php beacon.php 2 | php index.php
start
signal 0.12519300 1487511096
end
root@vultr:~/php7#
```

This time, the `while ((($line = fgets(STDIN)...` line did not block the execution by waiting for `beacon.php` to finish. The trick lies in the `stream_set_blocking()` function, as it enables us to control the stream blocking mode, which by default is set to block I/O. Let's go ahead and make a more PHP-like example, this time without using the console pipe. We will leave the `beacon.php` file as it is, but modify the `index.php` file as follows:

```php
<?php

echo 'start', PHP_EOL;

$process = proc_open('php beacon.php 2', [
  ['pipe', 'r'], // STDIN
  ['pipe', 'w'], // STDOUT
  ['file', './signals.log', 'a'] //STDERR
], $pipes);

//stream_set_blocking($pipes[1], 1); // Blocking I/O
//stream_set_blocking($pipes[1], 0); // Non-blocking I/O

while (proc_get_status($process)['running']) {
  usleep(100000); // 0.1s
  if ($signal = fgets($pipes[1])) {
    echo $signal;
  } else {
    echo '--- beacon lost ---', PHP_EOL;
  }
}

fclose($pipes[1]);
proc_close($process);

echo 'end', PHP_EOL;
```

We started off with a `proc_open()` function, which allows us to execute a command and open file pointers for standard input, output, and error. The `'php beacon.php 2'` argument does pretty much what our console command did, in regards to the part of command left of the pipe character. The way we catch an output of beacon script is using the `fgets()` function. However, we are not doing it directly, we are doing it through the while loop here, whereas the condition is the process `running` state. In other words, as long as the process is running, check whether there is any new output from the newly created process or not. If there is an output, show it; if not, show the **--- beacon lost ---** message. The following screenshot shows the resulting output with default (blocking) I/O:

If we now remove the comment in front of `stream_set_blocking($pipes[1], 0);`, the resulting output changes into this:

```
root@vultr:~/php7# php index.php
start
signal 0.21908400 1487512542
--- beacon lost ---
signal 0.41932000 1487512542
--- beacon lost ---
signal 0.61947000 1487512542
--- beacon lost ---
signal 0.81963700 1487512542
--- beacon lost ---
signal 0.01980000 1487512543
--- beacon lost ---
signal 0.21999000 1487512543
--- beacon lost ---
signal 0.42014000 1487512543
--- beacon lost ---
signal 0.62030500 1487512543
--- beacon lost ---
signal 0.82046500 1487512543
--- beacon lost ---
--- beacon lost ---
end
root@vultr:~/php7#
```

The output here shows the non-blocking relationship between the beacon and our running script. Unblocking the stream, we were able to utilize the `fgets()` function, which would normally block the script to periodically check on the standard input for as long as the process is running. In a nutshell, we are now able to read the output from a sub-process, while being able to initialize a few more of the sub-processes along the way. Although the example itself is a long-long way from the convenience of the jQuery promise/callback example, it is a first step towards the complexities behind blocking and non-blocking I/O, as it affects the way we write our code. This is where we will come to appreciate the role of the RxPHP observables and React event loops.

Using React

React is a library that makes it possible to event-driven programming in PHP, much like JavaScript does. Based on the reactor pattern, it essentially acts as an event loop, allowing various other third-party libraries using its components to write asynchronous code.

The page at `https://en.wikipedia.org/wiki/Reactor_pattern` states, *The reactor design pattern is an event handling pattern for handling service requests delivered concurrently to a service handler by one or more inputs.*

The library is available at `https://github.com/reactphp/react`

Installing React

The React library is available as a Composer `react/react` package. Assuming we are still in our project directory where we installed RxPHP, we can simply execute the following command in order to add React to our project:

```
composer require react/react
```

This should give us an output similar to the following one:

```
root@vultr:~/php7# composer require react/react
Running composer as root/super user is highly discouraged as packages, plugins and scripts cannot always be trusted
Using version ^0.4.2 for react/react
./composer.json has been updated
Loading composer repositories with package information
Updating dependencies (including require-dev)
  - Installing evenement/evenement (v2.0.0)
    Downloading: 100%

  - Installing react/stream (v0.4.6)
    Downloading: 100%

  - Installing react/promise (v2.5.0)
    Loading from cache

  - Installing react/event-loop (v0.4.2)
    Loading from cache

  - Installing react/socket (v0.4.6)
    Downloading: 100%

  - Installing react/cache (v0.4.1)
    Downloading: 100%

  - Installing react/dns (v0.4.4)
    Downloading: 100%

  - Installing react/socket-client (v0.4.6)
    Downloading: 100%

  - Installing psr/http-message (1.0.1)
    Downloading: 100%

  - Installing ringcentral/psr7 (1.2.1)
    Downloading: 100%

  - Installing react/http (v0.4.4)
    Downloading: 100%

  - Installing guzzlehttp/psr7 (1.3.1)
    Downloading: 100%

  - Installing react/http-client (v0.4.15)
    Downloading: 100%

  - Installing react/child-process (v0.4.1)
    Downloading: 100%

  - Installing react/react (v0.4.2)
    Downloading: 100%

react/event-loop suggests installing ext-libevent (>=0.1.0)
react/event-loop suggests installing ext-event (~1.0)
react/event-loop suggests installing ext-libev (*)
react/react suggests installing ext-libevent (Allows for use of a more performant event-loop implementation.)
react/react suggests installing ext-libev (Allows for use of a more performant event-loop implementation.)
react/react suggests installing ext-event (Allows for use of a more performant event-loop implementation.)
Writing lock file
Generating autoload files
root@vultr:~/php7#
```

We can see quite a few interesting `react/*` packages being pulled in, `react/event-loop` being one of them. The messages suggesting we should install one of the more performant loop implementations are definitely worthy of interest, though out of the scope of this book.

React event loop

Without any of the suggested event loop extensions, React event loop defaults to the `React\EventLoop\StreamSelectLoop` class, which is a `stream_select()` function-based event loop.

The page at `http://php.net/manual/en/function.stream-select.php` states, *The stream_select() function accepts arrays of streams and waits for them to change status*

As we already saw in our previous examples, making an event loop in React is simple

```php
<?php

require_once __DIR__ . '/vendor/autoload.php';

use \React\EventLoop\Factory;
use \Rx\Scheduler;

$loop = Factory::create();

Scheduler::setDefaultFactory(function () use ($loop) {
    return new Scheduler\EventLoopScheduler($loop);
});

// Within the loop

$loop->run();
```

We are using the `Factory::create()` static function, which is implemented as follows:

```php
class Factory
{
  public static function create()
  {
    if (function_exists('event_base_new')) {
      return new LibEventLoop();
    } elseif (class_exists('libev\EventLoop', false)) {
      return new LibEvLoop;
    } elseif (class_exists('EventBase', false)) {
      return new ExtEventLoop;
```

```
        }
        return new StreamSelectLoop();
    }
}
```

Here, we can see that unless we have ext-libevent, ext-event, or ext-libev installed, then the StreamSelectLoop implementation is used.

Each iteration of the loop is a tick. The event loop tracks timers and streams. Without either of these two, there are no ticks, and the loop simply

```php
<?php

require_once __DIR__ . '/vendor/autoload.php';

use \React\EventLoop\Factory;
use \Rx\Scheduler;

echo 'STEP#1 ', time(), PHP_EOL;

$loop = Factory::create();

Scheduler::setDefaultFactory(function () use ($loop) {
    return new Scheduler\EventLoopScheduler($loop);
});

echo 'STEP#2 ', time(), PHP_EOL;

$loop->run();

echo 'STEP#3 ', time(), PHP_EOL;
```

The preceding code gives us the following output:

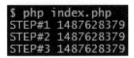

As soon as we add some timers, the situation ch

```php
<?php

require_once __DIR__ . '/vendor/autoload.php';

use \React\EventLoop\Factory;
use \Rx\Scheduler;

echo 'STEP#1 ', time(), PHP_EOL;

$loop = Factory::create();

Scheduler::setDefaultFactory(function () use ($loop) {
    return new Scheduler\EventLoopScheduler($loop);
});

echo 'STEP#2 ', PHP_EOL;

$loop->addTimer(2, function () {
    echo 'timer#1 ', time(), PHP_EOL;
});

echo 'STEP#3 ', time(), PHP_EOL;

$loop->addTimer(5, function () {
    echo 'timer#2 ', time(), PHP_EOL;
});

echo 'STEP#4 ', time(), PHP_EOL;

$loop->addTimer(3, function () {
    echo 'timer#3 ', time(), PHP_EOL;
});

echo 'STEP#5 ', time(), PHP_EOL;
$loop->run();

echo 'STEP#6 ', time(), PHP_EOL;
```

The preceding code gives us the following output:

```
$ php index.php
STEP#1 1487628504
STEP#2
STEP#3 1487628504
STEP#4 1487628504
STEP#5 1487628504
timer#1 1487628506
timer#3 1487628507
timer#2 1487628509
STEP#6 1487628509
```

Notice the order of the timer output, and the time next to each. Our loop still managed to end, as our timers expired. To keep the loop running constantly, we can add a *periodic timer*

```php
<?php

require_once __DIR__ . '/vendor/autoload.php';

use \React\EventLoop\Factory;
use \Rx\Scheduler;

echo 'STEP#1 ', time(), PHP_EOL;

$loop = Factory::create();

Scheduler::setDefaultFactory(function () use ($loop) {
    return new Scheduler\EventLoopScheduler($loop);
});

echo 'STEP#2 ', PHP_EOL;

$loop->addPeriodicTimer(1, function () {
    echo 'timer ', time(), PHP_EOL;
});

echo 'STEP#3 ', time(), PHP_EOL;

$loop->run();

echo 'STEP#4 ', time(), PHP_EOL;
```

The preceding code gives us the following output:

```
$ php index.php
STEP#1 1487628967
STEP#2
STEP#3 1487628967
timer 1487628968
timer 1487628969
timer 1487628970
timer 1487628971
timer 1487628972
timer 1487628973
```

This loop will now continue to produce the same **timer...** output until we hit *Ctrl + C* on the console. We might be wondering, how does this differ from a PHP `while` loop? Generally, the `while` loop is of polling type, as it continuously checks things, leaving little to no room for the processor to switch tasks. The event loop uses more efficient interrupt-driven I/O instead of polling. However, the default `StreamSelectLoop` uses the `while` loop for its event-loop implementation.

The addition of timers and streams is what makes it useful, as it abstracts the hard bits from us.

Observables and event loop

Let's go ahead and see how we can make our observables work with an event loop:

```php
<?php

require_once __DIR__ . '/vendor/autoload.php';

use \React\EventLoop\Factory;
use \Rx\Scheduler;
use \Rx\Observable;
use \Rx\Subject\Subject;
use \Rx\Scheduler\EventLoopScheduler;

$loop = Factory::create();

Scheduler::setDefaultFactory(function () use ($loop) {
    return new Scheduler\EventLoopScheduler($loop);
});

$stdin = fopen('php://stdin', 'r');

stream_set_blocking($stdin, 0);
```

```php
$observer = new class() extends Subject
{
    public function onCompleted()
    {
        echo '$observer.onCompleted: ', PHP_EOL;
        parent::onCompleted();
    }

    public function onNext($val)
    {
        echo '$observer.onNext: ', $val, PHP_EOL;
        parent::onNext($val);
    }

    public function onError(\Throwable $error)
    {
        echo '$observer.onError: ', $error->getMessage(), PHP_EOL;
        parent::onError($error);
    }
};

$loop = Factory::create();

$scheduler = new EventLoopScheduler($loop);

$disposable = Observable::interval(500, $scheduler)
    ->map(function () use ($stdin) {
        return trim(fread($stdin, 1024));
    })
    ->filter(function ($str) {
        return strlen($str) > 0;
    })
    ->subscribe($observer);

$observer->filter(function ($value) {
    return $value == 'quit';
})->subscribeCallback(function ($value) use ($disposable) {
    echo 'disposed!', PHP_EOL;
    $disposable->dispose();
});

$loop->run();
```

There is quite a lot going on here. We started off by creating a standard input and then flagging it as non-blocking. We then created the observer of the `Subject` type. This is because, as we will see later, we want our observer to behave like observer and observable. We then instantiated the loop, and passed onto `EventLoopScheduler`. In order for observables to work with the loop, we need to wrap them with a scheduler. We then used the instance of `IntervalObservable`, making its `map()` operator read the standard input, whereas the `filter()` operator was set to filter out any empty inputs (pressing Enter key on console with no text). We stored this observable into a `$disposable` variable. Finally, given that our `$observer` was an instance of `Subject`, we were able to attach the `filter()` operator to it as well as `subscribeCallback()`. We instructed the `filter()` operator here to only filter out the input with the **quit** string. Once `quit` was typed onto the console, followed by the *Enter* key, `subscribeCallback()` was executed. Within `subscribeCallback()`, we have a `$disposable->dispose()` expression. Calling the disposable's dispose method automatically unsubscribed `$observer` from `$observable`. Given that there were no other timers or streams within the loop, this automatically terminated the loop.

The following screenshot shows the console output of the preceding code:

```
$ php index.php
start
John
$observer.onNext: John
Mariya
$observer.onNext: Mariya
Marc
$observer.onNext: Marc
quit
$observer.onNext: quit
disposed!
end
```

When the code was run, we first saw the `start` string, then we typed in `John` and press , then we say **$observer.onNext...**, which repeated all the way until we typed `quit`.

The React event loop opens an interesting possibility for us, much like we are used to seeing in JavaScript and browser. While there is much more to be said about React, this should be enough to get us started with RxPHP and React combination.

Summary

In this chapter, we touched upon RxPHP and React, the two libraries that promise to bring reactive programming to PHP. While RxPHP brings the powerful observables packaged in composable-looking syntax, React enriches our experience with event-loop implementation. To carefully, we should emphasize that this is still a relatively experimental area for PHP, and far from ready for mainstream production use. It does, however, demonstrate that PHP is not limited with its runtime capabilities and shows promise in the reactive area.

Moving forward, we will shift our focus on common design patterns found in modern PHP applications.

10
Common Design Patterns

Those new to software development tend to focus their efforts on mastering the programming language. Once that barrier is passed, it is time to embrace **design patterns**, as writing high-quality and complex software is hardly possible without them. Mostly attributed to experienced developer use, design patterns represent a well established solution to common challenges faced in our applications. Successfully applying design patterns is likely to lead to more extensible, reusable, maintainable, and adaptable code.

The examples within this chapter are not meant to be copied and pasted. They merely serve a purpose of representing one possible implementation of design patterns. After all, real-life applications are all about details. Furthermore, there are plenty of other design patterns out there, with new ones being invented as technology and programming paradigms shift.

In this chapter, we will take a look at a few possible implementations of design patterns in PHP:

- Base patterns
    - The registry pattern
- Creational patterns
    - The singleton pattern
    - The prototype pattern
    - The abstract factory pattern
    - The builder pattern
    - The object pool pattern
- Behavioral patterns
    - The strategy pattern
    - The observer pattern
    - The lazy initialization pattern
    - The chain of responsibility pattern

- Structural patterns
    - The decorator pattern

Base patterns

In the coming section, we will take a look at the base pattern: the registry pattern.

The registry pattern

The registry pattern is an interesting one. It allows us to store and retrieve objects for later use. The process of storing and retrieving is based on the keys we define. Depending on the data scope, the association of keys and objects is made global across a process, thread, or a session, allowing us to retrieve the objects from anywhere within the data scope.

The following example demonstrates a possible registry pattern implementation:

```php
<?php

class Registry
{
    private
        $registry = [];

    public
    function get($key)
    {
        if (isset($this->registry[$key])) {
            return $this->registry[$key];
        }
        return null;
    }

    public
    function set($key, $value, $graceful = false)
    {
        if (isset($this->registry[$key])) {
            if ($graceful) {
                return;
            }
            throw new \RuntimeException('Registry key "' . $key . '"already
exists');
        }
        $this->registry[$key] = $value;
```

```
        }

        public
        function remove($key)
        {
            if (isset($this->registry[$key])) {
                unset($this->registry[$key]);
            }
        }

        public
        function __destruct()
        {
            $keys = array_keys($this->registry);
            array_walk($keys, [$this, 'remove']);
        }
    }

    // Client use
    class User
    {
        public $name;
    }

    $user1 = new User();
    $user1->name = 'John';
    $user2 = new User();
    $user2->name = 'Marc';

    $registry = new Registry();
    $registry->set('employee', $user1);
    $registry->set('director', $user2);
    echo $registry->get('director')->name; // Marc
```

Our `Registry` class implementation has three key methods: `get()`, `set()`, `remove()`. The `set()` method allows graceful behavior based on the `$graceful` parameter; otherwise, it triggers the `RuntimeException` for the existing key. We also defined a `__destruct` method, as a sort of a cleanup mechanism that removes each item in the registry when the `$registry` instance is destroyed.

Creational patterns

In this section, we will take a look at the creational patterns, such as the singleton, prototype, abstract factory, and builder patterns.

The singleton pattern

The singleton is among the first design patterns most developers learn. The goal of this design pattern is to limit the number of class instantiations to only one. What this means is that using the new keyword on a class will always return one and the same object instance. This is a powerful concept that allows us to implement all sorts of application-wide objects, such as loggers, mailers, registries, and other bits of functionality that we may want to act as singletons. However, as we will soon see, we will avoid the new keyword altogether, and instantiate an object via the static class method.

The following example demonstrates a possible singleton pattern implementation:

```php
<?php

class Logger
{
    private static $instance;

    const TYPE_ERROR = 'error';
    const TYPE_WARNING = 'warning';
    const TYPE_NOTICE = 'notice';

    protected function __construct()
    {
        // empty?!
    }

    private function __clone()
    {
        // empty?!
    }

    private function __wakeup()
    {
        // empty?!
    }

    public static function getInstance()
    {
        if (!isset(self::$instance)) {
            // late static binding
            self::$instance = new self;
        }
        return self::$instance;
    }

    public function log($type, $message)
```

```
    {
        return sprintf('Logging %s: %s', $type, $message);
    }
}

// Client use
echo Logger::getInstance()->log(Logger::TYPE_NOTICE, 'test');
```

The `Logger` class uses the static member `$instance` to keep an instance of one `self`, as per the implementation of the `getInstance()` method. We defined `__construct` as `protected` in order to prevent new instance creation via the `new` operator. The `__clone()` method was defined as `private` in order to prevent instance cloning via the `clone` operator. Similarly, the `__wakeup()` method was also defined as private, in order to prevent instance unserializing via the `unserialize()` function. These few simple restrictions make for a class that acts as a singleton. In order to fetch an instance, all it takes is calling the `getInstance()` class method.

The prototype pattern

The prototype pattern is about creating new objects by means of cloning them. This is quite a concept, as we are no longer using the `new` keyword to create new objects. The PHP language provides a special `clone` keyword to assist with object cloning.

The following example demonstrates a possible prototype pattern implementation:

```php
<?php

class Logger
{
    public $channel = 'N/A';
}

class SystemLogger extends Logger
{
    public function __construct()
    {
        $this->channel = 'STDIN';
    }

    public function log($data)
    {
        return sprintf('Logging %s to %s.', $data, $this->channel);
    }
}
```

```
    public function __clone()
    {
        /* additional changes for (after)clone behavior? */
    }
}

// Client use
$systemLogger = new SystemLogger();
echo $systemLogger->log('test');

$logger = clone $systemLogger;
echo $logger->log('test2');

$logger->channel = 'mail';
echo $logger->log('test3');

// Logging test to STDIN.
// Logging test2 to STDIN.
// Logging test3 to mail.
```

Normally, all it takes to clone an object is to use an expression such as `$clonedObj = clone $obj;`. This, however, does not give us any control over the cloning process. PHP objects can be heavy, with lots of members and references. Sometimes, we would like to impose certain limitations on the cloned object. This is where the magic `__clone()` method comes in handy. The `__clone()` method triggers after the cloning process is done, which is something to keep in mind for possible cleanup code implementations.

The abstract factory pattern

Abstract factory encapsulates a group of individual factories that have a common functionality. It does so without specifying their concrete classes. This makes it easier to write portable code, because clients can interchange concrete implementations without changing the code.

The following example demonstrates a possible abstract factory pattern implementation:

```
<?php

interface Button
{
    public function render();
}

interface FormFactory
{
```

```php
        public function createButton();
    }

    class LoginButton implements Button
    {
        public function render()
        {
            return '<button name="login">Login</button>';
        }
    }

    class RegisterButton implements Button
    {
        public function render()
        {
            return '<button name="register">Register</button>';
        }
    }

    class LoginFactory implements FormFactory
    {
        public function createButton()
        {
            return new LoginButton();
        }
    }

    class RegisterFactory implements FormFactory
    {
        public function createButton()
        {
            return new RegisterButton();
        }
    }

    // Client
    $loginButtonFactory = new LoginFactory();
    $button = $loginButtonFactory->createButton();
    echo $button->render();

    $registerButtonFactory = new RegisterFactory();
    $button = $registerButtonFactory->createButton();
    echo $button->render();
```

We started off by creating two simple interfaces, `Button` and `FormFactory`. The `Button` interface defines a single `render()` method, which we then implement through two concrete class implementations, `LoginButton` and `RegisterButton`. The two `FormFactory` implementations, `LoginFactory` and `RegisterFactory`, then instantiate the corresponding button classes as part of their `createButton()` method implementation. The client uses only the `LoginFactory` and `RegisterFactory` instances, thus avoiding directly instantiating concrete button classes.

The builder pattern

The builder pattern is quite a handy one, especially when it comes to large applications. It separates the construction of a complex object from its representation. This makes it possible for the same construction process to create numerous representations.

The following example demonstrates a possible *builder* pattern implementation using the `Image` class as an example:

```php
<?php

class Image
{
    private $width;
    private $height;

    public function getWidth()
    {
        return $this->width;
    }

    public function setWidth($width)
    {
        $this->width = $width;
        return $this;
    }

    public function getHeight()
    {
        return $this->height;
    }

    public function setHeight($height)
    {
        $this->height = $height;
        return $this;
```

```
        }
    }

    interface ImageBuilderInterface
    {
        public function setWidth($width);

        public function setHeight($height);

        public function getResult();
    }

    class ImageBuilder implements ImageBuilderInterface
    {
        private $image;

        public function __construct()
        {
            $this->image = new Image();
        }

        public function setWidth($width)
        {
            $this->image->setWidth($width);
            return $this;
        }

        public function setHeight($height)
        {
            $this->image->setHeight($height);
            return $this;
        }

        public function getResult()
        {
            return $this->image;
        }
    }

    class ImageBuildDirector
    {
        private $builder;

        public function __construct(ImageBuilder $builder)
        {
            $this->builder = $builder;
        }
```

```
    public function build()
    {
        $this->builder->setWidth(120);
        $this->builder->setHeight(80);
        return $this;
    }

    public function getImage()
    {
        return $this->builder->getResult();
    }
}

// Client use
$imageBuilder = new ImageBuilder();
$imageBuildDirector = new ImageBuildDirector($imageBuilder);
$image = $imageBuildDirector->build()->getImage();

var_dump($image);
// object(Image)#2 (2) { ["width":"Image":private]=> int(120)
["height":"Image":private]=> int(80) }
```

We started off with a simple Image class that provides width and height properties and corresponding getters and setters. We then created the ImageBuilderInterface interface, which defines the image width and height setter methods, along with the getResult() method. We then created an ImageBuilder concrete class that implements the ImageBuilderInterface interface. The client instantiates the ImageBuilder class. Another concrete class, ImageBuildDirector, wraps the creation or builder code within its build() method by working with the instance of ImageBuilder passed through its constructor.

The object pool pattern

The object pool pattern manages class instances--objects. It is used in situations where we would like to limit unnecessary class instantiation due to resource-intense operations. The object pool acts much like a registry for objects, from which clients can pick up necessary objects later on.

The following example demonstrates a possible object pool pattern implementation:

```php
<?php

class ObjectPool
{
    private $instances = [];

    public function load($key)
    {
        return $this->instances[$key];
    }

    public function save($object, $key)
    {
        $this->instances[$key] = $object;
    }
}

class User
{
    public function hello($name)
    {
        return 'Hello ' . $name;
    }
}

// Client use
$pool = new ObjectPool();

$user = new User();
$key = spl_object_hash($user);

$pool->save($user, $key);

// code...

$user = $pool->load($key);
echo $user->hello('John');
```

Using nothing but an array and two methods, we were able to implement a simple object pool. The save() method adds the object to the $instances array, while the load() method returns it to the client. The client, in this case, is in charge of keeping track of the key under which the object is saved. Objects themselves aren't destroyed after their use, as they remain in the pool.

Behavioral patterns

In this section, we will go through the behavioral patterns such as strategy, observer, lazy initialization, and chain of responsibility.

The strategy pattern

The strategy pattern comes in handy where we have multiple chunks of code performing similar operations. It defines an encapsulated and interchangeable family of algorithms. Imagine an order checkout process where we want to implement different shipment providers, such as UPS and FedEx.

The following example demonstrates a possible strategy pattern implementation:

```php
<?php

interface ShipmentStrategy
{
    public function calculate($amount);
}

class UPSShipment implements ShipmentStrategy
{
    public function calculate($amount)
    {
        return 'UPSShipment...';
    }
}

class FedExShipment implements ShipmentStrategy
{
    public function calculate($amount)
    {
        return 'FedExShipment...';
    }
}

class Checkout
{
    private $amount = 0;

    public function __construct($amount = 0)
    {
        $this->amount = $amount;
    }
```

```
    public function estimateShipment()
    {
        if ($this->amount > 199.99) {
            $shipment = new FedExShipment();
        } else {
            $shipment = new UPSShipment();
        }

        return $shipment->calculate($this->amount);
    }
}

// Client use
$checkout = new Checkout(19.99);
echo $checkout->estimateShipment(); // UPSShipment...

$checkout = new Checkout(499.99);
echo $checkout->estimateShipment(); // FedExShipment...
```

We started off by defining a `ShipmentStrategy` interface with a `calculate()` method. We then defined the `UPSShipment` and `FedExShipment` classes which implement the `ShipmentStrategy` interface. With these two concrete shipment classes in place, we made a `Checkout` class that encapsulates the two shipment options in its `estimateShipment()` method. The client then calls the `estimateShipment()` method on the `Checkout` instance. Depending on the amount passed on, a different shipment calculation kicks in. Using this pattern, we are free to add new shipment calculations without changing the client.

The observer pattern

The observer pattern is quite a popular one. It allows for an event subscription type of behavior. We differentiate the subject and observer(s) type of objects. The observer is an object subscribed to subject object state change. When the subject changes its state, it notifies all of its observers automatically.

The following example demonstrates a possible observer pattern implementation:

```
<?php

class CheckoutSuccess implements \SplSubject
{
    protected $salesOrder;
    protected $observers;
```

```php
    public function __construct($salesOrder)
    {
        $this->salesOrder = $salesOrder;
        $this->observers = new \SplObjectStorage();
    }

    public function attach(\SplObserver $observer)
    {
        $this->observers->attach($observer);
    }

    public function detach(\SplObserver $observer)
    {
        $this->observers->detach($observer);
    }

    public function notify()
    {
        foreach ($this->observers as $observer) {
            $observer->update($this);
        }
    }

    public function getSalesOrder()
    {
        return $this->salesOrder;
    }
}

class SalesOrder
{
}

class Mailer implements \SplObserver
{
    public function update(\SplSubject $subject)
    {
        echo 'Mailing ', get_class($subject->getSalesOrder()), PHP_EOL;
    }
}

class Logger implements \SplObserver
{
    public function update(\SplSubject $subject)
    {
        echo 'Logging ', get_class($subject->getSalesOrder()), PHP_EOL;
    }
}
```

```
$salesOrder = new SalesOrder();
$checkoutSuccess = new CheckoutSuccess($salesOrder);
// some code...
$checkoutSuccess->attach(new Mailer());
// some code...
$checkoutSuccess->attach(new Logger());
// some code...
$checkoutSuccess->notify();
```

The PHP `\SplSubject` and `\SplObserver` interfaces allow an observer pattern implementation. Our checkout success example uses these interfaces to implement `CheckoutSuccess` as a class for the subject type of object, and `Mailer` and `Logger` as classes for the observer type of object. Using the `attach()` method of a `CheckoutSuccess` instance, we attached both observers to the subject. Once the subject `notify()` method is called, the individual observer `update()` methods get triggered. The `getSalesOrder()` method calls might come as a surprise, as there is no actual `getSalesOrder()` method on direct instances of the `SplSubject` object. However, the two `update(\SplSubject $subject)` method calls in our example will be receiving an instance of `CheckoutSuccess`. Otherwise, type-casting the `$subject` argument directly to `CheckoutSuccess` would give us a PHP fatal error as follows.

```
PHP Fatal error: Declaration of Logger::update(CheckoutSuccess $subject)
must be compatible with SplObserver::update(SplSubject $SplSubject)
```

The lazy initialization pattern

The lazy initialization pattern is useful for addressing objects whose instantiation is likely to be resource-intense. The idea is to delay the actual resource intense operation until its result is actually required. The PDF generation is an example of a light to moderately resource-intense operation.

The following example demonstrates a possible lazy initialization pattern implementation based on PDF generation:

```php
<?php

interface PdfInterface
{
    public function generate();
}

class Pdf implements PdfInterface
{
    private $data;
```

```php
    public function __construct($data)
    {
        $this->data = $data;
        // Imagine resource intensive pdf generation here
        sleep(3);
    }

    public function generate()
    {
        echo 'pdf: ' . $this->data;
    }
}

class ProxyPdf implements PdfInterface
{
    private $pdf = null;
    private $data;

    public function __construct($data)
    {
        $this->data = $data;
    }

    public function generate()
    {
        if (is_null($this->pdf)) {
            $this->pdf = new Pdf($this->data);
        }
        $this->pdf->generate();
    }
}

// Client
$pdf = new Pdf('<h1>Hello</h1>'); // 3 seconds
// Some other code ...
$pdf->generate();

$pdf = new ProxyPdf('<h1>Hello</h1>'); // 0 seconds
// Some other code ...
$pdf->generate();
```

Depending on how the class is constructed, it might trigger the actual generation right after we call the `new` keyword, as we have done with the `new Pdf(...)` expression. The `new ProxyPdf(...)` expression behaves differently because it wraps around the `Pdf` class implementing the same `PdfInterface`, but providing a different `__construct()` method implementation.

The chain of responsibility pattern

The chain of responsibility pattern allows us to chain code in a sender-receiver manner, while the two are decoupled from each other. This makes it possible to have more than one object handle incoming requests.

The following example demonstrates a possible chain of responsibility pattern implementation using the logger functionality as an example:

```php
<?php

abstract class Logger
{
    private $logNext = null;

    public function logNext(Logger $logger)
    {
        $this->logNext = $logger;
        return $this->logNext;
    }

    final public function push($message)
    {
        $this->log($message);

        if ($this->logNext !== null) {
            $this->logNext->push($message);
        }
    }

    abstract protected function log($message);
}

class SystemLogger extends Logger
{
    public function log($message)
    {
        echo 'SystemLogger log!', PHP_EOL;
    }
}

class ElasticLogger extends Logger
{
    protected function log($message)
    {
        echo 'ElasticLogger log!', PHP_EOL;
    }
```

```
    }

    class MailLogger extends Logger
    {
        protected function log($message)
        {
            echo 'MailLogger log!', PHP_EOL;
        }
    }

    // Client use
    $systemLogger = new SystemLogger();
    $elasticLogger = new ElasticLogger();
    $mailLogger = new MailLogger();

    $systemLogger
        ->logNext($elasticLogger)
        ->logNext($mailLogger);

    $systemLogger->push('Stuff to log...');

    //SystemLogger log!
    //ElasticLogger log!
    //MailLogger log!
```

We started off by creating an abstract `Logger` class with three methods: `logNext()`, `push()`, and `log()`. The `log()` method was defined as abstract, which means the implementation is left to child classes. The `logNext()` method is the key ingredient as it moves the objects down the chain. We then created three concrete implementations of the `Logger` class: `SystemLogger`, `ElasticLogger`, and `MailLogger`. We then instantiated one of the concrete logger classes and passed the other two instances down the chain using the `logNext()` method. Finally, we called the `push()` method to trigger the chain.

Structural patterns

In this section, we will take a look at a structural pattern: the decorator pattern.

The decorator pattern

The decorator pattern is a simple one. It allows us to add new behavior to object instances without affecting other instances of the same class. It basically acts as a decorating wrapper around our object. We can imagine a simple use case with a Logger class instance, where we have a simple logger class that we would like to occasionally decorate, or wrap into a more specific error, warning, and notice level logger.

The following example demonstrates a possible decorator pattern implementation:

```php
<?php

interface LoggerInterface
{
    public function log($message);
}

class Logger implements LoggerInterface
{
    public function log($message)
    {
        file_put_contents('app.log', $message . PHP_EOL, FILE_APPEND);
    }
}

abstract class LoggerDecorator implements LoggerInterface
{
    protected $logger;

    public function __construct(Logger $logger)
    {
        $this->logger = $logger;
    }

    abstract public function log($message);
}

class ErrorLogger extends LoggerDecorator
{
    public function log($message)
    {
        $this->logger->log('ErrorLogger: ' . $message);
    }
}

class WarningLogger extends LoggerDecorator
{
```

```php
    public function log($message)
    {
        $this->logger->log('WarningLogger: ' . $message);
    }
}

class NoticeLogger extends LoggerDecorator
{
    public function log($message)
    {
        $this->logger->log('NoticeLogger: ' . $message);
    }
}

// Client use
(new Logger())->log('Test Logger.');

(new ErrorLogger(new Logger()))->log('Test ErrorLogger.');

(new WarningLogger(new Logger()))->log('Test WarningLogger.');

(new NoticeLogger(new Logger()))->log('Test NoticeLogger.');
```

Here, we started off by defining a `LoggerInterface` interface and a concrete `Logger` class that implements that interface. We then created an `abstract LoggerDecorator` class that also implements `LoggerInterface`. `LoggerDecorator` does not really implement the `log()` method itself; it defines it as `abstract` for future child classes to implement. Finally, we defined the concrete error, warning, and notice decorator classes. We can see their `log()` methods decorate the output according to their roles. The resulting output is shown as follows:

```
Test Logger.
ErrorLogger: Test ErrorLogger.
WarningLogger: Test WarningLogger.
NoticeLogger: Test NoticeLogger.
```

Summary

Throughout this chapter, we took an introductory hands-on approach with some of the most common design patterns used in PHP applications. The list is far from final, as there are other design patterns available. While some design patterns are quite general, others might be more suitable for GUIs or other areas of application programming. Understanding how to use and apply design patterns makes our code more extensible, reusable, maintainable, and adaptable.

Moving forward, we will take a closer look at building web services using SOAP, REST, and Apache Thrift.

11
Building Services

A great deal of modern applications use **HTTP** (**Hypertext Transfer Protocol**) nowadays. This stateless, application-layer protocol allows us to exchange messages between distributed systems. The message exchange process can be observed through a client-server computing model as it happens in the form of the request-response type of messages. This allows us to easily write a service, or web service to be more specific, that triggers various operations on server and feedback data back to the client.

In this chapter, we will take a closer look at this client-server relationship through the following sections:

- Understanding the client-server relationship
- Working with SOAP:
    - XML extensions
    - Creating server
    - Creating WSDL file
    - Creating client
- Working with REST:
    - JSON extensions
    - Creating server
    - Creating client
- Working with Apache Thrift (RPC):
    - Installing Apache Thrift
    - Defining service
    - Creating server
    - Creating client
- Understanding microservices

Understanding the client-server relationship

To easily visualize the client-server relationship and the request-response type of messaging, we can think of a mobile currency application acting as a client and some remote website, such as `http://api.fixer.io/`, being the server. The server exposes one or more URL endpoints, allowing communication exchange, such as `http://api.fixer.io/latest?symbols=USD,GBP`. The mobile application can easily issue a HTTP `GET http://api.fixer.io/latest?symbols=GBP,HRK,USD` request, which then results in a response like this:

```
{
  "base": "EUR",
  "date": "2017-03-10",
  "rates": {
    "GBP": 0.8725,
    "HRK": 7.419,
    "USD": 1.0606
  }
}
```

The HTTP `GET` keyword is used to denote the type of operation we want to perform on the receiver located on the remote (server) system that we contact via URL. The response contains JSON-formatted data, which our mobile currency application can easily digest and make use of. This specific message exchange example is what we flag as **representational state transfer** (**REST**) or RESTful service.

The REST service itself is not a protocol; it is an architectural style on top of HTTP's stateless protocol and standard operations (GET, POST, PUT, DELETE, and so on). There is much more to it, than showcased in this simple example, as we will get to see later on in the *Working with REST* section.

There are other forms of services that go beyond being just an architectural style, such as the SOAP service and Apache Thrift service. While they come with their own sets of protocols, they also play nicely with HTTP.

Working with SOAP

SOAP (**Simple Object Access Protocol**) is an XML-based message exchange protocol that relies on application layer protocols such as HTTP for message negotiation and transmission. The **World Wide Web Consortium** (**W3C**) maintains SOAP specification.

The SOAP specifications document is available at `https://www.w3.org/T R/soap/`.

The SOAP message is an XML document comprised of `Envelope`, `Header`, `Body`, and `Fault` elements:

```
<?xml version="1.0" ?>
<env:Envelope>
<env:Header>
<!-- ... -->
    </env:Header>
<env:Body>
<!-- ... -->
        <env:Fault>
<!-- ... -->
        </env:Fault>
</env:Body>
</env:Envelope>
```

`Envelope` is a required element of each SOAP request, as it envelops an entire SOAP message. Similarly, the `Body` element is also required as it contains request and response information. `Header` and `Fault`, on the other hand, are optional elements. Using merely XML-based request-response messages, we can establish client-server communication over HTTP. While trading XML messages may look simple, it can become cumbersome when one has to deal with a large number of method calls and data types.

This is where WSDL comes in play. WSDL is an interface definition language that can be used to define a web service's data types and operations. The W3C maintains WSDL specification.

 The WSDL specification document is available at `https://www.w3.org/TR /wsdl`.

A total of six major elements are used to describe the service, as per the following partial example:

```
<?xml version="1.0" ?>
<definitions>
<types>
<!-- ... -->
    </types>
```

```
<message>
<!-- ... -->
    </message>
<portType>
<!-- ... -->
    </portType>
<binding>
<!-- ... -->
    </binding>
<port>
<!-- ... -->
    </port>
<service>
<!-- ... -->
    </service>
</definitions>
```

While WSDL is not required for our service to be operational, it certainly comes in handy for clients consuming our SOAP service. Sadly, PHP lacks any official tooling for easy generation of WSDL files based on the PHP classes that our SOAP service uses. This makes it tedious and time consuming for PHP developers to write WSDL files manually, which is why some developers tend to overlook the WSDL completely.

Temporarily putting the WSDL file generation aside, it's safe to say that the only really challenging part of the SOAP service is writing and reading XML messages. This is where PHP extensions come in handy.

XML extensions

There are several ways to read and write XML documents in PHP, including regular expressions and specialized classes and methods. The regex approach is error-prone, especially with complex XML documents, which is why the use of extensions is advised. PHP provides several extensions for this purpose, the most common ones being as follows:

- **XMLWriter**: This allows us to generate streams or files of XML data
- **XMLReader**: This allows to read the XML data
- **SimpleXML**: This converts XML to an object and allows for an object to be processed with normal property selectors and array iterators
- **DOM**: This allows us to operate on XML documents through the DOM API

The basics of dealing with an XML document are about proper reading and writing of its elements and attributes. Let's assume the following `simple.xml` document:

```xml
<?xml version="1.0" encoding="UTF-8"?>
<customer>
  <name type="string"><![CDATA[John]]></name>
  <age type="integer">34</age>
  <addresses>
    <address><![CDATA[The Address #1]]></address>
  </addresses>
</customer>
```

Using `XMLWriter`, we can create the identical document by running the following code:

```php
<?php

$xml = new XMLWriter();
$xml->openMemory();
$xml->setIndent(true); // optional formatting

$xml->startDocument('1.0', 'UTF-8');
$xml->startElement('customer');

$xml->startElement('name');
$xml->writeAttribute('type', 'string');
$xml->writeCData('John');
$xml->endElement(); // </name>

$xml->startElement('age');
$xml->writeAttribute('type', 'integer');
$xml->writeRaw(34);
$xml->endElement(); // </age>

$xml->startElement('addresses');
$xml->startElement('address');
$xml->writeCData('The Address #1');
$xml->endElement(); // </address>
$xml->endElement(); // </addresses>

$xml->endElement(); // </customer>

$document = $xml->outputMemory();
```

We can see that writing down the necessary XML was a relatively straightforward operation with XMLWriter. The XMLWriter extension makes our code a bit hard to read at first. All those startElement() and endElement() methods make it a bit tedious to figure out where each element in XML resides. It takes a bit of getting used to it. However, it does allow us to easily generate simple XML documents. Using XMLReader, we can now output the Customer John, at age 34, living at The Address #1 string based on data from the given XML document using the following code block:

```php
<?php

$xml = new XMLReader();
$xml->open(__DIR__ . '/simple.xml');

$name = '';
$age = '';
$address = '';

while ($xml->read()) {
    if ($xml->name == 'name') {
        $name = $xml->readString();
        $xml->next();
    } elseif ($xml->name == 'age') {
        $age = $xml->readString();
        $xml->next();
    } elseif ($xml->name == 'address') {
        $address = $xml->readString();
        $xml->next();
    }
}

echo sprintf(
    'Customer %s, at age %s, living at %s',
    $name, $age, $address
);
```

Although the code itself looks pretty simple, the while loop reveals an interesting nature of XMLReader. The XMLReader reads the XML document top to bottom. While this approach is a great choice for efficiently parsing large and complex XML documents in a stream-based manner, it seems a bit of an overkill for simpler XML documents.

Let's see how SimpleXML handles writing of the same simple.xml file. The following code generates nearly the same XML content as XMLWriter:

```php
<?php
```

```php
$document = new SimpleXMLElement(
    '<?xml version="1.0" encoding="UTF-8"?><customer></customer>'
);

$name = $document->addChild('name', 'John');
$age = $document->addChild('age', 34);
$addresses = $document->addChild('addresses');
$address = $addresses->addChild('address', 'The Address #1');

echo $document->asXML();
```

The difference here is that we cannot specifically pass `<![CDATA[...]]>` to our elements. There are workarounds using the `dom_import_simplexml()` function, but that's a function from the `DOM` extension. Not that there is anything bad about it, but let's keep our examples nicely separated. Now that we know we can write XML documents with `SimpleXML`, let's see about reading from them. Using `SimpleXML`, we can now output the same `Customer John, at age 34, living at The Address #1` string using the following code:

```php
<?php

$document = new SimpleXMLElement(__DIR__ . '/simple.xml', null, true);

$name = (string)$document->name;
$age = (string)$document->age;
$address = (string)$document->addresses[0]->address;

echo sprintf(
    'Customer %s, at age %s, living at %s',
    $name, $age, $address
);
```

The XML reading process seems somewhat shorter with `SimpleXML` than it is with `XMLReader`, although none of the examples have any error handling in them.

Let's take a look at using the `DOMDocument` class to write down an XML document:

```php
<?php

$document = new DOMDocument('1.0', 'UTF-8');
$document->formatOutput = true; // optional

$customer = $document->createElement('customer');
$customer = $document->appendChild($customer);

$name = $document->createElement('name');
$name = $customer->appendChild($name);
```

```php
$nameTypeAttr = $document->createAttribute('type');
$nameTypeAttr->value = 'string';
$name->appendChild($nameTypeAttr);
$name->appendChild($document->createCDATASection('John'));

$age = $document->createElement('age');
$age = $customer->appendChild($age);
$ageTypeAttr = $document->createAttribute('type');
$ageTypeAttr->value = 'integer';
$age->appendChild($ageTypeAttr);
$age->appendChild($document->createTextNode(34));

$addresses = $document->createElement('addresses');
$addresses = $customer->appendChild($addresses);

$address = $document->createElement('address');
$address = $addresses->appendChild($address);
$address->appendChild($document->createCDATASection('The Address #1'));

echo $document->saveXML();
```

Finally, let's see how `DOMDocument` handles the reading of XML documents:

```php
<?php

$document = new DOMDocument();
$document->load(__DIR__ . '/simple.xml');

$name = $document->getElementsByTagName('name')[0]->nodeValue;
$age = $document->getElementsByTagName('age')[0]->nodeValue;
$address = $document->getElementsByTagName('address')[0]->nodeValue;

echo sprintf(
    'Customer %s, at age %s, living at %s',
    $name, $age, $address
);
```

The `DOM` and `SimpleXMLElement` extensions make it quite easy to read the values from the XML document, as long as we are confident about the integrity of its structure. When dealing with XML documents, we should evaluate our use case based on factors such as document size. While the `XMLReader` and `XMLWriter` classes are more verbose to deal with, they tend to be more performance efficient when used properly.

Now that we have gained a basic insight into dealing with XML documents in PHP, let's create our first SOAP server.

Creating server

The PHP `soap` extension provides `SoapClient` and `SoapServer` classes. We can use the `SoapServer` class to set up a SOAP service server with or without a WSDL service description file.

 When used without WSDL (non-WSDL mode), `SoapClient` and `SoapServer` use a common exchange format, which removes the need for a WSDL file.

Before moving forward, we should make sure we have the `soap` extension installed. We can do so by observing the output of the `php -m` console command or taking a look at the `phpinfo()` function output:

soap		
Soap Client	enabled	
Soap Server	enabled	

Directive	Local Value	Master Value
soap.wsdl_cache	1	1
soap.wsdl_cache_dir	/var/lib/php-fpm/wsdlcache	/var/lib/php-fpm/wsdlcache
soap.wsdl_cache_enabled	1	1
soap.wsdl_cache_limit	5	5
soap.wsdl_cache_ttl	86400	86400

With the soap extension available and loaded, we can prepare our `soap-service` project directory as per the following structure:

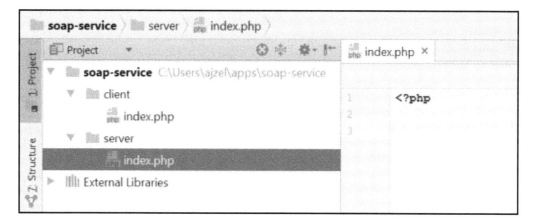

Moving forward, we will assume that the web server is configured to serve content from the `soap-service/server` directory to `http://soap-service.server` requests, and content from the `soap-service/client` directory to `http://soap-service.client` requests.

Let's create a small SOAP service with two different classes, each with the same `welcome()` method. We can start off by creating the `soap-service/server/services/Foggyline/Customer.php` file with the following content:

```php
<?php

namespace Foggyline;

class Customer
{
    /**
     * Says "Welcome customer..."
     * @param $name
     * @return string
     */
    function welcome($name)
    {
        return 'Welcome customer: ' . $name;
    }
}
```

Now, let's create the `soap-service/server/services/Foggyline/User.php` file with the following content:

```php
<?php

namespace Foggyline;

class User
{
    /**
     * Says "Welcome user..."
     * @param $name
     * @return string
     */
    function welcome($name)
    {
        return 'Welcome user: ' . $name;
    }
}
```

With the two classes in place, let's create a proxy class to wrap around them. We do so by creating the `soap-service/server/ServiceProxy.php` file with the following content:

```php
<?php

require_once __DIR__ . '/services/Foggyline/Customer.php';
require_once __DIR__ . '/services/Foggyline/User.php';

class ServiceProxy
{
    private $customerService;
    private $userService;

    public function __construct()
    {
        $this->customerService = new Foggyline\Customer();
        $this->userService = new Foggyline\User();
    }

    /**
     * Says "Welcome customer..."
     * @soap
     * @param $name
     * @return string
     */
    public function customerWelcome($name)
    {
        return $this->customerService->welcome($name);
    }

    /**
     * Says "Welcome user..."
     * @soap
     * @param $name
     * @return string
     */
    public function userWelcome($name)
    {
        return $this->userService->welcome($name);
    }
}
```

Now that we have our proxy class, we can create the actual `SoapServer` instance. We do so by creating the `soap-service/server/index.php` file with the following content:

```php
<?php

require_once __DIR__ . '/ServiceProxy.php';

$options = [
    'uri' => 'http://soap-service.server/index.php'
];

$server = new SoapServer(null, $options);

$server->setClass('ServiceProxy');

$server->handle();
```

Here, we are instantiating the `SoapServer` instance, passing it null for the `$wsdl` parameter and only a `'uri'` option under the `$options` parameter. The URI must be specified in a non-wsdl mode. We then use the `setClass()` instance method to set the class that will handle incoming SOAP requests. Unfortunately, we cannot pass an array of classes or call the `setClass()` method multiple times to add several different handling classes at once, which is why we created the `ServiceProxy` class to wrap around both `Customer` and `User` classes. Finally, we called the `handle()` method of the `$server` instance, which handles a SOAP request. At this point, our SOAP service server should be fully operational.

Creating WSDL file

However, before we move onto the client, let's take a quick look at WSDL. The `@soap` tag used on the `ServiceProxy` class methods has nothing to do with the functioning of `SoapServer` as it is now. We used it merely because of the php2wsdl library that enables us to auto-generate a WSDL file based on the provided class. The php2wsdl library is provided as a composer package, which means we can install it by simply running the following command within the `soap-service/server` directory:

```
composer require php2wsdl/php2wsdl
```

Once installed, we can create the `soap-service\server\wsdl-auto-gen.php` file with the following content:

```php
<?php

require_once __DIR__ . '/vendor/autoload.php';
require_once __DIR__ . '/ServiceProxy.php';

$class = 'ServiceProxy';
$serviceURI = 'http://soap-service.server/index.php';

$wsdlGenerator = new PHP2WSDL\PHPClass2WSDL($class, $serviceURI);
$wsdlGenerator->generateWSDL(true);

file_put_contents(__DIR__ . '/wsdl.xml', $wsdlGenerator->dump());
```

Once we execute `wsdl-auto-gen.php`, either in the console or in the browser, it will generate the `soap-service/server/wsdl.xml` file with the following content:

```xml
<?xml version="1.0"?>
<definitions xmlns="http://schemas.xmlsoap.org/wsdl/"
xmlns:tns="http://soap-service.server/index.php"
xmlns:soap="http://schemas.xmlsoap.org/wsdl/soap/"
xmlns:xsd="http://www.w3.org/2001/XMLSchema"
xmlns:soap-enc="http://schemas.xmlsoap.org/soap/encoding/"
xmlns:wsdl="http://schemas.xmlsoap.org/wsdl/" name="ServiceProxy"
targetNamespace="http://soap-service.server/index.php">
<types>
<xsd:schema targetNamespace="http://soap-service.server/index.php">
<xsd:import namespace="http://schemas.xmlsoap.org/soap/encoding/"/>
</xsd:schema>
</types>
<portType name="ServiceProxyPort">
  <operation name="customerWelcome">
  <documentation>Says "Welcome customer..."</documentation>
  <input message="tns:customerWelcomeIn"/>
  <output message="tns:customerWelcomeOut"/>
  </operation>
    <operation name="userWelcome">
    <documentation>Says "Welcome user..."</documentation>
    <input message="tns:userWelcomeIn"/>
  <output message="tns:userWelcomeOut"/>
</operation>
</portType>
<binding name="ServiceProxyBinding" type="tns:ServiceProxyPort">
<soap:binding style="rpc"
transport="http://schemas.xmlsoap.org/soap/http"/>
<operation name="customerWelcome">
```

```
<soap:operation
soapAction="http://soap-service.server/index.php#customerWelcome"/>
<input>
<soap:body use="encoded"
encodingStyle="http://schemas.xmlsoap.org/soap/encoding/"
namespace="http://soap-service.server/index.php"/>
</input>
<output>
<soap:body use="encoded"
encodingStyle="http://schemas.xmlsoap.org/soap/encoding/"
namespace="http://soap-service.server/index.php"/>
</output>
</operation>
<operation name="userWelcome">
<soap:operation
soapAction="http://soap-service.server/index.php#userWelcome"/>
<input>
<soap:body use="encoded"
encodingStyle="http://schemas.xmlsoap.org/soap/encoding/"
namespace="http://soap-service.server/index.php"/>
</input>
<output>
<soap:body use="encoded"
encodingStyle="http://schemas.xmlsoap.org/soap/encoding/"
namespace="http://soap-service.server/index.php"/>
</output>
</operation>
</binding>
<service name="ServiceProxyService">
<port name="ServiceProxyPort" binding="tns:ServiceProxyBinding">
   <soap:address location="http://soap-service.server/index.php"/>
</port>
</service>
<message name="customerWelcomeIn">
  <part name="name" type="xsd:anyType"/>
</message>
<message name="customerWelcomeOut">
  <part name="return" type="xsd:string"/>
</message>
<message name="userWelcomeIn">
  <part name="name" type="xsd:anyType"/>
</message>
<message name="userWelcomeOut">
  <part name="return" type="xsd:string"/>
</message>
</definitions>
```

This is quite a long file to write manually. The benefit of it is that various third-party tools and other language libraries can easily consume our service once we set the WSDL file. As an example, this is a screenshot of the Wizdler extension for the Chrome browser, interpreting the WSDL file content:

With WSDL in place, we can now easily modify the `soap-service/server/index.php` file as follows:

```
// NON-WSDL MODE: $server = new SoapServer(null, $options);

// WSDL MODE: $server = new
SoapServer('http://soap-service.server/wsdl.xml');

$server = new SoapServer('http://soap-service.server/wsdl.xml');
```

Now that we have the SOAP server bits sorted out, let's create a client.

Creating client

Creating a SOAP client in PHP is a relatively simple task when we are using
the `SoapClient` class. Let's create the `soap-service/client/index.php` file with the
following content:

```php
<?php

$options = [
    'location' => 'http://soap-service.server/index.php',
    'uri' => 'http://soap-service.server/index.php',
    'trace ' => true,
];

// NON-WSDL MODE: $client = new SoapClient($wsdl = null, $options);
// WSDL MODE: $client = new
SoapClient('http://soap-service.server/wsdl.xml', $options);

$client = new SoapClient('http://soap-service.server/wsdl.xml', $options);

echo $client->customerWelcome('John');
echo $client->userWelcome('Mariya');
```

Executing the client code should result in the following output:

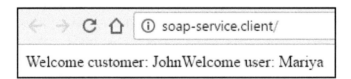

What happens under the hood when the SOAP request is issued can be observed with
networking tools such as Wireshark:

This shows us the exact content of an individual SOAP request, such as that for
`$client->customerWelcome('John')`:

```
POST /index.php HTTP/1.1
Host: soap-service.server
Connection: Keep-Alive
User-Agent: PHP-SOAP/7.0.10
Content-Type: text/xml; charset=utf-8
SOAPAction: "http://soap-service.server/index.php#customerWelcome"
Content-Length: 525
```

```
<?xml version="1.0" encoding="UTF-8"?>
<SOAP-ENV:Envelope xmlns:SOAP-
ENV="http://schemas.xmlsoap.org/soap/envelope/"
 xmlns:ns1="http://soap-service.server/index.php"
xmlns:xsd="http://www.w3.org/2001/XMLSchema"
 xmlns:xsi="http://www.w3.org/2001/XMLSchema-instance"
 xmlns:SOAP-ENC="http://schemas.xmlsoap.org/soap/encoding/"
 SOAP-ENV:encodingStyle="http://schemas.xmlsoap.org/soap/encoding/">
 <SOAP-ENV:Body>
 <ns1:customerWelcome>
 <name xsi:type="xsd:string">John</name>
 </ns1:customerWelcome>
 </SOAP-ENV:Body>
</SOAP-ENV:Envelope>
```

Understanding the structure and content of the SOAP request makes it possible to even use the cURL functions to handle request-response communication, although that would be much more cumbersome and error-prone than dealing with the `SoapClient` and `SoapServer` classes.

Throughout this section, we have touched upon some of the key points of SOAP services. While there is much more to be said about the SOAP specification, the examples presented here are a nice starting point to writing SOAP services.

A somewhat simpler variant of a web service would be REST.

Working with REST

Unlike SOAP, REST is an architectural style. It has no protocols or standards of its own. It relies on URLs and HTTP verbs, such as POST, GET, PUT, and DELETE, in order to establish a message exchange process. The lack of standard makes it somewhat challenging to talk about, as various REST service implementations may present a client with different ways to consume services. When it comes to juggling data back and forth, we are free to choose over JSON, XML, or any other format we prefer. The simplicity and lightweightness of JSON made it a popular choice among many users and frameworks.

Loosely speaking, the very act of opening a web page in the browser can be interpreted as a REST call, where the browser acts as a client and server acts as a REST service. Unlike browser pages that may involve cookies and sessions, REST relies on stateless operations.

Moving forward, we will assume that our web server is configured to serve content of the `rest-service/server` directory for `http://rest-service.server` requests, and content of the `rest-service/client` directory for `http://rest-service.client` requests.

JSON extensions

Over the years, the JSON data format has become somewhat of a default data exchange format for REST. The simplicity of JSON made it quite popular with PHP developers. Out of the box, the PHP language provides the `json_encode()` and `json_decode()` functions. Using these functions, we can easily encode PHP arrays and objects as well as decode various JSON structures.

The following example demonstrates the simplicity of using the `json_encode()` function:

```php
<?php

class User
{
    public $name;
    public $age;
    public $salary;
}

$user = new User();
$user->name = 'John';
$user->age = 34;
$user->salary = 4200.50;

echo json_encode($user);
// {"name":"John","age":34,"salary":4200.5}

$employees = ['John', 'Mariya', 'Sarah', 'Marc'];

echo json_encode($employees);
// ["John","Mariya","Sarah","Marc"]
```

The following example demonstrates the simplicity of using the `json_decode()` function:

```php
<?php

$user = json_decode('{"name":"John","age":34,"salary":4200.5}');

print_r($user);
```

```
//     stdClass Object
//     (
//         [name] => John
//         [age] => 34
//         [salary] => 4200.5
//     )
```

This is where limitations kick in. Notice how the JSON object was converted to a `stdClass` type object in PHP. There is no direct way to pour this into a `User` type of object. We could, of course, write a custom functionality that tries to convert a `stdClass` object to an instance of `User` if needed.

Creating server

Put simply, REST servers send HTTP responses based on a given URL and HTTP verb. Keeping that in mind, let's start with the following chunk of code added to the `rest-service/server/customer/index.php` file:

```php
<?php

if ('POST' == $_SERVER['REQUEST_METHOD']) {
    header('Content-type: application/json');
    echo json_encode(['data' => 'Triggered customer POST!']);
}

if ('GET' == $_SERVER['REQUEST_METHOD']) {
    header('Content-type: application/json');
    echo json_encode(['data' => 'Triggered customer GET!']);
}

if ('PUT' == $_SERVER['REQUEST_METHOD']) {
    header('Content-type: application/json');
    echo json_encode(['data' => 'Triggered customer PUT!']);
}

if ('DELETE' == $_SERVER['REQUEST_METHOD']) {
    header('Content-type: application/json');
    echo json_encode(['data' => 'Triggered customer DELETE!']);
}
```

Funny as it looks, this, here, is already a simple REST service example--one that handles four different operations for a single resource. Using a tool such as Postman, we can trigger the `DELETE` operation on the `http://rest-service.server/customer/index.php`resource

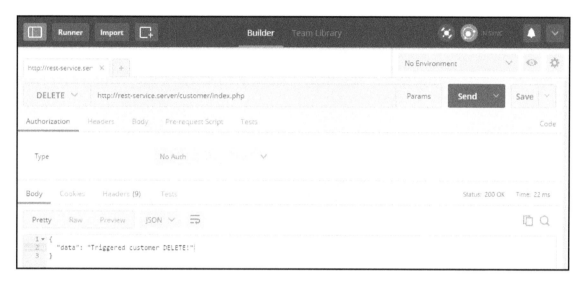

Obviously, this simplified implementation does not deal with any of the things you would normally find in REST services, such as versioning, normalization, validation, **Cross-Origin Resource Sharing** (**CORS**), authentication, and others. Implementing all of these REST features from scratch is a time-consuming task, which is why we might want to take a look at solutions provided by existing frameworks.

The Silex micro-frameworks is a neat solution for quickly getting started with REST services. We can add Silex to our project simply by running the following command on console, within the `rest-service/server` directory:

```
composer require silex/silex "~2.0"
```

Once we get it installed, we can dump the following code into the `rest-service/server/index.php` file:

```php
<?php

require_once __DIR__ . '/vendor/autoload.php';

use Silex\Application;
use Symfony\Component\HttpFoundation\Request;
use Symfony\Component\HttpFoundation\Response;
```

```
$app = new Silex\Application();

// The "before" middleware, convenient for auth and request data check
$app->before(function (Request $request, Application $app) {
    // Some auth token control
    if (!$request->headers->get('X-AUTH-TOKEN')) {
        // todo: Implement
    }
    // JSON content type control
    if ($request->headers->get('Content-Type') != 'application/json') {
        // todo: Implement
    }
});

// The "error" middleware, convenient for service wide error handling
$app->error(function (\Exception $e, Request $request, $code) {
    // todo: Implement
});

// The "OPTIONS" route, set to trigger for any URL
$app->options('{url}', function ($url) use ($app) {
    return new Response('', 204, ['Allow' => 'POST, GET, PUT, DELETE,
OPTIONS']);
})->assert('url', '.+');

// The "after" middleware, convenient for CORS control
$app->after(function (Request $request, Response $response) {
    $response->headers->set('Access-Control-Allow-Headers', 'origin,
content-type, accept, X-AUTH-TOKEN');
    $response->headers->set('Access-Control-Allow-Origin', '*');
    $response->headers->set('Access-Control-Allow-Methods', 'POST, GET,
PUT, DELETE');
});

// The "POST /user/welcome" REST service endpoint
$app->post('/user/welcome', function (Request $request, Application $app) {
    $data = json_decode($request->getContent(), true);
    return $app->json(['data' => 'Welcome ' . $data['name']]);
})->bind('user_welcome');

$app->run();
```

This too is a relatively simple example of the REST service, but one that does much more than our initial example. The Silex framework, in this case, introduces several key concepts that we can use to our advantage as we build our REST server. The `before`, `after`, and `error` middleware enable us to hook into three distinctive stages of the request handling process. Using the `before` middleware, we are able to inject an authentication code for example, as well as various checks for the validity of incoming data. REST services usually build their authentication around tokens, which are then passed along individual requests. The general idea is to have an endpoint such as `POST user/login`, where the user logs in with their username and password, and is then given an authentication token for use with the rest of the REST service calls. This token then usually gets passed around as a part of the request header. Now, every time the user tries to access a protected resource, a token is extracted from the header and looked into the database (or any other storage where it might be stored), to find out the user behind the token. The system then either allows the user to continue with the original request or blocks it out. This is where middleware comes in handy.

The web service authentication is an enormous topic by itself--one that won't be covered in this book. OAuth is the industry-standard protocol for authorization that is quite often used with REST style services. For more information about OAuth, check out `https://oauth.net`.

The way we wrap our responses is entirely up to us. Unlike with the SOAP, there is no long-established standard that defines the data structure of the REST service response. However, there are several initiatives in the last few years that try to tackle that challenge.

JSON API is an attempt to formalize client-server interfaces that use exchange JSON data; check out `http://jsonapi.org/format/` for more information.

To get the server working properly, we also need to add the `rest-service\server\.htaccess` file with the following content:

```
<IfModule mod_rewrite.c>
Options -MultiViews
    RewriteEngine On
    RewriteCond %{REQUEST_FILENAME} !-d
    RewriteCond %{REQUEST_FILENAME} !-f
    RewriteRule ^ index.php [QSA,L]
</IfModule>
```

Silex conveniently supports several key HTTP verbs (GET, POST, PUT, DELETE, PATCH, and OPTIONS), for which, we can easily implement logic in a *resource path + callback function* syntax:

```
$app->get('/resource/path', function () { /* todo: logic */ });
$app->post('/resource/path', function () { /* todo: logic */ });
$app->put('/resource/path', function () { /* todo: logic */ });
$app->delete('/resource/path', function () { /* todo: logic */ });
$app->patch('/resource/path', function () { /* todo: logic */ });
$app->options('/resource/path', function () { /* todo: logic */ });
```

This makes it easy to quickly draft a REST service, with merely a few lines of code. Our server example does little to nothing in terms of server security. Its purpose is to merely emphasize the usefulness of middleware when building REST services. Security aspects, such as authentication, authorization, CORS, HTTPS, and others should be given utmost attention.

 Frameworks such as http://silex.sensiolabs.org and https://apigil ity.org provide a great solution to write high-quality feature-rich REST services.

Creating client

Given that REST services rely on HTTP, it's safe to assume that writing clients with PHP CURL should be quite a straightforward process. Let's create a rest-service/client/index.php file with the following content:

```php
<?php

$ch = curl_init();

$headers = [
    'Content-Type: application/json',
    'X-AUTH-TOKEN: some-auth-token-here'
];

curl_setopt($ch, CURLOPT_URL, 'http://rest-service.server/user/welcome');
curl_setopt($ch, CURLOPT_POST, true);
curl_setopt($ch, CURLOPT_POSTFIELDS, json_encode(['name' => 'John']));
curl_setopt($ch, CURLOPT_HTTPHEADER, $headers);
curl_setopt($ch, CURLOPT_RETURNTRANSFER, true);

$result = curl_exec($ch);
```

```
curl_close($ch);

echo $result;
```

The Wireshark network tool tells us that this code generates the following HTTP request to a REST service:

```
POST /user/welcome HTTP/1.1
Host: rest-service.server
Accept: */*
Content-Type: application/json
X-AUTH-TOKEN: some-auth-token-here
Content-Length: 15

{"name":"John"}
```

While the CURL approach works just fine, it can quickly become cumbersome and error-prone. This implies the challenges of having to deal with various types of error responses, SSL certificates, and so on. A more elegant solution would be to use the HTTP client library, such as Guzzle.

 Guzzle is an MIT-licensed HTTP client written in PHP. It can easily be installed through composer, by running the `composer require guzzlehttp/guzzle` command.

Chances are that our REST services will be contacted more often by non-PHP clients than by PHP clients. With that in mind, let's see how a simple HTML/jQuery client can talk to our REST service. We do so by adding the following code to `rest-service/client/index.html`:

```html
<!DOCTYPE html>
<html lang="en">
  <head>
    <meta charset="UTF-8">
    <title>Client App</title>
    <script src="https://code.jquery.com/jquery-3.1.1.min.js"
      integrity="sha256-hVVnYaiADRTO2PzUGmuLJr8BLUSjGIZsDYGmIJLv2b8="
      crossorigin="anonymous"></script>
  </head>
<body>
  <script>
    jQuery.ajax({
      method: 'POST',
      url: 'http://rest-service.server/user/welcome',
      headers: {'X-AUTH-TOKEN': 'some-auth-token-here'},
      data: JSON.stringify({name: 'John'}),
```

```
        dataType: 'json',
        contentType: 'application/json',
        success: function (response) {
          console.log(response.data);
        }
      });
      </script>
    </body>
  </html>
```

The jQuery `ajax()` method acts as an HTTP client. Passing it the proper parameter values, it was able to successfully establish request-response communication with the REST service.

Throughout this section, we have touched upon some of the key points of REST services. Although we have barely scratched the surface of the overall REST architecture, the examples presented here should be enough to get us started. The ease of implementation and simplicity of JSON and HTTP make REST quite an appealing choice for modern applications.

Working with Apache Thrift (RPC)

Apache Thrift is an open source framework to build scalable cross-language services. It was originally developed by Facebook, then entered the Apache Incubator around May 2008. Simplicity, transparency, consistency, and performance are the four key values behind the framework.

Unlike the REST and SOAP type of services, Thrift services use a binary form of communication. Luckily for us, Thrift provides a code generation engine to get us started. The code generation engine can pick up any **interface definition language** (**IDL**) file and generate PHP or other language bindings from it.

Before we start writing our first service definition, we need to install Apache Thrift.

Installing Apache Thrift

Apache Thrift can be installed from source files. Assuming that we have a fresh Ubuntu 16.10 installation, we can kick off the Apache Thrift installation steps using the following set of commands:

```
sudo apt-get update
sudo apt-get -y install php automake bison flex g++ git libboost-all-dev
libevent-dev libssl-dev libtool make pkg-config
```

These two commands should get us the necessary tooling to compile our Apache Thrift source files. Once this is done, we can pull the actual source files on our machine:

```
wget http://apache.mirror.anlx.net/thrift/0.10.0/thrift-0.10.0.tar.gz
tar -xvf thrift-0.10.0.tar.gz
cd thrift-0.10.0/
```

With the source files unpacked, we can trigger the `configure` and `make` commands, as follows:

```
./configure
make
make install
```

Finally, we need to make sure we have the `/usr/local/lib/` directory on our `LD_LIBRARY_PATH` path:

```
echo "export LD_LIBRARY_PATH=$LD_LIBRARY_PATH:/usr/local/lib/" >> ~/.bashrc
```

We should now log out of the shell and then log back in. Using the following command, we confirm that the Apache Thrift is installed:

```
thrift -version
```

This should give us the following output:

```
root@vultr:~# thrift -version
Thrift version 0.10.0
root@vultr:~#
```

With the `thrift` tool installed and available through the console, we can prepare our `thrift-service` project:

```
mkdir thrift-service
cd thrift-service/
mkdir client
mkdir server
mkdir vendor
cd vendor
git clone https://github.com/apache/thrift.git
```

Moving forward, we will assume that the web server is configured to serve content of the `thrift-service/client` directory to `http://thrift-service.client` requests, and content of the `thrift-service/server` directory to `http://thrift-service.server` requests.

Defining service

Working with Apache Thrift in PHP can be described through the following few steps:

- Defining the services through the IDL file
- Autogenerating language bindings
- Providing PHP implementation of defined interfaces
- Exposing provided service implementation through the server
- Consuming exposed services via client

Thrift services begin their life as `.thrift` files, that is, files described by IDL.

The IDL files support definition of several data types:

- `bool`: This is a Boolean value (true or false)
- `byte`: This is an 8-bit signed integer
- `i16`: This is a 16-bit signed integer
- `i32`: This is a 32-bit signed integer
- `i64`: This is a 64-bit signed integer
- `double`: This is a 64-bit floating point number
- `string`: This is a UTF-8 encoded text string
- `binary`: This is a sequence of unencoded bytes
- `struct`: This is essentially equivalent to classes in OOP languages, but without inheritance
- Container (`list`, `set`, `map`): This maps to common container types in most programming languages

To keep things simple, we will focus our use on the `string` type. Let's create our first Apache Thrift service. We do so by creating a `Greeting.thrift` file within the `thrift-service/` directory, as follows:

```
namespace php user

service GreetingService
{
  string hello(1: string name),
  string goodbye()
}
```

We can see that the Thrift file is a pure interface--there is no implementation here. The `namespace php user` syntax translates to *when code generation engine runs, generate GreetingService within user namespace for PHP type of generated code*. If we were using another language alongside PHP, let's say Java, we could easily add another line saying `namespace java customer`. This would then generate PHP bindings in one namespace, and Java in another.

We can see that the `service` keyword is being used to specify the `GreetingService` interface. Within the interface, we then have two method definitions. The `hello(1: string name)` string receives a single name parameter, whereas `goodbye()` receives no parameters.

 See `https://thrift.apache.org/docs/idl` for more details about IDL syntax.

With the `Greeting.thrift` file in place, we can trigger code generation to get us the necessary PHP bindings. We can do so by executing the following code on the console:

```
thrift -r -gen php:server Greeting.thrift
```

At this point, we should have our folder structure similar to the following screenshot:

We can see that the `thrift` command generated two files for us under the `gen-php/user` directory. The `GreetingService.php` is file quite a large one; with nearly 500 lines of code, it defines various helper functions and structures needed to work with our Thrift service:

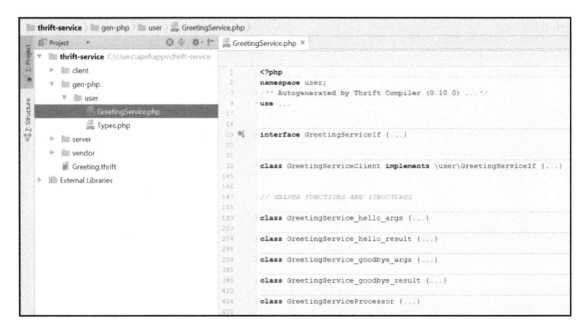

Whereas, the `Types.php` file defines several different types for use:

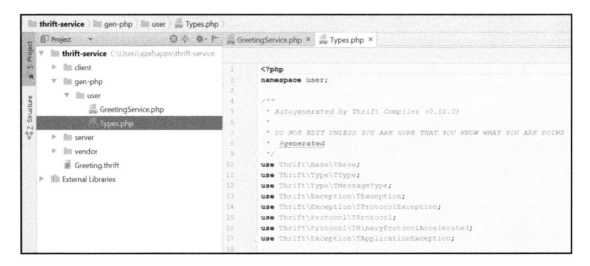

All of these types reside in `thrift-service/vendor/thrift/lib/php/lib/Thrift`, which is why we did the `git clone` `https://github.com/apache/thrift.git` command earlier. Up to this point, our `thrift-service/gen-php/user/GreetingService.php` service still does not really do anything in terms of the `hello()` and `goodbye()` method logic.

Creating server

The `thrift-service/server/` directory is where we will implement our project's server bits. Let's create a single all-in-one `thrift-service/server/index.php` file that implements the `hello()` and `goodbye()` methods and exposes them through the `http://thrift-service.server/index.php` for any thrift request that may come in:

```php
<?php

require_once __DIR__ .
'/../vendor/thrift/lib/php/lib/Thrift/ClassLoader/ThriftClassLoader.php';

use Thrift\ClassLoader\ThriftClassLoader;
use Thrift\Transport\TPhpStream;
use Thrift\Transport\TBufferedTransport;
use Thrift\Protocol\TBinaryProtocol;
use user\GreetingServiceProcessor;
use user\GreetingServiceIf;

$loader = new ThriftClassLoader();
$loader->registerNamespace('Thrift', __DIR__ .
'/../vendor/thrift/lib/php/lib');
$loader->registerDefinition('user', __DIR__ . '/../gen-php');
$loader->register();

class GreetingServiceImpl implements GreetingServiceIf
{
  public function hello($name)
  {
    return 'Hello ' . $name . '!';
  }

  public function goodbye()
  {
    return 'Goodbye!';
  }
}

header('Content-Type', 'application/x-thrift');
```

```php
$handler = new GreetingServiceImpl();
$processor = new GreetingServiceProcessor($handler);
$transport = new TBufferedTransport(new TPhpStream(TPhpStream::MODE_R |
TPhpStream::MODE_W));
$protocol = new TBinaryProtocol($transport, true, true);

$transport->open();
$processor->process($protocol, $protocol);
$transport->close();
```

We started off by including the ThriftClassLoader class. This loader class then enabled us to set the auto-loading for the entire Thrift and user namespaces. We then moved onto the hello() and goodbye() method implementations through the GreetingServiceImpl class. Finally, we instantiated the appropriate *handler, processor, transport,* and *protocol* in order to be able to process incoming requests.

Creating client

The thrift-service/client/ directory is where we will implement our project's client. Let's create a single *all-in-one* thrift-service/client/index.php file that calls the hello() and goodbye() methods from the Thrift service exposed on http://thrift-service.server/index.php:

```php
<?php

require_once __DIR__ .
'/../vendor/thrift/lib/php/lib/Thrift/ClassLoader/ThriftClassLoader.php';

use Thrift\ClassLoader\ThriftClassLoader;
use Thrift\Transport\THttpClient;
use Thrift\Transport\TBufferedTransport;
use Thrift\Protocol\TBinaryProtocol;
use user\GreetingServiceClient;

$loader = new ThriftClassLoader();
$loader->registerNamespace('Thrift', __DIR__ .
'/../vendor/thrift/lib/php/lib');
$loader->registerDefinition('user', __DIR__ . '/../gen-php');
$loader->register();

$socket = new THttpClient('thrift-service.server', 80, '/index.php');
$transport = new TBufferedTransport($socket);
$protocol = new TBinaryProtocol($transport);
$client = new GreetingServiceClient($protocol);
```

```
$transport->open();

echo $client->hello('John');
echo $client->goodbye();

$transport->close();
```

Much like with the server example, here, we also started by including the `ThriftClassLoader` class, which in turn enabled us to set the auto-loading for the entire `Thrift` and `user` namespaces. We then instantiated the socket, transport, protocol, and client, thus making a connection with the Thrift service. Both client and server are using the same `thrift-service/gen-php/user/GreetingService.php` file. Given that `GreetingServiceClient` resides within the auto-generated `GreetingService.php` file, this makes it easy for the client to instantly be aware of any method `GreetingService` may expose.

To test our client, all we need to do is open `http://thrift-service.client/index.php` in the browser. This should give us the following output:

Throughout this section, we touched upon some of the key points of Apache Thrift services. Although there is plenty more to be said about the Thrift's IDL and type system, the examples presented here are a step in the right direction.

Understanding microservices

The term microservices denotes an architectural style of building applications taking the form of loosely coupled services. These independently deployable services are tiny applications most often built via a web service technology. While one service can communicate via SOAP, the other can be do so via REST, Apache Thrift, or something else. There is no standard to specify the firm requirements here. The general idea is to take a large monolithic application and slice it down into several smaller applications, that is, services, but doing so in a manner that serves a business goal.

The following diagram tries to visualize this concept:

Popularized by the likes of Netflix and Amazon, the microservices style sets out to solve a few key challenges of modern application development, some of which include the following:

- **Development team size**: This is a single microservice that can be developed by a relatively small team
- **Diversity of development skills**: These are different services that can be written in different programming languages
- **Change/upgrade**: These smaller pieces of code are easier to change or update
- **Integration and deployment**: These smaller pieces of code are easier to deploy
- **Easier for newcomers**: These smaller pieces of code are easier to catch up with
- **Business capabilities focus**: This individual service code is organized around specific business capability
- **Scalability**: Not everything scales equally; smaller chunks of code can be scaled more easily
- **Fault handling**: This single faulty service does not bring an entire application down
- **Technology stack**: This is less dependency on fast-chaining technology stacks

At the same time, they induce several new challenges, some of which include the following:

- **Service communication**: This is an extra effort involved around service communication
- **Distributed transactions**: These are challenges caused by business requirements spanning across several services
- **Testing and monitoring**: These are somewhat more challenging than with monolith applications
- **Network latency**: Every microservice introduces an extra bit of network latency
- **Fault tolerance**: These are microservices that have to be designed for failure from the ground up

That being said, building microservices is all but an easy task. Going *monolith first*, with a carefully decoupled and modular structure, may be a better starting point for most of the applications. Once a monolithic grows to the point where its complexities begin to affect the way we manage it, then it's time to consider slicing it into microservices.

Summary

Throughout this chapter, we took a look at two of the most common and well-established web services: SOAP and REST. We also looked into a rising new star called Apache Thrift. Once we pass the barrier of initial Apache Thrift installation and setup, features such as simplicity, scalability, speed, and portability certainly come into focus. As we saw in our client example, the RPC calls can easily be implemented with a central code repository-- the `thrift-service/gen-php/` directory in our case.

While Apache Thrift has yet to catch up in terms of popularity, the fact that it is being used by the likes of Facebook, Evernote, Pinterest, Quora, Uber, and other well-known names, certainly speaks for itself. This is not to say that future-wise SOAP or REST are less important. Choosing the right type of service is a matter of *careful planning* and *forward thinking*.

Finally, we glossed over some of the key points of an emerging a new architectural style called microservices.

Moving forward, we will take a closer look at working with some of the most commonly used databases in PHP applications: MySQL, Mongo, Elasticsearch, and Redis.

12
Working with Databases

The PHP language has a pretty good support for several different databases. MySQL has been embraced by PHP developers as the go-to database ever since the early days of the PHP language. While the initial emphasis was mostly on **relational database management systems** (**RDBMS**), other types of databases proved to be equally (or more) important for modern applications. The document and data key-value databases have been growing in popularity ever since.

Nowadays, it is not uncommon to see a PHP application making use of MySQL, Mongo, Redis, and possibly a few more databases or data stores all at once.

The NoSQL ("non SQL", "non relational" or "not only SQL") nature of Mongo allows building applications that generate massive volumes of new and possibly rapidly changing data types. Relieved from the strictness of **SQL** (**Structured Query Language**), working with structured, semi-structured, unstructured, and polymorphic data becomes a whole new experience with the Mongo database. The in-memory data structure stores such as Redis strive on speed, which makes them great to cache and message broker systems.

In this chapter, we will take a closer look at MySQL, Mongo, and Redis through the following sections:

- Working with MySQL
    - Installing MySQL
    - Setting up sample data
    - Querying via the mysqli driver extension
    - Querying via the PHP Data Objects driver extension
- Working with MongoDB
    - Installing MongoDB
    - Setting up sample data
    - Querying via the MongoDB driver extension

- Working with Redis
    - Installing Redis
    - Setting up sample data
    - Querying via the phpredis driver extension

Throughout this chapter, we provide quick installation instructions for each of the three database servers. These instructions are given on a relatively basic level, without any post-installation configuration or tuning that is usually done on production-type machines. The general idea here was to merely get the developer machine up and running with each of the database servers.

Working with MySQL

MySQL is an open source RDBMS that has been around for over 20 years now. Originally developed and owned by the Swedish company MySQL AB, it is now owned by Oracle Corporation. The current stable version of MySQL is 5.7.

Some of the key strengths of MySQL can be outlined as follows:

- Cross-platform, runs on server
- Can be used for desktop and web applications
- Fast, reliable, and easy to use
- Good for small and large applications
- Uses standard SQL
- Supports query caching
- Supports Unicode
- ACID compliance when using InnoDB
- Transactions when using InnoDB

Installing MySQL

Assuming we are using the fresh Ubuntu 16.10 (Yakkety Yak) installation, the following steps outline how we can set up MySQL:

1. To install MySQL, we execute the following console commands:

   ```
   sudo apt-get update
   sudo apt-get -y install mysql-server
   ```

2. The installation process triggers a console GUI interface that asks us to enter a root user password:

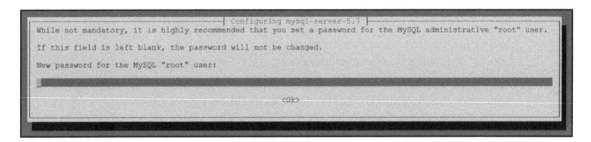

3. The provided password needs to be repeated for confirmation purposes:

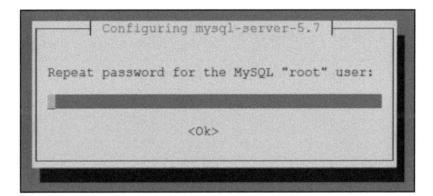

4. Once the installation is done, we can execute the following `mysql --version` command to confirm if the MySQL server is up and running:

```
root@vultr:~# mysql --version
mysql Ver 14.14 Distrib 5.7.17, for Linux (x86_64) using EditLine
wrapper
```

5. Once the server is running, we need to secure the installation. This is done by running the following command:

```
sudo mysql_secure_installation
```

6. The secure installation process triggers an interactive shell with several prompts, asking for the following information:
    - **Enter password for user root:**
    - **Would you like to setup VALIDATE PASSWORD plugin?**
    - **Please enter 0 = LOW, 1 = MEDIUM and 2 = STRONG:**
    - **New password:**
    - **Re-enter new password:**
    - **Remove anonymous users?**
    - **Disallow root login remotely?**
    - **Remove test database and access to it?**
    - **Reload privilege tables now?**

The following screenshot depicts this process:

```
root@vultr:~# sudo mysql_secure_installation

Securing the MySQL server deployment.

Enter password for user root:

VALIDATE PASSWORD PLUGIN can be used to test passwords
and improve security. It checks the strength of password
and allows the users to set only those passwords which are
secure enough. Would you like to setup VALIDATE PASSWORD plugin?

Press y|Y for Yes, any other key for No: Y

There are three levels of password validation policy:

LOW    Length >= 8
MEDIUM Length >= 8, numeric, mixed case, and special characters
STRONG Length >= 8, numeric, mixed case, special characters and dictionary                file

Please enter 0 = LOW, 1 = MEDIUM and 2 = STRONG: 2
Using existing password for root.

Estimated strength of the password: 50
Change the password for root ? ((Press y|Y for Yes, any other key for No) : y

New password:

Re-enter new password:

Estimated strength of the password: 100
Do you wish to continue with the password provided?(Press y|Y for Yes, any other key for No) : y
By default, a MySQL installation has an anonymous user,
allowing anyone to log into MySQL without having to have
a user account created for them. This is intended only for
testing, and to make the installation go a bit smoother.
You should remove them before moving into a production
environment.

Remove anonymous users? (Press y|Y for Yes, any other key for No) : y
Success.


Normally, root should only be allowed to connect from
'localhost'. This ensures that someone cannot guess at
the root password from the network.

Disallow root login remotely? (Press y|Y for Yes, any other key for No) : y
Success.

By default, MySQL comes with a database named 'test' that
anyone can access. This is also intended only for testing,
and should be removed before moving into a production
environment.

Remove test database and access to it? (Press y|Y for Yes, any other key for No) : y
 - Dropping test database...
Success.

 - Removing privileges on test database...
Success.

Reloading the privilege tables will ensure that all changes
made so far will take effect immediately.

Reload privilege tables now? (Press y|Y for Yes, any other key for No) : y
Success.

All done!
```

Check out `https://dev.mysql.com/doc/refman/5.7/en/validate-pass word-plugin.html`for more information about the password validation plugin.

7. Once the secure installation process is done, we can go ahead and connect to MySQL using the `mysql` console tool, as follows:

```
// INSECURE WAY (bare passwords in a command)
mysql -uroot -p'mL08e!Tq'
mysql --user=root --password='mL08e!Tq'

// SECURE WAY (triggers "enter password" prompt)
mysql -uroot -p
mysql --user=root --password
```

Notice the use of the single quote character (`'`) around the password. While normally we could use the `"` or `'` quotes, the `!` char used in password forces us to use `'`. Without wrapping the password in a single quote, in this case, we will be seeing an error like **!Tq: event not found**. This is because the exclamation mark (`!`) is a part of the history expansion in bash. To use it as a part of the password, we need to enclose it in single quotes. Furthermore, our passwords can contain the `'` or `"` characters. To escape these quotes in the password, we can either use a leading backslash (), or enclose the entire argument in the opposite style of quotes. However, the simplest and safest way to get around quirky password characters is to avoid assigning the password value with `-p` or `--password` arguments, and provide the password through the **Enter password:** prompt.

This should give us the following output:

```
root@vultr:~# mysql -uroot -p
Enter password:
Welcome to the MySQL monitor.  Commands end with ; or \g.
Your MySQL connection id is 11
Server version: 5.7.17-0ubuntu0.16.10.1 (Ubuntu)

Copyright (c) 2000, 2016, Oracle and/or its affiliates. All rights reserved.

Oracle is a registered trademark of Oracle Corporation and/or its
affiliates. Other names may be trademarks of their respective
owners.

Type 'help;' or '\h' for help. Type '\c' to clear the current input statement.

mysql> quit
Bye
root@vultr:~#
```

Check out `https://dev.mysql.com/doc/refman/5.7/en/mysql-shell.h tml`for more information about the MySQL shell.

Setting up sample data

Before we move onto querying MySQL, let's go ahead and set up some sample data. MySQL provides a sample database called Sakila, which we can download from the official MySQL site, as follows:

```
cd ~
wget http://downloads.mysql.com/docs/sakila-db.tar.gz
tar -xzf sakila-db.tar.gz
cd sakila-db/
```

Once downloaded and unpacked, this should give us the following three files:

```
root@vultr:~/sakila-db# ls -al
total 3404
drwxr-xr-x 2  500  500     4096 Jul 20  2016 .
drwx------ 4 root root     4096 Mar 18 09:18 ..
-rw-r--r-- 1  500  500 3398148 Jul 20  2016 sakila-data.sql
-rw-r--r-- 1  500  500   50019 Jul 20  2016 sakila.mwb
-rw-r--r-- 1  500  500   23424 Jul 20  2016 sakila-schema.sql
root@vultr:~/sakila-db#
```

Moving forward, we need to see how we can import `sakila-schema.sql` and `sakila-data.sql`. Luckily, MySQL provides several ways to do this. A quick look at the `sakila-schema.sql` file shows the following entries at the top of the file:

```
DROP SCHEMA IF EXISTS sakila;
CREATE SCHEMA sakila;
USE sakila;
```

This means that the `sakila-schema.sql` file will create a schema (database) for us, as well as set it as currently used database. This is an important bit to understand, as not all of the `.sql` / backup files will have this, and we will be forced to do this part manually. Knowing how `sakila-schema.sql` handles everything we need to import it, the following commands show three different approaches we can use:

```
// Either this command
mysql -uroot -p < sakila-schema.sql

// Either this command
mysql -uroot -p -e "SOURCE sakila-schema.sql"
```

The second command uses the `-e` (`--execute`) argument to pass SQL statements to the server. We could have easily used the `mysql` tool interactively and then executed `SOURCE sakila-schema.sql` within it. With the schema in place, we can go ahead and import the actual data:

```
// Either this command
mysql -uroot -p < sakila-data.sql

// Either this command
mysql -uroot -p -e "SOURCE sakila-data.sql"
```

If we now use the `mysql` tool interactively, we can check if the database is imported successfully:

```
show databases;
use sakila;
show tables;
```

This should give us the following output:

```
mysql> show databases;
+--------------------+
| Database           |
+--------------------+
| information_schema |
| mysql              |
| performance_schema |
| sakila             |
| sys                |
+--------------------+
5 rows in set (0.00 sec)

mysql> use sakila;
Reading table information for completion of table and column names
You can turn off this feature to get a quicker startup with -A

Database changed
mysql> show tables;
+----------------------------+
| Tables_in_sakila           |
+----------------------------+
| actor                      |
| actor_info                 |
| address                    |
| category                   |
| city                       |
| country                    |
| customer                   |
| customer_list              |
| film                       |
| film_actor                 |
| film_category              |
| film_list                  |
| film_text                  |
| inventory                  |
| language                   |
| nicer_but_slower_film_list |
| payment                    |
| rental                     |
| sales_by_film_category     |
| sales_by_store             |
| staff                      |
| staff_list                 |
| store                      |
+----------------------------+
23 rows in set (0.00 sec)

mysql>
```

Check out `https://dev.mysql.com/doc/sakila/en/` for more information about the Sakila sample database.

Querying via the MySQLi driver extension

There are several driver extensions that allow us to query MySQL. MySQLi is one of them. In order to use MySQLi on the console, we need to ensure that we have the PHP CLI and `mysql` driver extension installed:

```
sudo apt-get -y install php7.0-cli php7.0-mysql
```

Note that the name of the extension lacks the `i` suffix. Once the `mysql` driver extension is installed, we can go ahead and start querying the MySQL server.

Connecting

We can either use the MySQLi functions or classes to interact with MySQL. In the spirit of OOP, we will use the class approach for all of our examples. Using the `mysqli` class, we can establish a MySQL connection from PHP, as follows:

```
$mysqli = new mysqli('127.0.0.1', 'root', 'mL08e!Tq', 'sakila');
```

This single line expression will look for MySQL on the `127.0.0.1` host and try to connect to its `sakila` database using the `root` username and `mL08e!Tq` as its password.

Error handling

Handling errors around `mysqli` is relatively easy as we can use a simple `try...catch` block, as follows:

```php
<?php

mysqli_report(MYSQLI_REPORT_ALL);

try {
    $mysqli = new mysqli('127.0.0.1', 'root', 'mL08e!Tq', 'sakila');
} catch (Throwable $t) {
    exit($t->getMessage());
}
```

Ideally, we would want to use `mysqli_sql_exception` for more targeted MySQL exceptions-only handling:

```php
<?php

mysqli_report(MYSQLI_REPORT_ALL);

try {
  $mysqli = new mysqli('127.0.0.1', 'root', 'mL08e!Tq', 'sakila');
} catch (mysqli_sql_exception $e) {
  exit($e->getMessage());
}
```

We can pass one of the following report levels to the `mysqli_report()` function:

- `MYSQLI_REPORT_INDEX`: This reports if a bad index or no index at all was used in a query
- `MYSQLI_REPORT_ERROR`: This reports errors from the MySQL function calls
- `MYSQLI_REPORT_STRICT`: This reports `mysqli_sql_exception` instead of possible warnings
- `MYSQLI_REPORT_ALL`: This reports everything
- `MYSQLI_REPORT_OFF`: This reports nothing

While `MYSQLI_REPORT_ALL` may seem like an overkill, using it may pinpoint MySQL errors that are not obvious on the application level, such as the lack of an index on a column.

Selecting

We can select data from MySQL using the `query()` method of a `mysqli` instance, as follows:

```php
<?php

try {
    // Report on all types of errors
    mysqli_report(MYSQLI_REPORT_ALL);

    // Open a new connection to the MySQL server
    $mysqli = new mysqli('127.0.0.1', 'root', 'mL08e!Tq', 'sakila');

    // Perform a query on the database
    $result = $mysqli->query('SELECT * FROM customer WHERE email LIKE
```

```
"MARIA.MILLER@sakilacustomer.org"');

    // Return the current row of a result set as an object
    $customer = $result->fetch_object();

    // Close opened database connection
    $mysqli->close();

    // Output customer info
    echo $customer->first_name, ' ', $customer->last_name, PHP_EOL;
} catch (mysqli_sql_exception $e) {
    // Output error and exit upon exception
    echo $e->getMessage(), PHP_EOL;
    exit;
}
```

The preceding example gives the following error:

```
No index used in query/prepared statement SELECT * FROM customer WHERE
email = "MARIA.MILLER@sakilacustomer.org"
```

If we have used MYSQLI_REPORT_STRICT instead of MYSQLI_REPORT_ALL, we would not have got the error. However, using less restrictive error reporting is not a solution for mitigating the error. Even though we might not be in charge of the database architecture and maintenance, it is our duty as a developer to report overlooks like these as they will most definitely affect our application performance. A solution, in this case, is to actually create an index on the email column. We can do so easily via the following query:

```
ALTER TABLE customer ADD INDEX idx_email (email);
```

```
mysql> use sakila;
Reading table information for completion of table and column names
You can turn off this feature to get a quicker startup with -A

Database changed
mysql> ALTER TABLE customer ADD INDEX idx_email (email);
Query OK, 0 rows affected (0.02 sec)
Records: 0  Duplicates: 0  Warnings: 0

mysql>
```

idx_email is the freely given name of the index we are creating, while email is the column for which we are creating an index. The idx_ prefix is merely a matter of convention some developers use; the index can easily be named xyz or just email.

With the index in place, if we now try to execute the previous code, it should output **MARIA MILLER**, as shown in the following screenshot:

The query() method returns either the mysqli_result object or the True and False Boolean value, based on the following type:

- SELECT type of query - mysqli_result object or Boolean False
- SHOW type of query - mysqli_result object or Boolean False
- DESCRIBE type of query - mysqli_result object or Boolean False
- EXPLAIN type of query - mysqli_result object or Boolean False
- other types of queries - Boolean True or False

The instance of the mysqli_result object has several different result fetching methods:

- fetch_object(): This fetches the current row of a result set as an object, and allows being called repeatedly
- fetch_all(): This fetches all result rows as either MYSQLI_ASSOC, MYSQLI_NUM, or MYSQLI_BOTH
- fetch_array(): This fetches a single result row as either MYSQLI_ASSOC, MYSQLI_NUM, or MYSQLI_BOTH
- fetch_assoc(): This fetches a single result row as an associative array, and allows being called repeatedly
- fetch_field(): This fetches the next field in the result set, and allows being called repeatedly
- fetch_field_direct(): This fetches meta-data for a single field
- fetch_fields(): This fetches meta-data for fields in an entire result set
- fetch_row(): This fetches a single result row as an enumerated array and allows being called repeatedly

Binding parameters

More often than not, querying data comes with data binding. Security-wise, data binding is the way to go, as we should never concatenate query string with variables on our own. This leads to SQL injection attacks. We can bind data into a query using the `prepare()` and `bind_param()` methods of the respective `mysqli` and `mysqli_stmt` instances, as follows:

```php
<?php

try {
    // Report on all types of errors
    mysqli_report(MYSQLI_REPORT_ALL);

    // Open a new connection to the MySQL server
    $mysqli = new mysqli('127.0.0.1', 'root', 'mL08e!Tq', 'sakila');

    $customerIdGt = 100;
    $storeId = 2;
    $email = "%ANN%";

    // Prepare an SQL statement for execution
    $statement = $mysqli->prepare('SELECT * FROM customer WHERE customer_id
> ? AND store_id = ? AND email LIKE ?');

    // Binds variables to a prepared statement as parameters
    $statement->bind_param('iis', $customerIdGt, $storeId, $email);

    // Execute a prepared query
    $statement->execute();

    // Gets a result set from a prepared statement
    $result = $statement->get_result();

    // Fetch object from row/entry in result set
    while ($customer = $result->fetch_object()) {
        // Output customer info
        echo $customer->first_name, ' ', $customer->last_name, PHP_EOL;
    }

    // Close a prepared statement
    $statement->close();

    // Close database connection
    $mysqli->close();
} catch (mysqli_sql_exception $e) {
    // Output error and exit upon exception
    echo $e->getMessage();
    exit;
```

```
}
```

This should give us the following output:

The `bind_param()` method has an interesting syntax. It accepts two or more parameters. The first parameter--the `$types` string--contains one or more characters. These characters specify the types for the corresponding bind variables:

- `i`: This is the variable of a type integer
- `d`: This is the variable of a type double
- `s`: This is the variable of a type string
- `b`: This is the variable of a type blob

The second and all of the following parameters represent the binding variables. Our example uses `'iis'` for the `$types` parameter, which basically reads the `bind_param()` method and its parameters as: bind integer type (`$customerIdGt`), integer type (`$storeId`), and string type (`$email`).

Inserting

Now that we have learned how to prepare a query and bind data to it, inserting new records becomes pretty easy:

```php
<?php

try {
    // Report on all types of errors
    mysqli_report(MYSQLI_REPORT_ALL);

    // Open a new connection to the MySQL server
    $mysqli = new mysqli('127.0.0.1', 'root', 'mL08e!Tq', 'sakila');
```

```
    // Prepare some teat address data
    $address = 'The street';
    $district = 'The district';
    $cityId = 135; // Matches the Dallas city in Sakila DB
    $postalCode = '31000';
    $phone = '123456789';

    // Prepare an SQL statement for execution
    $statement = $mysqli->prepare('INSERT INTO address (
            address,
            district,
            city_id,
            postal_code,
            phone
        ) VALUES (
            ?,
            ?,
            ?,
            ?,
            ?
        );
    ');

    // Bind variables to a prepared statement as parameters
    $statement->bind_param('ssiss', $address, $district, $cityId,
$postalCode, $phone);

    // Execute a prepared Query
    $statement->execute();

    // Close a prepared statement
    $statement->close();

    // Quick & "dirty" way to fetch newly created address id
    $addressId = $mysqli->insert_id;

    // Close database connection
    $mysqli->close();
} catch (mysqli_sql_exception $e) {
    // Output error and exit upon exception
    echo $e->getMessage();
    exit;
}
```

The example here pretty much follows the previous one where we introduced binding. The obvious difference merely lies in the actual INSERT INTO SQL expression. It goes without saying that mysqli does not have separate PHP classes or methods to handle selecting, inserting, or any other action.

Updating

Much like selecting and inserting, we can also use the prepare(), bind_param(), and execute() methods to handle record updating, as follows:

```php
<?php

try {
    // Report on all types of errors
    mysqli_report(MYSQL_REPORT_ALL);

    // Open a new connection to the MySQL server
    $mysqli = new mysqli('127.0.0.1', 'root', 'mL08e!Tq', 'sakila');

    // Prepare some teat address data
    $address = 'The new street';
    $addressId = 600;

    // Prepare an SQL statement for execution
    $statement = $mysqli->prepare('UPDATE address SET address = ? WHERE
address_id = ?');

    // Bind variables to a prepared statement as parameters
    $statement->bind_param('si', $address, $addressId);

    // Execute a prepared Query
    $statement->execute();

    // Close a prepared statement
    $statement->close();

    // Close database connection
    $mysqli->close();
} catch (mysqli_sql_exception $e) {
    // Output error and exit upon exception
    echo $e->getMessage();
    exit;
}
```

Deleting

Again, we can use the `prepare()`, `bind_param()`, and `execute()` methods to handle record deleting, as shown here:

```php
<?php

try {
    // Report on all types of errors
    mysqli_report(MYSQLI_REPORT_ALL);

    // Open a new connection to the MySQL server
    $mysqli = new mysqli('127.0.0.1', 'root', 'mL08e!Tq', 'sakila');

    // Prepare some teat address data
    $paymentId = 500;

    // Prepare an SQL statement for execution
    $statement = $mysqli->prepare('DELETE FROM payment WHERE payment_id = ?');

    // Bind variables to a prepared statement as parameters
    $statement->bind_param('i', $paymentId);

    // Execute a prepared Query
    $statement->execute();

    // Close a prepared statement
    $statement->close();

    // Close database connection
    $mysqli->close();
} catch (mysqli_sql_exception $e) {
    // Output error and exit upon exception
    echo $e->getMessage();
    exit;
}
```

Transactions

While the SELECT, INSERT, UPDATE, and DELETE methods allow us to manipulate data in a step-by-step manner, the real strength of MySQL lies in transactions. Using the `begin_transaction()`, `commit()`, `commit()`, and `rollback()` methods of an `mysqli` instance, we are able to control the transaction features of MySQL:

```php
<?php

mysqli_report(MYSQLI_REPORT_ALL);
$mysqli = new mysqli('127.0.0.1', 'root', 'mL08e!Tq', 'sakila');

try {
    // Start new transaction
    $mysqli->begin_transaction(MYSQLI_TRANS_START_READ_WRITE);

    // Create new address
    $result = $mysqli->query('INSERT INTO address (
            address,
            district,
            city_id,
            postal_code,
            phone
        ) VALUES (
            "The street",
            "The district",
            333,
            "31000",
            "123456789"
        );
    ');

    // Fetch newly created address id
    $addressId = $mysqli->insert_id;

    // Create new customer
    $statement = $mysqli->prepare('INSERT INTO customer (
            store_id,
            first_name,
            last_name,
            email,
            address_id
        ) VALUES (
            2,
            "John",
            "Doe",
            "john@test.it",
            ?
        )
    ');
    $statement->bind_param('i', $addressId);
    $statement->execute();

    // Fetch newly created customer id
    $customerId = $mysqli->insert_id;
```

```
    // Select newly created customer info
    $statement = $mysqli->prepare('SELECT * FROM customer WHERE customer_id
= ?');
    $statement->bind_param('i', $customerId);
    $statement->execute();
    $result = $statement->get_result();
    $customer = $result->fetch_object();

    // Commit transaction
    $mysqli->commit();

    echo $customer->first_name, ' ', $customer->last_name, PHP_EOL;
} catch (mysqli_sql_exception $t) {
    // We MUST be careful with non-db try block operations that throw
exceptions
    // As they might cause a rollback inadvertently
    $mysqli->rollback();
    echo $t->getMessage(), PHP_EOL;
}

// Close database connection
$mysqli->close();
```

The valid transaction flags are as follows:

- `MYSQLI_TRANS_START_READ_ONLY`: This matches the MySQL `START TRANSACTION READ ONLY` query
- `MYSQLI_TRANS_START_READ_WRITE`: This matches the MySQL `START TRANSACTION READ WRITE` query
- `MYSQLI_TRANS_START_WITH_CONSISTENT_SNAPSHOT`: This matches the MySQL `START TRANSACTION WITH CONSISTENT SNAPSHOT` query

 Check out `https://dev.mysql.com/doc/refman/5.7/en/commit.html` for more information about the MySQL transaction syntax and meaning.

Querying via the PHP Data Objects driver extension

The **PHP Data Objects** (**PDO**) driver extension comes with PHP by default, ever since PHP 5.1.0.

Connecting

Using the PDO driver extension, we can connect to a MySQL database from PHP using the PDO class, as follows:

```php
<?php

$host = '127.0.0.1';
$dbname = 'sakila';
$username = 'root';
$password = 'mL08e!Tq';

$conn = new PDO(
    "mysql:host=$host;dbname=$dbname",
    $username,
    $password
);
```

This simple multiline expression will look for MySQL on the 127.0.0.1 host and try to connect to its sakila database using the root username and mL08e!Tq password.

Error handling

Handling errors around PDO can be done using the special PDOException class, as follows:

```php
<?php

try {
    $host = '127.0.0.1';
    $dbname = 'sakila';
    $username = 'root';
    $password = 'mL08e!Tq';

    $conn = new PDO(
        "mysql:host=$host;dbname=$dbname",
        $username,
        $password,
        [PDO::ATTR_ERRMODE => PDO::ERRMODE_EXCEPTION]
    );
} catch (PDOException $e) {
    echo $e->getMessage(), PHP_EOL;
}
```

There are three different error modes:

- ERRMODE_SILENT
- ERRMODE_WARNING
- ERRMODE_EXCEPTION

Here, we are using ERRMODE_EXCEPTION in order to utilize the try...catch blocks.

Selecting

Querying for records with PDO is somewhat similar to querying for records with mysqli. We use raw SQL statements in both cases. The difference lies in the convenience of PHP methods and the subtle differences they provide. The following example demonstrates how we can select records from a MySQL table:

```php
<?php

try {
    $conn = new PDO(
        "mysql:host=127.0.0.1;dbname=sakila", 'root', 'mL08e!Tq',
        [PDO::ATTR_ERRMODE => PDO::ERRMODE_EXCEPTION]
    );

    $result = $conn->query('SELECT * FROM customer LIMIT 5');
    $customers = $result->fetchAll(PDO::FETCH_OBJ);

    foreach ($customers as $customer) {
        echo $customer->first_name, ' ', $customer->last_name, PHP_EOL;
    }
} catch (PDOException $e) {
    echo $e->getMessage(), PHP_EOL;
}
```

This gives the following output:

```
root@vultr:~/querying# php pdo.php
MARY SMITH
PATRICIA JOHNSON
LINDA WILLIAMS
BARBARA JONES
ELIZABETH BROWN
root@vultr:~/querying# 
```

The instance of the PDOStatement and $result object has several different result-fetching methods:

- fetch(): This fetches the next row from a result set, allows being called repeatedly, and returns a value depending on the fetch style
- fetchAll(): This fetches all of the result set rows as an array, and returns a value depending on the fetch style
- fetchObject(): This fetches the next row from a result set as an object, and allows being called repeatedly
- fetchColumn(): This fetches a single column from the next row of a result set, and allows being called repeatedly

The following list shows available PDO fetch styles:

- PDO::FETCH_LAZY
- PDO::FETCH_ASSOC
- PDO::FETCH_NUM
- PDO::FETCH_BOTH
- PDO::FETCH_OBJ
- PDO::FETCH_BOUND
- PDO::FETCH_COLUMN
- PDO::FETCH_CLASS
- PDO::FETCH_INTO
- PDO::FETCH_FUNC
- PDO::FETCH_GROUP
- PDO::FETCH_UNIQUE
- PDO::FETCH_KEY_PAIR
- PDO::FETCH_CLASSTYPE
- PDO::FETCH_SERIALIZE
- PDO::FETCH_PROPS_LATE
- PDO::FETCH_NAMED

While most of these fetch styles are quite self-explanatory, we can consult http://php.net/manual/en/pdo.constants.php for further details.

The following example demonstrates a more elaborate select approach, one with parameter binding in the mix:

```php
<?php

try {
    $conn = new PDO(
        "mysql:host=127.0.0.1;dbname=sakila", 'root', 'mL08e!Tq',
        [PDO::ATTR_ERRMODE => PDO::ERRMODE_EXCEPTION]
    );

    $statement = $conn->prepare('SELECT * FROM customer
        WHERE customer_id > :customer_id AND store_id = :store_id AND email
LIKE :email');

    $statement->execute([
        ':customer_id' => 100,
        ':store_id' => 2,
        ':email' => '%ANN%',
    ]);

    $customers = $statement->fetchAll(PDO::FETCH_OBJ);

    foreach ($customers as $customer) {
        echo $customer->first_name, ' ', $customer->last_name, PHP_EOL;
    }
} catch (PDOException $e) {
    echo $e->getMessage(), PHP_EOL;
}
```

This gives the following output:

```
root@vultr:~/querying# php pdo.php
SHANNON FREEMAN
JOANNE ROBERTSON
SUZANNE NICHOLS
JOANN GARDNER
JEANNE LAWSON
DIANNE SHELTON
JAMES GANNON
RANDALL NEUMANN
SETH HANNON
root@vultr:~/querying#
```

The most obvious difference between binding with `PDO` and binding with `mysqli` is that `PDO` allows named parameter binding. This makes for much more readable queries.

Inserting

Much like selecting, inserting involves the same set of PDO methods wrapped around the `INSERT INTO` SQL statement:

```php
<?php

try {
    $conn = new PDO(
        "mysql:host=127.0.0.1;dbname=sakila", 'root', 'mL08e!Tq',
        [PDO::ATTR_ERRMODE => PDO::ERRMODE_EXCEPTION]
    );

    $statement = $conn->prepare('INSERT INTO address (
            address,
            district,
            city_id,
            postal_code,
            phone,
            location
        ) VALUES (
            :address,
            :district,
            :city_id,
            :postal_code,
            :phone,
            POINT(:longitude, :latitude)
        );
    ');

    $statement->execute([
        ':address' => 'The street',
        ':district' => 'The district',
        ':city_id' => '537',
        ':postal_code' => '31000',
        ':phone' => '888777666333',
        ':longitude' => 45.55111,
        ':latitude' => 18.69389
    ]);
} catch (PDOException $e) {
    echo $e->getMessage(), PHP_EOL;
}
```

Updating

Much like selecting and inserting, updating involves the same set of PDO methods wrapped around the UPDATE SQL statement:

```php
<?php

try {
    $conn = new PDO(
        "mysql:host=127.0.0.1;dbname=sakila", 'root', 'mL08e!Tq',
        [PDO::ATTR_ERRMODE => PDO::ERRMODE_EXCEPTION]
    );

    $statement = $conn->prepare('UPDATE address SET phone = :phone WHERE
address_id = :address_id');

    $statement->execute([
        ':phone' => '888777666555',
        ':address_id' => 600,
    ]);
} catch (PDOException $e) {
    echo $e->getMessage(), PHP_EOL;
}
```

Deleting

Much like selecting, inserting, and updating, deleting involves the same set of PDO methods wrapped around the DELETE FROM SQL statement:

```php
<?php

try {
    $conn = new PDO(
        "mysql:host=127.0.0.1;dbname=sakila", 'root', 'mL08e!Tq',
        [PDO::ATTR_ERRMODE => PDO::ERRMODE_EXCEPTION]
    );
    $statement = $conn->prepare('DELETE FROM payment WHERE payment_id =
:payment_id');
    $statement->execute([
        ':payment_id' => 16046
    ]);
} catch (PDOException $e) {
    echo $e->getMessage(), PHP_EOL;
}
```

Transactions

Transactions with PDO are not much different from those with MySQLi. Utilizing the `beginTransaction()`, `commit()`, and `rollback()` methods of the PDO instance, we are able to control the transaction features of MySQLi:

```php
<?php

$conn = new PDO(
    "mysql:host=127.0.0.1;dbname=sakila", 'root', 'mL08e!Tq',
    [PDO::ATTR_ERRMODE => PDO::ERRMODE_EXCEPTION]
);

try {
    // Start new transaction
    $conn->beginTransaction();

    // Create new address
    $result = $conn->query('INSERT INTO address (
            address,
            district,
            city_id,
            postal_code,
            phone,
            location
        ) VALUES (
            "The street",
            "The district",
            537,
            "27107",
            "888777666555",
            POINT(45.55111, 18.69389)
        );
    ');

    // Fetch newly created address id
    $addressId = $conn->lastInsertId();

    // Create new customer
    $statement = $conn->prepare('INSERT INTO customer (
            store_id,
            first_name,
            last_name,
            email,
            address_id
        ) VALUES (
            2,
            "John",
```

```
                    "Doe",
                    "john-pdo@test.it",
                    :address_id
            )
    ');

    $statement->execute([':address_id' => $addressId]);

    // Fetch newly created customer id
    $customerId = $conn->lastInsertId();

    // Select newly created customer info
    $statement = $conn->prepare('SELECT * FROM customer WHERE customer_id =
:customer_id');
    $statement->execute([':customer_id' => $customerId]);
    $customer = $statement->fetchObject();

    // Commit transaction
    $conn->commit();

    echo $customer->first_name, ' ', $customer->last_name, PHP_EOL;
} catch (PDOException $e) {
    $conn->rollback();
    echo $e->getMessage(), PHP_EOL;
}
```

Working with MongoDB

MongoDB is a free and open source NoSQL database developed by MongoDB Inc.

Some of the key strengths of MongoDB can be outlined as follows:

- It is a document-based database
- It is cross-platform
- It runs on a single server as well as on distributed architectures
- It can be used for desktop and web applications
- It uses JSON objects to store data
- It can use JavaScript map-reduce for information processing at the server side
- It processes large volumes of data
- It aggregates calculations
- It supports fields, range queries, and regular expression searches
- It is a native replication

Installing MongoDB

Assuming we are using the fresh Ubuntu 16.10 (Yakkety Yak) installation, the following steps outline how we can setup MongoDB:

1. We will install MongoDB using the following console command:

   ```
   sudo apt-get update
   sudo apt-get install -y mongodb
   ```

2. To further check that MongoDB is successfully installed and running, we can execute the following command:

   ```
   sudo systemctl status mongodb.service
   ```

3. This should give us the following output:

```
root@vultr:~/querying# sudo systemctl status mongodb.service
• mongodb.service - An object/document-oriented database
   Loaded: loaded (/lib/systemd/system/mongodb.service; enabled; vendor preset: enabled)
   Active: active (running) since Sun 2017-03-19 12:01:05 UTC; 1min 34s ago
     Docs: man:mongod(1)
 Main PID: 19161 (mongod)
   CGroup: /system.slice/mongodb.service
           └─19161 /usr/bin/mongod --unixSocketPrefix=/run/mongodb --config /etc/mongodb.conf

Mar 19 12:01:05 vultr.guest systemd[1]: Started An object/document-oriented database.
root@vultr:~/querying# 
```

Setting up sample data

Running the `mongo` command on the Ubuntu terminal gets us into a mongo interactive shell. From here on, with a simple few commands, we can add the sample data:

```
use foggyline
db.products.insert({name: "iPhone 7", price: 650, weight: "138g"});
db.products.insert({name: "Samsung Galaxy S7", price: 670, weight: "152g"
});
db.products.insert({name: "Motorola Moto Z Play", price: 449.99, weight:
"165g" });
db.products.insert({name: "Google Pixel", price: 649.99, weight: "168g" });
db.products.insert({name: "HTC 10", price: 799, weight: "161g" });
show dbs
show collections
```

This should give us an output much like the following screenshot:

```
root@vultr:~/querying# mongo
MongoDB shell version: 2.6.11
connecting to: test
> use foggyline
switched to db foggyline
> db.products.insert({name: "iPhone 7", price: 650, weight: "138g"});
WriteResult({ "nInserted" : 1 })
> db.products.insert({name: "Samsung Galaxy S7", price: 670, weight: "152g" });
WriteResult({ "nInserted" : 1 })
> db.products.insert({name: "Motorola Moto Z Play", price: 449.99, weight: "165g" });
WriteResult({ "nInserted" : 1 })
> db.products.insert({name: "Google Pixel", price: 649.99, weight: "168g" });
WriteResult({ "nInserted" : 1 })
> db.products.insert({name: "HTC 10", price: 799, weight: "161g" });
WriteResult({ "nInserted" : 1 })
> show dbs
admin        (empty)
foggyline   0.078GB
local       0.078GB
test        (empty)
> show collections
products
system.indexes
>
```

Using `use foggyline` and `db.products.find()`, we are able to now list all the entries added to the `products` collection:

```
root@vultr:~/querying# mongo
MongoDB shell version: 2.6.11
connecting to: test
> use foggyline
switched to db foggyline
> db.products.find()
{ "_id" : ObjectId("58ce900780b38d0018d17a6a"), "name" : "iPhone 7", "price" : 650, "weight" : "138g" }
{ "_id" : ObjectId("58ce900a80b38d0018d17a6b"), "name" : "Samsung Galaxy S7", "price" : 670, "weight" : "152g" }
{ "_id" : ObjectId("58ce901080b38d0018d17a6c"), "name" : "Motorola Moto Z Play", "price" : 449.99, "weight" : "165g" }
{ "_id" : ObjectId("58ce901680b38d0018d17a6d"), "name" : "Google Pixel", "price" : 649.99, "weight" : "168g" }
{ "_id" : ObjectId("58ce901a80b38d0018d17a6e"), "name" : "HTC 10", "price" : 799, "weight" : "161g" }
>
```

Querying via the MongoDB driver extension

We need to make sure we have the PHP CLI and MongoDB driver extension installed:

```
sudo apt-get -y install php-pear
sudo apt-get -y install php7.0-dev
```

```
sudo apt-get -y install libcurl4-openssl-dev pkg-config libssl-dev
libsslcommon2-dev
sudo pecl install mongodb
```

Upon successful execution of these commands, we can confirm that the `mongodb` driver extension is installed, as shown in the following screenshot:

Aside from the driver extension, we also need a `mongodb/mongodb` composer package added to our project directory. We can do so by running the following console command:

```
sudo apt-get -y install composer
composer require mongodb/mongodb
```

Assuming we have the `mongo.php` file within our project directory, all it takes is to load the MongoDB library, and start working with Mongo database:

```php
<?php

require_once __DIR__ . '/vendor/autoload.php';

// Code...
```

Connecting

Using the `mongodb` driver extension and the `mongodb/mongodb` PHP library, we can connect to the Mongo database from PHP using the `MongoDBDriverManager` class, as follows:

```php
<?php

require_once __DIR__ . '/vendor/autoload.php';

$manager = new MongoDBDriverManager('mongodb://localhost:27017');
```

This single-line expression will look for MongoDB on `localhost` under port `27017`.

Error handling

Handling errors is pretty straightforward with the `try...catch` blocks, as `MongoDBDriverExceptionException` is being thrown whenever an error occurs:

```php
<?php

require_once __DIR__ . '/vendor/autoload.php';

try {
    $manager = new MongoDBDriverManager('mongodb://localhost:27017');
} catch (MongoDBDriverExceptionException $e) {
    echo $e->getMessage(), PHP_EOL;
    exit;
}
```

Selecting

Fetching data with MongoDB comes down to working with three different classes, `MongoDBDriverManager`, `MongoDBDriverQuery`, and `MongoDBDriverReadPreference`:

```php
<?php

require_once __DIR__ . '/vendor/autoload.php';

try {
    $manager = new MongoDBDriverManager('mongodb://localhost:27017');

    /* Select only the matching documents */
    $filter = [
        'price' => [
            '$gte' => 619.99,
        ],
    ];

    $queryOptions = [
        /* Return only the following fields in the matching documents */
        'projection' => [
            'name' => 1,
            'price' => 1,
        ],
        /* Return the documents in descending order of price */
        'sort' => [
            'price' => -1
        ]
    ];
```

```
    $query = new MongoDBDriverQuery($filter, $queryOptions);

    $readPreference = new
MongoDBDriverReadPreference(MongoDBDriverReadPreference::RP_PRIMARY);

    $products = $manager->executeQuery('foggyline.products', $query,
$readPreference);

    foreach ($products as $product) {
        echo $product->name, ': ', $product->price, PHP_EOL;
    }
} catch (MongoDBDriverExceptionException $e) {
    echo $e->getMessage(), PHP_EOL;
    exit;
}
```

This gives the following output:

```
root@vultr:~/querying# php mongo.php
HTC 10: 799
Samsung Galaxy S7: 670
iPhone 7: 650
Google Pixel: 649.99
root@vultr:~/querying# 
```

The list of query operators we can pass onto $filter is quite an extensive one, but the following comparison operators may be the most interesting ones:

- $eq: These match all values that are equal to a specified value
- $gt: These match all values that are greater than a specified value
- $gte: These match all values that are greater than or equal to a specified value
- $lt: These match all values that are less than a specified value
- $lte: These match all values that are less than or equal to a specified value
- $ne: These match all values that are not equal to a specified value
- $in: These match all values that are specified in an array
- $nin: These match the none values that are specified in an array

 Check out ttps://docs.mongodb.com/manual/reference/operator/que ry/ for a full list of MongoDB query and projection operators.

The list of query options we can pass onto `$queryOptions` is equally impressive, but the following options may be the essential ones:

- `collation`: These allow specifying language-specific rules for string comparison
- `limit`: These allow specifying the maximum number of documents to return
- `maxTimeMS`: These set the processing operations time limit in milliseconds
- `projection`: These allow specifying which fields to include in the returned documents
- `sort`: These allow specifying sort ordering of the results

Check out `http://php.net/manual/en/mongodb-driver-query.construct.php` for a full list of the `MongoDBDriverQuery` query options.

Inserting

Writing new data with MongoDB comes down to working with three different classes, `MongoDBDriverManager`, `MongoDBDriverBulkWrite`, and `MongoDBDriverWriteConcern`:

```php
<?php

require_once __DIR__ . '/vendor/autoload.php';

try {
    $manager = new MongoDBDriverManager('mongodb://localhost:27017');

    $bulkWrite = new MongoDBDriverBulkWrite;

    $bulkWrite->insert([
        'name' => 'iPhone 7 Black White',
        'price' => 650,
        'weight' => '138g'
    ]);

    $bulkWrite->insert([
        'name' => 'Samsung Galaxy S7 White',
        'price' => 670,
        'weight' => '152g'
    ]);

    $writeConcern = new
```

```
MongoDBDriverWriteConcern(MongoDBDriverWriteConcern::MAJORITY, 1000);

    $result = $manager->executeBulkWrite('foggyline.products', $bulkWrite,
$writeConcern);

    if ($result->getInsertedCount()) {
        echo 'Record(s) saved successfully.', PHP_EOL;
    } else {
        echo 'Error occurred.', PHP_EOL;
    }
} catch (MongoDBDriverExceptionException $e) {
    echo $e->getMessage(), PHP_EOL;
    exit;
}
```

The instance of `BulkWrite` can store one or more insert statements through the `insert()`
method. We then simply pass `$bulkWrite` and `$writeConcern` to `executeBulkWrite()`
on the `$manager` instance. Once executed, we can observe the newly added records
through the `mongo` shell:

```
root@vultr:~/querying# mongo
MongoDB shell version: 2.6.11
connecting to: test
> use foggyline
switched to db foggyline
> db.products.find()
{ "_id" : ObjectId("58ce900780b38d0018d17a6a"), "name" : "iPhone 7", "price" : 650, "weight" : "138g" }
{ "_id" : ObjectId("58ce900a80b38d0018d17a6b"), "name" : "Samsung Galaxy S7", "price" : 670, "weight" : "152g" }
{ "_id" : ObjectId("58ce901080b38d0018d17a6c"), "name" : "Motorola Moto Z Play", "price" : 449.99, "weight" : "165g" }
{ "_id" : ObjectId("58ce901680b38d0018d17a6d"), "name" : "Google Pixel", "price" : 649.99, "weight" : "168g" }
{ "_id" : ObjectId("58ce901a80b38d0018d17a6e"), "name" : "HTC 10", "price" : 799, "weight" : "161g" }
{ "_id" : ObjectId("58ce975365d440035061b832"), "name" : "iPhone 7 Black White", "price" : 650, "weight" : "138g" }
{ "_id" : ObjectId("58ce975365d440035061b833"), "name" : "Samsung Galaxy S7 White", "price" : 670, "weight" : "152g" }
>
```

Updating

Updating existing data is a nearly identical process as writing new data. The obvious
difference being the use of the `update()` method on the `MongoDBDriverBulkWrite`
instance:

```php
<?php

require_once __DIR__ . '/vendor/autoload.php';

try {
    $manager = new MongoDBDriverManager('mongodb://localhost:27017');

    $bulkWrite = new MongoDBDriverBulkWrite;
```

```
    $bulkWrite->update(
        ['name' => 'iPhone 7 Black White'],
        ['$set' => [
            'name' => 'iPhone 7 Black Black',
            'price' => 649.99
        ]],
        ['multi' => true, 'upsert' => false]
    );

    $bulkWrite->update(
        ['name' => 'Samsung Galaxy S7 White'],
        ['$set' => [
            'name' => 'Samsung Galaxy S7 Black',
            'price' => 669.99
        ]],
        ['multi' => true, 'upsert' => false]
    );

    $writeConcern = new
MongoDBDriverWriteConcern(MongoDBDriverWriteConcern::MAJORITY, 1000);

    $result = $manager->executeBulkWrite('foggyline.products', $bulkWrite,
$writeConcern);

    if ($result->getModifiedCount()) {
        echo 'Record(s) saved updated.', PHP_EOL;
    } else {
        echo 'Error occurred.', PHP_EOL;
    }
} catch (MongoDBDriverExceptionException $e) {
    echo $e->getMessage(), PHP_EOL;
    exit;
}
```

The `update()` method accepts three different parameters: filter, a new object, and update options. The `multi` option passed under update options, tells if all documents' matching criteria will be updated. The `upsert` option passed under update options, controls the creation of a new record if the existing record is not found. The resulting change can be observed through the `mongo` shell:

```
root@vultr:~/querying# mongo
MongoDB shell version: 2.6.11
connecting to: test
> use foggyline
switched to db foggyline
> db.products.find()
{ "_id" : ObjectId("58ce900780b38d0018d17a6a"), "name" : "iPhone 7", "price" : 650, "weight" : "138g" }
{ "_id" : ObjectId("58ce900a80b38d0018d17a6b"), "name" : "Samsung Galaxy S7", "price" : 670, "weight" : "152g" }
{ "_id" : ObjectId("58ce901080b38d0018d17a6c"), "name" : "Motorola Moto Z Play", "price" : 449.99, "weight" : "165g" }
{ "_id" : ObjectId("58ce901680b38d0018d17a6d"), "name" : "Google Pixel", "price" : 649.99, "weight" : "168g" }
{ "_id" : ObjectId("58ce901a80b38d0018d17a6e"), "name" : "HTC 10", "price" : 799, "weight" : "161g" }
{ "_id" : ObjectId("58ce975365d440035061b832"), "name" : "iPhone 7 Black", "price" : 649.99, "weight" : "138g" }
{ "_id" : ObjectId("58ce975365d440035061b833"), "name" : "Samsung Galaxy S7 Black", "price" : 669.99, "weight" : "152g" }
>
```

Deleting

Deletion is done in a manner similar to write and update, in that it uses an instance of the `MongoDBDriverBulkWrite` object. This time, we are using the instance `delete()` method, which accepts filter and delete options:

```php
<?php

require_once __DIR__ . '/vendor/autoload.php';

try {
    $manager = new MongoDBDriverManager('mongodb://localhost:27017');

    $bulkWrite = new MongoDBDriverBulkWrite;

    $bulkWrite->delete(
        // filter
        [
            'name' => [
                '$regex' => '^iPhone'
            ]
        ],
        // Delete options
        ['limit' => false]
    );

    $writeConcern = new
MongoDBDriverWriteConcern(MongoDBDriverWriteConcern::MAJORITY, 1000);

    $result = $manager->executeBulkWrite('foggyline.products', $bulkWrite,
$writeConcern);

    if ($result->getDeletedCount()) {
        echo 'Record(s) deleted.', PHP_EOL;
    } else {
```

```
            echo 'Error occurred.', PHP_EOL;
    }
} catch (MongoDBDriverExceptionException $e) {
    echo $e->getMessage(), PHP_EOL;
    exit;
}
```

Using the `false` value for the `limit` option, we are effectively asking to delete all matching documents. Using the `mongo` shell, we can observe the changes shown in the following screenshot:

```
root@vultr:~/querying# mongo
MongoDB shell version: 2.6.11
connecting to: test
> use foggyline
switched to db foggyline
> db.products.find()
{ "_id" : ObjectId("58ce900a80b38d0018d17a6b"), "name" : "Samsung Galaxy S7", "price" : 670, "weight" : "152g" }
{ "_id" : ObjectId("58ce901080b38d0018d17a6c"), "name" : "Motorola Moto Z Play", "price" : 449.99, "weight" : "165g" }
{ "_id" : ObjectId("58ce901680b38d0018d17a6d"), "name" : "Google Pixel", "price" : 649.99, "weight" : "168g" }
{ "_id" : ObjectId("58ce901a80b38d0018d17a6e"), "name" : "HTC 10", "price" : 799, "weight" : "161g" }
{ "_id" : ObjectId("58ce975365d440035061b833"), "name" : "Samsung Galaxy S7 Black", "price" : 669.99, "weight" : "152g" }
>
```

Transactions

MongoDB does not have a full **ACID** (**Atomicity, Consistency, Isolation, Durability**) support in a sense that MySQL has. It supports ACID transactions only at the document level. The multi-document transactions are not supported. The lack of ACID compliance certainly limits its use with platforms that depend on this feature. This is not to say that MongoDB cannot be used with such platforms. Let's consider a popular Magento e-commerce platform. There is nothing preventing Magento from adding MongoDB to the mix. While the MySQL features can guarantee ACID compliance around sales-related functionality, MongoDB can be used within the conjunction to cover bits around catalog functionality. This type of symbiosis can then easily bring the best of both database features to our platform.

Working with Redis

Redis is an open source, in-memory data structure store, whose development is sponsored by Redis Labs. The name originated from **REmote DIctionary Server**. It currently ranks as one of the most popular key-value databases.

Some of the key strengths of Redis can be outlined as follows:

- In-memory data structure store
- Key-value data store
- Keys with a limited time-to-live
- Publish/subscribe messaging
- It can be used for cache data stores
- Transactions
- Master-slave replication

Installing Redis

Assuming we are using the fresh Ubuntu 16.10 (Yakkety Yak) installation, the following steps outline how we can setup the Redis server:

1. We can install the Redis server using the following console commands:

```
sudo apt-get update
sudo apt-get -y install build-essential tcl
wget http://download.redis.io/redis-stable.tar.gz
tar xzf redis-stable.tar.gz
cd redis-stable
make
make test
sudo make install
./src/redis-server
```

2. This should give us the following output:

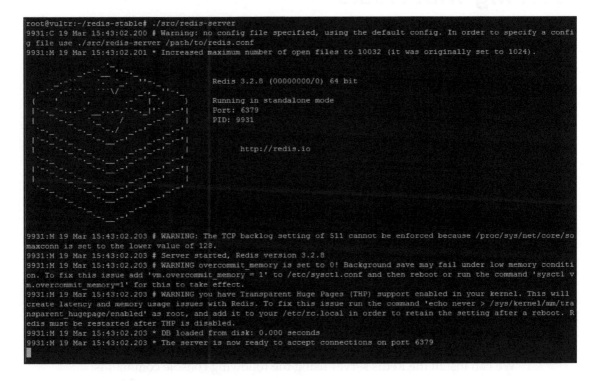

Setting up sample data

Running the `redis-cli` command on the Ubuntu terminal gets us into the
Redis interactive shell. From here on, with a simple few commands, we can add the
following sample data:

```
SET Key1 10
SET Key2 20
SET Key3 30
SET Key4 40
SET Key5 50
```

This should give us the following output:

```
root@vultr:~# cd redis-stable/src/
root@vultr:~/redis-stable/src# ./redis-cli
127.0.0.1:6379> SET Key1 10
OK
127.0.0.1:6379> SET Key2 20
OK
127.0.0.1:6379> SET Key3 30
OK
127.0.0.1:6379> SET Key4 40
OK
127.0.0.1:6379> SET Key5 50
OK
```

Using the KEYS * command within the redis-cli shell, we are able to now list all the entries added by Redis:

```
root@vultr:~/redis-stable/src# ./redis-cli
127.0.0.1:6379> KEYS *
1) "Key1"
2) "Key3"
3) "Key4"
4) "Key2"
5) "Key5"
127.0.0.1:6379> 
```

Querying via the phpredis driver extension

Before we start querying, we need to ensure that we have the PHP CLI and phpredis driver extension installed:

```
sudo apt-get -y install php7.0-dev
sudo apt-get -y install unzip
wget https://github.com/phpredis/phpredis/archive/php7.zip -O phpredis.zip
unzip phpredis.zip
cd phpredis-php7/
phpize
./configure
make
sudo make install
echo extension=redis.so >> /etc/php/7.0/cli/php.ini
```

Upon successful execution of these commands, we can confirm that the `phpredis` driver extension is installed as follows:

```
root@vultr:~# php -m | grep redis
redis
root@vultr:~#
```

Connecting

Using the `phpredis` driver extension, we can connect to Redis from PHP using the `Redis` class, as follows:

```php
<?php

$client = new Redis();

$client->connect('localhost', 6379);
```

This single-line expression will look for Redis on localhost under port 6379.

Error handling

The `phpredis` driver extension throws `RedisException` for every error that occurs using the `Redis` class. This makes it easy to handle errors via simple `try...catch` blocks:

```php
<?php

try {
    $client = new Redis();
    $client->connect('localhost', 6379);
    // Code...
} catch (RedisException $e) {
    echo $e->getMessage(), PHP_EOL;
}
```

Selecting

Given that Redis is a key value store, selecting keys is as easy as using a single `get()` method of the `Redis` instance:

```php
<?php
```

```
try {
    $client = new Redis();
    $client->connect('localhost', 6379);
    echo $client->get('Key3'), PHP_EOL;
    echo $client->get('Key5'), PHP_EOL;
} catch (RedisException $e) {
    echo $e->getMessage(), PHP_EOL;
}
```

This should give us the following output:

```
root@vultr:~/querying# php redis.php
30
50
root@vultr:~/querying#
```

The Redis client class also provides the mget() method, which is able to fetch more than one key value at a time:

```
<?php

try {
    $client = new Redis();
    $client->connect('localhost', 6379);

    $values = $client->mget(['Key1', 'Key2', 'Key4']);
    print_r($values);
} catch (RedisException $e) {
    echo $e->getMessage(), PHP_EOL;
}
```

This should give us the following output:

```
root@vultr:~/querying# php redis.php
Array
(
    [0] => 10
    [1] => 20
    [2] => 40
)
root@vultr:~/querying#
```

Inserting

The simplicity behind the Redis key-value mechanism makes for a simple and straightforward `set()` method, through which we insert new entries, as shown in the following example:

```php
<?php

try {
    $client = new Redis();
    $client->connect('localhost', 6379);

    $client->set('user', [
        'name' => 'John',
        'age' => 34,
        'salary' => 4200.00
    ]);

    // $client->get('user');
    // returns string containing "Array" chars

    $client->set('customer', json_encode([
        'name' => 'Marc',
        'age' => 43,
        'salary' => 3600.00
    ]));

    // $client->get('customer');
    // returns json looking string, which we can simply json_decode()
} catch (RedisException $e) {
    echo $e->getMessage(), PHP_EOL;
}
```

This should give us the following output:

```
root@vultr:~/redis-stable/src# ./redis-cli
127.0.0.1:6379> KEYS *
1) "user"
2) "Key5"
3) "customer"
4) "Key1"
5) "Key2"
6) "Key4"
7) "Key3"
127.0.0.1:6379> GET user
"Array"
127.0.0.1:6379> GET customer
"{\"name\":\"Marc\",\"age\":43,\"salary\":3600}"
127.0.0.1:6379>
```

We should be careful when using the set methods with non-string like structures. The `user` key value resulted in the **Array** string being stored in Redis, and not the actual array structure. This is easily sorted by converting our array structure to JSON using `json_encode()`, right before we pass it onto the `set()` method.

One great benefit of the `set()` method is that it supports the timeout in seconds, so we can easily write expressions such as the following:

```
$client->set('test', 'test2', 3600);
```

Although, calling the `setex()` method is the preferred way for when we want to add a timeout to our keys:

```
$client->setex('key', 3600, 'value');
```

> Timeouts are a great feature to use when using Redis as a cache database. They basically automate the cache lifetime for us.

Updating

Updating a value via the Redis client is the same as inserting it. We use the same `set()` method, with the same key. The new value simply overwrites the previous one, if any exists:

```php
<?php

try {
    $client = new Redis();
    $client->connect('localhost', 6379);

    $client->set('test', 'test1');
    $client->set('test', 'test2');

    // $client->get('test');
    // returns string containing "test2" chars
} catch (RedisException $e) {
    echo $e->getMessage(), PHP_EOL;
}
```

Deleting

Removing records from Redis is as easy as calling the Redis client `del()` method and passing it the key that we want to delete:

```php
<?php

try {
    $client = new Redis();
    $client->connect('localhost', 6379);
    $client->del('user');
} catch (RedisException $e) {
    echo $e->getMessage(), PHP_EOL;
}
```

Transactions

Much like MongoDB, Redis also does not have ACID support in a sense that MySQL has, which is alright really, as Redis is just a key/value store and not a relational database. Redis, however, provides a level of atomicity. Using MULTI, EXEC, DISCARD, and WATCH, we are able to execute a group of commands within a single step, during which Redis makes the following two guarantees:

- Another client request can never be served in the middle of our group-commands execution
- Either all or none of the commands are processed

Let's take a look at the following example:

```php
<?php

try {
    $client = new Redis();
    $client->connect('localhost', 6379);

    $client->multi();

    $result1 = $client->set('tKey1', 'Test#1'); // Valid command
    $result2 = $client->zadd('tKey2', null); // Invalid command

    if ($result1 == false || $result2 == false) {
        $client->discard();
        echo 'Transaction aborted.', PHP_EOL;
    } else {
        $client->exec();
        echo 'Transaction commited.', PHP_EOL;
    }
} catch (RedisException $e) {
    echo $e->getMessage(), PHP_EOL;
}
```

The $result2 value comes out as false, which triggers $client->discard();. Although, result1 is a valid expression, it came after the $client->multi(); call, which means that its command is not really processed; so, we don't get to see the Test#1 value stored in Redis. Although there is no classically looking rollback mechanism, like we had with MySQL, this makes for a nice transaction model.

Summary

Throughout this chapter, we touched upon the basics of querying three very different database systems.

The MySQL database has been around for a very long time, and is likely the number one database for most PHP applications. Its ACID compliance makes it irreplaceable for applications dealing with financial or other sensitive data where atomicity, consistency, isolation, and durability are key factors.

Mongo, on the other hand, tackles data storage through a schema-less approach. This makes it much easier for developers to pace up application development, although the lack of ACID compliance across documents limits its use in certain types of applications.

Finally, the Redis data store serves as a great caching, or even a session-storing solution for our applications.

Moving forward, we will take a closer look at dependency injection, what it is, and what role does it have within modular applications.

13
Resolving Dependencies

Writing a loosely coupled code has become an essential skill for any professional developer. While legacy applications had a tendency to pack it all up, thus ending in one big solid block of code, modern applications take a more gradient approach as they largely rely on third-party libraries and other components. Nowadays, hardly anyone builds their own mailer, logger, router, template engine, and so on. Great deal of these components are out there, waiting to be consumed by our application through Composer. As individual components themselves are tested and maintained by various community or commercial entities, the cost of maintaining our application is significantly reduced. The overall code quality itself improves as an indirect consequence of more specialized developers addressing specific functionalities that otherwise might fall out of the area of our expertise. Harmony that has been made possible via loosely coupled code.

There are a multitude of positive side-effects of loosely coupled code, some of which include the following:

- Easier refactoring
- Improved code maintainability
- Easier cross-platform utilization
- Easier cross-framework utilization
- Aspiration towards a single responsibility principle compliance
- Easier testing

This magic of loose coupling is easily achieved by utilizing various language features, such as interfaces, and design patterns, such as dependency injection. Moving forward, we will take a look at the basic aspects of dependency injection through the following sections:

- Mitigating the common problem
- Understanding dependency injection

- Understanding dependency injection container

Mitigating the common problem

The dependency injection is a well-established software technique that deals with the problem of object dependencies, allowing us to write loosely coupled classes. While the pattern itself has been around for quite some time, the PHP ecosystem hasn't really picked it up until major frameworks such as Symfony started implementing it. Nowadays, it is a de facto standard for anything other than trivial types of application. The whole dependency problem is easily observed through a simple example:

```php
<?php

class Customer
{
    protected $name;

    public function loadByEmail($email)
    {
        $mysqli = new mysqli('127.0.0.1', 'foggy', 'h4P9niq5', 'sakila');

        $statement = $mysqli->prepare('SELECT * FROM customer WHERE email = ?');
        $statement->bind_param('s', $email);
        $statement->execute();

        $customer = $statement->get_result()->fetch_object();

        $this->name = $customer->first_name . ' ' . $customer->last_name;

        return $this;
    }
}

$customer = new Customer();
$customer->loadByEmail('MARY.SMITH@sakilacustomer.org');
```

Here, we have a simple `Customer` class with a single `loadByEmail()` method. The troubling part is the dependency on the database `$mysqli` object being locked in a `loadByEmail()` instance method. This makes for tight coupling, which reduces code reusability and opens the door for possible system-wide side-effects to be induced by later code changes. To mitigate the problem, we need to inject the database `$mysqli` object into `$customer`.

The MySQL Sakila database can be obtained from `https://dev.mysql.co m/doc/sakila/en/`.

There are three ways to inject the dependency into an object:

- Through an instance method
- Through a class constructor
- Through instance property

Whereas the instance method and class constructor approach seem slightly more popular than instance property injection.

The following example demonstrates the approach of using an instance method for dependency injection:

```php
<?php

class Customer
{
    public function loadByEmail($email, $mysqli)
    {
        // ...
    }
}

$mysqli = new mysqli('127.0.0.1', 'foggy', 'h4P9niq5', 'sakila');

$customer = new Customer();
$customer->loadByEmail('MARY.SMITH@sakilacustomer.org', $mysqli);
```

Here, we are injecting an instance of the `$mysqli` object into an instance of the `Customer` object through the customer's `loadByEmail()` instance method. While this is certainly a better way than instantiating the `$mysqli` object within the `loadByEmail()` method itself, it is easy to imagine how quickly our client code might become clumsy if our class were to have a dozen of methods, each requiring different objects to be passed to it. While this approach might seem tempting, injecting dependencies through instance methods violates OOP's principle of encapsulation. Furthermore, adding arguments to methods for the sake of dependency is anything but an example of best practice.

Another approach would be to utilize the class constructor method as per the following example:

```php
<?php
```

```php
class Customer
{
    public function __construct($mysqli)
    {
        // ...
    }

    public function loadByEmail($email)
    {
        // ...
    }
}

$mysqli = new mysqli('127.0.0.1', 'foggy', 'h4P9niq5', 'sakila');

$customer = new Customer($mysqli);
$customer->loadByEmail('MARY.SMITH@sakilacustomer.org');
```

Here, we are injecting an instance of the $mysqli object into an instance of the Customer object through the customer's __constructor() method. Whether a single or a dozen objects are being injected, the constructor injection comes out as the clear winner here. The client application has a single entry point for all injections, making it easy to keep a track of things.

Without the notion of dependency injection, a loosely coupled code would be impossible to achieve.

Understanding dependency injection

Throughout the introductory section, we touched upon passing dependency through the class __construct() method. There is more to it than just passing the dependent object. Let's consider the following three seemingly similar but different examples.

Though PHP has been supporting type hinting for quite a while now, it isn't uncommon to come across pieces of code, which are as follows:

```php
<?php

class App
{
    protected $config;
    protected $logger;

    public function __construct($config, $logger)
    {
```

```php
        $this->config = $config;
        $this->logger = $logger;
    }

    public function run()
    {
        $this->config->setValue('executed_at', time());
        $this->logger->log('executed');
    }
}

class Config
{
    protected $config = [];

    public function setValue($path, $value)
    {
        // implementation
    }
}

class Logger
{
    public function log($message)
    {
        // implementation
    }
}

$config = new Config();
$logger = new Logger();

$app = new App($config, $logger);
$app->run();
```

We can see that the App class __construct() method does not utilize the PHP type hinting feature. The $config and $logger variables are assumed by the developer to be of a certain type. While this example will work just fine, it still keeps our classes tightly coupled. There really is not that much difference between this example and the previous one where we had the $msqli dependency within the loadByEmail() method.

Adding type hinting to the mix allows us to force the types we pass into the App class __construct() method:

```php
<?php

class App
```

```
{
    protected $config;
    protected $logger;

    public function __construct(Config $config, Logger $logger)
    {
        $this->config = $config;
        $this->logger = $logger;
    }

    public function run()
    {
        $this->config->setValue('executed_at', time());
        $this->logger->log('executed');
    }
}

class Config
{
    protected $config = [];

    public function setValue($path, $value)
    {
        // implementation
    }
}

class Logger
{
    public function log($message)
    {
        // implementation
    }
}

$config = new Config();
$logger = new Logger();

$app = new App($config, $logger);
$app->run();
```

This simple move sets us halfway through making our code loosely coupled. Although we are now instructing our injectable objects to be of an exact type, we are still locked onto a specific type, that is, implementation. Striving for loose coupling should not get us locked into a specific implementation; otherwise, there would not be much use of a dependency injection pattern.

This third example sets an important differentiation in regards to the first two examples:

```php
<?php

class App
{
    protected $config;
    protected $logger;

    public function __construct(ConfigInterface $config, LoggerInterface
$logger)
    {
        $this->config = $config;
        $this->logger = $logger;
    }

    public function run()
    {
        $this->config->setValue('executed_at', time());
        $this->logger->log('executed');
    }
}

interface ConfigInterface
{
    public function getValue($value);

    public function setValue($path, $value);
}

interface LoggerInterface
{
    public function log($message);
}

class Config implements ConfigInterface
{
    protected $config = [];

    public function getValue($value)
    {
        // implementation
    }

    public function setValue($path, $value)
    {
        // implementation
    }
```

```
    }

    class Logger implements LoggerInterface
    {
        public function log($message)
        {
            // implementation
        }
    }

    $config = new Config();
    $logger = new Logger();

    $app = new App($config, $logger);
    $app->run();
```

Favoring interface type hints instead of concrete class type hints is among the key ingredients to write loosely coupled code. Although we are still injecting dependencies through the class __construct(), we are now doing so in a *program to an interface, not an implementation* manner. This allows us to avoid tight coupling, making our code more reusable.

Clearly, these examples are ultimately simple. We can imagine how quickly things start to complicate when the number of injected objects increase, where each of the injected objects might need one, two, or even a dozen of the __construct() parameters itself. This is where the dependency injection container comes in handy.

Understanding dependency injection container

A dependency injection container is an object that knows how to auto-wire classes together. The **auto-wire** term implies both instantiating and properly configuring objects. This is by no means an easy task, which is why there are several libraries addressing this functionality.

The DependencyInjection component provided by the Symfony framework is a neat dependency injection container that can be easily installed by Composer. Moving forward, let's go ahead and create a di-container directory where we will execute these commands and set up our project:

```
composer require symfony/dependency-injection
```

The resulting output suggests we should install some additional packages:

```
root@sightsdigital:~/di-container# composer require symfony/dependency-injection
Using version ^3.2 for symfony/dependency-injection
./composer.json has been created
Loading composer repositories with package information
Updating dependencies (including require-dev)
  - Installing symfony/dependency-injection (v3.2.6)
    Downloading: 100%

symfony/dependency-injection suggests installing symfony/yaml ()
symfony/dependency-injection suggests installing symfony/config ()
symfony/dependency-injection suggests installing symfony/expression-language (For using expressions in service container configuration)
symfony/dependency-injection suggests installing symfony/proxy-manager-bridge (Generate service proxies to lazy load them)
Writing lock file
Generating autoload files
root@sightsdigital:~/di-container#
```

We need to make sure we add the `symfony/yaml` and `symfony/config` packages by running the following console commands:

```
composer require symfony/yaml
composer require symfony/config
```

The `symfony/yaml` package installs the Symfony Yaml component. This component parses the YAML strings into PHP arrays and the other way around. The `symfony/config` package installs the Symfony Config component. This component provides classes to help us find, load, combine, autofill, and validate configuration values from sources, such as YAML, XML, INI files, or even a database itself. The `symfony/dependency-injection`, `symfony/yaml`, and `symfony/config` packages themselves stand as a nice example of loosely coupled components. While the three work hand in hand to deliver the full scope of dependency injection functionality, components themselves follow the principles of loose coupling.

 Check out `http://symfony.com/doc/current/components/dependency_injection.html` for more information about the Symfony's DependencyInjection component.

Now let's go ahead and create the `container.yml` configuration file within the `di-container` directory:

```
services:
  config:
    class: Config
  logger:
    class: Logger
  app:
    class: App
    autowire: true
```

The `container.yml` file has a specific structure that begins with the keyword `services`. Without delving any deeper into it, suffice it to say that the service container is the Symfony's name for dependency injection container, while the service is any PHP object performing some task--basically, an instance of a class of any sort.

Right below the `services` tag, we have the `config`, `logger`, and `app` tags. These denote a declaration of three distinctive services. We could have easily named them `the_config`, `the_logger`, `the_app`, or whatever else we prefer. Drilling deeper into individual services, we see the `class` tag being common to all three services. The `class` tag tells the container what class to instantiate when a given service instance is asked for. Finally, the `autowire` feature used within the `app` service definition allows the autowiring subsystem to detect the dependencies of the `App` class by parsing its constructor. This makes it dead simple for a client code to get an instance of the `App` class without even being aware of the `$config` and `$logger` requirements on the `App` class `__construct()`.

With the `container.yml` file in place, let's go ahead and create the `index.php` file within the `di-container` directory:

```php
<?php

require_once __DIR__ . '/vendor/autoload.php';

use Symfony\Component\DependencyInjection\ContainerBuilder;
use Symfony\Component\Config\FileLocator;
use Symfony\Component\DependencyInjection\Loader\YamlFileLoader;

interface ConfigInterface { /* ... */}
interface LoggerInterface { /* ... */}
class Config implements ConfigInterface { /* ... */}
class Logger implements LoggerInterface { /* ... */}
class App { /* ... */}

// Bootstrapping
$container = new ContainerBuilder();

$loader = new YamlFileLoader($container, new FileLocator(__DIR__));
$loader->load('container.yml');

$container->compile();

// Client code
$app = $container->get('app');
$app->run();
```

Be sure to replace everything from `ConfigInterface` to `App` with the exact code we had in our third example from within the **Understanding dependency injection** section.

We started off by including the `autoload.php` file so we get the auto-loading for our dependency container component working. The code following the `use` statements is the same code we had in the **Understanding dependency injection** section. The interesting part comes after it. The instance of `ContainerBuilder` is created and passed onto `YamlFileLoader`, which loads the `container.yml` file. Right after the file is loaded, we call the `compile()` method on the `$container` instance. Running `compile()` allows the container to pick up on the `autowire` service tag, among other things. Finally, we are using the `get()` method on the `$container` instance to fetch an instance of the `app` service. The client, in this case, has no upfront knowledge of arguments being passed to the `App` instance; the dependency container handled it all by itself based on a `container.yml` configuration.

Using interface type hints and the container, we are able to write more reusable, testable, and decoupled code.

Check out `http://symfony.com/doc/current/service_container.html` for more information about the Symfony service container.

Summary

The dependency injection is a simple technique that allows us to escape from the shackles of tight coupling. Combined with interface type hints, we get a powerful technique to write loosely coupled code. This isolates and minimizes the impact of possible future application design changes as well as its defects. Nowadays, it is considered irresponsible to even write modular and large code base applications without embracing these simple techniques.

Moving forward, we will take a closer look at the state of the ecosystem around PHP packages, their creation, and distribution.

14
Working with Packages

Modern PHP applications tend to be comprised of a large number of files. Take the Magento 2 eCommerce platform as an example. Once installed, its `vendor` directory contains over thirty thousand of the PHP class files. The sheer size of it is enough to stunt anyone. Why so many files, one might wonder? Nowadays, it is popular, if not mandatory, to make use of preexisting libraries and packages other developers have written before us. It would not make much sense to *reinvent the wheel* all the time. This is why package managers such as Composer are ever so popular among the PHP developers. Making use of these package managers usually means pulling in a diverse set of third-party packages into our project. While this usually hints increased application size, it also allows us to jump-start our application development. The added benefit being the quality and continuous maintenance of these packages by third parties, which we then merely update into our application.

In this chapter, we will look into Composer, the most popular PHP package manager:

- Understanding Composer
- Understanding Packagist
- Using third-party packages
- Creating your own package
- Distributing your package

 Throughout the previous chapters, we already had certain touching points with Composer, as we used some of its packages. The following sections are to add some extra clarity on top of that, as well as showcase how we can create our own packages.

Understanding Composer

Composer is a *per-project* package manager for PHP. Originally released in 2011, it quickly caught up and became a favorite package manager among PHP developers. Just by looking at its GitHub statistics, we can see the project is being actively developed by the community:

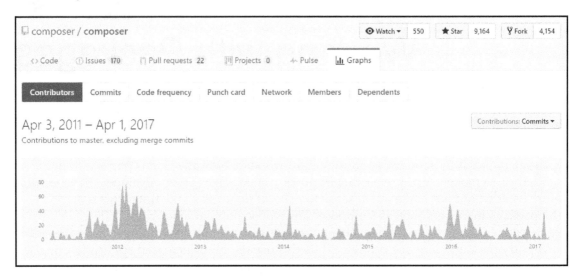

Nowadays, it is an integral part of almost every popular PHP project. Installing Composer is a pretty straightforward task. Assuming we are using the fresh Ubuntu 16.10 (Yakkety Yak) installation, the following command outlines how we can install Composer:

```
sudo apt-get -y install composer
```

Running composer -v after the installation should show the output similar to the following screenshot:

```
   /  __ __ \ / ___ _ __ ___ / __  ___ ___ __ __
  /  / ___  ___/ __  ___  ___   __/  __/ __/  \ \
  \  \ \___ \ \_____/ \_____/ \__/  \__/ \__/ \ \
    \____/ _/
Composer version 1.1.3 2016-06-26 15:42:08

Usage:
  command [options] [arguments]

Options:
  -h, --help                    Display this help message
  -q, --quiet                   Do not output any message
  -V, --version                 Display this application version
      --ansi                    Force ANSI output
      --no-ansi                 Disable ANSI output
  -n, --no-interaction          Do not ask any interactive question
      --profile                 Display timing and memory usage information
      --no-plugins              Whether to disable plugins.
  -d, --working-dir=WORKING-DIR If specified, use the given directory as working directory.
  -v|vv|vvv, --verbose          Increase the verbosity of messages: 1 for normal output, 2 for more verbose output and 3 for debug

Available commands:
  about            Short information about Composer
  archive          Create an archive of this composer package
  browse           Opens the package's repository URL or homepage in your browser.
  clear-cache      Clears composer's internal package cache.
  clearcache       Clears composer's internal package cache.
  config           Set config options
```

Now that we have it installed, using Composer is quite simple. Assuming we have an existing project to which we would like to add the Twig library, we can do so just by running the following command within our project root directory:

```
composer require "twig/twig:^2.0"
```

```
$ composer require "twig/twig:^2.0"
Running composer as root/super user is highly discouraged as packages, plugins and scripts cannot always be trusted
./composer.json has been created
Loading composer repositories with package information
Updating dependencies (including require-dev)
  - Installing symfony/polyfill-mbstring (v1.3.0)
    Downloading: 100%

  - Installing twig/twig (v2.3.0)
    Downloading: 100%

symfony/polyfill-mbstring suggests installing ext-mbstring (For best performance)
Writing lock file
Generating autoload files
$ ls
composer.json  composer.lock  vendor
$
```

Upon execution, two files and a directory are created/modified: `composer.json`, `composer.lock`, and `vendor`. The `vendor` directory is the physical location where Composer places the packages we choose to install. We could have easily started off by manually creating the same `composer.json` file with the content as follows, and then running the `composer install` command within the project directory:

```
{
  "require": {
```

```
    "twig/twig": "^2.0"
  }
}
```

 Check out `https://getcomposer.org/doc/04-schema.md`for full information on possible `composer.json` content.

Now we could easily modify `index.php` or any other entry-point file to our root project directory and include all of the installed composer packages by adding the following entry to it as follows:

```
require_once __DIR__ . '/vendor/autoload.php';
```

The `vendor/autoload.php` file is created by the composer tool, which handles the autoloading of all the packages we pulled in through composer, the content of which looks like this:

```
<?php

// autoload.php @generated by Composer

require_once __DIR__ . '/composer/autoload_real.php';

return ComposerAutoloaderInitea5a081b69b5068b6eadbd8b638d57b2::getLoader();
```

This file is not something we should really concern ourselves with, aside from knowing where it is.

 Both PSR-4 and PSR-0 autoloading are supported, although PSR-4 is the recommended way as it offers a greater ease of use.

As soon as we include `/vendor/autoload.php` into our script, all of the pulled in packages become available to our application. Whether it is a new or existing project, Composer makes it quite easy to add packages to it.

 Learning about Composer in full is out of the scope of this section. Consult the original documentation (`https://getcomposer.org/`) for more details on Composer.

Understanding Packagist

Much like the Git and GitHub relationship, we have the Composer and Packagist relationship. While **Composer** itself is the actual tool, **Packagist** is the default repository service that provides packages for Composer. Service is easy enough to let us find packages we would like to use for our project. Without getting into the internals, it is suffice to say that the composer tool understands where to get the code for each of the packages hosted on Packagist.

The Packagist repository service is hosted at `https://packagist.org`:

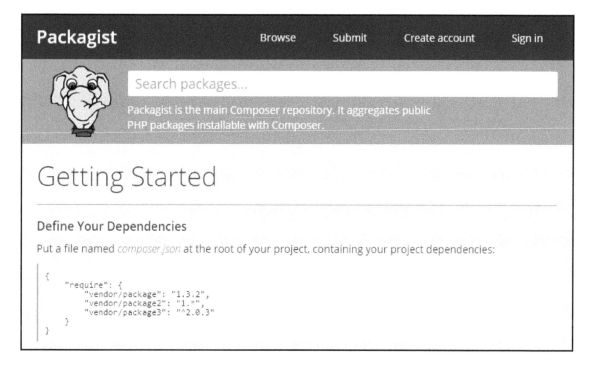

The popularity of Composer over time can be easily observed through the `https://packag ist.org/statistics` page, which shows the rapidly increasing number of packages in the Packagist repository over the course of few years:

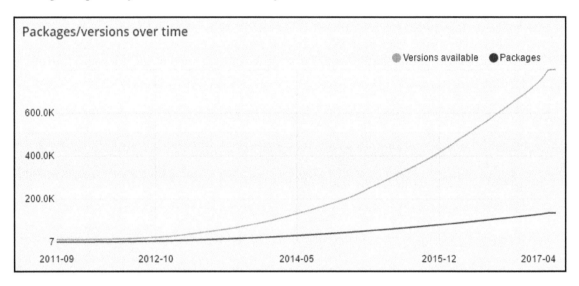

Using third-party packages

We already saw how easy it is to install the composer package via one of the following two options:

- Executing a command such as `require vendor/package:2.* vendor/package2:dev-master`
- Adding a package link information under `composer.json require`, and executing `composer install` on console

Without knowing which package exactly we might need, we could use the `https://packag ist.org`search tool to find it. Let's consider, for example, we are looking for a package with an e-mail sending functionality. This is where the sheer size of the Packagist repository might take us some time to find the right package. Luckily, we can use **Sort by downloads** or **Sort by favorites** to help ourselves out:

Once we click on the individual package, we get to see the available versions we can install:

Running `composer require swiftmailer/swiftmailer` in this case would give us the latest stable version 5.4.6.

Once installed, packages can later be updated to possible new stable versions simply by running the `composer update` command within the project root.

Creating your own package

Using the `composer init` command, we can kick off the interactive `composer.json` generator that we will use later on to distribute our package. The interactive generator raises several questions, as per the following output:

```
$ composer init
Running composer as root/super user is highly discouraged as packages, plugins and scripts cannot always be trusted

   Welcome to the Composer config generator


This command will guide you through creating your composer.json config.

Package name (<vendor>/<name>) [root/mp7]: foggyline/mp7
Description []: Just a test package.
Author [, n to skip]: Branko Ajzele <ajzele@gmail.com>
Minimum Stability []:
Package Type []: library
License []: MIT

Define your dependencies.

Would you like to define your dependencies (require) interactively [yes]? no
Would you like to define your dev dependencies (require-dev) interactively [yes]? no

{
    "name": "foggyline/mp7",
    "description": "Just a test package.",
    "type": "library",
    "license": "MIT",
    "authors": [
        {
            "name": "Branko Ajzele",
            "email": "ajzele@gmail.com"
        }
    ],
    "require": {}
}

Do you confirm generation [yes]? yes
$
```

We used `foggyline` as our vendor name here, whereas `mp7` (short for Mastering PHP 7) was used for the package name. Upon completion, the `composer.json` file is generated with the following content:

```
{
"name": "foggyline/mp7",
"description": "Just a test package.",
"type": "library",
"license": "MIT",
"authors": [
    {
"name": "Branko Ajzele",
"email": "ajzele@gmail.com"
    }
  ],
"require": {}
}
```

Now, let's go ahead and create the `src/Foggyline/MP7/Greeting/Goodbye.php` file, relative to the project root directory, with the following content:

```php
<?php

namespace FoggylineMP7Greeting;

class Welcome
{
    public function generate($name)
    {
        return 'Welcome ' . $name;
    }
}
```

This is our dummy library class that we will soon distribute as the composer package. Before we do so, we need to amend `composer.json` by adding the top-level `autoload` entry to it, as follows:

```json
"autoload": {
  "psr-4": {
    "FoggylineMP7": "src/Foggyline/MP7/"
  }
}
```

To test if `autoload` is set right, we run the `composer dump-autoload --optimize` console command and create the `index.php` file with the following content. We deliberately use the full path to the `MP7` directory, as this will be our individual library, that is, package:

```php
<?php

require_once __DIR__ . '/vendor/autoload.php';

use FoggylineMP7GreetingWelcome;

$greeting = new Welcome();

echo $greeting->generate('John');
```

If all went well, running this script should give us a **Welcome John** output. Now that we have `composer.json` describing our project, and `src/Foggyline/MP7/` containing our library code, we can go ahead and distribute this.

Distributing your package

We first need to push `composer.json` and our library code from within `src/Foggyline/MP7/`, into the GitHub repository. Assuming we have an empty GitHub repository, such as `git@github.com:ajzele/foggyline_mp7.git`, waiting for us, we can easily do so through the following few commands:

```
git init
git remote add origin git@github.com:ajzele/foggyline_mp7.git
git add composer.json
git add src/Foggyline/MP7/
git commit -m "Initial commit"
git push origin master
```

This should show up in GitHub, as follows:

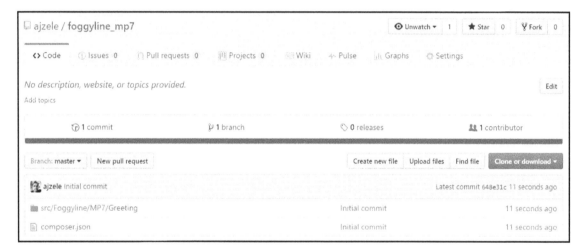

With the files in the GitHub repository, we can now visit the `https://packagist.org` page and **Submit** our package:

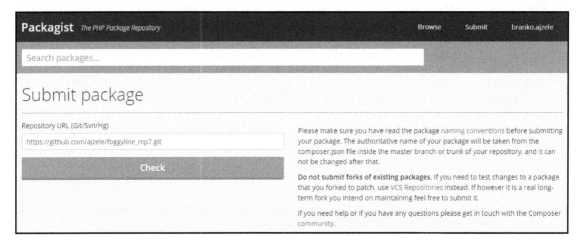

Once the **Check** is done, we should be able to see a screen similar to the following one:

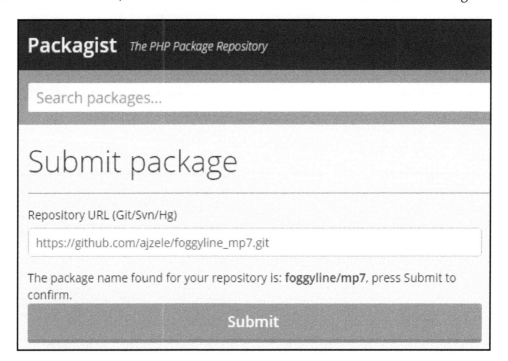

Once we hit the **Submit** button, we should be able to see a screen similar to the following one:

We should now be able to use the `foggyline/mp7` package within any project just by running the following console command:

```
composer require foggyline/mp7:dev-master
```

 Notice the `dev-master` suffix here. Our package is flagged as `dev-master` only. This is because our `https://github.com/ajzele/foggyline_mp7` repository has no tags defined on it.

Let's go ahead and add a `v1.5` tag to our repository. We will do so by running the following console commands:

```
git tag -a v1.5 -m "my version 1.4" 648e31cc4a
git push origin v1.5
```

Since we are adding a tag to an already made commit, we use the commit ID `648e31cc4a` to attach the tag to it. Once the tag is pushed to the GitHub repository, we can go back to Packagist and hit the **Update** button on the package edit screen. This should instantly update the package versions list to show `v1.5`:

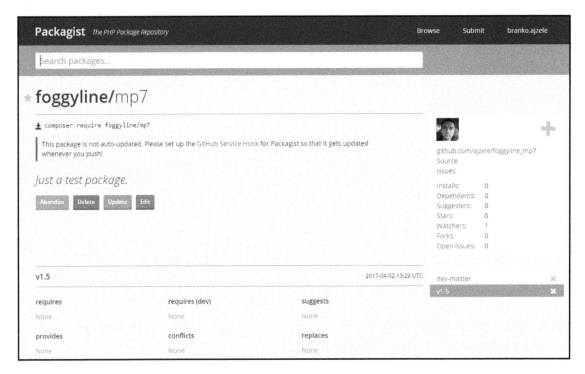

Assuming we have some project directory with merely an `index.php` file within it, we should be able to use the `foggyline/mp7` package by running the following console command:

```
composer require foggyline/mp7
```

This should result in a directory structure, as follows:

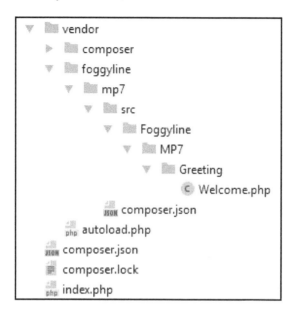

The `index.php` script can then start using our MP7 library just by including `/vendor/autoload.php`.

Summary

Throughout this chapter, we took a look at PHP's most popular package manager-- Composer. We saw how easy it is to add third-party packages to our application, as well as distribute our own packages using the Packagist repository. A great deal of modern PHP applications rely on Composer, which is why understanding how to make the best of it is crucial to our day-to-day development efforts.

Moving forward, we will take a look at the types of testing applicable to PHP applications.

15
Testing the Important Bits

Writing quality software is a technically challenging and expensive activity. The technically challenging part comes from the need to understand and implement more than one type of application testing. Whereas, the expensive part comes from the fact that proper testing usually yields more code than the code we are testing, which translates to more time needed to get the job done.

Unlike developers, businesses don't care as much about technicalities, as they care about reducing cost. This is where the two worlds clash at the expense of quality. While both understand the implications of a *technical debt* concept, rarely few take it seriously. Web applications come to mind as a nice example of this clash. The good enough UX and design is often sufficient to meet the needs of shareholders, while many of the internals and far-from-the-eye parts of the software are left untested.

 Check out `https://en.wikipedia.org/wiki/Technical_debt` for more information on the technical debt concept.

There are many types of testing we can apply to our application, some of which are as follows:

- Unit Testing
- Functional Testing
- Performance Testing
- Usability Testing
- Acceptance Testing

It would be unjust to say that one is more important than the other, as each addresses a very distinct segment of the application. The current state of the PHP ecosystem and tooling indicates *unit*, *functional*, and *performance testing* to be among the popular ones. In this chapter, we will take a quick look at a few of the tools and libraries that accommodate these types of testing:

- PHPUnit
- Behat
- phpspec
- jMeter

Software that a typical programmer believes to be thoroughly tested has often had only about 55 to 60 percent of its logic paths executed. Using automated support, such as coverage analyzers, can raise that roughly to 85 to 90 percent. It is nearly impossible to test software at the level of 100 percent of its logic paths.

- Facts and Fallacies of Software Engineering

book.

PHPUnit

PHPUnit is a representative of unit testing frameworks, whose overall idea is to provide a *strict contract* over an isolated piece of code that must be satisfied. This piece of code is what we call *unit*, which translates to the class and its methods in PHP. Using the *assertions* functionality, the PHPUnit framework verifies that these units behave as expected. The benefit of unit testing is that its early problem detection helps mitigate *compound* or *down-the-line* errors that might not be obvious initially. The more possible paths of a program the unit test covers, the better.

Setting up the PHPUnit

PHPUnit can be installed as, provisionally named, a tool or a library. Both are the same things actually, just differing in a way we install and use them. The *tool* version is really just a PHP *phar* archive we can run via console, which then provides a set of console commands we can execute globally. The *library* version on the other hand is a set of PHPUnit libraries packed as a Composer package, as well as a binary that gets dumped into the project's `vendor/bin/` directory.

Assuming that we are using the Ubuntu 16.10 (Yakkety Yak) installation, installing the PHPUnit as a tool is easy via the following commands:

```
wget https://phar.phpunit.de/phpunit.phar
chmod +x phpunit.phar
sudo mv phpunit.phar /usr/local/bin/phpunit
phpunit --version
```

This should give us the final output, much like the following screenshot:

The PHPUnit becomes a system-wide accessible console tool, not related to any project specifically.

Installing PHPUnit as a library is easy as running the following console command within the root of our project:

```
composer require phpunit/phpunit
```

This should give us the final output, much like the following screenshot:

```
$ composer require phpunit/phpunit
Using version ^6.1 for phpunit/phpunit
./composer.json has been created
Loading composer repositories with package information
Updating dependencies (including require-dev)
Package operations: 27 installs, 0 updates, 0 removals
  - Installing sebastian/version (2.0.1) Loading from cache
  - Installing sebastian/resource-operations (1.0.0) Loading from cache
  - Installing sebastian/recursion-context (3.0.0) Loading from cache
  - Installing sebastian/object-reflector (1.1.1) Loading from cache
  - Installing sebastian/object-enumerator (3.0.2) Loading from cache
  - Installing sebastian/global-state (1.1.1) Loading from cache
  - Installing sebastian/exporter (3.1.0) Loading from cache
  - Installing sebastian/environment (2.0.0) Loading from cache
  - Installing sebastian/diff (1.4.1) Loading from cache
  - Installing sebastian/comparator (2.0.0) Loading from cache
  - Installing doctrine/instantiator (1.0.5) Loading from cache
  - Installing phpunit/php-text-template (1.2.1) Loading from cache
  - Installing phpunit/phpunit-mock-objects (4.0.1) Loading from cache
  - Installing phpunit/php-timer (1.0.9) Loading from cache
  - Installing phpunit/php-file-iterator (1.4.2) Loading from cache
  - Installing sebastian/code-unit-reverse-lookup (1.0.1) Loading from cache
  - Installing phpunit/php-token-stream (1.4.11) Loading from cache
  - Installing phpunit/php-code-coverage (5.1.1) Loading from cache
  - Installing webmozart/assert (1.2.0) Loading from cache
  - Installing phpdocumentor/reflection-common (1.0) Loading from cache
  - Installing phpdocumentor/type-resolver (0.2.1) Loading from cache
  - Installing phpdocumentor/reflection-docblock (3.1.1) Loading from cache
  - Installing phpspec/prophecy (v1.7.0) Loading from cache
  - Installing phar-io/version (1.0.1) Loading from cache
  - Installing phar-io/manifest (1.0.1) Loading from cache
  - Installing myclabs/deep-copy (1.6.0) Loading from cache
  - Installing phpunit/phpunit (6.1.0) Loading from cache
sebastian/global-state suggests installing ext-uopz (*)
phpunit/phpunit suggests installing phpunit/php-invoker (^1.1)
Writing lock file
Generating autoload files
```

This installs all the PHPUnit library files within our project's vendor/phpunit/ directory, as well as the phpunit executable file under the vendor/bin/ directory.

Setting up a sample application

Before we start writing some PHPUnit test scripts, let's go ahead and create a very simple application consisting of merely a few files. This will allow us to focus on the essence of writing a test later on.

Test driven development (TDD), such as the one done with PHPUnit, encourages writing tests before the implementations. This way, the tests set the expectations for the functionality and not the other way around. This approach requires a certain level of experience and discipline, which might not sit well with newcomers to PHPUnit.

Let's assume that we are making a part of the web shopping functionality, thus dealing with product and category entities for a start. The first class we address is the Product model. We will do so by creating the src\Foggyline\Catalog\Model\Product.php file, with its content as follows:

```php
<?php

declare(strict_types=1);

namespace Foggyline\Catalog\Model;

class Product
{
    protected $id;
    protected $title;
    protected $price;
    protected $taxRate;

    public function __construct(string $id, string $title, float $price,
int $taxRate)
    {
        $this->id = $id;
        $this->title = $title;
        $this->price = $price;
        $this->taxRate = $taxRate;
    }

    public function getId(): string
    {
        return $this->id;
    }

    public function getTitle(): string
    {
        return $this->title;
    }

    public function getPrice(): float
    {
        return $this->price;
    }
```

```
        public function getTaxRate(): int
        {
            return $this->taxRate;
        }
    }
```

The Product class relies on the constructor for setting up the product's ID, title, price, and tax rate. Other than that, there is no actual logic to the class, aside from the simple getter methods. With the Product class in place, let's go ahead and create a Category class. We will add it to the src\Foggyline\Catalog\Model\Category.php file, with its content as follows:

```php
<?php

declare(strict_types=1);

namespace Foggyline\Catalog\Model;

class Category
{
    protected $title;
    protected $products;

    public function __construct(string $title, array $products)
    {
        $this->title = $title;
        $this->products = $products;
    }

    public function getTitle(): string
    {
        return $this->title;
    }

    public function getProducts(): array
    {
        return $this->products;
    }
}
```

The Category class relies on the constructor for setting up the category title and its products. Other than that, there is no logic in it, aside from the two getter methods, which merely return the values set through the constructor.

To spice things up a bit, for testing purposes, let's go ahead and create a dummy Layer class as a part of the src\Foggyline\Catalog\Model\Layer.php file, with its content as follows:

```php
<?php

namespace Foggyline\Catalog\Model;

// Just a dummy class, for testing purpose
class Layer
{
    public function dummy()
    {
        $time = time();
        sleep(2);
        $time = time() - $time;
        return $time;
    }
}
```

We will use this class merely as an example, with the code coverage analysis later on.

With the Product and Category models, let's go ahead and create the Block\Category\View class as a part of the src\Foggyline\Catalog\Block\Category\View.php file, with its content as follows:

```php
<?php

declare(strict_types=1);

namespace Foggyline\Catalog\Block\Category;

use Foggyline\Catalog\Model\Category;
class View
{
    protected $category;

    public function __construct(Category $category)
    {
        $this->category = $category;
    }

    public function render(): string
    {
        $products = '';
```

```
        foreach ($this->category->getProducts() as $product) {
          if ($product instanceof \Foggyline\Catalog\Model\Product) {
            $products .= '<div class="product">
             <h1 class="product-title">' . $product->getTitle() . '</h1>
             <div class="product-price">' .
number_format($product->getPrice(), 2, ',', '.') . '</h1>
               </div>';
          }
        }

        return '<div class="category">
           <h1 class="category-title">' . $this->category->getTitle() .
'</h1>
           <div class="category-products">' . $products . '</div>
        </div>';
    }
}
```

We are using the `render()` method to render the entire category page. The page itself consists of a category title, and a container of all of its products with their individual titles and prices. Now that we have our truly basic application classes outlined, let's add a simple PSR4 type loader to the `autoload.php` file, with its content as follows:

```php
<?php

$loader = require __DIR__ . '/vendor/autoload.php';
$loader->addPsr4('Foggyline\\', __DIR__ . '/src/Foggyline');
```

Finally, we set up the entry point to our application as a part of the `index.php` file, with its content as follows:

```php
<?php

require __DIR__ . '/autoload.php';

use Foggyline\Catalog\Model\Product;
use Foggyline\Catalog\Model\Category;
use Foggyline\Catalog\Block\Category\View as CategoryView;

$category = new Category('Laptops', [
    new Product('RL', 'Red Laptop', 1499.99, 25),
    new Product('YL', 'Yellow Laptop', 2499.99, 25),
    new Product('BL', 'Blue Laptop', 3499.99, 25),
]);

$categoryView = new CategoryView($category);
echo $categoryView->render();
```

We will be using this utterly simple application across other types of tests as well, so it's worth keeping its files and structure in mind.

Writing test

Getting started with writing PHPUnit tests requires grasping a few basic concepts, such as the following:

- **The setUp() method**: Analogous to the constructor, this is where we create the objects against which we will perform the test.
- **The tearDown() method**: Analogous to the destructor, this is where we clean up objects against which we performed the test.
- **The test*() methods**: Every public method whose name begins with test, for example, testSomething(), testItAgain(), and so on, is considered a single test. The same effect can be achieved by adding the @test annotation in a method's docblock; although, this seems to be a less used case.
- **The @depends annotation**: This allows expressing dependencies between the test methods.
- **Assertions**: The heart of the PHPUnit, this set of methods allows us to reason about correctness.

 The vendor\phpunit\phpunit\src\Framework\Assert\Functions.php file contains an extensive list of the assert* function declarations, such as assertEquals(), assertContains(), assertLessThan(), and others, totaling to over 90 different assert functions.

With these in mind, let's go ahead and write the src\Foggyline\Catalog\Test\Unit\Model\ProductTest.php file, with its content as follows:

```php
<?php

namespace Foggyline\Catalog\Test\Unit\Model;

use PHPUnit\Framework\TestCase;
use Foggyline\Catalog\Model\Product;

class ProductTest extends TestCase
{
    protected $product;
```

```
    public function setUp()
    {
        $this->product = new Product('SL', 'Silver Laptop', 4599.99, 25);
    }

    public function testTitle()
    {
        $this->assertEquals(
            'Silver Laptop',
            $this->product->getTitle()
        );
    }

    public function testPrice()
    {
        $this->assertEquals(
            4599.99,
            $this->product->getPrice()
        );
    }
}
```

Our `ProductTest` class is using a `setUp()` method to set up an instance of a `Product` class. The two `test*()` methods then use the PHPUnit's built-in `assertEquals()` method to test the value of the product title and price.

We then add the `src\Foggyline\Catalog\Test\Unit\Model\CategoryTest.php` file, with its content as follows:

```php
<?php

namespace Foggyline\Catalog\Test\Unit\Model;

use PHPUnit\Framework\TestCase;
use Foggyline\Catalog\Model\Product;
use Foggyline\Catalog\Model\Category;

class CategoryTest extends TestCase
{
    protected $category;

    public function setUp()
    {
        $this->category = new Category('Laptops', [
            new Product('TRL', 'Test Red Laptop', 1499.99, 25),
            new Product('TYL', 'Test Yellow Laptop', 2499.99, 25),
        ]);
    }
```

```
    public function testTotalProductsCount()
    {
        $this->assertCount(2, $this->category->getProducts());
    }

    public function testTitle()
    {
        $this->assertEquals('Laptops', $this->category->getTitle());
    }
}
```

Our `CategoryTest` class is using a `setUp()` method to set up an instance of a `Category` class, along with the two products passed onto the `Category` class constructor. The two `test*()` methods then use the PHPUnit's built-in `assertCount()` and `assertEquals()` methods to test the instantiated values.

We then add the `src\Foggyline\Catalog\Test\Unit\Block\Category\ViewTest.php` file, with its content as follows:

```php
<?php

namespace Foggyline\Catalog\Test\Unit\Block\Category;

use PHPUnit\Framework\TestCase;
use Foggyline\Catalog\Model\Product;
use Foggyline\Catalog\Model\Category;
use Foggyline\Catalog\Block\Category\View as CategoryView;

class ViewTest extends TestCase
{
    protected $category;
    protected $categoryView;

    public function setUp()
    {
        $this->category = new Category('Laptops', [
            new Product('TRL', 'Test Red Laptop', 1499.99, 25),
            new Product('TYL', 'Test Yellow Laptop', 2499.99, 25),
        ]);

        $this->categoryView = new CategoryView($this->category);
    }

    public function testCategoryTitle()
    {
        $this->assertContains(
```

```
                '<h1 class="category-title">Laptops',
                $this->categoryView->render()
            );
        }

        public function testProductsContainer()
        {
            $this->assertContains(
                '<h1 class="product-title">Test Yellow',
                $this->categoryView->render()
            );
        }
    }
```

Our `ViewTest` class is using a `setUp()` method to set up an instance of a `Category` class, alongside with the two products passed onto the `Category` class constructor. The two `test*()` methods then use the PHPUnit's built-in `assertContains()` method to test the presence of the value that should be returned through the category view `render()` method call.

We then add the `phpunit.xml` file, with its content as follows:

```
<phpunit bootstrap="autoload.php">
  <testsuites>
    <testsuite name="foggyline">
      <directory>src/Foggyline/*/Test/Unit/*</directory>
    </testsuite>
  </testsuites>
</phpunit>
```

The `phpunit.xml` configuration file supports quite a robust list of options. Using the bootstrap attribute of a PHPUnit element, we are instructing the PHPUnit tool to load the `autoload.php` file prior to running the tests. This ensures that our PSR4 autoloader will kick in, and that our test classes will see our classes within the `src/Foggyline` directory. The `foggyline` test suite we defined within `testsuites` uses the directory option to specify, in regex form, the path to our unit tests. The path we used was such so that all of the files under both `src/Foggyline/Catalog/Test/Unit/` and possibly `src/Foggyline/Checkout/Test/Unit/` directories are picked up.

Check out `https://phpunit.de/manual/current/en/appendixes.confi guration.html`for more information on `phpunit.xml` configuration options.

Executing tests

Running the test suite we have just written is as easy as executing the `phpunit` command within our project root directory.

Upon execution, `phpunit` will look for the `phpunit.xml` file and act accordingly. This means that `phpunit` will know where to look for the test files. Successfully executed tests show an output like the following screenshot:

```
$ php phpunit.phar --coverage-html log/report
PHPUnit 6.1.0 by Sebastian Bergmann and contributors.

........                                                    8 / 8 (100%)

Time: 254 ms, Memory: 10.00MB

OK (8 tests, 8 assertions)
```

However, the unsuccessfully executed tests show an output like the following screenshot:

```
PHPUnit 6.1.0 by Sebastian Bergmann and contributors.

.F......                                                    8 / 8 (100%)

Time: 143 ms, Memory: 8.00MB

There was 1 failure:

1) Foggyline\Catalog\Test\Unit\Block\Category\ViewTest::testProductsContainer
Failed asserting that '<div class="category">\r\n
        <h1 class="category-title">Laptops</h1>\r\n
        <div class="category-products"><div class="product">\r\n
            <h1 class="product-title">Test Red Laptop</h1>\r\n
            <div class="product-price">1.499,99</h1>\r\n
        </div><div class="product">\r\n
            <h1 class="product-title">Test Yellow Laptop</h1>\r\n
            <div class="product-price">2.499,99</h1>\r\n
        </div></div>\r\n
    </div>' contains "<h1 class="product-title">Tes Yellow".

C:\Users\ajzel\apps\php7\src\Foggyline\Catalog\Test\Unit\Block\Category\ViewTest.php:37

FAILURES!
Tests: 8, Assertions: 8, Failures: 1.
```

We can easily modify one of the test classes, as we did with the preceding `ViewTest`, in order to trigger and observe the reactions of `phpunit` to failures.

Code coverage

The great thing about PHPUnit is its code coverage reporting functionality. We can easily add code coverage to our testing suite just by extending the `phpunit.xml` file as follows:

```xml
<phpunit bootstrap="autoload.php">
  <testsuites>
    <testsuite name="foggyline">
      <directory>src/Foggyline/*/Test/Unit/*</directory>
    </testsuite>
  </testsuites>
  <filter>
    <whitelist>
      <directory>src/Foggyline/</directory>
      <exclude>
        <file>src/config.php</file>
        <file>src/auth.php</file>
        <directory>src/Foggyline/*/Test/</directory>
      </exclude>
    </whitelist>
    <logging>
      <log type="coverage-html" target="log/report" lowUpperBound="50"
        highLowerBound="80"/>
    </logging>
  </filter>
</phpunit>
```

Here, we added the `filter` element, with an extra `whitelist` and `logging` element. We can now trigger the testing again, but, this time, with a slightly modified command, as follows:

```
phpunit --coverage-html log/report
```

This should give us the final output, as shown in the following screenshot:

```
$ php phpunit.phar --coverage-html log/report
PHPUnit 6.1.0 by Sebastian Bergmann and contributors.

........                                                    8 / 8 (100%)

Time: 254 ms, Memory: 10.00MB

OK (8 tests, 8 assertions)

Generating code coverage report in HTML format ... done
```

The `log/report` directory should now be filled with HTML report files. If we expose it to the browser, we can see a nicely generated report with valuable pieces of information about our code base, as shown in the following screenshot:

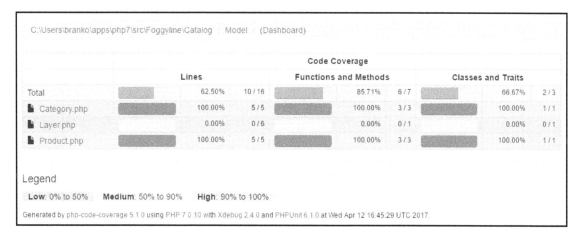

The preceding screenshot shows a code coverage percentage across the `src/Foggyline/Catalog/` directory structure. Drilling further down into a `Model` directory, we see our `Layer` class having 0% code coverage, which is expected, as we haven't written any test for it:

C:\Users\branko\apps\php7\src\Foggyline\Catalog   Model   (Dashboard)

	Code Coverage							
	Lines			Functions and Methods			Classes and Traits	
Total		62.50%	10 / 16		85.71%	6 / 7		66.67%	2 / 3
Category.php		100.00%	5 / 5		100.00%	3 / 3		100.00%	1 / 1
Layer.php		0.00%	0 / 6		0.00%	0 / 1		0.00%	0 / 1
Product.php		100.00%	5 / 5		100.00%	3 / 3		100.00%	1 / 1

Legend

Low: 0% to 50%   **Medium**: 50% to 90%   **High**: 90% to 100%

Generated by php-code-coverage 5.1.0 using PHP 7.0.10 with Xdebug 2.4.0 and PHPUnit 6.1.0 at Wed Apr 12 16:45:29 UTC 2017.

Drilling further down into the actual `Product` class itself, we can see the PHPUnit code coverage outlining each and every line of code covered by our test:

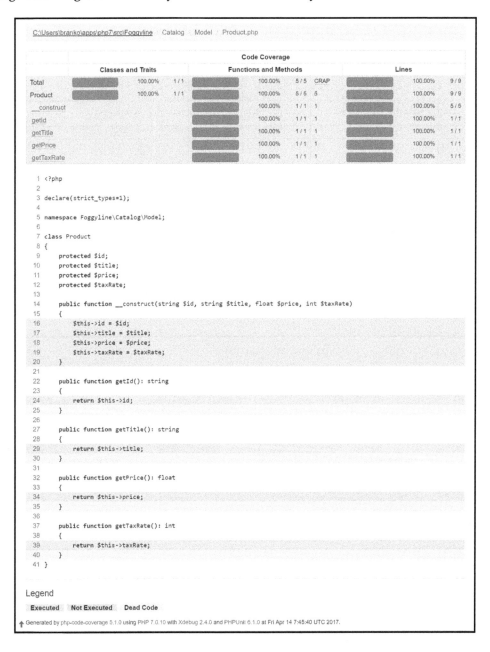

Looking directly into the actual `Layer` class gives us a nice visual on the lack of any code coverage within this class:

C:\Users\branko\apps\php7\src\Foggyline\Catalog / Model / Layer.php

	Code Coverage								
	Classes and Traits			Functions and Methods				Lines	
Total	0.00%	0 / 1		0.00%	0 / 1	CRAP		0.00%	0 / 6
Layer	0.00%	0 / 1		0.00%	0 / 1	2		0.00%	0 / 6
dummy				0.00%	0 / 1	2		0.00%	0 / 6

```php
1  <?php
2
3  namespace Foggyline\Catalog\Model;
4
5  // Just a dummy class, for testing purpose
6  class Layer
7  {
8      public function dummy()
9      {
10         $time = time();
11         sleep(2);
12         $time = time() - $time;
13         return $time;
14     }
15 }
```

Legend

Executed   **Not Executed**   **Dead Code**

Generated by php-code-coverage 5.1.0 using PHP 7.0.10 with Xdebug 2.4.0 and PHPUnit 6.1.0 at Wed Apr 12 16.45.29 UTC 2017.

Code coverage provides valuable visual and statistical information about the amount of code we have covered with tests. Although this information is easily misinterpreted, having 100% code coverage is by no means a measure of our individual test quality. Writing quality tests requires the writer, that is, the developer, to have a clear understanding of what exactly is the unit testing. It goes to say that we can easily have 100% code coverage, with 100% passing tests, and yet fail to address certain test cases or paths of logic.

Behat

Behat is an open source and free testing framework based on a notion of **behavior-driven development** (**BDD**). The great benefit of the BDD frameworks, including Behat, is that a significant portion of the functional documentation gets poured into the actual user stories we end up testing. That is, to some extent, the documentation itself becomes a test.

Setting up Behat

Much like PHPUnit, Behat can be installed as a tool and library. The tool version being the .phar archive, we can download it from the official GitHub repository, where the library version comes packed as a Composer package.

Assuming that we are using the Ubuntu 16.10 (Yakkety Yak) installation, installing the Behat as a tool is easy through the following commands:

```
wget https://github.com/Behat/Behat/releases/download/v3.3.0/behat.phar
chmod +x behat.phar
sudo mv behat.phar /usr/local/bin/behat
behat --version
```

This should give us the following output:

```
root@vultr:~# behat --version
behat 3.3.0
root@vultr:~#
```

Installing Behat as a library is as easy as running the following console command within the root of our project:

```
composer require behat/behat
```

This should give us the final output, as shown in the following screenshot:

```
$ composer require behat/behat
Using version ^3.3 for behat/behat
./composer.json has been updated
Loading composer repositories with package information
Updating dependencies (including require-dev)
Package operations: 16 installs, 0 updates, 0 removals
  - Installing symfony/yaml (v3.2.7) Downloading: 100%
  - Installing symfony/polyfill-mbstring (v1.3.0) Loading from cache
  - Installing symfony/translation (v3.2.7) Downloading: 100%
  - Installing symfony/event-dispatcher (v3.2.7) Downloading: 100%
  - Installing symfony/dependency-injection (v3.2.7) Downloading: 100%
  - Installing psr/log (1.0.2) Loading from cache
  - Installing symfony/debug (v3.2.7) Downloading: 100%
  - Installing symfony/console (v3.2.7) Downloading: 100%
  - Installing symfony/filesystem (v3.2.7) Downloading: 100%
  - Installing symfony/config (v3.2.7) Downloading: 100%
  - Installing symfony/class-loader (v3.2.7) Downloading: 100%
  - Installing psr/container (1.0.0) Downloading: 100%
  - Installing container-interop/container-interop (1.2.0) Downloading: 100%
  - Installing behat/transliterator (v1.2.0) Downloading: 100%
  - Installing behat/gherkin (v4.4.5) Downloading: 100%
  - Installing behat/behat (v3.3.0) Downloading: 100%
symfony/event-dispatcher suggests installing symfony/http-kernel ()
symfony/dependency-injection suggests installing symfony/expression-language (For using expressions in service container configuration)
symfony/dependency-injection suggests installing symfony/proxy-manager-bridge (Generate service proxies to lazy load them)
symfony/console suggests installing symfony/process ()
symfony/class-loader suggests installing symfony/polyfill-apcu (For using ApcClassLoader on HHVM)
behat/behat suggests installing behat/symfony2-extension (for integration with Symfony2 web framework)
behat/behat suggests installing behat/yii-extension (for integration with Yii web framework)
behat/behat suggests installing behat/mink-extension (for integration with Mink testing framework)
Writing lock file
Generating autoload files
```

The Behat library now becomes available under the `vendor/behat` directory and its console tool executable under the `vendor/bin/behat` file.

Setting up a sample application

The sample application for Behat testing is the same one we used for PHPUnit testing. We will merely extend it a bit by adding an extra class to it. Given the lack of any real "behavior" in our PHPUnit sample application, our extension here will include a dummy shopping cart functionality.

Therefore, we will add the `src\Foggyline\Checkout\Model\Cart.php` file, with its content as follows:

```php
<?php

declare(strict_types=1);

namespace Foggyline\Checkout\Model;

class Cart implements \Countable
{
    protected $productQtyMapping = [];

    public function addProduct(\Foggyline\Catalog\Model\Product $product,
int $qty): self
    {
        $this->productQtyMapping[$product->getId()]['product'] = $product;
        $this->productQtyMapping[$product->getId()]['qty'] = $qty;
        return $this;
    }

    public function removeProduct($productId): self
    {
        if (isset($this->productQtyMapping[$productId])) {
            unset($this->productQtyMapping[$productId]);
        }

        return $this;
    }

    public function getSubtotal()
    {
        $subtotal = 0.0;

        foreach ($this->productQtyMapping as $mapping) {
```

```
                    $subtotal += ($mapping['qty'] *
$mapping['product']->getPrice());
        }

        return $subtotal;
    }

    public function getTotal()
    {
        $total = 0.0;

        foreach ($this->productQtyMapping as $mapping) {
            $total += ($mapping['qty'] * ($mapping['product']->getPrice() +
($mapping['product']->getPrice() * ($mapping['product']->getTaxRate() /
100))));
        }

        return $total;
    }

    public function count()
    {
        return count($this->productQtyMapping);
    }
}
```

Leaving the original `index.php` file as it is, let's go ahead and create the `index_2.php` file, with its content as follows:

```php
<?php

$loader = require __DIR__ . '/vendor/autoload.php';
$loader->addPsr4('Foggyline\\', __DIR__ . '/src/Foggyline');

use Foggyline\Catalog\Model\Product;
use \Foggyline\Checkout\Model\Cart;

$cart = new Cart();
$cart->addProduct(new Product('RL', 'Red Laptop', 75.00, 25), 1);
$cart->addProduct(new Product('YL', 'Yellow Laptop', 100.00, 25), 1);

echo $cart->getSubtotal(), PHP_EOL;
echo $cart->getTotal(), PHP_EOL;

$cart->removeProduct('YL');

echo $cart->getSubtotal(), PHP_EOL;
echo $cart->getTotal(), PHP_EOL;
```

We won't actually be needing this one for testing, but it goes to show how our dummy cart can be utilized.

Writing test

Getting started with writing the Behat tests requires grasping a few basic concepts, such as the following:

- **Gherkin language**: This is a whitespace, business-readable, domain-specific language created for behavior descriptions, with the ability to be used for a project's documentation and automated test at once through its *Given-When-Then* concept.
- **Features**: This is a list of one or more scenarios saved under the `*.feature` file. By default, the Behat features are to be stored and found in the `features/` directory relative to our project.
- **Scenarios**: These are the core Gherkin structures, consisting of one or more steps.
- **Steps**: These are also known as *Givens*, *Whens*, and *Thens*. Indistinguishable to Behat, they should be distinguishable to developers as they are carefully selected for their purpose. The *Given* steps put the system in a known state, prior to any user interaction. The *When* steps describe the key action that the user performs. The *Then* step observes the outcomes.

With these in mind, let's go ahead and write and kick off our Behat tests.

 The `vendor\phpunit\phpunit\src\Framework\Assert\Functions.php` file contains an extensive list of `asert*` function declarations, such as `assertEquals()`, `assertContains()`, `assertLessThan()`, and others, totaling to over 90 different assert functions.

Within the root of our project directory, if we run the `behat --init` console command, it will generate a `features/` directory, and, within it, a `features/bootstrap/FeatureContext.php` file with the following content:

```php
<?php

use Behat\Behat\Context\Context;
use Behat\Gherkin\Node\PyStringNode;
use Behat\Gherkin\Node\TableNode;

/**
 * Defines application features from the specific context.
 */
```

```
class FeatureContext implements Context
{
    /**
     * Initializes context.
     *
     * Every scenario gets its own context instance.
     * You can also pass arbitrary arguments to the
     * context constructor through behat.yml.
     */
    public function __construct()
    {
    }
}
```

The newly created `features/` directory is where we write our tests. Ignoring the newly generated `FeatureContext` for the moment, let's go ahead and create our first `.feature`. As we mentioned earlier, Behat tests are written in a special format called **Gherkin**. Let's go ahead and write down our `features/checkout-cart.feature` file as follows:

```
Feature: Checkout cart
  In order to buy products
  As a customer
  I need to be able to put products into a cart

  Rules:
  - Each product TAX rate is 25%
  - Delivery for basket under $100 is $10
  - Delivery for basket over $100 is $5

Scenario: Buying a single product under $100
Given there is a "Red Laptop", which costs $75.00 and has a tax rate of 25
When I add the "Red Laptop" to the cart
Then I should have 1 product in the cart
And the overall subtotal cart price should be $75.00
And the delivery cost should be $10.00
And the overall total cart price should be $103.75

Scenario: Buying two products over $100
Given there is a "Red Laptop", which costs $75.00 and has a tax rate of 25
And there is a "Yellow Laptop", which costs $100.00 and has a tax rate of
25
When I add the "Red Laptop" to the cart
And I add the "Yellow Laptop" to the cart
Then I should have 2 product in the cart
And the overall subtotal cart price should be $175.00
And the delivery cost should be $5.00
And the overall total cart price should be $223.75
```

We can see the `Given`, `When`, and `Then` keywords being put to use. However, there are also several occurrences of `And`. When there are several `Given`, `When`, and `Then` steps, we are free to use additional keywords such as `And` or `But` to flag a step, thus allowing our Scenario to be read more fluently. Behat does not differentiate any of these keywords; they are only meant to be differentiated and experienced by the developer.

Now, we can update our `FeatureContext` class with the tests, that is, steps, from `checkout-cart.feature`. All it takes is to run the following command, and the Behat tool will do this for us:

```
behat --dry-run --append-snippets
```

This should give us the following output:

```
In order to buy products
As a customer
I need to be able to put products into a cart

Rules:
- Each product TAX rate is 25%
- Delivery for basket under $100 is $10
- Delivery for basket over $100 is $5

Scenario: Buying a single product under $100
  Given there is a "Red Laptop", which costs $75.00 and has a tax rate of 25
  When I add the "Red Laptop" to the cart
  Then I should have 1 product in the cart
  And the overall subtotal cart price should be $75.00
  And the delivery cost should be $10.00
  And the overall total cart price should be $103.75

Scenario: Buying two products over $100
  Given there is a "Red Laptop", which costs $75.00 and has a tax rate of 25
  And there is a "Yellow Laptop", which costs $100.00 and has a tax rate of 25
  When I add the "Red Laptop" to the cart
  And I add the "Yellow Laptop" to the cart
  Then I should have 2 product in the cart
  And the overall subtotal cart price should be $175.00
  And the delivery cost should be $5.00
  And the overall total cart price should be $223.75

2 scenarios (2 undefined)
14 steps (14 undefined)
0m0.01s (7.65Mb)

>> default suite has undefined steps. Please choose the context to generate snippets:

  [0] None
  [1] FeatureContext
 > 1

u features/bootstrap/FeatureContext.php - `there is a "Red Laptop", which costs $75.00 and has a tax rate of 25` definition added
u features/bootstrap/FeatureContext.php - `I add the "Red Laptop" to the cart` definition added
u features/bootstrap/FeatureContext.php - `I should have 1 product in the cart` definition added
u features/bootstrap/FeatureContext.php - `the overall subtotal cart price should be $75.00` definition added
u features/bootstrap/FeatureContext.php - `the delivery cost should be $10.00` definition added
u features/bootstrap/FeatureContext.php - `the overall total cart price should be $103.75` definition added
root@vultr:~/behat-test#
```

After executing this command, Behat automatically appends all the missing step methods into our `FeatureContext` class, which now looks like the following code block:

```php
<?php

use Behat\Behat\Tester\Exception\PendingException;
use Behat\Behat\Context\Context;
use Behat\Gherkin\Node\PyStringNode;
use Behat\Gherkin\Node\TableNode;

/**
 * Defines application features from the specific context.
 */
class FeatureContext implements Context
{
    /**
     * Initializes context.
     *
     * Every scenario gets its own context instance.
     * You can also pass arbitrary arguments to the
     * context constructor through behat.yml.
     */
    public function __construct()
    {
    }

    /**
     * @Given there is a :arg1, which costs $:arg2 and has a tax rate of
:arg3
     */
    public function thereIsAWhichCostsAndHasATaxRateOf($arg1, $arg2, $arg3)
    {
        throw new PendingException();
    }

    /**
     * @When I add the :arg1 to the cart
     */
    public function iAddTheToTheCart($arg1)
    {
        throw new PendingException();
    }

    /**
     * @Then I should have :arg1 product in the cart
     */
    public function iShouldHaveProductInTheCart($arg1)
    {
```

```
            throw new PendingException();
    }

    /**
     * @Then the overall subtotal cart price should be $:arg1
     */
    public function theOverallSubtotalCartPriceShouldBe($arg1)
    {
        throw new PendingException();
    }

    /**
     * @Then the delivery cost should be $:arg1
     */
    public function theDeliveryCostShouldBe($arg1)
    {
        throw new PendingException();
    }

    /**
     * @Then the overall total cart price should be $:arg1
     */
    public function theOverallTotalCartPriceShouldBe($arg1)
    {
        throw new PendingException();
    }
}
```

Now, we need to go in and edit these stub methods to reflect on the classes we are testing this behavior against. This means replacing all of the `throw new PendingException()` expressions with the proper logic and assertions:

```php
<?php

$loader = require __DIR__ . '/../../vendor/autoload.php';
$loader->addPsr4('Foggyline\\', __DIR__ . '/../../src/Foggyline');

use Behat\Behat\Tester\Exception\PendingException;
use Behat\Behat\Context\Context;
use Behat\Gherkin\Node\PyStringNode;
use Behat\Gherkin\Node\TableNode;

use Foggyline\Catalog\Model\Product;
use \Foggyline\Checkout\Model\Cart;
use \PHPUnit\Framework\Assert;

/**
```

```
 * Defines application features from the specific context.
 */
class FeatureContext implements Context
{
    protected $cart;
    protected $products = [];

    /**
     * Initializes context.
     *
     * Every scenario gets its own context instance.
     * You can also pass arbitrary arguments to the
     * context constructor through behat.yml.
     */
    public function __construct()
    {
        $this->cart = new Cart();
    }

    /**
     * @Given there is a :arg1, which costs $:arg2 and has a tax rate of
:arg3
     */
    public function thereIsAWhichCostsAndHasATaxRateOf($arg1, $arg2, $arg3)
    {
        $this->products[$arg1] = new Product($arg1, $arg1, $arg2, $arg3);
    }

    /**
     * @When I add the :arg1 to the cart
     */
    public function iAddTheToTheCart($arg1)
    {
        $this->cart->addProduct($this->products[$arg1], 1);
    }

    /**
     * @Then I should have :arg1 product in the cart
     */
    public function iShouldHaveProductInTheCart($arg1)
    {
        Assert::assertCount((int)$arg1, $this->cart);
    }

    /**
     * @Then the overall subtotal cart price should be $:arg1
     */
    public function theOverallSubtotalCartPriceShouldBe($arg1)
```

```
    {
        Assert::assertEquals($arg1, $this->cart->getSubtotal());
    }

    /**
     * @Then the delivery cost should be $:arg1
     */
    public function theDeliveryCostShouldBe($arg1)
    {
        Assert::assertEquals($arg1, $this->cart->getDeliveryCost());
    }

    /**
     * @Then the overall total cart price should be $:arg1
     */
    public function theOverallTotalCartPriceShouldBe($arg1)
    {
        Assert::assertEquals($arg1, $this->cart->getTotal());
    }
}
```

Note the use of the PHPUnit framework for asserting. Using Behat does not mean we have to stop using the PHPUnit library. It would be a shame not to reuse the wast number of the assert functions available in PHPUnit. Adding it to the project is easy, as shown in the following line of code:

```
composer require phpunit/phpunit
```

Executing tests

Once we sort out all of the stub methods within the `features\bootstrap\FeatureContext.php` file, we can simply run the `behat` command in our project root to execute tests. This should give us the following output:

```
root@vultr:~/behat-test# behat
Feature: Checkout cart
  In order to buy products
  As a customer
  I need to be able to put products into a cart

  Rules:
  - Each product TAX rate is 25%
  - Delivery for basket under $100 is $10
  - Delivery for basket over $100 is $5

  Scenario: Buying a single product under $100
    Given there is a "Red Laptop", which costs $75.00 and has a tax rate of 25
    When I add the "Red Laptop" to the cart
    Then I should have 1 product in the cart
    And the overall subtotal cart price should be $75.00
    And the delivery cost should be $10.00
    And the overall total cart price should be $103.75

  Scenario: Buying two products over $100
    Given there is a "Red Laptop", which costs $75.00 and has a tax rate of 25
    And there is a "Yellow Laptop", which costs $100.00 and has a tax rate of 25
    When I add the "Red Laptop" to the cart
    And I add the "Yellow Laptop" to the cart
    Then I should have 2 product in the cart
    And the overall subtotal cart price should be $175.00
    And the delivery cost should be $5.00
    And the overall total cart price should be $223.75

2 scenarios (2 passed)
14 steps (14 passed)
0m0.02s (8.26Mb)
```

The output indicates a total of 2 scenarios and 14 different steps, all of which are confirmed to be working.

phpspec

Like Behat, **phpspec** is an open source and free testing framework based on the notion of BDD. However, its approach to testing is quite different than that of Behat; we may even say it sits somewhere in the middle of PHPUnit and Behat. Unlike Behat, phpspec does not use the Gherkin format stories to describe its tests. Doing so, phpspec shifts its focus on internal, rather than external application behavior. Much like PHPUnit, phpspec allows us to instantiate objects, call its methods, and perform various assertions on the results. The part where it differs is in its "think of specification", and not of "think of test" approach.

Setting up phpspec

Much like PHPUnit and Behat, phpspec can be installed as a tool and a library. The tool version being the .phar archive, we can download it from the official GitHub repository, whereas the library version comes packed as a Composer package.

Assuming that we are using the Ubuntu 16.10 (Yakkety Yak) installation, installing phpspec as a tool is easy, as shown in the following commands:

```
wget
https://github.com/phpspec/phpspec/releases/download/3.2.3/phpspec.phar
chmod +x phpspec.phar
sudo mv phpspec.phar /usr/local/bin/phpspec
phpspec --version
```

This should give us the following output:

Installing phpspec as a library is as easy as running the following console command within the root of our project:

```
composer require phpspec/phpspec
```

This should give us the final output, which looks like the following screenshot:

```
$ composer require phpspec/phpspec
Using version ^3.2 for phpspec/phpspec
./composer.json has been created
Loading composer repositories with package information
Updating dependencies (including require-dev)
Package operations: 20 installs, 0 updates, 0 removals
  - Installing symfony/yaml (v3.2.7) Loading from cache
  - Installing symfony/process (v3.2.7) Downloading: 100%
  - Installing symfony/finder (v3.2.7) Downloading: 100%
  - Installing symfony/event-dispatcher (v3.2.7) Loading from cache
  - Installing psr/log (1.0.2) Loading from cache
  - Installing symfony/debug (v3.2.7) Loading from cache
  - Installing symfony/polyfill-mbstring (v1.3.0) Loading from cache
  - Installing symfony/console (v3.2.7) Loading from cache
  - Installing sebastian/recursion-context (2.0.0) Downloading: 100%
  - Installing sebastian/exporter (2.0.0) Downloading: 100%
  - Installing doctrine/instantiator (1.0.5) Loading from cache
  - Installing sebastian/diff (1.4.1) Loading from cache
  - Installing sebastian/comparator (1.2.4) Downloading: 100%
  - Installing webmozart/assert (1.2.0) Loading from cache
  - Installing phpdocumentor/reflection-common (1.0) Loading from cache
  - Installing phpdocumentor/type-resolver (0.2.1) Loading from cache
  - Installing phpdocumentor/reflection-docblock (3.1.1) Loading from cache
  - Installing phpspec/prophecy (v1.7.0) Loading from cache
  - Installing phpspec/php-diff (v1.1.0) Downloading: 100%
  - Installing phpspec/phpspec (3.2.3) Downloading: 100%
symfony/event-dispatcher suggests installing symfony/dependency-injection ()
symfony/event-dispatcher suggests installing symfony/http-kernel ()
symfony/console suggests installing symfony/filesystem ()
phpspec/phpspec suggests installing phpspec/nyan-formatters (Adds Nyan formatters)
Writing lock file
Generating autoload files
```

The phpspec library now becomes available under the `vendor/phpspec` directory and its console tool is executable under the `vendor/bin/phpspec` file.

Writing test

Getting started with writing phpspec tests requires grasping a few basic concepts, such as the following:

- **The it_*() and its_*() methods**: This object behavior is made up of individual examples, each one being flagged with the `it_*()` or `its_*()` methods. We can have one or more of these methods defined per single specification. Each defined method gets triggered when a test is run.
- **Matchers methods**: These are analogous to assertions in PHPUnit. They describe how an object should behave.

- **Object construction methods**: Every object we describe in phpspec is not a separate variable, but is `$this`. Sometimes, however, getting the proper `$this` variable requires managing constructor parameters. This is where the `beConstructedWith()`, `beConstructedThrough()`, `let()`, and `letGo()` methods come in handy.
- **The let() method**: This runs before each example.
- **The letGo() method**: This runs after each example.

The matchers are likely something we will have most contact with, so it is worth knowing there are several different matchers in phpspec, all of which implement the `Matcher` interface declared in the `src\PhpSpec\Matcher\Matcher.php` file:

```php
<?php
namespace PhpSpec\Matcher;
interface Matcher
{
  public function supports($name, $subject, array $arguments);
  public function positiveMatch($name, $subject, array $arguments);
  public function negativeMatch($name, $subject, array $arguments);
  public function getPriority();
}
```

Using the `phpspec describe` command, we can create a specification for either one of the existing or new concrete classes we are yet to write. Since we already have our project set, let's go ahead and generate a specification for our `Cart` and `Product` classes.

We will do so by running the following two commands within the root directory of our project:

```
phpspec describe Foggyline/Checkout/Model/Cart
phpspec describe Foggyline/Catalog/Model/Product
```

The first command generates the `spec/Foggyline/Checkout/Model/CartSpec.php` file, with its initial content as follows:

```php
<?php

namespace spec\Foggyline\Checkout\Model;

use Foggyline\Checkout\Model\Cart;
use PhpSpec\ObjectBehavior;
use Prophecy\Argument;

class CartSpec extends ObjectBehavior
```

```php
{
    function it_is_initializable()
    {
        $this->shouldHaveType(Cart::class);
    }
}
```

The second command generates the `spec/Foggyline/Catalog/Model/ProductSpec.php` file, with its initial content as follows:

```php
<?php

namespace spec\Foggyline\Catalog\Model;

use Foggyline\Catalog\Model\Product;
use PhpSpec\ObjectBehavior;
use Prophecy\Argument;

class ProductSpec extends ObjectBehavior
{
    function it_is_initializable()
    {
        $this->shouldHaveType(Product::class);
    }
}
```

The generated `CartSpec` and `ProductSpec` classes are nearly identical. The difference lies in the concrete classes they reference through the `shouldHaveType()` method call. Moving forward, we will try to write a few simple tests only for the `Cart` and `Product` models. That being said, let's go ahead and modify our `CartSpec` and `ProductSpec` classes to reflect upon the use of matchers: the `it_*()` and `its_*()` functions.

We will modify the `spec\Foggyline\Checkout\Model\CartSpec.php` file with the following content:

```php
<?php

namespace spec\Foggyline\Checkout\Model;

use Foggyline\Checkout\Model\Cart;
use PhpSpec\ObjectBehavior;
use Prophecy\Argument;
use Foggyline\Catalog\Model\Product;

class CartSpec extends ObjectBehavior
{
```

```php
    function it_is_initializable()
    {
        $this->shouldHaveType(Cart::class);
    }

    function it_adds_single_product_to_cart()
    {
        $this->addProduct(
            new Product('YL', 'Yellow Laptop', 1499.99, 25),
            2
        );

        $this->count()->shouldBeLike(1);
    }

    function it_adds_two_products_to_cart()
    {
        $this->addProduct(
            new Product('YL', 'Yellow Laptop', 1499.99, 25),
            2
        );

        $this->addProduct(
            new Product('RL', 'Red Laptop', 2499.99, 25),
            2
        );

        $this->count()->shouldBeLike(2);
    }
}
```

We will modify the `spec\Foggyline\Catalog\Model\ProductSpec.php` file with the following content:

```php
<?php

namespace spec\Foggyline\Catalog\Model;

use Foggyline\Catalog\Model\Product;
use PhpSpec\ObjectBehavior;
use Prophecy\Argument;

class ProductSpec extends ObjectBehavior
{
    function it_is_initializable()
    {
        $this->shouldHaveType(Product::class);
```

```
    }

    function let()
    {
        $this->beConstructedWith(
            'YL', 'Yellow Laptop', 1499.99, 25
        );
    }

    function its_price_should_be_like()
    {
        $this->getPrice()->shouldBeLike(1499.99);
    }

    function its_title_should_be_like()
    {
        $this->getTitle()->shouldBeLike('Yellow Laptop');
    }
}
```

Here, we are making use of the let() method, as it triggers before any of the it_*() or its_*() methods are executed. Within the let() method, we are calling beConstructedWith() with arguments we would normally pass to a new Product(...) expression. This builds our product instance, and allows all of the it_*() or its_*() methods to execute successfully.

Check out http://www.phpspec.net/en/stable/manual/introduction.html for more information on the advanced phpspec concepts.

Executing tests

Running only a phpspec run command at this point will likely fail with something like a **class ... does not exist** message, because phpspec assumes a PSR-0 mapping by default. To be able to work with the application we have done so far, we need to tell phpspec to include our src/Foggyline/* classes. We can do so either through a phpspec.yml configuration file, or using the --bootstrap option. Since we have already created the autoload.php file, let's go ahead and run phpspec by bootstrapping this file as follows:

phpspec run --bootstrap=autoload.php

This generates the following output:

```
root@vultr:~/phpspec-test# phpspec run --bootstrap=autoload.php
                                                                        6
2 specs
6 examples (6 passed)
7ms
```

We have involved these two specs using `phpspec describe` on the existing class. We could easily pass on the non-existing class name to the same command, as per the following example:

phpspec describe Foggyline/Checkout/Model/Guest/Cart

The `Guest\Cart` class does not really exist in our `src/` directory. phpspec has no trouble creating a `spec/Foggyline/Checkout/Model/Guest/CartSpec.php` specification file, just like it did for `Cart` and `Product`. However, running the phpspec describe now raises a **class ... does not exist error** message, along with the interactive generator, as per the following output:

```
root@vultr:~/phpspec-test# phpspec describe Foggyline/Checkout/Model/Guest/Cart
Specification for Foggyline\Checkout\Model\Guest\Cart created in /root/phpspec-test/spec/Foggyline/Checkout/Model/Guest/CartSpec.php.

root@vultr:~/phpspec-test# phpspec run --bootstrap=autoload.php
Foggyline/Checkout/Model/Guest/Cart
  11  - it is initializable
        class Foggyline\Checkout\Model\Guest\Cart does not exist.

                                                          14%      7
3 specs
7 examples (6 passed, 1 broken)
8ms

  Do you want me to create `Foggyline\Checkout\Model\Guest\Cart` for you?
                                                          [Y/n]
Y
Class Foggyline\Checkout\Model\Guest\Cart created in /root/phpspec-test/src/Foggyline/Checkout/Model/Guest/Cart.php.

                                                                   7
3 specs
7 examples (7 passed)
7ms
```

As a result, the `src\Foggyline\Checkout\Model\Guest\Cart.php` file is additionally generated with the following content:

```php
<?php

namespace Foggyline\Checkout\Model\Guest;

class Cart
{
}
```

While all of these are simple examples, it goes to show that phpspec works both ways:

- Creating specifications based on existing concrete classes
- Generating concrete classes based on a specification

Running our test now should give us the following output:

```
root@vultr:~/phpspec-test# phpspec run --bootstrap=autoload.php -v

                                                                          7
3 specs
7 examples (7 passed)
7ms

root@vultr:~/phpspec-test#
```

Now, lets's deliberately fail a test by changing the `its_title_should_be_like()` method of `spec\Foggyline\Catalog\Model\ProductSpec.php` into the following line of code:

```
$this->getTitle()->shouldBeLike('Yellow');
```

Running the test now should give us the following output:

```
root@vultr:~/phpspec-test# phpspec run --bootstrap=autoload.php
Foggyline/Catalog/Model/Product
   28   - its title should be like
        expected "Yellow", but got "Yellow Laptop".

                                                            14%       7
3 specs
7 examples (6 passed, 1 failed)
8ms
```

There is much more to be said about phpspec. Things such as Stubs, Mocks, Spies, templates, and extensions further enrich our phpspec testing experience. This section, however, focuses on the basics to get us started.

jMeter

The Apache jMeter is a free and open source application designed for load and performance testing. The functionality of jMeter extends across many different applications, servers, and protocol types. In the context of web applications, we might be tempted to compare it to the browser. However, jMeter works with HTTP and https at a protocol level. It does not render HTML or execute JavaScript. Although jMeter is primarily a GUI application, it can easily be installed and have its tests run in console mode. This makes it a convenient tool of choice for quickly building our tests in GUI mode, and then running them on a server console later on.

Assuming that we are using the Ubuntu 16.10 (Yakkety Yak) installation, installing jMeter as a tool is easy, as shown in the following command line:

```
sudo apt-get -y install jmeter
```

However, this might not give us the latest version of jMeter, in which case, we can get one from the official jMeter download page (`http://jmeter.apache.org/download_jmeter.cgi`):

```
wget
http://ftp.carnet.hr/misc/apache//jmeter/binaries/apache-jmeter-3.2.tgz
tar -xf apache-jmeter-3.2.tgz
```

Using this second method of installation, we will find the jMeter executable at `apache-jmeter-3.2/bin/jmeter`.

Writing test

Throughout this chapter, we used a simple project with a few classes in the `src/Foggyline` directory to demonstrate the use of PHPUnit, Behat, and phpspec testing. Those, however, can't quite serve the purpose of this type of testing. Since we don't have any HTML pages to showcase in the browser, our focus with jMeter is on kicking off a simple built-in web test plan in order to understand its components and how we can run it later on.

Writing jMeter tests for web applications requires a basic understanding of several key concepts, which are as follows:

- **Thread Group**: This defines a pool of users who execute a specific test case against our web server. The GUI allows us to control the several **Thread Group** options, as shown in the following screenshot:

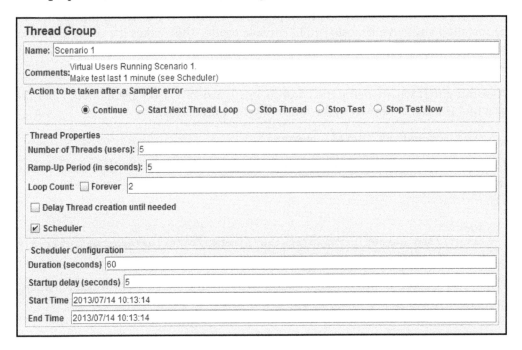

- **HTTP Request Defaults**: This sets the default values that our **HTTP Request** controllers use. The GUI allows us to control the several **HTTP Request Defaults** options, as shown in the following screenshot:

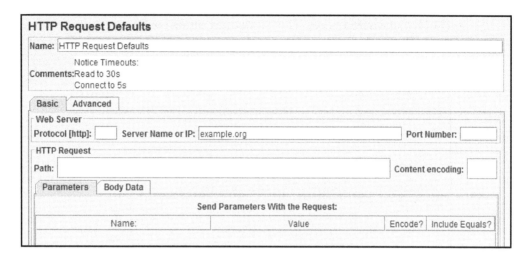

- **HTTP Request**: This sends the HTTP/HTTPS request to a web server. The GUI allows us to control the several **HTTP Request** options, as shown in the following screenshot:

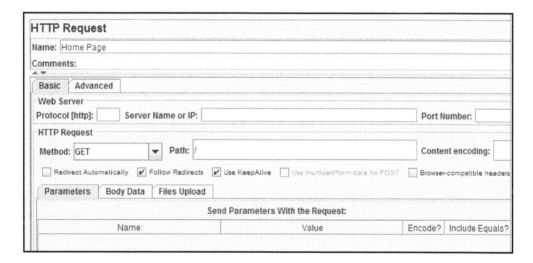

- **HTTP Cookie Manager**: This stores and sends cookies, just like a web browser does. The GUI allows us to control the several **HTTP Cookie Manager** options, as shown in the following screenshot:

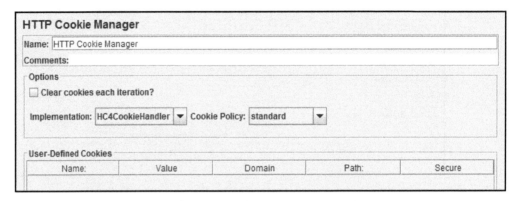

- **HTTP Header Manager**: This adds or overrides HTTP request headers. The GUI allows us to control the several **HTTP Header Manager** options, as shown in the following screenshot:

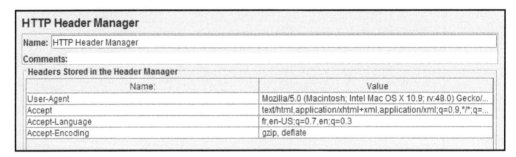

- **Graph Results**: This generates a graph with all the sample times plotted out. The GUI allows us to control the several **Graph Results** options, as shown in the following screenshot:

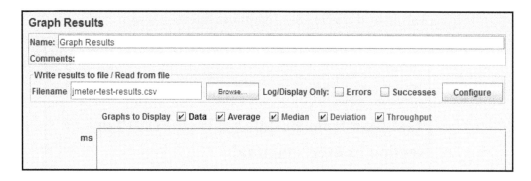

We should never use the **Graph Results** listener component during production load tests as it consumes a lot of memory and CPU resources.

The great thing about jMeter is that it already provides several different test plan templates. We can easily generate a **Web Test Plan** simply by following these steps:

1. Click on the **File** | **Templates...** menu under the main application menu, as shown here:

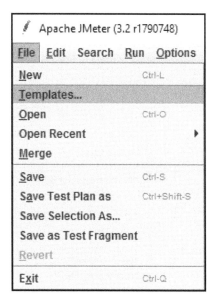

This in turn triggers the **Templates** selection screen:

2. Clicking on the **Create** button should kick off a new test plan, as shown in the following screenshot:

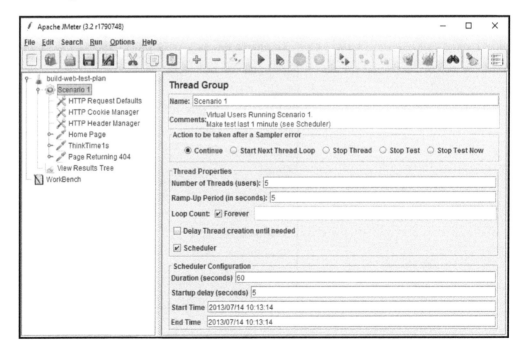

While the test is just fine as it is, let's go ahead and change a few things before we run it:

1. Right-click on **View Results Tree** and click on **Remove**.
2. Right-click on **build-web-test-plan** and **Add** | **Listener** | **Graph Results**, then set **Filename** to `jmeter-result-tests.csv`, as follows:

3. Click on **Scenario 1** and edit **Loop Count** to value 2:

4. With these modifications in place, let's click on **File** | **Save** under the main menu and name our test `web-test-plan.jmx`.

Out test is now ready to be run. While the test itself won't be load testing our own server in this case, rather `example.org`, the value of this exercise lies in understanding how to build the test via a GUI tool, run it via console, and generate the test results log for later inspection.

Executing tests

Running a jMeter test via a console is quite easy, as the following command shows:

```
jmeter -n -t web-test-plan.jmx
```

The `-n` parameter, also works with `--nongui`, stands for **run JMeter in nongui mode**. Whereas,, the `-t` parameter that also works with `--testfile`, stands for **the jmeter test(.jmx) file to run**.

The resulting output should look the following screenshot:

```
root@vultr:~# ./apache-jmeter-3.2/bin/jmeter -n -t web-test-plan.jmx
Creating summariser <summary>
Created the tree successfully using web-test-plan.jmx
Starting the test @ Sun Apr 16 17:56:52 UTC 2017 (1492365412851)
Waiting for possible Shutdown/StopTestNow/Heapdump message on port 4445
summary +      3 in 00:00:07 =    0.5/s Avg:    169 Min:    84 Max:    248 Err:     0 (0.00%) Active: 2 Started: 2 Finished: 0
summary +     17 in 00:00:05 =    3.3/s Avg:    124 Min:    83 Max:    171 Err:     0 (0.00%) Active: 0 Started: 5 Finished: 5
summary =     20 in 00:00:12 =    1.7/s Avg:    131 Min:    83 Max:    248 Err:     0 (0.00%)
Tidying up ...    @ Sun Apr 16 17:57:05 UTC 2017 (1492365425371)
... end of run
root@vultr:~#
```

A quick look into the `jmeter-result-tests.csv` file reveals the structure and data captured:

```
jmeter-result-tests.csv  ✕
    1    timeStamp,elapsed,label,responseCode,responseMessage,threadName,dataType,success,failureMessage
    2    1492365418836,248,Home Page,200,OK,Scenario 1 1-1,text,true,,956,307,1,1,247,0,142
    3    1492365419738,175,Home Page,200,OK,Scenario 1 1-2,text,true,,956,307,2,2,175,0,86
    4    1492365420146,84,Page Returning 404,404,Not Found,Scenario 1 1-1,text,true,,961,311,2,2,84,0,0
    5    1492365420235,86,Home Page,200,OK,Scenario 1 1-1,text,true,,956,307,2,2,86,0,0
    6    1492365420738,167,Home Page,200,OK,Scenario 1 1-3,text,true,,956,307,3,3,167,0,83
    7    1492365420999,83,Page Returning 404,404,Not Found,Scenario 1 1-2,text,true,,961,311,3,3,83,0,0
    8    1492365421083,84,Home Page,200,OK,Scenario 1 1-2,text,true,,956,307,3,3,84,0,0
```

While the example demonstrated here relies on a default test plan with some minor modifications, the overall capabilities of Apache jMeter can enrich the whole testing experience by multiple factors.

Summary

Throughout this chapter, we very briefly scratched the surface of some of the most popular types of PHP application testing. The test driven development (TDD) and behaviour driven development comprise of a very large and important chunk of it. Luckily, the PHP ecosystem provides two excellent frameworks, PHPUnit and Behat, which makes these types of testing easy to work with. Although fundamentally different, PHPUnit and Behat complete each other in a sense that they ensure our application is tested both from the smallest unit of functionality to a logical outcome of overall functionality point of view. phpspec on the other hand seems to sit in the middle of the two, trying to address these two challenges in its own uniform way. We further glossed over Apache jMeter, seeing how easy it is to kick off a performance test with a simple web test plan. This allows us to take an important step forward and confirms that our application not only works, but works fast enough to meet user expectations.

Moving forward, we will take a closer look at the debugging, tracing, and profiling PHP applications.

16
Debugging, Tracing, and Profiling

Tools such as PHPUnit and Behat take an automated approach to testing software. They give us a great level of reassurance that our application will deliver according to the tests. The tests, however, like the code itself, are subject to flaws. Be it a faulty test code or an incomplete test case, having a fully written test for something does not necessarily mean our code is perfect in a bug-free and performance-optimized way.

More often than not, there are unexpected bugs and performance issues that are far from obvious during development cycles, only to occasionally resurface at production stage. While perfect code is a far-reaching concept or, at the very least, a subject for debate, there certainly is more we can do to improve the quality of our software. To complete the canvas of software testing, a more methodical process and thorough insight into the application is required during its runtime.

This is where debugging kicks in. The term is so common among developers that it usually indicates the following three distinctive processes:

- **Debugging**: This is process of detecting and fixing an application's bugs
- **Tracing**: This is a process of logging an application's chronologically relevant information
- **Profiling**: This is a process of logging an application's performance-relevant information

While the tracing and profiling processes automatically log the relevant information every time an application is run, the debugging process is more of a manual undertaking.

In this chapter, we will take a closer look at the two PHP extensions that deal with the debugging, tracing, and profiling functionalities:

- Xdebug
    - Installation
    - Debugging
    - Tracing
    - Profiling
- Zend Z-Ray
    - Installing Zend Server
    - Setting up the virtual host
    - Using Z-Ray

Xdebug

Xdebug is a PHP extension that provides debugging, tracing, and profiling capabilities. The debugger component uses the DBGp debugging protocol in order to establish the communication between a PHP scripting engine and a debugger IDE. There are several IDEs and text editors that support the DBGp debugging protocol; the following are merely a few of the more popular ones:

- **NetBeans**: This is a free cross-platform IDE available at `https://netbeans.org/`
- **Eclipse PDT**: This is a free cross-platform IDE available at `https://eclipse.org/pdt/`
- **PhpStorm**: This is a commercial cross-platform IDE available at `https://www.jetbrains.com/phpstorm/`
- **Zend Studio**: This is a commercial cross-platform IDE available at `http://www.zend.com/en/products/studio`
- **Sublime Text 3** : This is a commercial cross-platform text editor available at `https://www.sublimetext.com/3`
- **Notepad++**: This is a free Windows platform text editor available at `https://notepad-plus-plus.org/`
- **Vim**: This is a free cross-platform text editor available at `http://www.vim.org/`

While the DBGp debugging protocol support may seem sufficient as a debugger selection factor, what really differentiates these IDEs and text editors is their level of support for latest versions of PHP.

With its cutting-edge PHP support and innovative solutions, PhpStorm is likely the most popular commercial choice among professional PHP developers. Considering the average hourly rate of a skilled PHP developer, the cost of tool seems all but expensive with regards to the abundance of features that speed up the development work.

To get a better understanding of the Xdebug capabilities, let's go ahead and perform the following steps:

1. Install LAMP stack.
2. Install the Xdebug extension.
3. Install NetBeans.
4. Pull in the sample PHP application as our playground for debugging.
5. Configure debugging.
6. Configure tracing.
7. Configure profiling.

Installation

Assuming that we have a fresh Ubuntu 17.04 (Zesty Zapus) installation, installing the complete LAMP stack and Xdebug extension is easy via the following commands:

```
apt-get update
apt-get -y install lamp-server^
apt-get -y install php-xdebug
sudo service apache2 restart
```

Once this process is done, opening `http://localhost/index.html` in our browser should give us a default Apache page. Now, let's go ahead and do some permission changes:

```
sudo adduser user_name www-data
sudo chown -R www-data:www-data /var/www
sudo chmod -R g+rwX /var/www
```

Be sure to replace `user_name` with the name of the actual user on the system.

The reason for doing this permissions update is to make it possible for a user's NetBeans IDE to access the /var/www/html/ directory, where our project will be located. Once these commands are executed, we need to log out and log in, or restart the computer for permissions to kick in.

We can now execute the following command on the console and then open http://localhost/index.php in order to confirm whether PHP and Xdebug are up and running:

```
rm /var/www/html/index.html
echo "<?php phpinfo(); ?>" > /var/www/html/index.php
```

This should give us an output indicating the presence of the Xdebug extension, much like the following screenshot:

xdebug		
xdebug support	enabled	
Version	2.4.0	
IDE Key	*no value*	
Supported protocols	**Revision**	
DBGp - Common DeBuGger Protocol	$Revision: 1.145 $	
Directive	**Local Value**	**Master Value**
xdebug.auto_trace	Off	Off
xdebug.cli_color	0	0
xdebug.collect_assignments	Off	Off
xdebug.collect_includes	On	On
xdebug.collect_params	0	0
xdebug.collect_return	Off	Off
xdebug.collect_vars	Off	Off

To this point, we have merely installed the extension, but haven't really enabled any of its three core features: debugging, tracing, and profiling. Before we go ahead with debugging, let's quickly install NetBeans IDE. This will make our debugging efforts much easier. We will first need to download NetBeans for PHP from https://netbeans.org/downloads/. Once downloaded and unpacked, we can execute the following command:

```
chmod +x netbeans-8.2-php-linux-x64.sh
./netbeans-8.2-php-linux-x64.sh
```

It is worth noting that the use of NetBeans IDE here is completely optional. We could have easily used one of the other free or even commercial solutions. Now would be a good time to open NetBeans IDE; click on **File | New Project | Categories [PHP] | Projects [PHP Application with Existing Sources]** and point it to our /var/www/html/ directory, as shown in the following screenshot:

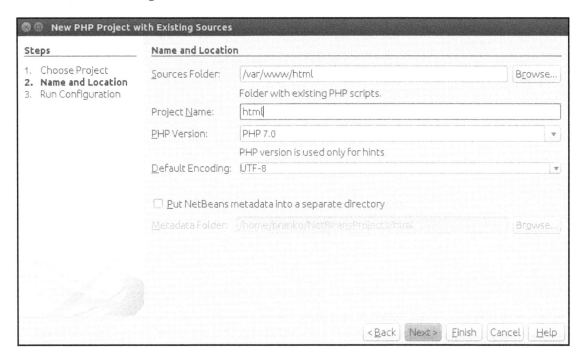

Once we fill in the required data on the **Name and Location** screen, clicking on **Next** brings us to the **Run Configuration** setup:

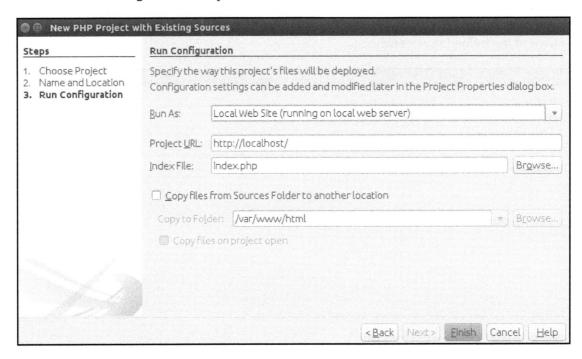

Clicking on the **Finish** button finishes the project setup, and we should now be able to see our index.php file:

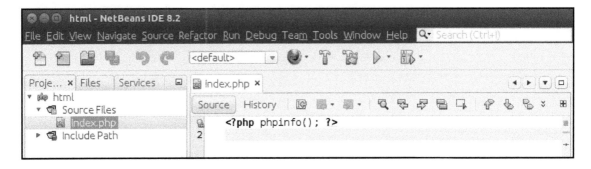

Finally, let's go ahead and pull in our sample application by executing the following console commands:

```
rm /var/www/html/index.php
cd /var/www/html/
git init
git remote add origin git@github.com:ajzele/MPHP7-CH16.git
git pull origin master
```

The NetBeans IDE should be able to instantly pick up these changes in its **Projects** tab. To this point, we haven't really actually done any configuration or setup related to Xdebug's debugging, tracing, or profiling components. We merely installed LAMP stack, Xdebug itself, NetBeans IDE and pulled in the sample application. Now, let's go ahead and look into the debugging component of Xdebug.

Debugging

The debugging feature of Xdebug can be easily turned on with the `xdebug.remote_enable=1` option. With modern PHP, there is usually a special `xdebug.ini` configuration file; otherwise, we would edit the default `php.ini` file. With our Ubuntu installation, we add this to the `/etc/php/7.0/apache2/conf.d/20-xdebug.ini` file as follows:

```
zend_extension=xdebug.so
xdebug.remote_enable=1
```

Once the file has been modified, we need to make sure the Apache server is restarted:

```
service apache2 restart
```

While `xdebug.remote_enable` is the required option to turn on the debugging feature, other related options include the following:

- `xdebug.extended_info`
- `xdebug.idekey`
- `xdebug.remote_addr_header`
- `xdebug.remote_autostart`
- `xdebug.remote_connect_back`
- `xdebug.remote_cookie_expire_time`
- `xdebug.remote_enable`
- `xdebug.remote_handler`

- xdebug.remote_host
- xdebug.remote_log
- xdebug.remote_mode
- xdebug.remote_port

 Supplemental information about individual debugger configuration options can be found under https://xdebug.org/docs/all_settings.

Back in NetBeans, we can turn our focus on the **Debug** toolbar:

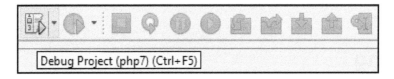

When we click on the **Debug Project** button, NetBeans kicks off a browser with the URL http://localhost/index.php?XDEBUG_SESSION_START=netbeans-xdebug and activates the previously disabled buttons.

The buttons available on the Debug toolbar present us with several debugging options:

- **Step Into**: This tells the debugger to go into the next function call and break there.
- **Step Over**: This tells the debugger to execute the next function and break afterwards.
- **Step Out**: This tells the debugger to finish the current function and break after it.
- **Run to Cursor**: This has a bit of a dual role. When used in combination with enabled breakpoints, it jumps directly from one breakpoint to another. When breakpoints are disabled, it jumps straight to the line where we positioned our cursor. We can, therefore, debug in a sort of free manner, as we decide on the next breakpoint dynamically after the debugging process is started, simply by placing our cursor where needed.

The **Run to Cursor** option seems like a sensible and straightforward first approach. Let's go ahead and set several breakpoints in our sample application as follows:

- `index.php`: This is a total of six breakpoints:

```
3     require_once __DIR__ . '/src/Foggyline/Catalog/Model/Product.php';
4     require_once __DIR__ . '/src/Foggyline/Catalog/Model/Category.php';
5     require_once __DIR__ . '/src/Foggyline/Catalog/Block/Category/View.php';
6
7     use Foggyline\Catalog\Model\Product;
8     use Foggyline\Catalog\Model\Category;
9     use Foggyline\Catalog\Block\Category\View as CategoryView;
10
□     $x = 'test-X';
12
13    $category = new Category('Laptops');
14
□     $y = 'test-Y';
16
17    $category->addProduct(new Product('RL', 'Red Laptop', 1499.99, 25));
□     $category->addProduct(new Product('YL', 'Yellow Laptop', 2499.99, 25));
19    $category->addProduct(new Product('BL', 'Blue Laptop', 3499.99, 25));
20
21    $categoryView = new CategoryView($category);
22
□     $z = 'test-Z';
24
□     echo $categoryView->render();
26
□     $q = 'test-Q';
```

- `src/Foggyline/Catalog/Model/Category.php`: This is a total of one breakpoint:

```php
<?php

declare(strict_types = 1);

namespace Foggyline\Catalog\Model;

use Foggyline\Catalog\Model\Product;

class Category {

    protected $title;
    protected $products = [];

    public function __construct(string $title) {
        $this->title = $title;
    }
```

- `src/Foggyline/Catalog/Block/Category/View.php`: This is a total of one breakpoint:

```php
declare(strict_types = 1);

namespace Foggyline\Catalog\Block\Category;

use Foggyline\Catalog\Model\Category;

class View {

    protected $category;

    public function __construct(Category $category) {
        $this->category = $category;
    }

    public function render(): string {
        $products = '';

        foreach ($this->category->getProducts() as $product) {
            if ($product instanceof \Foggyline\Catalog\Model\Product) {
                $formattedPrice = number_format($product->getPrice(), 2, '.', ',');
                $products .= '<div class="product">
                    <h1 class="product-title">' . $product->getTitle() . '</h1>
                    <div class="product-price">' . $formattedPrice . '</h1>
                </div>';
            }
        }
```

The following steps outline a debugging using only the **Run to Cursor** button:

1. Click on **Debug Project**. This jumps to line 3 of `index.php` and records the following:

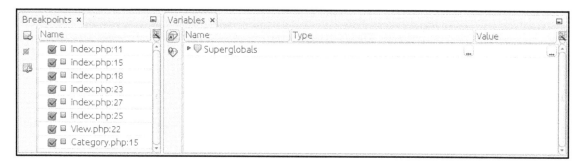

2. Click on **Run to Cursor**. This jumps to line 11 of `index.php` and records the following:

Notice how the **Breakpoints** tab now shows a green arrow next to **index.php:11**.

3. Click on **Run to Cursor**. This jumps to line 15 of `src/Foggyline/Catalog/Model/Category.php` and records the following:

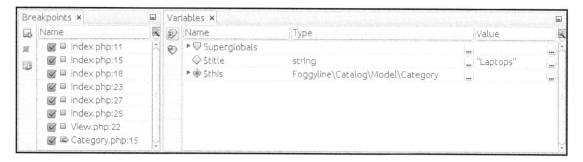

4. Click on **Run to Cursor**. This jumps to line15 of the `index.php` file and records the following:

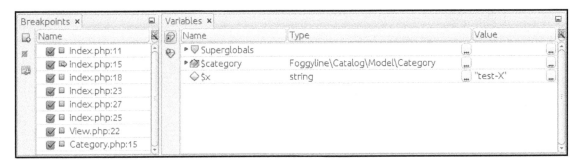

5. Click on **Run to Cursor**. This jumps to line 18 of the `index.php` file and records the following:

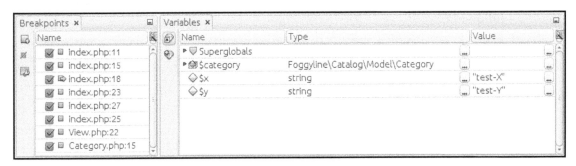

6. Click on **Run to Cursor**. This jumps to line 23 of the `index.php` file and records the following:

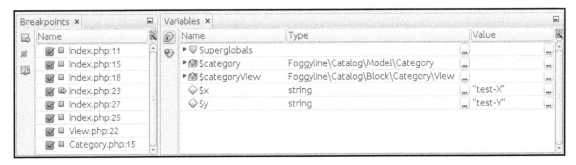

7. Click on **Run to Cursor**. This jumps to line 25 of the `index.php` file and records the following:

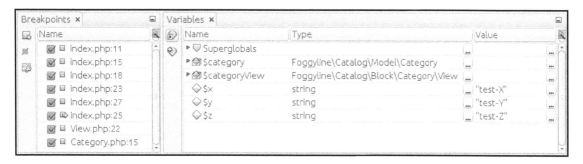

8. Click on **Run to Cursor**. This jumps to line 22 of the `src/Foggyline/Catalog/Block/Category/View.php` file and records the following:

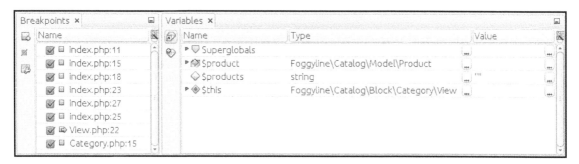

9. Click on **Run to Cursor**. This jumps to line 22 of the `src/Foggyline/Catalog/Block/Category/View.php` file and records the following:

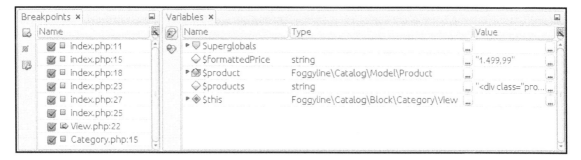

10. Click on **Run to Cursor**. This jumps to line 22 of
    the `src/Foggyline/Catalog/Block/Category/View.php` file and records the
    following:

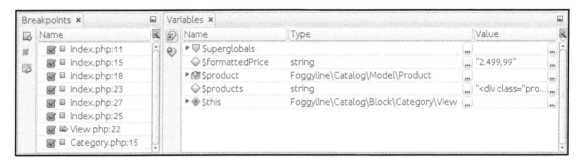

11. Click on **Run to Cursor**. This jumps to line 27 of the `index.php` file and records
    the following:

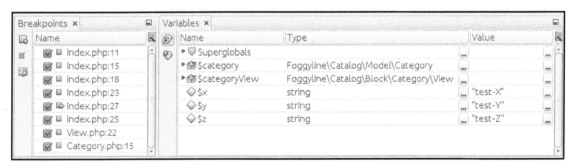

12. Click on **Run to Cursor**. This leaves us at line 27 of the `index.php` file as it
    reaches our last debug point where it records the following:

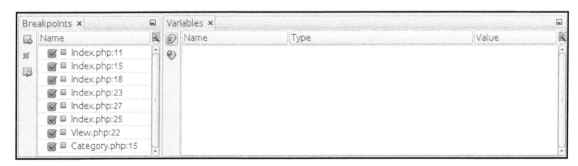

Now we can click on the **Finish Debugger Session** button.

Throughout this twelve-step process, we can clearly observe a behavior of IDE and the values it manages to record. It makes it easy to target specific bits and pieces of our code and then observe the variables as they change during the debugging process.

Note that in between steps 10 and 11, we never see the **Variables** tab recording values for our third product. This is because variables get recorded after we move past the given debug breakpoint, which, in this case, shifts the context from the View.php class file onto an index.php file. This is where clicking on the **Step Into** button might have come in handy, as it would enable us to drill further down the code within the body of while during the execution of the third loop, thus yielding values for the third product.

We should encourage mixing and using all of the debugging options in order to properly reach and read-out the variables of interest.

Tracing

The tracing feature of Xdebug can be easily turned on with the xdebug.auto_trace=1 option. With our Ubuntu installation, we add this to the /etc/php/7.0/apache2/conf.d/20-xdebug.ini file as follows:

```
zend_extension=xdebug.so
xdebug.remote_enable=1
xdebug.auto_trace=1
```

Once the file has been modified, we need to make sure the Apache server is re started :

```
service apache2 restart
```

While xdebug.auto_trace is the required option to turn on the tracing feature, other related options include the following:

- xdebug.collect_assignments
- xdebug.collect_includes
- xdebug.collect_params
- xdebug.collect_return
- xdebug.show_mem_delta
- xdebug.trace_enable_trigger
- xdebug.trace_enable_trigger_value
- xdebug.trace_format

- xdebug.trace_options
- xdebug.trace_output_dir
- xdebug.trace_output_name
- xdebug.var_display_max_children
- xdebug.var_display_max_data
- xdebug.var_display_max_depth

 Supplemental information about individual *tracing* configuration options can be found at https://xdebug.org/docs/execution_trace.

Unlike the debugging feature, which we control from IDE or text editor, we don't get to control tracing. By default, the tracing feature creates a different trace.%c file under the /tmp directory each time an application is run. What this means in the context of web application is that, each time we refresh the page in the browser, the tracing feature creates a trace.%c file for us.

Our specific example application, once executed, results in a trace file, much like the following screenshot:

```
TRACE START [2017-04-23 12:27:04]
    0.0001     363448       -> {main}() /var/www/html/index.php:0
    0.0002     368336         -> require_once(/var/www/html/src/Foggyline/Catalog/Model/Product.php) /var/www/html/index.php:3
    0.0003     371192         -> require_once(/var/www/html/src/Foggyline/Catalog/Model/Category.php) /var/www/html/index.php:4
    0.0004     375768         -> require_once(/var/www/html/src/Foggyline/Catalog/Block/Category/View.php) /var/www/html/index.php:5
    0.0004     375400         -> Foggyline\Catalog\Model\Category->__construct() /var/www/html/index.php:13
    0.0005     375512         -> Foggyline\Catalog\Model\Product->__construct() /var/www/html/index.php:17
    0.0006     375512         -> Foggyline\Catalog\Model\Category->addProduct() /var/www/html/index.php:17
    0.0006     376000         -> Foggyline\Catalog\Model\Product->__construct() /var/www/html/index.php:18
    0.0006     376000         -> Foggyline\Catalog\Model\Category->addProduct() /var/www/html/index.php:18
    0.0006     376112         -> Foggyline\Catalog\Model\Product->__construct() /var/www/html/index.php:19
    0.0007     376112         -> Foggyline\Catalog\Model\Category->addProduct() /var/www/html/index.php:19
    0.0007     376168         -> Foggyline\Catalog\Block\Category\View->__construct() /var/www/html/index.php:21
    0.0007     376168         -> Foggyline\Catalog\Block\Category\View->render() /var/www/html/index.php:25
    0.0008     376168           -> Foggyline\Catalog\Model\Category->getProducts() /var/www/html/src/Foggyline/Catalog/Block/Category/View.php:20
    0.0008     376168           -> Foggyline\Catalog\Model\Product->getPrice() /var/www/html/src/Foggyline/Catalog/Block/Category/View.php:22
    0.0008     376168           -> number_format() /var/www/html/src/Foggyline/Catalog/Block/Category/View.php:22
    0.0009     376208           -> Foggyline\Catalog\Model\Product->getTitle() /var/www/html/src/Foggyline/Catalog/Block/Category/View.php:24
    0.0009     376400           -> Foggyline\Catalog\Model\Product->getPrice() /var/www/html/src/Foggyline/Catalog/Block/Category/View.php:22
    0.0009     376400           -> number_format() /var/www/html/src/Foggyline/Catalog/Block/Category/View.php:22
    0.0009     376400           -> Foggyline\Catalog\Model\Product->getTitle() /var/www/html/src/Foggyline/Catalog/Block/Category/View.php:24
    0.0010     376592           -> Foggyline\Catalog\Model\Product->getPrice() /var/www/html/src/Foggyline/Catalog/Block/Category/View.php:22
    0.0011     376592           -> number_format() /var/www/html/src/Foggyline/Catalog/Block/Category/View.php:22
    0.0011     376592           -> Foggyline\Catalog\Model\Product->getTitle() /var/www/html/src/Foggyline/Catalog/Block/Category/View.php:24
    0.0011     376848           -> Foggyline\Catalog\Model\Category->getTitle() /var/www/html/src/Foggyline/Catalog/Block/Category/View.php:31
    0.0014       3240
TRACE END   [2017-04-23 12:27:04]
```

The output itself is relatively easy for a developer to read and understand. Surely, this gets a bit clunky when it comes to large applications, as we end up with a large trace file. Still, knowing the bits of code we are targeting, we can search the file and find the needed occurrences of the code. Let's assume that we are looking for the use of the `number_format()` function throughout our code. A quick search for `number_format` would point us to line 22 of `Category/View.php`, with an execution time next to it. This is a valuable piece of information for the overall debugging efforts.

Profiling

The profiling feature of Xdebug can be easily turned on with the `xdebug.profiler_enable=1` option. With our Ubuntu installation, we will modify the `/etc/php/7.0/apache2/conf.d/20-xdebug.ini` file as follows:

```
zend_extension=xdebug.so
xdebug.remote_enable=1
xdebug.auto_trace=1
xdebug.profiler_enable=1
```

Once the file has been modified, we need to make sure the Apache server is restarted :

```
service apache2 restart
```

While `xdebug.profiler_enable` is the required option to turn on the profiling feature, other related options include the following:

- `xdebug.profiler_aggregate`
- `xdebug.profiler_append`
- `xdebug.profiler_enable`
- `xdebug.profiler_enable_trigger`
- `xdebug.profiler_enable_trigger_value`
- `xdebug.profiler_output_dir`
- `xdebug.profiler_output_name`

 Supplemental information about individual profiler configuration options can be found at `https://xdebug.org/docs/profiler`.

Similar to tracing, we don't get to control the profiling feature from IDE or text editor. By default, the profiling feature creates a different `cachegrind.out.%p` file under the `/tmp` directory each time an application is executed.

Our specific example application, once executed, results in a cachegrind file, much like the following screenshot (partial output):

```
version: 1
creator: xdebug 2.5.0 (PHP 7.0.13-2ubuntu1)
cmd: /var/www/html/index.php
part: 1
positions: line

events: Time

fl=(1) /var/www/html/src/Foggyline/Catalog/Model/Product.php
fn=(1) require_once::/var/www/html/src/Foggyline/Catalog/Model/Product.php
1 1

fl=(2) /var/www/html/src/Foggyline/Catalog/Model/Category.php
fn=(2) require_once::/var/www/html/src/Foggyline/Catalog/Model/Category.php
1 0

fl=(3) /var/www/html/src/Foggyline/Catalog/Block/Category/View.php
fn=(3) require_once::/var/www/html/src/Foggyline/Catalog/Block/Category/View.php
1 1
```

The information contained here is far less readable than that of a tracing file, which is alright as the two target different types of information. The cachegrind file can be pulled into an application such as KCachegrind or QCacheGrind, which then gives us a much more user -friendly and visual representation of the captured information :

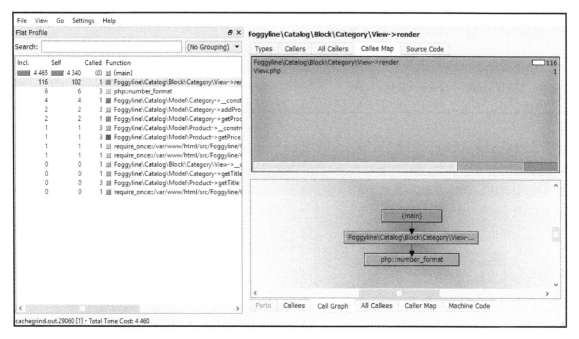

The cachegrind file output delivers an important performance-related information. We get an insight into all of the functions used within the application, sorted by time spent within an individual function and all of its children. This allows us to spot performance bottlenecks, even if it is within the millisecond time frame.

Zend Z-Ray

The *Rougue Wave Software* company offers a commercial PHP server called Zend Server. One of Zend Server's outstanding features is its **Z-Ray** extension. Seemingly analogous to Xdebug's tracing and profiling functionality, Z-Ray offers comprehensive information capturing and an improved user experience. Captured information ranges from execution times, errors and warnings, database queries, and function calls to request information. These are provided in a form that resembles a built-in browser's developer tools, making it easy for the developer to retrieve a vital piece of profiling information within seconds.

The Z-Ray extension itself is free, and can be used independently off the commercially available Zend Server. We can install it just like any other PHP extension. Although, at the time of writing, the stand-alone Z-Ray extension is available only for the PHP 5.5 and 5.6 versions, which are now considered outdated.

Installing Zend Server

Given that this book is targeting PHP 7, moving forward, we will grab a free trial version of the Zend Server and install it. We can do so by opening the official Zend page and clicking on the **Download Free Trial** button:

Assuming that we are using the fresh Ubuntu 17.04 installation, Zend's download service is likely to offer us a `tar.gz` archive download:

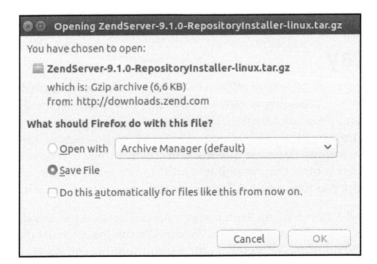

Once downloaded and unpacked, we need to trigger the `install_zs.sh` command with the PHP version argument as follows:

```
branko@devbox:~/Downloads/ZendServer-RepositoryInstaller-linux$ sudo ./install_zs.sh 7.1
[sudo] password for branko:

Running this script will perform the following:
* Configure your package manager to use Zend Server repository
* Install Zend Server (PHP 7.1) on your system using your package manager

Hit ENTER to install Zend Server (PHP 7.1), or Ctrl+C to abort now.
```

Upon installation completion, the console gives us information about how to access the server administration interface through the browser :

```
Zend Server started...
Processing triggers for libc-bin (2.24-9ubuntu2) ...

**********************************************************
* Zend Server was successfully installed.               *
*                                                        *
* To access the Zend Server UI open your browser at:     *
* https://<hostname>:10082/ZendServer (secure)           *
* or                                                     *
* http://<hostname>:10081/ZendServer                     *
**********************************************************

Log file is kept at /tmp/install_zs.log.2364
```

Opening `https://localhost:10082/ZendServer` triggers the **License Agreement** step of the **Launch Zend Server** process:

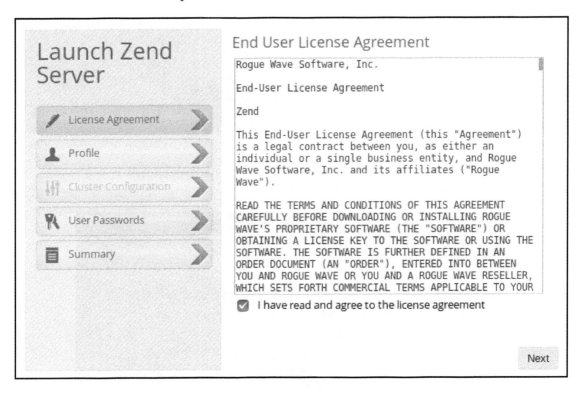

Agreeing to the license agreement and clicking on the **Next** button takes us to the **Profile** step of the **Launch Zend Server** process:

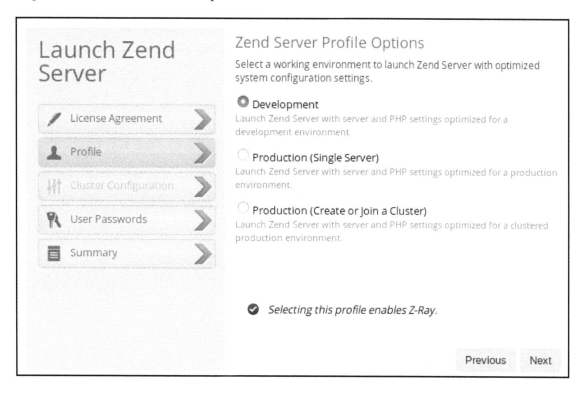

The Profile step offers three distinctive options: **Development, Production (Single Server)**, and **Production (Create or Join a Cluster)**. Choosing the **Development** option, we click on the **Next** button, which takes us to the **User Passwords** step of the **Launch Zend Server** process:

Launch Zend Server

- ✏ License Agreement ❯
- 👤 Profile ❯
- ⋔ Cluster Configuration ❯
- 🔧 User Passwords ❯
- 📋 Summary ❯

Set the passwords for accessing Zend Server

Enter password for user 'admin':

| Password | •••••••• |
| Confirm Password | •••••••• |

Enter password for user 'developer' (Optional):

| Password | •••••••• |
| Confirm Password | •••••••• |

Previous   Next

Here we provide **admin** and **developer** with user passwords. Clicking on the **Next** button takes us to the **Summary** step of the **Launch Zend Server** process:

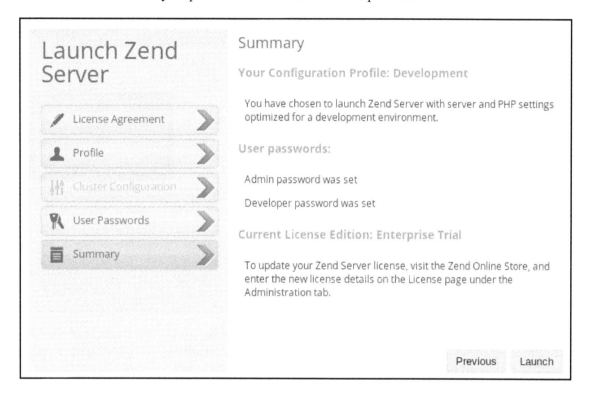

The summary step merely confirms our previous selections and entries. By clicking on the **Launch** button, we finalize the **Launch Zend Server** process and land on the **Getting Started** page:

The Zend Server provides a rich interface for managing pretty much every aspect of the running sever. From here, we can manage virtual hosts, applications, job queues, caching, security, and other bits. Before we can focus on Z-Ray functionality, we need to set up our test application. We will use the same application we used with Xdebug, mapped on the test.loc domain.

Setting up the virtual host

We first amend the /etc/hosts file by adding the 127.0.0.1 test.loc line entry to it.

With the `test.loc` host now added to the hosts file, we turn back to the Zend Server and click on the **Add virtual host** button under the **Applications | Virtual Hosts** screen. This takes us to the **Properties** step of the **Add Virtual Host** process:

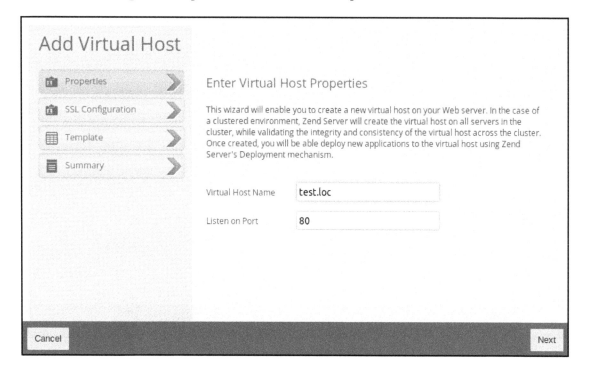

Here we enter `test.loc` for **Virtual Host Name** and `80` for **Listen on Port**. Clicking on the **Next** button takes us to the **SSL Configuration** step of the **Add Virtual Host** process:

To keep things simple, let's just leave the **This virtual host does not use SSL** selection active and click on the **Next** button. This takes us to the **Template** step of the **Add Virtual Host** process:

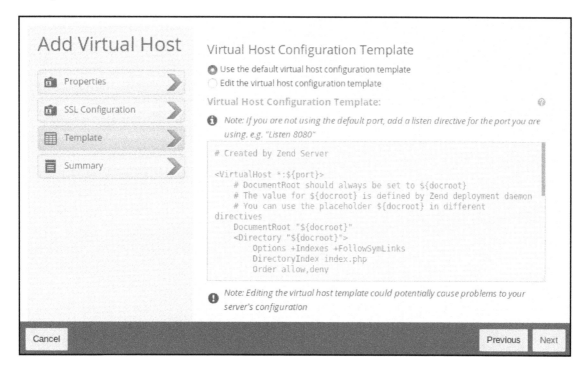

Likewise, let's just leave the **Use the default virtual host configuration template** selection active and click on the **Next** button. This takes us to the **Summary** step of the **Add Virtual Host** process:

To complete the virtual host setup, we click on the **Finish** button. Our `test.loc` virtual host should now be created, showing details such as the following:

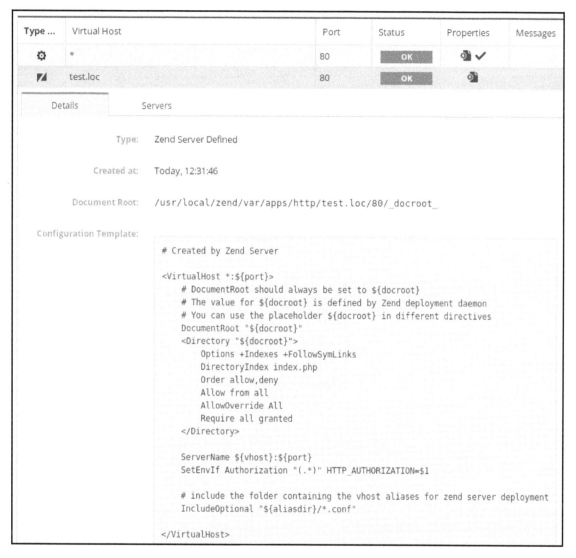

The document root used for our newly created virtual host points to the `/usr/local/zend/var/apps/http/test.loc/80/_docroot_` directory. This is where we will dump our sample application using the following `git clone` command:

```
sudo git clone https://github.com/ajzele/MPHP7-CH16.git .
```

The output of the preceding command is as follows:

```
branko@devbox:/usr/local/zend/var/apps/http/test.loc/80/_docroot_$ sudo git clone https://github.com/ajzele/MPHP7-CH16.git .
Cloning into '.'...
remote: Counting objects: 46, done.
remote: Compressing objects: 100% (22/22), done.
remote: Total 46 (delta 9), reused 45 (delta 8), pack-reused 0
Unpacking objects: 100% (46/46), done.
branko@devbox:/usr/local/zend/var/apps/http/test.loc/80/_docroot_$ ls -al
total 24
drwxr-xr-x 4 zend zend 4096 Tra 27 12:43 .
drwxr-xr-x 3 zend zend 4096 Tra 27 12:31 ..
drwxr-xr-x 8 root root 4096 Tra 27 12:43 .git
-rw-r--r-- 1 root root   10 Tra 27 12:43 .gitignore
-rw-r--r-- 1 root root  741 Tra 27 12:43 index.php
drwxr-xr-x 3 root root 4096 Tra 27 12:43 src
branko@devbox:/usr/local/zend/var/apps/http/test.loc/80/_docroot_$ []
```

With the code in place, accessing the `http://test.loc` URL within the browser should give us the following output:

Using Z-Ray

Now that we have our test application up and running, we can finally focus on the Z-Ray functionality. Within the Zend Server administration interface, under **Z-Ray** | **Mode**, we need to make sure that the **Enabled** option is the active one. Now, if we access the `http://test.loc` URL within the browser, we should be able to see the Z-Ray toolbar at the bottom of the page:

The toolbar itself consists of several key sections, each of which gathers a specific metric:

- **Page Requests** :

- **Execution Time and Memory Peak**:

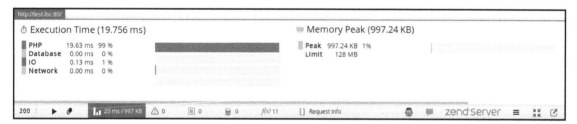

- **Monitor Events**:

- **Errors & Warnings**:

- **Database Queries:**

While our specific sample application has no database interactions, the following output illustrates Z-Ray capturing raw SQL database queries as well as their execution times from a resource-intense Magento eCommerce platform:

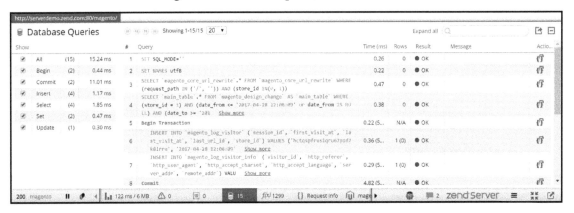

- **Functions**:

- **Request Info**:

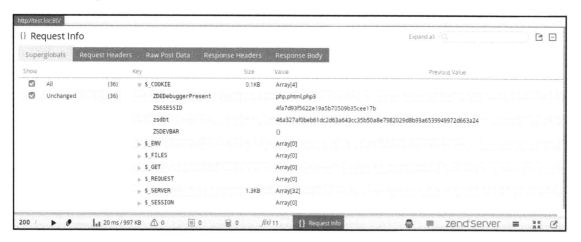

Z-Ray acts like a mix of Xdebug's trace and profile functionalities, delivered straight into the browser. This makes it an extremely handy tool for developers. Capturing rawSQL queries adds even more value to the tool, as, usually, these tend to be the unexpected performance bottlenecks.

The Z-Ray feature can be easily enabled only for a specific host. The way to do this is by activating the Selective option under the **Z-Ray | Mode** screen. This type of setup makes it convenient to profile production sites.

Summary

Throughout this section, we touched upon three unique types of process we contribute to overall application testing. Distinctively labeled as debugging, tracing, and profiling, these processes provide a unique and remarkably informative perspective on our application inner bits. While tracing and profiling gather application performance and path-of-execution data for us in a sort of hands-free mode, debugging allows for a unique experience of tapping into a specific bit of code. Whether we are a seasonal or a full-time software developer, debugging, tracing, and profiling are absolutely essential skills to master. Without them, resolving the really nasty bugs or writing performance-optimized applications becomes a whole new challenge.

Moving forward, we will take a closer look at the landscape and available choices around PHP application hosting, provisioning, and deployment.

17
Hosting, Provisioning, and Deployment

Hosting, provisioning, and deployment are admittedly three very distinct activities that often go hand in hand with the overall application life cycle management. Whereas, some types of hosting solutions make it near impossible to achieve seamless deployments, others make it an ultimately joyful and time-effective experience for developers. This brings us to the most important point of all, which is, *Why would developers even bother with these system operations things*? There are plenty of answers for this one. Whereas, the real sales pitch is simple as: market demands it. Nowadays, developers are tangled in a web of multidisciplinary activities, which often goes beyond coding skills itself and into system operations at some level. The *not my job* mantra is all but reserved for us here, which is ultimately alright, as having a strong knowledge about activities supporting an entire application life cycle makes us more responsive in the face of possible outages.

In this chapter, we will take a high-level overview on some of these activities through the following few sections:

- Choosing the right hosting plan
- Automating provisioning
- Automating deployment
- Continuous integration

Choosing the right hosting plan

Choosing the right hosting plan for our next project can be a tedious challenge. There are many types of solutions to choose from, some of which include the following:

- Shared server
- Virtual private server
- Dedicated server
- PaaS

They all have their *pros* and *cons*. Whereas once decision factors were dominated by features such as memory, CPU, bandwidth, and disk storage, those became ever *cheaper* over the years. Nowadays, **auto-scaling** and **ease of deployment** emerged as an equally important metrics. While ultimately the pricing plays a crucial role, great deal of modern hosting solutions have a lot to offer for an affordable price.

Shared server

The shared web hosting service is the one where many different users host their applications. The hosting provider usually provides a well-tuned web server with MySQL or PostgreSQL database and an FTP access. On top of that, there is usually a web-based control panel system, such as cPanel, Plesk, H-Sphere, or alike. This allows us to manage a limited set of features through a nice graphical interface, right from our browser.

The popular PC Mag magazine (http://www.pcmag.com) shares the list of the **best web hosting services of 2017** as follows:

- **HostGator Web Hosting**: http://www.hostgator.com
- **1&1 Web Hosting**: https://www.1and1.com
- **InMotion Web Hosting**: https://www.inmotionhosting.com/
- **DreamHost Web Hosting**: https://www.dreamhost.com
- **GoDaddy Web Hosting**: https://www.godaddy.com
- **Bluehost Web Hosting**: https://www.bluehost.com
- **Hostwinds Web Hosting**: https://www.hostwinds.com
- **Liquid Web Hosting**: https://www.liquidweb.com
- **A2 Web Hosting**: https://www.a2hosting.com
- **Arvixe Web Hosting**: https://www.arvixe.com

Each of these web hosting services seems to provide a similar set of functionalities, as shown in the following screenshot:

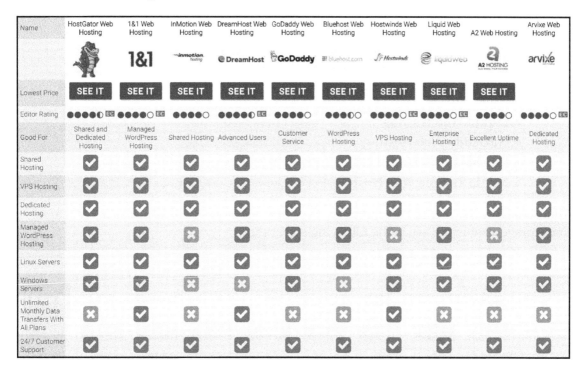

While the affordable shared server price might seem tempting, the lack of control over the server limits its use with any serious applications. Our application shares the same CPU, memory, and storage as a dozen, a hundred, or even a thousand other applications. We don't get to install any software we want, which might even turn into a deal breaker if our application requires some fancy PHP extension, which is why this type of a poor man's hosting is something we should wholeheartedly try to avoid for anything other than the business card or blog type of applications.

Virtual private server

The **virtual private server** (**VPS**) is a virtual machine provided by the hosting provider. This machine then runs its own operating system to which we often have a full super-user access. The VPS itself shares the same set of physical hardware resources as other VPS machines. This means that our VPS performance can easily be impaired by other VPS machines' processes.

The popular PCMag magazine (`http://www.pcmag.com`) shares the list of the **best VPS web hosting services of 2017** as follows:

- **HostGator Web Hosting**: `http://www.hostgator.com`
- **InMotion Web Hosting**: `https://www.inmotionhosting.com/`
- **1&1 Web Hosting**: `https://www.1and1.com`
- **DreamHost Web Hosting**: `https://www.dreamhost.com`
- **Hostwinds Web Hosting**: `https://www.hostwinds.com`
- **Liquid Web Hosting**: `https://www.liquidweb.com`
- **GoDaddy Web Hosting**: `https://www.godaddy.com`
- **Bluehost Web Hosting**: `https://www.bluehost.com`
- **Media Temple Web Hosting**: `https://mediatemple.net`

There are quite a few variations between these hosting services, mostly in terms of memory and storage, as you can see in the following screenshot:

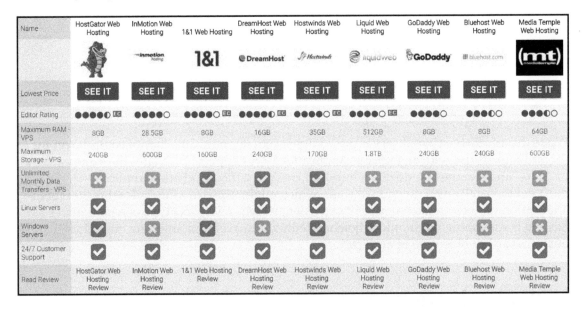

While VPS is still a form of shared resources, it allows us a much greater degree of freedom than conventional shared hosting. Having full super-user access to the machine means we can install pretty much any piece of software we want to. This also means a greater degree of responsibility for us.

Dedicated server

The dedicated server assumes a real physical machine provided by the hosting provider. Such a machine does not share resources with anyone else other than us. This makes it a viable option for high-performance and mission-critical applications.

The popular PCMag magazine (`http://www.pcmag.com`)shares the list of the **best dedicated web hosting services of 2017** as follows:

- **HostGator Web Hosting**: `http://www.hostgator.com`
- **DreamHost Web Hosting**: `https://www.dreamhost.com`
- **InMotion Web Hosting**: `https://www.inmotionhosting.com/`
- **1&1 Web Hosting**: `https://www.1and1.com`
- **Liquid Web Hosting**: `https://www.liquidweb.com`
- **Hostwinds Web Hosting**: `https://www.hostwinds.com`
- **GoDaddy Web Hosting**: `https://www.godaddy.com`
- **Bluehost Web Hosting**: `https://www.bluehost.com`
- **SiteGround Web Hosting**: `https://www.siteground.com`
- **iPage Web Hosting**: `http://www.ipage.com`

There are quite a few variations between these hosting services, mostly in terms of memory and storage, as you can see in this screenshot:

Name	HostGator Web Hosting	DreamHost Web Hosting	InMotion Web Hosting	1&1 Web Hosting	Liquid Web Hosting	Hostwinds Web Hosting	GoDaddy Web Hosting	Bluehost Web Hosting	SiteGround Web Hosting	iPage Web Hosting
Lowest Price	SEE IT	SEE IT	SEE IT	SEE IT	SEE IT	SEE IT	SEE IT	SEE IT	SEE IT	SEE IT
Editor Rating	●●●●◐ EC	●●●●◐ EC	●●●●○	●●●●◐ EC	●●●●○ EC	●●●●◐ EC	●●●●○	●●●○○	●●●●○	●●●○○
Maximum RAM - Dedicated	16GB	16GB	64GB	128GB	512GB	96GB	32GB	16GB	16GB	16GB
Maximum Storage - Dedicated	1TB	1TB	1.2TB	6TB	12TB	6TB	2TB	1TB	2TB	1TB
Unlimited Monthly Data Transfers - Dedicated	✗	✓	✗	✓	✗	✗	✗	✗	✗	✗
Linux Servers	✓	✓	✓	✓	✓	✓	✓	✓	✓	✓
Windows Servers	✓	✗	✗	✓	✓	✓	✓	✓	✗	✓
24/7 Customer Support	✓	✓	✓	✓	✓	✓	✓	✓	✓	✓
Read Review	HostGator Web Hosting Review	DreamHost Web Hosting Review	InMotion Web Hosting Review	1&1 Web Hosting Review	Liquid Web Hosting Review	Hostwinds Web Hosting Review	GoDaddy Web Hosting Review	Bluehost Web Hosting Review	SiteGround Web Hosting Review	iPage Web Hosting Review

While they come at a higher cost, dedicated servers guarantee a level of performance and full control over the machine. At the same time, managing scalability and redundancy can easily turn into a challenge of its own.

PaaS

The **platform as a service** (**PaaS**) is a special type of hosting where a provider delivers hardware and software tools needed to speed up application development. We may go so far as to compare PaaS with the power and flexibility of dedicated servers backed by dozens of easily connected services assisting the availability, reliability, scalability, and application development activities. This makes it a popular choice among developers.

The popular *IT Central Station* site (`https://www.itcentralstation.com`) shares the list of the **best PaaS clouds vendors** of 2017 as follows:

- **Amazon AWS**: `https://aws.amazon.com`
- **Microsoft Azure**: `https://azure.microsoft.com`
- **Heroku**: `https://www.heroku.com`
- **Mendix**: `https://www.mendix.com`
- **Salesforce App Cloud**: `https://www.salesforce.com`
- **Oracle Java Cloud Service**: `https://cloud.oracle.com/java`

- **HPE Helion**: `https://www.hpe.com`
- **Rackspace Cloud**: `https://www.rackspace.com`
- **Google App Engine**: `https://cloud.google.com`
- **Oracle Cloud Platform**: `http://www.oracle.com/solutions/cloud/platform/`

The following report has been taken for April 2017:

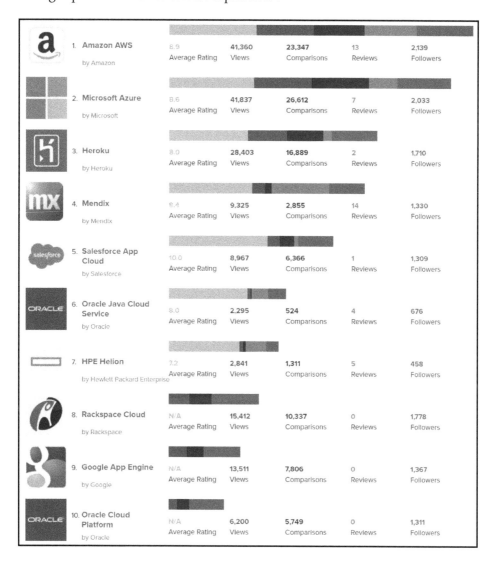

While all of these services have much to offer, it is worth pointing out Amazon AWS, which was named by Gartner in 2016 **Magic Quadrant for Cloud Infrastructure as a Service** as having the furthest completeness of vision. The evaluation criteria are based on several key factors:

- Market understanding
- Marketing strategy
- Sales strategy
- Offering (product) strategy
- Business model
- Vertical/industry strategy
- Innovation
- Geographic strategy

The great starting point with Amazon AWS is its EC2 service, which provides resizable virtual servers. These act much like the dedicated server, but in cloud, where we get to choose the region of the world we would like to deploy these. On top of that, there are dozens of other services within the Amazon AWS offering that enrich the overall application management:

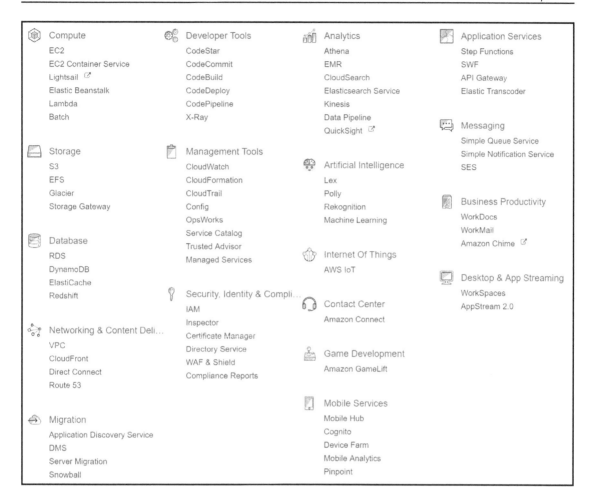

An easy-to-use interface, rich service offering, affordable price, great documentation, certification, and available tooling are some of the *selling points* for developers when it comes to Amazon AWS.

Automating provisioning

The provisioning is a term that has gained a lot of traction among developers lately. It refers to the activity of setting up and configuring *servers* with every bit of required software, making it ready for application use. While this sounds a lot like the system operations type of work, developers found it interesting with the rise of cloud services and the tooling surrounding it.

Historically, provisioning implied a lot of manual type of work. There were not as many general purpose automated provisioning tools as there is today. This meant that there were times when provisioning took days or even weeks. Looking through the prism of today's market demands, such a scenario is hardly imaginable. Nowadays, a single application is usually served by several different servers, each of which is targeting a single functionality, such as web (Apache, Nginx, ...), storage (MySQL, Redis, ...), session (Redis, Memcached, ...), static content (Nginx), and so on. We simply cannot afford to spend days setting up each of the servers.

There are several popular tools we can use to automate provisioning, some of which include these popular four:

- **Ansible**: https://www.ansible.com.
- **Chef**: https://www.chef.io/chef/
- **Puppet**: https://puppet.com
- **SaltStack**: https://saltstack.com

Like others tools of the same type, these are all built with the goal of making it easier to configure and maintain dozens, hundreds, or even thousands of servers. While all of these tools are more likely to get any provisioning job done with equal effect, let's take a closer look at one of them. Released in 2012, **Ansible** is the youngest of the four. It is an open source tool that automates software provisioning, configuration management, and application deployment. This tool performs all of its functions over SSH, without requiring any agent software installation on the target node/server. This alone makes it a favorable choice among developers.

There are several key concepts around Ansible, some of which are as follows:

- **Inventories**: This is the list of Ansible managed servers
- **Playbooks**: This is Ansible's configuration expressed in YAML format
- **Roles**: This is automation around include directives based on a file structure
- **Tasks**: This is the possible actions that Ansible can execute

 The https://galaxy.ansible.comservice acts as a hub that provides ready-to-use roles.

To get a very basic understanding of Ansible, let's do a very simple and quick demonstration based on the following:

- Ubuntu workstation machine
- Ubuntu server machine

We will use the `ansible` tool to provision software on the server machine.

Setting up the workstation machine

Using Ubuntu powered workstation, we can easily install the Ansible tool just by running the following set of commands:

```
sudo apt-get install software-properties-common
sudo apt-add-repository ppa:ansible/ansible
sudo apt-get update
sudo apt-get install ansible
```

If all went well, `ansible --version` should give us an output much like this screenshot:

```
$ ansible --version
ansible 2.2.1.0
   config file = /root/mphp7/ansible.cfg
   configured module search path = Default w/o overrides
$
```

The Ansible is a console tool for running ad-hoc tasks. Whereas ad-hoc implies on something we do quickly, without writing the entire playbook for it.

Likewise, `ansible-galaxy --version` should give us an output much like the following screenshot:

```
$ ansible-galaxy --version
ansible-galaxy 2.2.1.0
   config file = /root/mphp7/ansible.cfg
   configured module search path = Default w/o overrides
$
```

The `ansible-galaxy` is a console tool we can use to install, create, and remove roles, or perform tasks on the Galaxy website. By default, tool communicates with the Galaxy website API using the server address `https://galaxy.ansible.com`.

Also, `ansible-playbook --version` should give us an output much like the following screenshot:

```
$ ansible-playbook --version
ansible-playbook 2.2.1.0
  config file = /root/mphp7/ansible.cfg
  configured module search path = Default w/o overrides
$
```

The `ansible-playbook` is a console tool used for configuration management and deployments.

With the Ansible tool in place, let's make sure our workstation has a proper SSH key, which we will use later on to connect to the server machine. We can easily generate the SSH key by simply running the following command, followed by hitting the *Enter* key when asked for a file and passphrase:

```
ssh-keygen -t rsa
```

This should give us an output much like the following one:

```
$ ssh-keygen -t rsa
Generating public/private rsa key pair.
Enter file in which to save the key (/root/.ssh/id_rsa):
Created directory '/root/.ssh'.
Enter passphrase (empty for no passphrase):
Enter same passphrase again:
Your identification has been saved in /root/.ssh/id_rsa.
Your public key has been saved in /root/.ssh/id_rsa.pub.
The key fingerprint is:
SHA256:Vb+Qx8zp3mw699NoFosPMpLYn+pNiHB3YB1v5Vu94vU root@vultr.guest
The key's randomart image is:
+---[RSA 2048]----+
|         . . .   |
|        . + O ..|
|       o o = O o|
|      . o . + +.|
|     . . S .  .+o |
|      o = +  ..+o.|
|      o = + .o.+E|
|       = +..*+o|
|        .o.+  +oo+|
+----[SHA256]-----+
```

Using the Ansible playbooks, we can define various provisioning steps in the easy-to-read YAML format.

Setting up the server machine

We previously mentioned there are several hosting solutions that allow full control over the server machine. These solutions come in form of VPS, dedicated and cloud services. For the purpose of this example, we will be using the **Vultr Cloud Compute** (**VC2**), which is available at `https://www.vultr.com`. Without going too deep into the ins and outs of the **Vultr** service, it's suffice to say it provides an affordable cloud compute service via an easy-to-use administration interface.

Assuming we have created a Vultr account, the first thing we want to do now is to add our workstation SSH public key to it. We can easily do so through Vultr's **Servers** | **SSH Keys** interface:

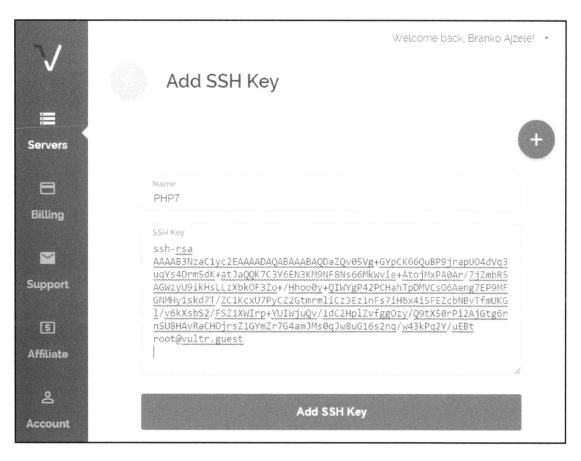

Once the **SSH Key** is saved, we can go back to the Servers screen and click on the **Deploy New Server** button. This brings us to the **Deploy New Instance** interface, which presents us with several steps. The steps we focus our attention on are **Server Type** and **SSH Keys**.

For **Server Type**, let's go ahead and choose **Ubuntu 16.04 x64**:

For SSH Keys, let's go ahead and choose the SSH key we just added to Vultr:

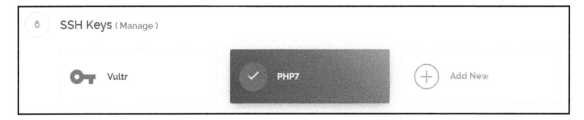

With these two selected, we can click on the **Deploy Now** button, which should trigger deployment of our server machine.

To this point, we might wonder, what the purpose of this exercise might be, as we have clearly created a server machine pretty much manually. After all, Ansible has a module to manage servers on Vultr so we could have easily used that for server creation. The exercise here, however, is around the basics of understanding how easily it is to "hook" Ansible to an existing server machine and then use it to provision further software to it. Now that we have a server machine running, let's move on to the further configuration of Ansible on the workstation.

Configuring Ansible

Back on our workstation machine, let's go ahead and create a project directory:

```
mkdir mphp7
cd mphp7/
```

Now, let's go ahead and create an `ansible.cfg` file with its content as follows:

```
[defaults]
hostfile = hosts
```

Next, let's go ahead and create the `hosts` file with its content as follows:

```
[mphp7]
45.76.88.214 ansible_ssh_user=root
```

In the preceding lines of code, `45.76.88.214` is the IP address of our server machine.

We should now be able to run the `ansible` tool as follows:

```
ansible mphp7 -m ping
```

Ideally, this should give us the following output:

The `ansible` tool might throw a **MODULE FAILURE** message in the case of a missing Python installation on our server machine:

```
$ ansible mphp7 -m ping
The authenticity of host '45.76.88.214 (45.76.88.214)' can't be established.
ECDSA key fingerprint is SHA256:hxvskg5G9ruBSi5OO6MNNIraov6W+b8I+1J6UvUsVYc.
Are you sure you want to continue connecting (yes/no)? yes
45.76.88.214 | FAILED! => {
    "changed": false,
    "failed": true,
    "module_stderr": "Shared connection to 45.76.88.214 closed.\r\n",
    "module_stdout": "/bin/sh: 1: /usr/bin/python: not found\r\n",
    "msg": "MODULE FAILURE"
}
$
```

If this happens, we should SSH into our server machine and install Python as follows:

```
sudo apt-get -y install python
```

At this point, our workstation `ansible` tool should be set to have clear communication with our *server* machine.

Now, let's go ahead and do a quick lookup for the LAMP server role on the Galaxy hub:

Clicking on one of the results gives us information on how to install it:

By running the following command on the workstation, we install the existing `fvarovillodres.lamp` role:

```
ansible-galaxy install fvarovillodres.lamp
```

Provisioning a web server

With the newly pulled `fvarovillodres.lamp` rule, we should be able to effortlessly deploy a new web server. To do so, all it takes is creating a playbook, such as `lamp.yaml`, with its content as follows:

```
- hosts: mphp7
  roles:
    - role: fvarovillodres.lamp
      become: yes
```

Now, we can easily run our `lamp.yaml` playbook via the following command:

```
ansible-playbook lamp.yml
```

This should trigger the tasks within the `fvarovillodres.lamp` role that we pulled from the Galaxy hub upon completion:

```
PLAY RECAP ********************************************************************
45.76.88.214               : ok=18    changed=4    unreachable=0    failed=0
```

Finally, opening a `http://45.76.88.214/` URL should give us an Apache page.

The overall topic of provisioning, or even Ansible, is a broad subject worth a book of its own. The example given here is merely to showcase the ease of use of the available tooling in order to address the provisioning in an automated way. There is one important takeaway here, which is that we need full control over the server/node in order to utilize the provisioning. This is why shared types of hosting are excluded from any such discussions.

The exact example given here uses a single server box. However, it is not hard to imagine how easily this approach can be scaled up to a dozen or even hundreds of server machines just by amending the Ansible configuration. We could have easily used Ansible itself to automate the deployment for our application, where each deployment, for instance, might trigger a new server creation process with code being pulled from some Git repository or alike. There are, however, more simpler, specialized tools to handle automated deployments.

Automating the deployment

Deploying a PHP application primarily implies deploying PHP code. Since PHP is an interpreted and not compiled language, the PHP applications deploy their code as-is, in source files. This means that there is no real build process involved when deploying an application, which further means that application deployment can be as easy as doing a `git pull` within a server web directory. Surely, things are never that simple, as we often have various other bits that need to fit in place when the code is deployed, such as databases, mounted drives, shared files, permissions, other services connected to our server, and so on.

We can easily imagine the complexity of having to manually deploy code from a single git repository onto dozens of web servers behind some load balancer at the same time. Such manual deployments will surely have negative implications, as we end up with a time in-between overall deployments, where one server might have newer versions of an application code, while others still serve the old application. The lack of consistency is, therefore, just a one of the impacting challenges to worry about.

Luckily, there are a dozen of tools that address the challenges of automated deployments. While we won't be getting into the ins and outs of any of them specifically, for the sake of a quick comparison, let's just mention the following two:

- **Deployer**: This is an open source PHP-based tool suited for automating deployments, available at `https://deployer.org`
- **AWS CodeDeploy**: This is a code deployment service offered by AWS, available at `https://aws.amazon.com/codedeploy/`

Unlike AWS CodeDeploy, the Deployer tool is service-independent. That is, we can use it to deploy code to any server upon which we have control, including the AWS EC2 instances. The AWS CodeDeploy, on the other hand, is a service tightly integrated into an AWS itself, meaning we cannot use it outside of the AWS. This does not mean Deployer is better than AWS CodeDeploy in this case. It simply goes to show that some cloud and PaaS services offer their own integrated solutions to automated deployments.

Moving forward, let's take a quick look at how easily we can set Deployer to deploy code to our server machine.

Installing Deployer

Installing Deployer is quite easy via the following few commands:

```
curl -LO https://deployer.org/releases/v4.3.0/deployer.phar
mv deployer.phar /usr/local/bin/dep
chmod +x /usr/local/bin/dep
```

Running the dep console command now gives us the following output:

```
$ dep
Deployer 4.3.0

Usage:
  command [options] [arguments]

Options:
  -h, --help            Display this help message
  -q, --quiet           Do not output any message
  -V, --version         Display this application version
      --ansi            Force ANSI output
      --no-ansi         Disable ANSI output
  -n, --no-interaction  Do not ask any interactive question
  -f, --file[=FILE]     Specify Deployer file
  -v|vv|vvv, --verbose  Increase the verbosity of messages: 1 for normal output
  2 for more verbose output and 3 for debug

Available commands:
  help         Displays help for a command
  init         Initialize deployer system in your project
  list         Lists commands
  self-update  Updates deployer.phar to the latest version
$
```

Using Deployer

There are several key concepts that comprise of the Deployer applications:

- **Configuration**: Using the set() and get() functions, we set and fetch one or more configurations options:

    ```
    set('color', 'Yellow');
    set('hello', function () {
       return run(...)->toString();
    });
    ```

- **Tasks**: These are units of work defined via the task() function, used together with the desc() method that sets the task description. Within the task, there is usually one or more functions, such as run():

    ```
    desc('Foggyline task #1');
    task('update', 'apt-get update');
    ```

```
desc('Foggyline task #2');
task('task_2', function () {
  run(...);
});
```

- **Servers**: This is the list of servers defined via the server() function, as shown in the following code snippet:

```
server('mphp7_staging', 'mphp7.staging.foggyline.net')
 ->user('user')
 ->password('pass')
 ->set('deploy_path', '/home/www')
 ->set('branch', 'stage')
 ->stage('staging');

server('mphp7_prod', 'mphp7.foggyline.net')
 ->user('user')
 ->identityFile()
 ->set('deploy_path', '/home/www')
 ->set('branch', 'master')
 ->stage('production');
```

- **Flow**: This represents a group of tasks. The common type project uses a default flow as follows:

```
task('deploy', [
    'deploy:prepare',
    'deploy:lock',
    'deploy:release',
    'deploy:update_code',
    'deploy:shared',
    'deploy:writable',
    'deploy:vendors',
    'deploy:clear_paths',
    'deploy:symlink',
    'deploy:unlock',
    'cleanup',
    'success'
]);
```

We could easily create our own flow by changing this flow from the auto-generated deploy.php file.

- **Functions**: This is a group of utility functions that provide useful functionality, such as run(), upload(), ask(), and others.

Using the Deployer tool is quite straightforward. Unless we already have some previously created recipes, we can create one simply by running the following console command:

```
dep init
```

This kicks off an interactive process, asking us to choose the type of project we are working with. Let's proceed with the idea of deploying our **MPHP7-CH16** application from `https ://github.com/ajzele/MPHP7-CH16` repository, flagging it as **[0] Common**:

```
$ dep init
Please select your project type (defaults to common):
  [0] Common
  [1] Laravel
  [2] Symfony
  [3] Yii
  [4] Zend Framework
  [5] CakePHP
  [6] CodeIgniter
  [7] Drupal
 > 0
Successfully created: /root/mphp7/deploy.php
$
```

This command generates the `deploy.php` file with its content as follows:

```php
<?php
namespace Deployer;
require 'recipe/common.php';

// Configuration

set('ssh_type', 'native');
set('ssh_multiplexing', true);

set('repository', 'git@domain.com:username/repository.git');
set('shared_files', []);
set('shared_dirs', []);
set('writable_dirs', []);

// Servers

server('production', 'domain.com')
    ->user('username')
    ->identityFile()
    ->set('deploy_path', '/var/www/domain.com');
```

```
// Tasks

desc('Restart PHP-FPM service');
task('php-fpm:restart', function () {
    // The user must have rights for restart service
    // /etc/sudoers: username ALL=NOPASSWD:/bin/systemctl restart php-
fpm.service
    run('sudo systemctl restart php-fpm.service');
});
after('deploy:symlink', 'php-fpm:restart');

desc('Deploy your project');
task('deploy', [
    'deploy:prepare',
    'deploy:lock',
    'deploy:release',
    'deploy:update_code',
    'deploy:shared',
    'deploy:writable',
    'deploy:vendors',
    'deploy:clear_paths',
    'deploy:symlink',
    'deploy:unlock',
    'cleanup',
    'success'
]);

// [Optional] if deploy fails automatically unlock.
after('deploy:failed', 'deploy:unlock');
```

We should approach this file as a template that needs adjusting to our real servers. Assuming we wish to deploy our **MPHP7-CH16** application to our previously provisioned 45.76.88.214 server, we can do so by adjusting the deploy.php file as follows:

```
<?php

namespace Deployer;
require 'recipe/common.php';

set('repository', 'https://github.com/ajzele/MPHP7-CH16.git');

server('production', '45.76.88.214')
    ->user('root')
    ->identityFile()
    ->set('deploy_path', '/var/www/MPHP7')
    ->set('branch', 'master')
    ->stage('production');
```

```
desc('Symlink html directory');
task('web:symlink', function () {
    run('ln -sf /var/www/MPHP7/current /var/www/html');
});

desc('Restart Apache service');
task('apache:restart', function () {
    run('service apache2 restart');
});

after('deploy:symlink', 'web:symlink');
after('web:symlink', 'apache:restart');

desc('Deploy your project');
task('deploy', [
    'deploy:prepare',
    'deploy:lock',
    'deploy:release',
    'deploy:update_code',
    'deploy:shared',
    'deploy:writable',
    //'deploy:vendors',
    'deploy:clear_paths',
    'deploy:symlink',
    'deploy:unlock',
    'cleanup',
    'success'
]);

after('deploy:failed', 'deploy:unlock');
```

We used the set() function to configure the location of the git repository. The server() function then defines the individual server we called production, behind a 45.76.88.214 IP. The identityFile() simply tells the system to use the SSH key instead of the password for the SSH connection. Next to the server, we defined two custom tasks, web:symlink and apache:restart. These make sure proper mapping is done from the Deployer's /var/www/MPHP7/current/ directory to our /var/www/html/ directory. The after() function calls simply define the order when our two custom jobs are supposed to execute, which is after the Deployer's deploy:symlink event.

To execute the amended deploy.php, we use the following console command:

```
dep deploy production
```

This should give us the following output:

```
$ dep deploy production
Warning: ssh type `phpseclib` will be deprecated in Deployer 5.
Add this lines to your deploy.php file:

    set('ssh_type', 'native');
    set('ssh_multiplexing', true);

More info here: https://goo.gl/ya8rKW
√ Executing task deploy:prepare
√ Executing task deploy:lock
√ Executing task deploy:release
√ Executing task web:symlink
√ Executing task apache:restart
√ Executing task deploy:update_code
√ Executing task deploy:shared
√ Executing task deploy:writable
√ Executing task deploy:clear_paths
√ Executing task deploy:symlink
√ Executing task deploy:unlock
√ Executing task cleanup
√ Executing task success
Successfully deployed!
```

To confirm that the deployment was successful, opening `http://45.76.88.214/` should give us the following page:

This simple Deployer script gave us a powerful way of automatically deploying code from our repository into a server. Scaling this to multiple servers is imaginably easy, given the Deployer's `server()` functions.

Continuous integration

The idea behind continuous integration is to bind together the building, testing, and releasing processes in an easy-to-oversee manner. As we mentioned before, the notion of building is a bit of a specific one when it comes to PHP, given the interpreted nature of the language itself; we are not talking about compiling code here. With PHP, we tend to relate it to various configurations required by our application.

That being said, some of the strong points of continuous integration include the following:

- Automated code coverage and quality check through static code analysis
- Automation by running after each developer code push
- Automated faulty code detection through unit and behavior testing
- Reduced application release cycle
- Increased visibility across project

There are a dozen of continuous integration tools to chose from, some of which include the following:

- **PHPCI**: https://www.phptesting.org
- **Jenkins**: http://jenkins-php.org
- **Travis CI**: https://travis-ci.org
- **TeamCity**: https://www.jetbrains.com/teamcity/
- **Bamboo**: https://www.atlassian.com/software/bamboo
- **AWS CodePipeline**: https://aws.amazon.com/codepipeline/

It would be unfair to say one of these tools is better than the others. Though Jenkins seems to resurface slightly more than others when it comes to PHP.

Jenkins

Jenkins is an open source, self-contained, cross-platform, ready to run Java-based automation server. There are regularly two versions of Jenkins being released: **long term support** (**LTS**) and weekly releases. The LTS version gives it a bit of an enterprise-friendly feel, among other things:

Out-of-the-box, Jenkins does not really do anything for PHP code specifically, which is where plugins come into the mix.

The rich Jenkins plugin system enables us to easily install the plugins to work with the following PHP tools:

- **PHPUnit**: This is a unit testing framework that is available at `https://phpunit.de/`
- **PHP_CodeSniffer**: This is a tool that detects violations against a certain set of coding standards, available at `https://github.com/squizlabs/PHP_CodeSniffer`
- **PHPLOC**: This is a tool to quickly measure the size of a PHP project, which is available at `https://github.com/sebastianbergmann/phploc`

- **PHP_Depend**: This shows the quality of code design in the terms of extensibility, reusability, and maintainability, which is available at `https://github.com/pdepend/pdepend`
- **PHPMD**: This is the PHP mess detector, which is available at `https://phpmd.org/`
- **PHPCPD**: This is the copy/paste detector for PHP code, which is available at `https://github.com/sebastianbergmann/phpcpd`
- **phpDox**: This is a documentation generator for PHP projects, which is available at `http://phpdox.de/`

Plugins for these tools affect the automated testing bits that Jenkins is able to continuously run for us. The bits about code deployments are generally language-agnostic. Going into the details of plugin installation and the overall use of Jenkins, it is a topic for a book of its own. The takeaway here is to understand the importance and role of of continuous integration over the application life cycle, as well as to raise awareness of available tools.

 See `https://jenkins.io/doc/` and `https://plugins.jenkins.io/` for more information.

Summary

In this chapter, we touched upon some of the non-coding essentials surrounding our application. While developers tend to avoid much of these system operations related activities, the hands-on experience with servers and their setups have a massive advantage with deployments and quick outage responses. Drawing a not-my-job line within our line of work is always a slippery slope. Working closely with system operations adds a layer of quality around our applications. The layer which the end-user might otherwise perceive as a fault in the application itself, rather than its infrastructure. Hosting, provisioning, and deployment have become topics every developer needs to be familiar with. The tools offering around these activities seem quite satisfactory in terms of availability and ease of use.

Throughout the book, we covered a wide and seemingly independent range of topics. These show us that building applications is all but an easy and quick task. Knowing the ins and outs of the PHP language itself does not imply quality software. Giving structure to our code is among the first signs of modularity, which, in turn, reduces the impact of technical debt. This is where standards and design patterns play an important role. Testing, without a doubt, proved to be an essential part of every application. Luckily the PHP ecosystem provides rich testing frameworks to easily cover both the TDD and BDD styles. With the great new features added in PHP 7, writing quality PHP applications has never been easier.

Hopefully, by now, we know enough about PHP, its ecosystem, and various other essential bits and pieces that comprise quality applications, in order to become proficient at developing them. With all being said, we conclude our journey.

Index

Lightning Source UK Ltd.
Milton Keynes UK
UKHW03f0615180518
322796UK00011B/283/P